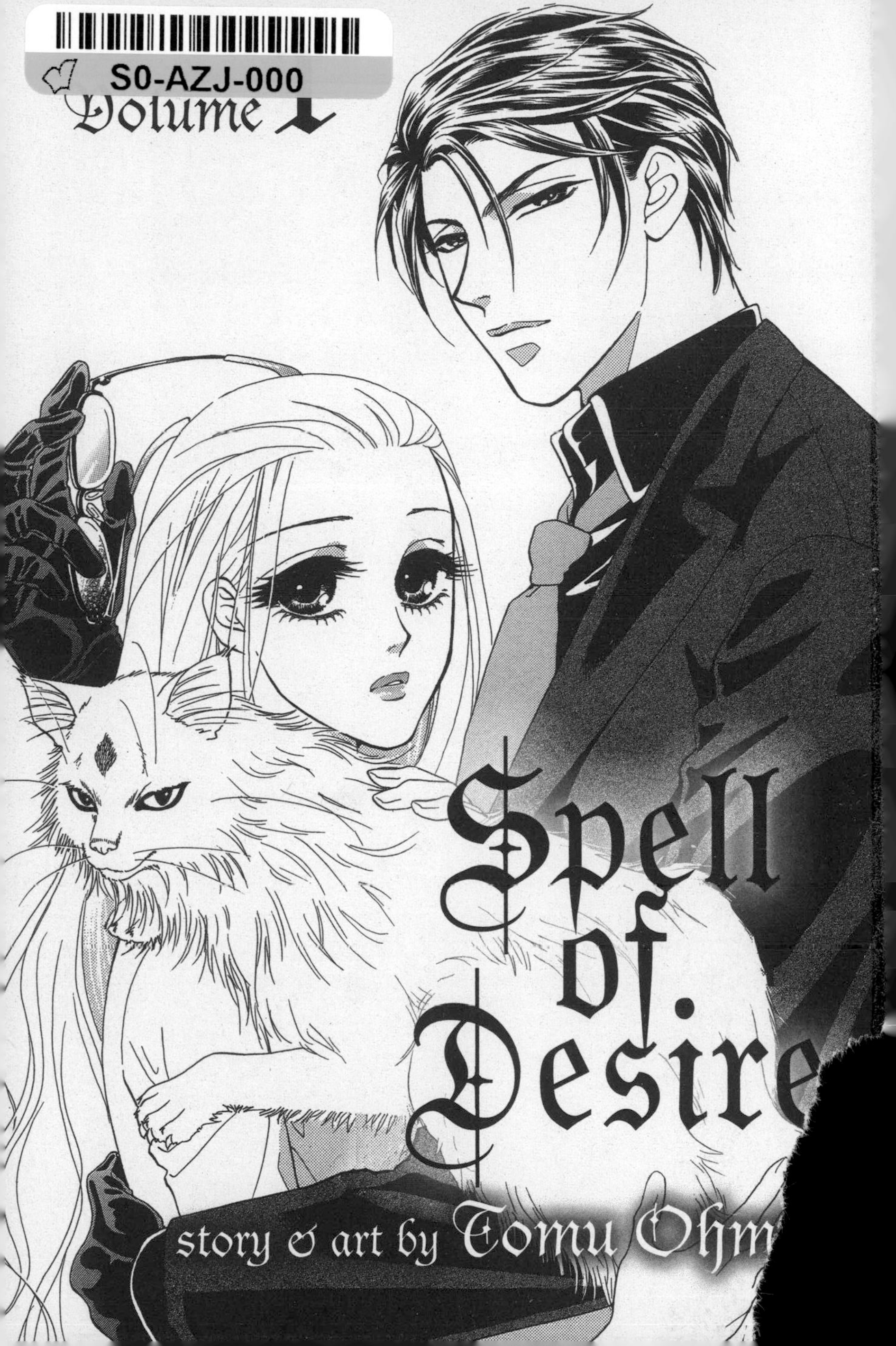
Volume 1
Spell of Desire
story & art by Tomu Ohm

Spell of Desire
Volume 1

Contents

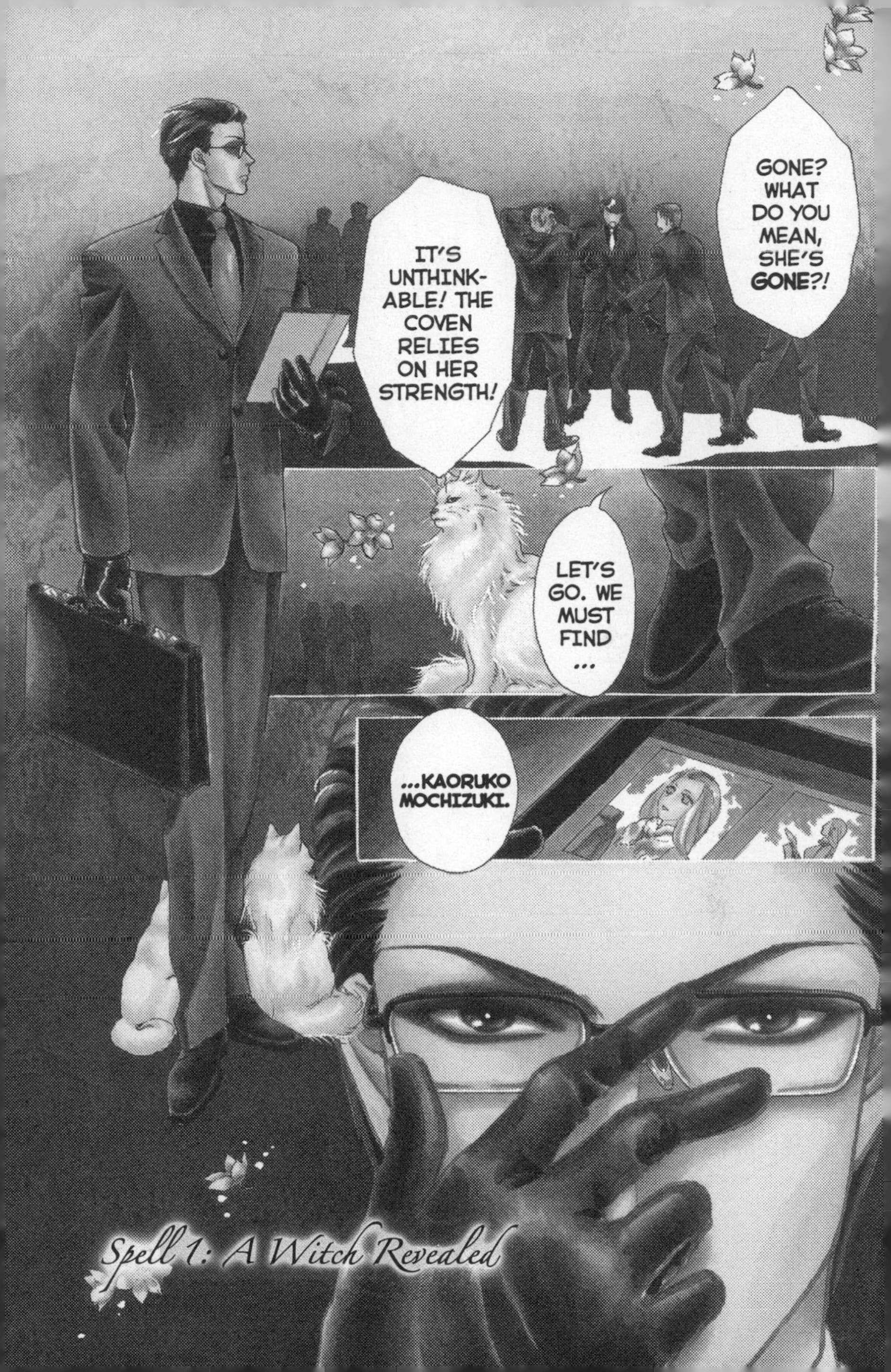
GONE? WHAT DO YOU MEAN, SHE'S GONE?!
IT'S UNTHINK-ABLE! THE COVEN RELIES ON HER STRENGTH!
LET'S GO. WE MUST FIND ...
...KAORUKO MOCHIZUKI.
Spell 1: A Witch Revealed

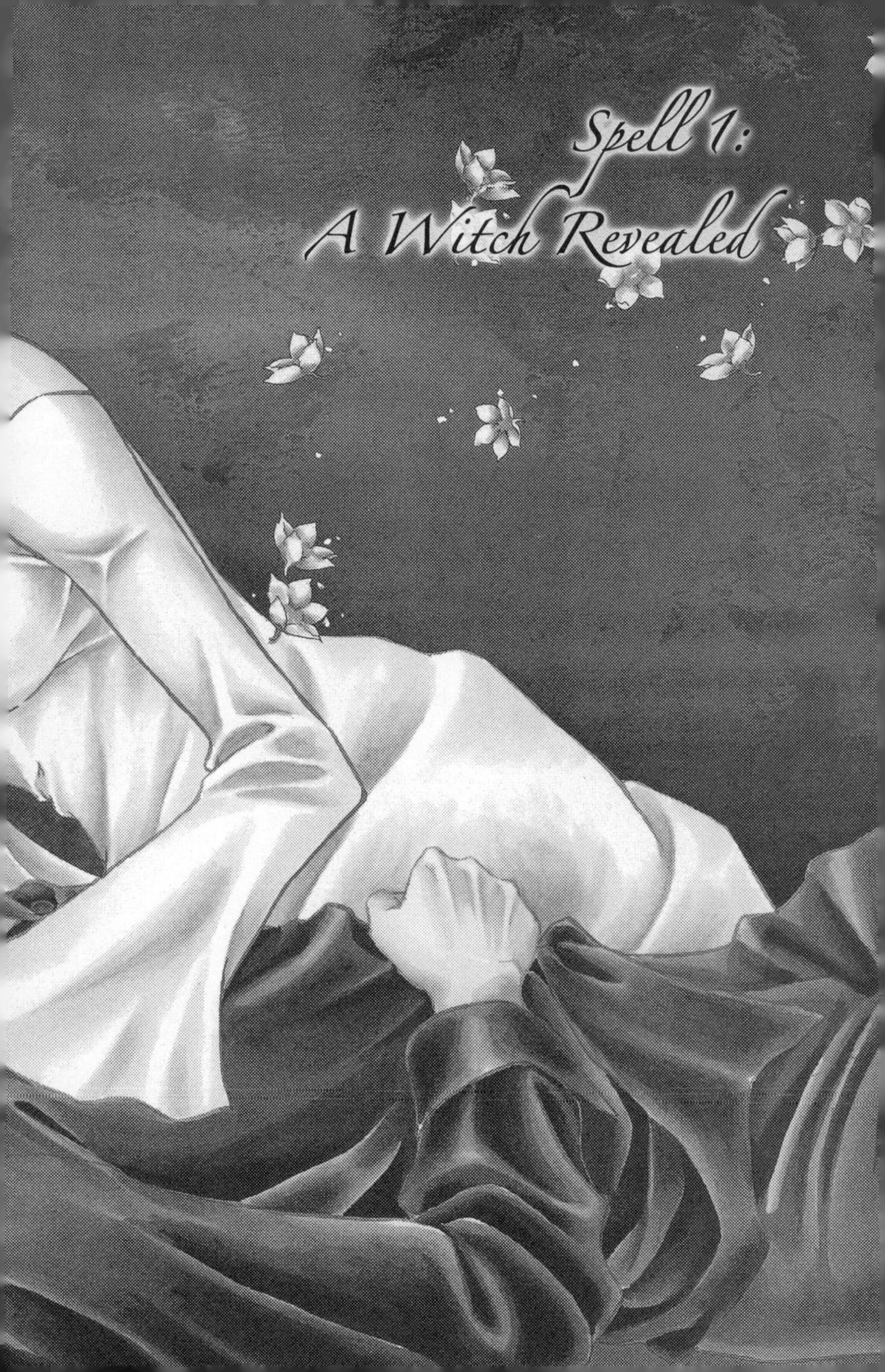
Spell 1:
A Witch Revealed

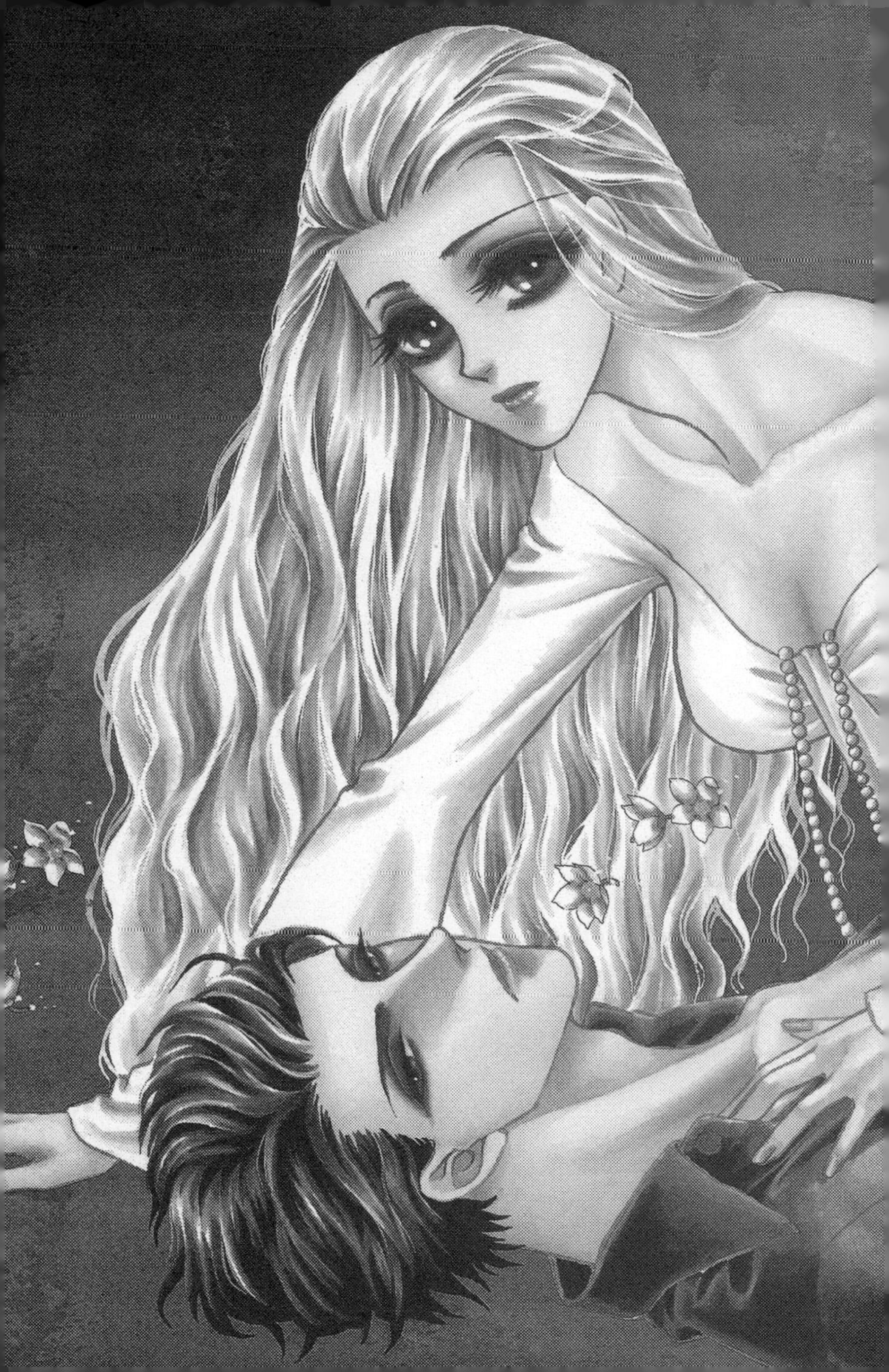

I'm so happy to be able to see you all in a new series! This story is jam-packed with so many of my favorite things. I'm really looking forward to developing it further. (Smile) I hope you all have fun too!

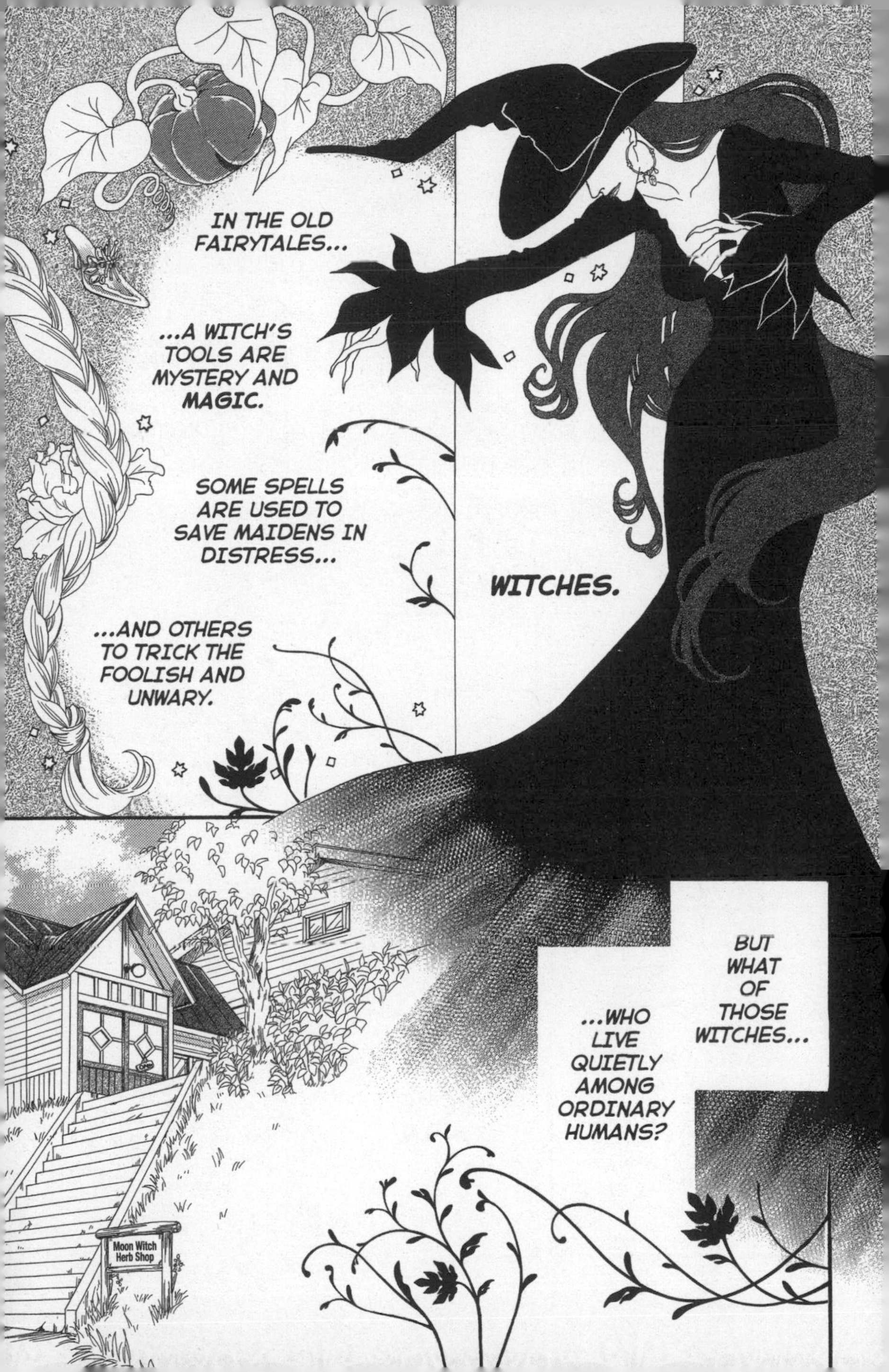
WITCHES.
IN THE OLD FAIRYTALES...
...A WITCH'S TOOLS ARE MYSTERY AND MAGIC.
SOME SPELLS ARE USED TO SAVE MAIDENS IN DISTRESS...
...AND OTHERS TO TRICK THE FOOLISH AND UNWARY.
BUT WHAT OF THOSE WITCHES...
...WHO LIVE QUIETLY AMONG ORDINARY HUMANS?
Moon Witch Herb Shop

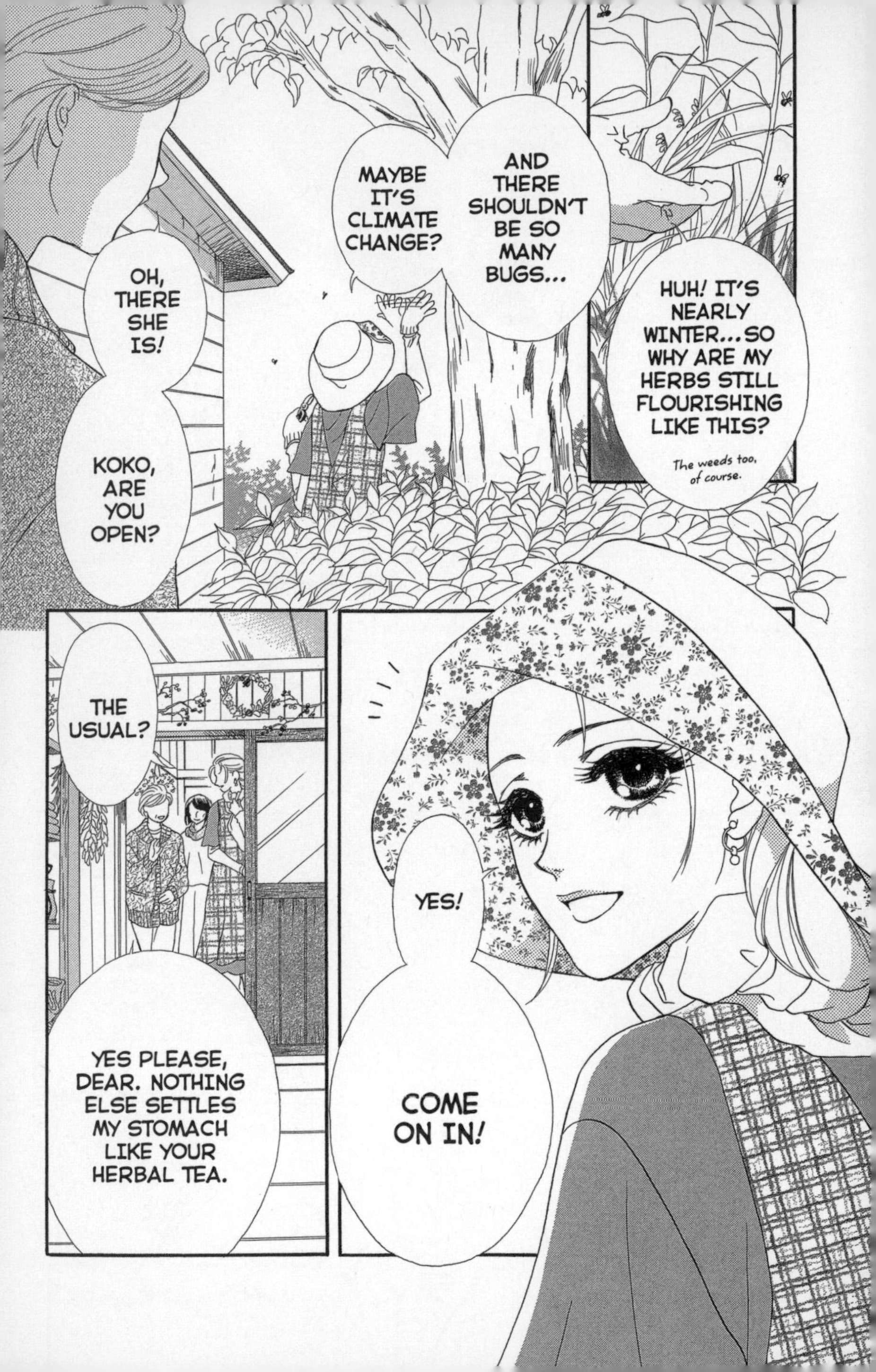
HUH! IT'S NEARLY WINTER...SO WHY ARE MY HERBS STILL FLOURISHING LIKE THIS?
The weeds too, of course.
AND THERE SHOULDN'T BE SO MANY BUGS...
MAYBE IT'S CLIMATE CHANGE?
OH, THERE SHE IS!
KOKO, ARE YOU OPEN?
YES!
COME ON IN!
THE USUAL?
YES PLEASE, DEAR. NOTHING ELSE SETTLES MY STOMACH LIKE YOUR HERBAL TEA.

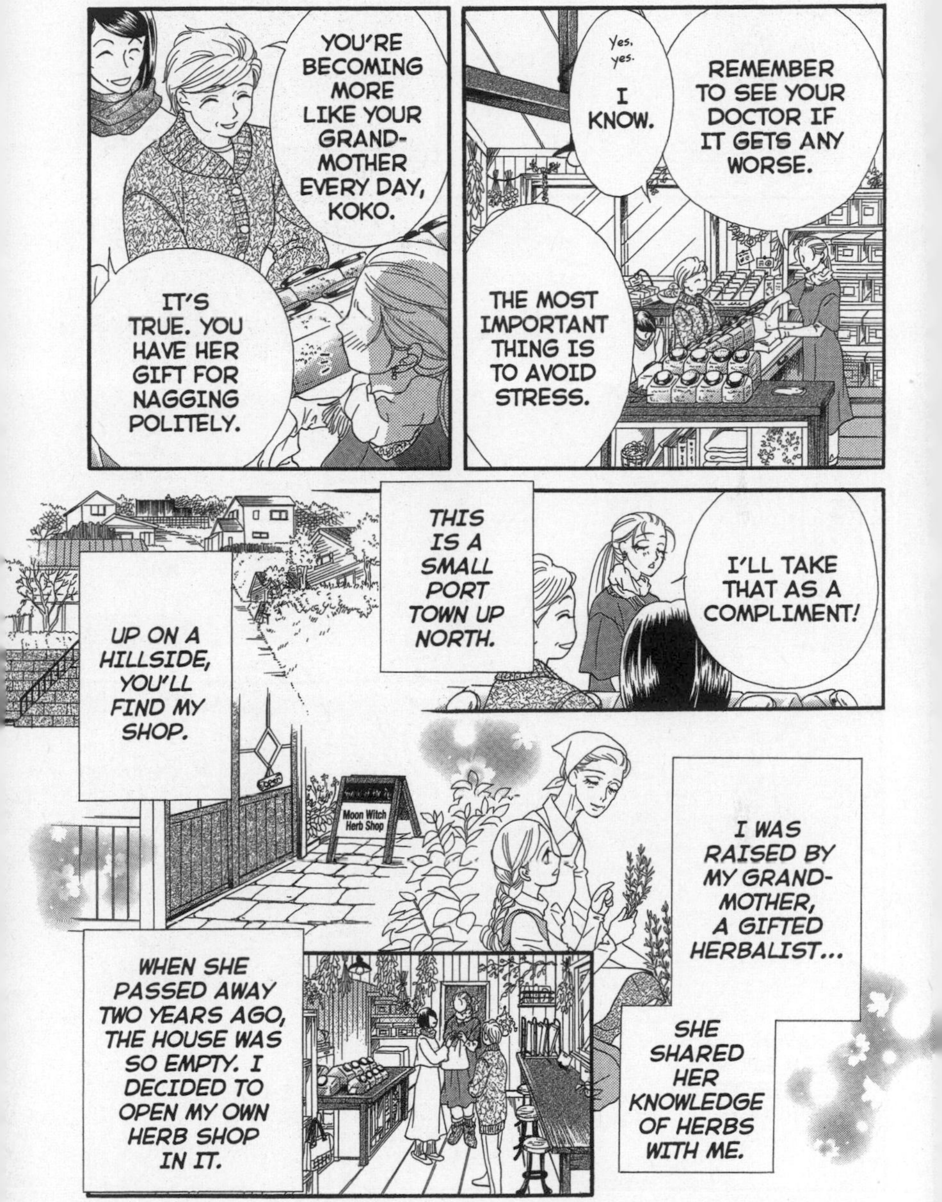
REMEMBER TO SEE YOUR DOCTOR IF IT GETS ANY WORSE.
Yes, yes.
I KNOW.
THE MOST IMPORTANT THING IS TO AVOID STRESS.
YOU'RE BECOMING MORE LIKE YOUR GRAND-MOTHER EVERY DAY, KOKO.
IT'S TRUE. YOU HAVE HER GIFT FOR NAGGING POLITELY.
I'LL TAKE THAT AS A COMPLIMENT!
THIS IS A SMALL PORT TOWN UP NORTH.
UP ON A HILLSIDE, YOU'LL FIND MY SHOP.
Moon Witch Herb Shop
I WAS RAISED BY MY GRAND-MOTHER, A GIFTED HERBALIST...
SHE SHARED HER KNOWLEDGE OF HERBS WITH ME.
WHEN SHE PASSED AWAY TWO YEARS AGO, THE HOUSE WAS SO EMPTY. I DECIDED TO OPEN MY OWN HERB SHOP IN IT.

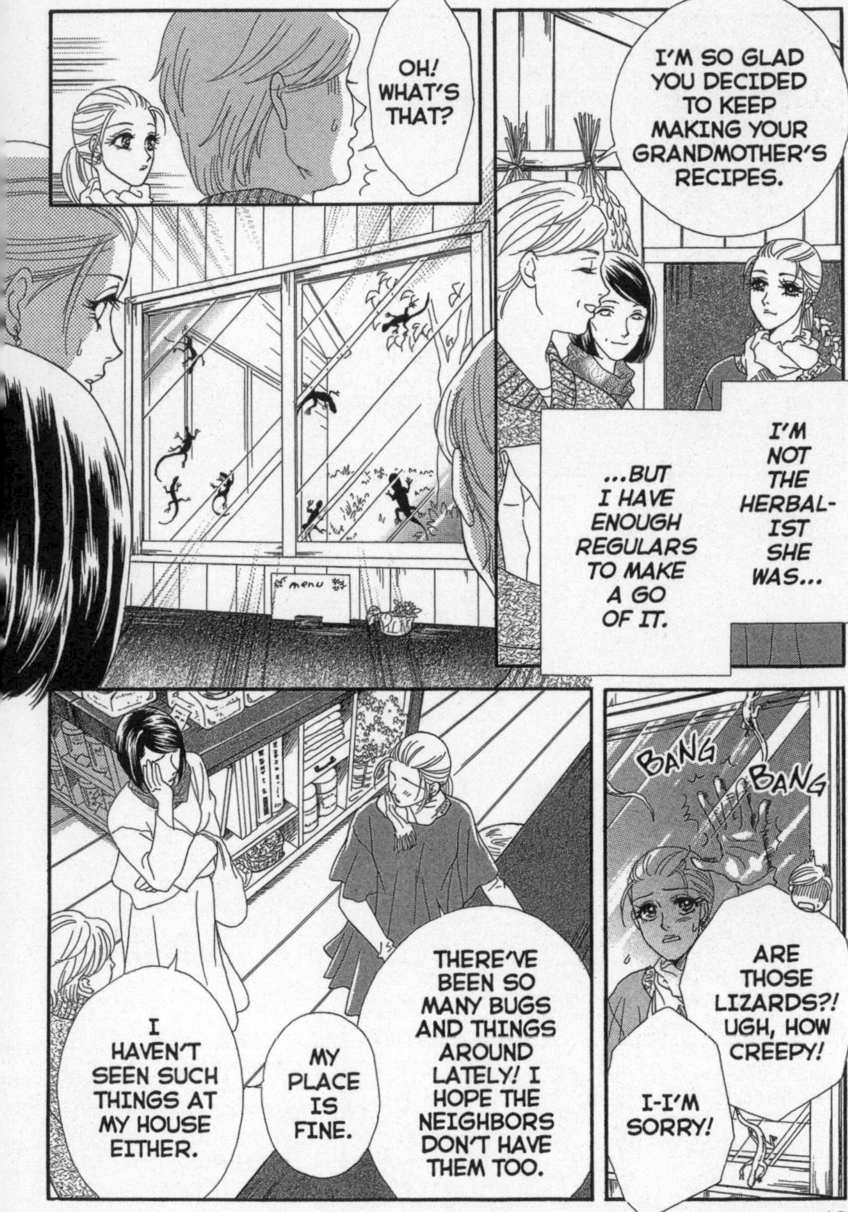
I'M SO GLAD YOU DECIDED TO KEEP MAKING YOUR GRANDMOTHER'S RECIPES.
I'M NOT THE HERBAL-IST SHE WAS...
...BUT I HAVE ENOUGH REGULARS TO MAKE A GO OF IT.
OH! WHAT'S THAT?
menu
BANG
BANG
ARE THOSE LIZARDS?! UGH, HOW CREEPY!
I-I'M SORRY!
THERE'VE BEEN SO MANY BUGS AND THINGS AROUND LATELY! I HOPE THE NEIGHBORS DON'T HAVE THEM TOO.
MY PLACE IS FINE.
I HAVEN'T SEEN SUCH THINGS AT MY HOUSE EITHER.

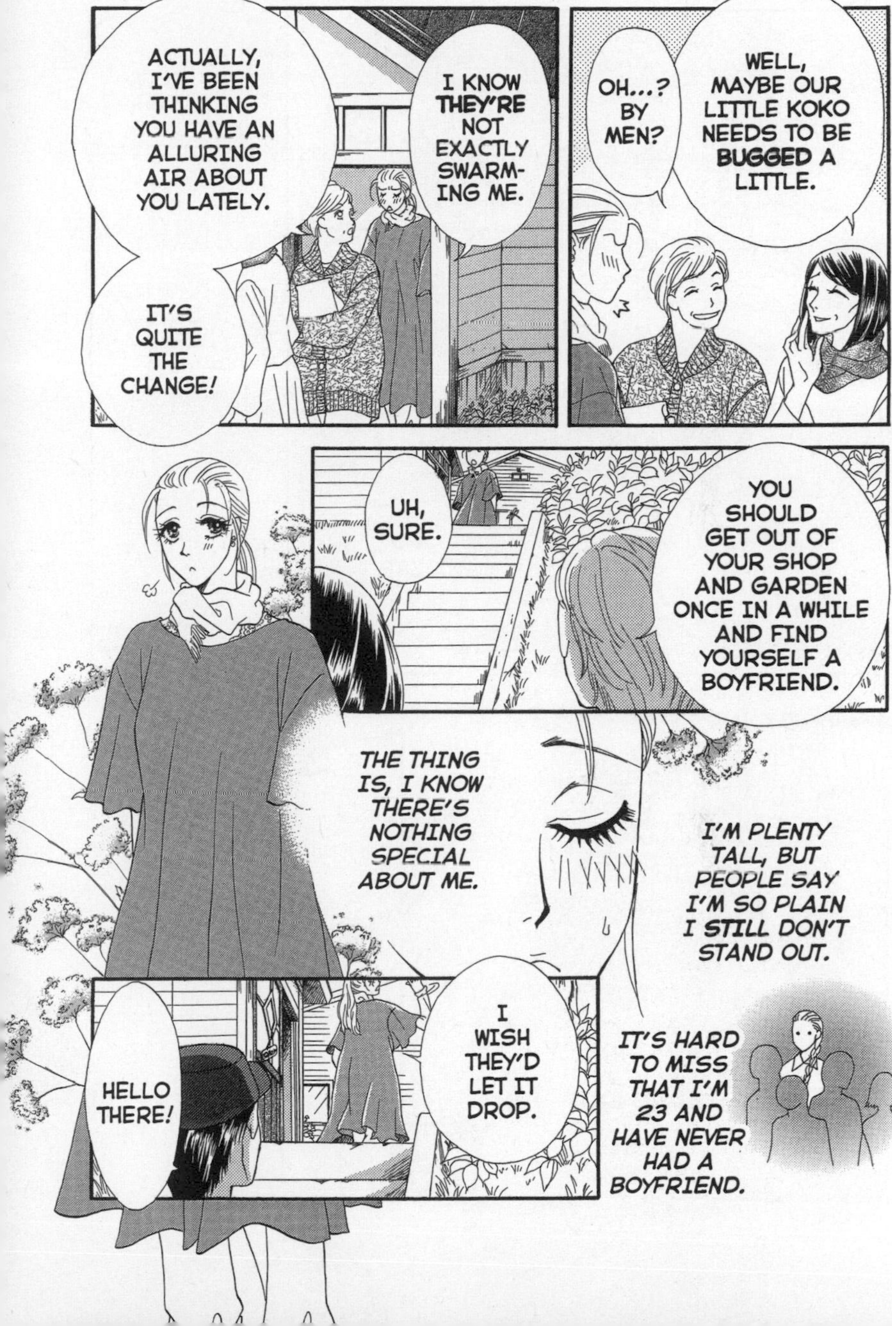
WELL, MAYBE OUR LITTLE KOKO NEEDS TO BE BUGGED A LITTLE.
OH...? BY MEN?
ACTUALLY, I'VE BEEN THINKING YOU HAVE AN ALLURING AIR ABOUT YOU LATELY.
IT'S QUITE THE CHANGE!
I KNOW THEY'RE NOT EXACTLY SWARMING ME.
YOU SHOULD GET OUT OF YOUR SHOP AND GARDEN ONCE IN A WHILE AND FIND YOURSELF A BOYFRIEND.
UH, SURE.
THE THING IS, I KNOW THERE'S NOTHING SPECIAL ABOUT ME.
I'M PLENTY TALL, BUT PEOPLE SAY I'M SO PLAIN I STILL DON'T STAND OUT.
IT'S HARD TO MISS THAT I'M 23 AND HAVE NEVER HAD A BOYFRIEND.
I WISH THEY'D LET IT DROP.
HELLO THERE!

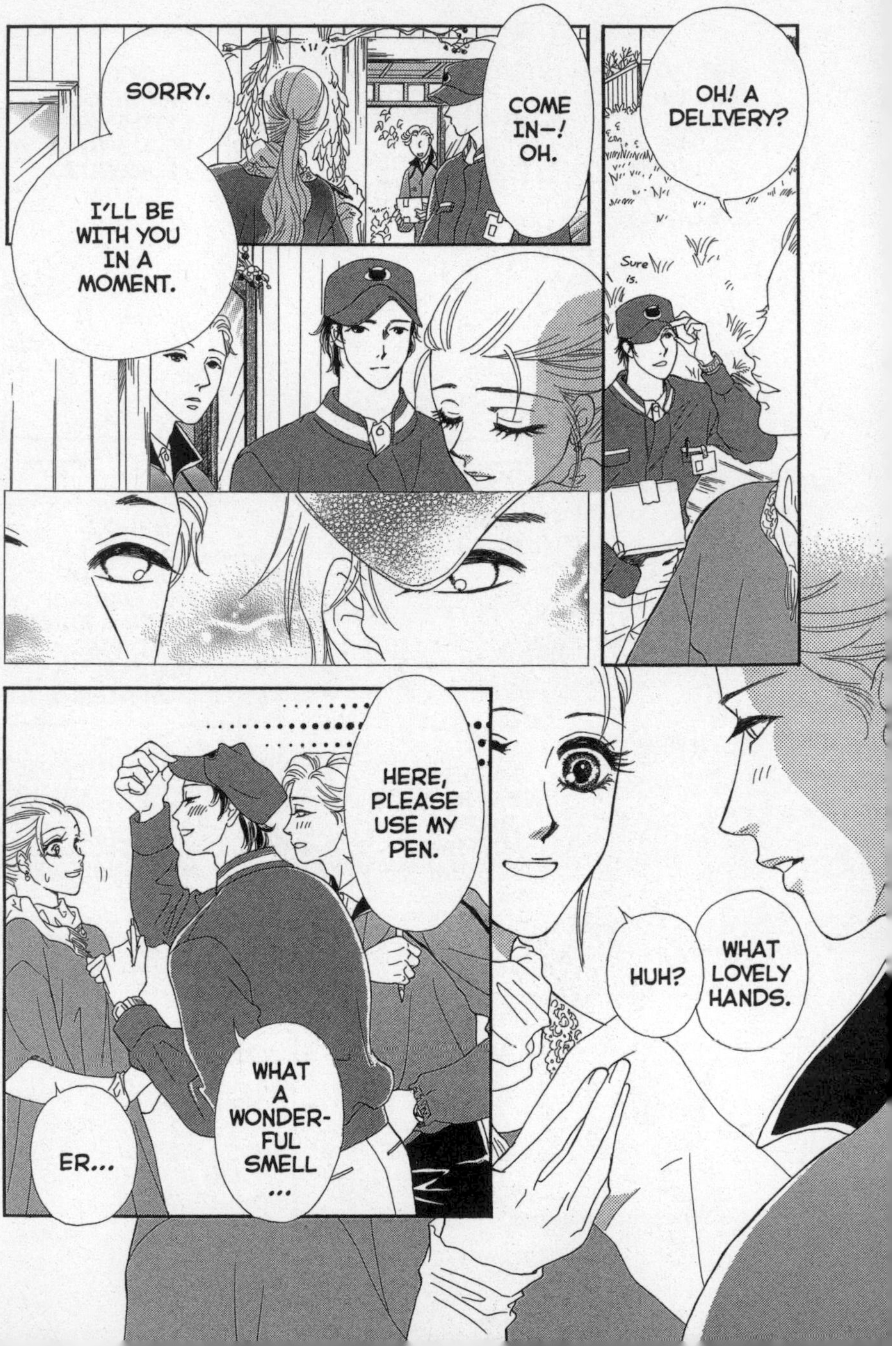
OH! A DELIVERY?
Sure is.
COME IN—! OH.
SORRY.
I'LL BE WITH YOU IN A MOMENT.
WHAT LOVELY HANDS.
HUH?
HERE, PLEASE USE MY PEN.
WHAT A WONDER-FUL SMELL ...
ER...

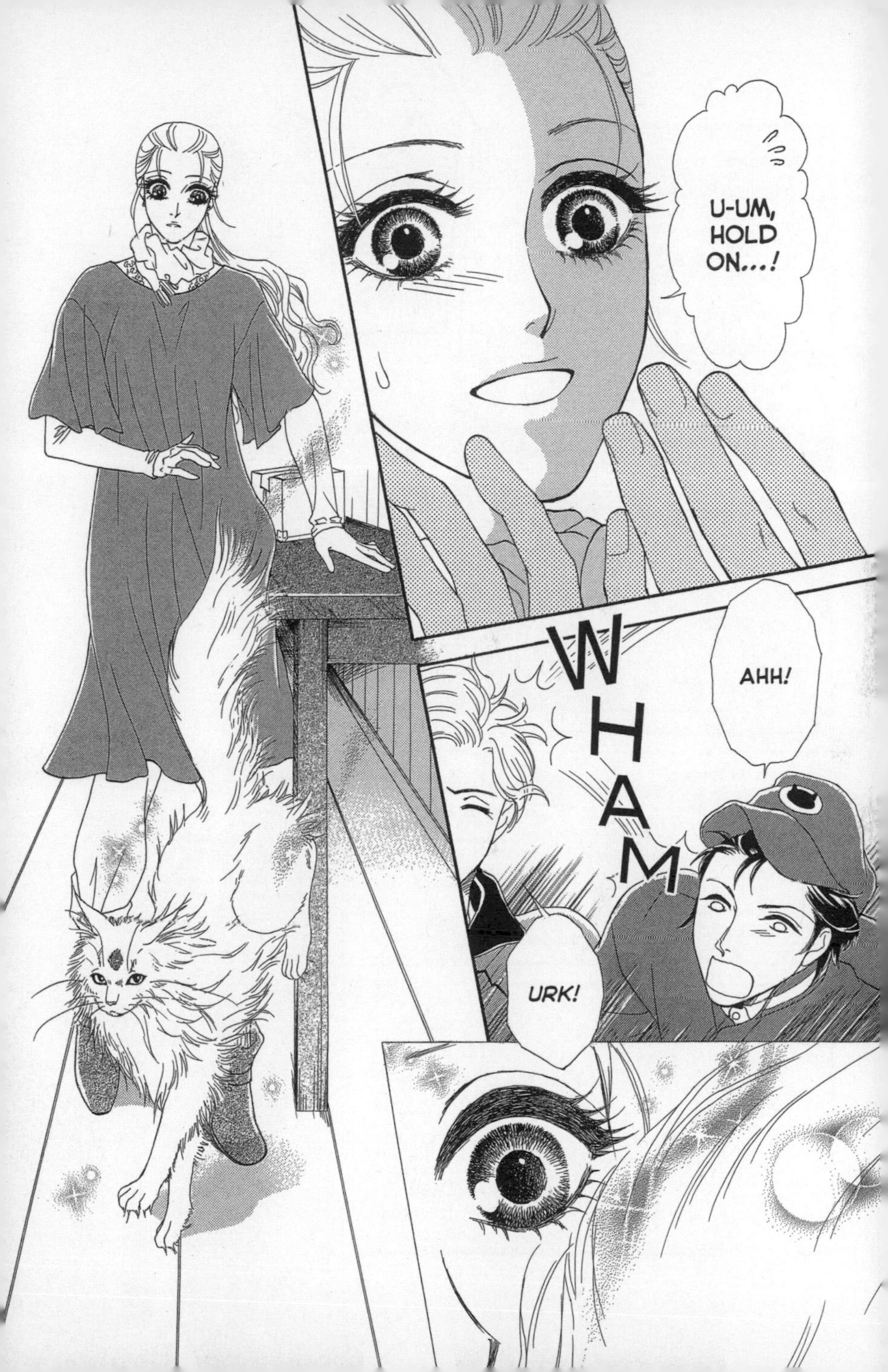
U-UM, HOLD ON...!
WHAM
AHH!
URK!

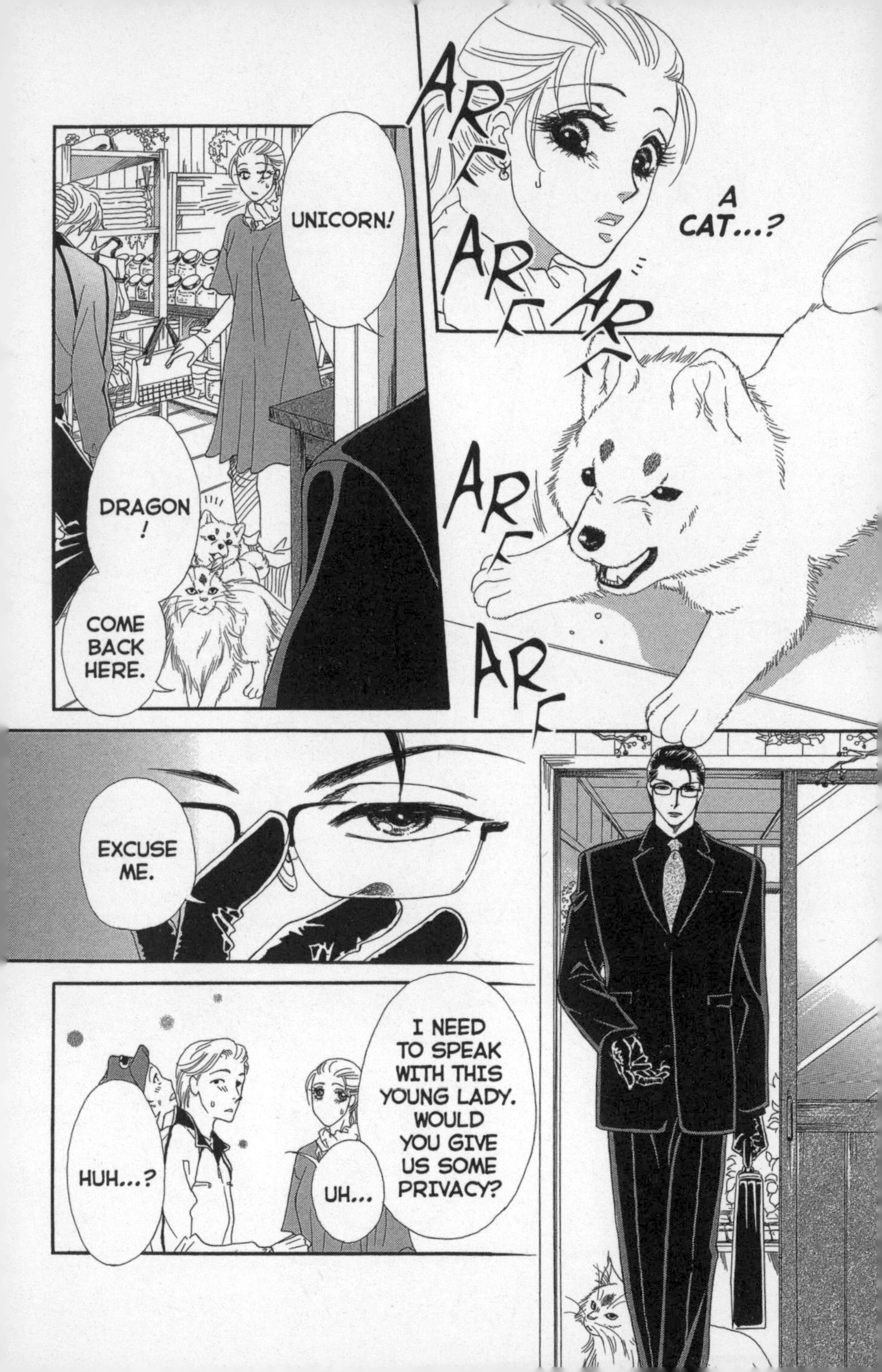
ARF
A CAT...?
ARF
ARF
ARF
ARF
UNICORN!
DRAGON!
COME BACK HERE.
EXCUSE ME.
I NEED TO SPEAK WITH THIS YOUNG LADY. WOULD YOU GIVE US SOME PRIVACY?
UH...
HUH...?

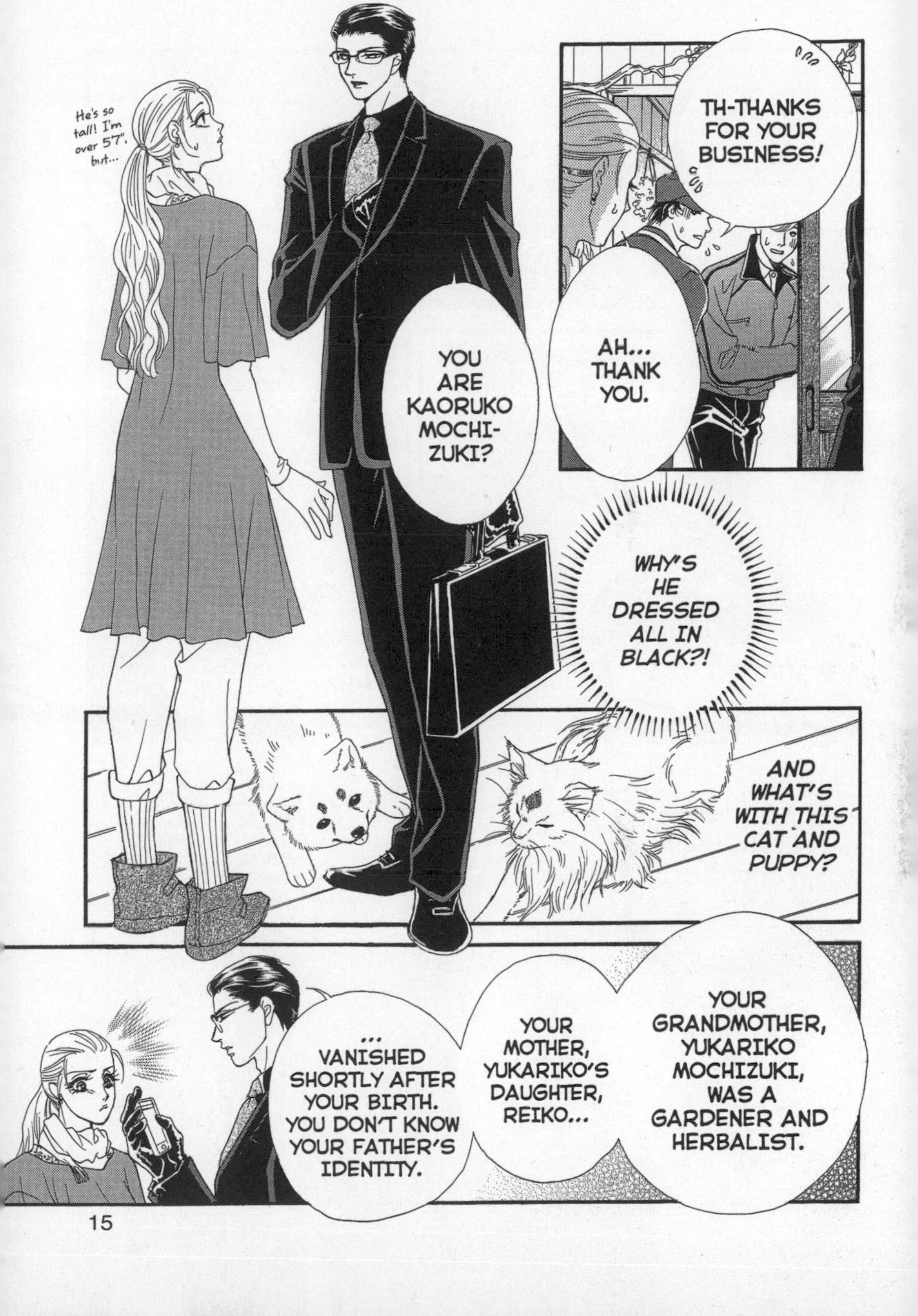

TH-THANKS FOR YOUR BUSINESS!
AH... THANK YOU.
YOU ARE KAORUKO MOCHI-ZUKI?
He's so tall! I'm over 5'7", but...
WHY'S HE DRESSED ALL IN BLACK?!
AND WHAT'S WITH THIS CAT AND PUPPY?
YOUR GRANDMOTHER, YUKARIKO MOCHIZUKI, WAS A GARDENER AND HERBALIST.
YOUR MOTHER, YUKARIKO'S DAUGHTER, REIKO...
... VANISHED SHORTLY AFTER YOUR BIRTH. YOU DON'T KNOW YOUR FATHER'S IDENTITY.

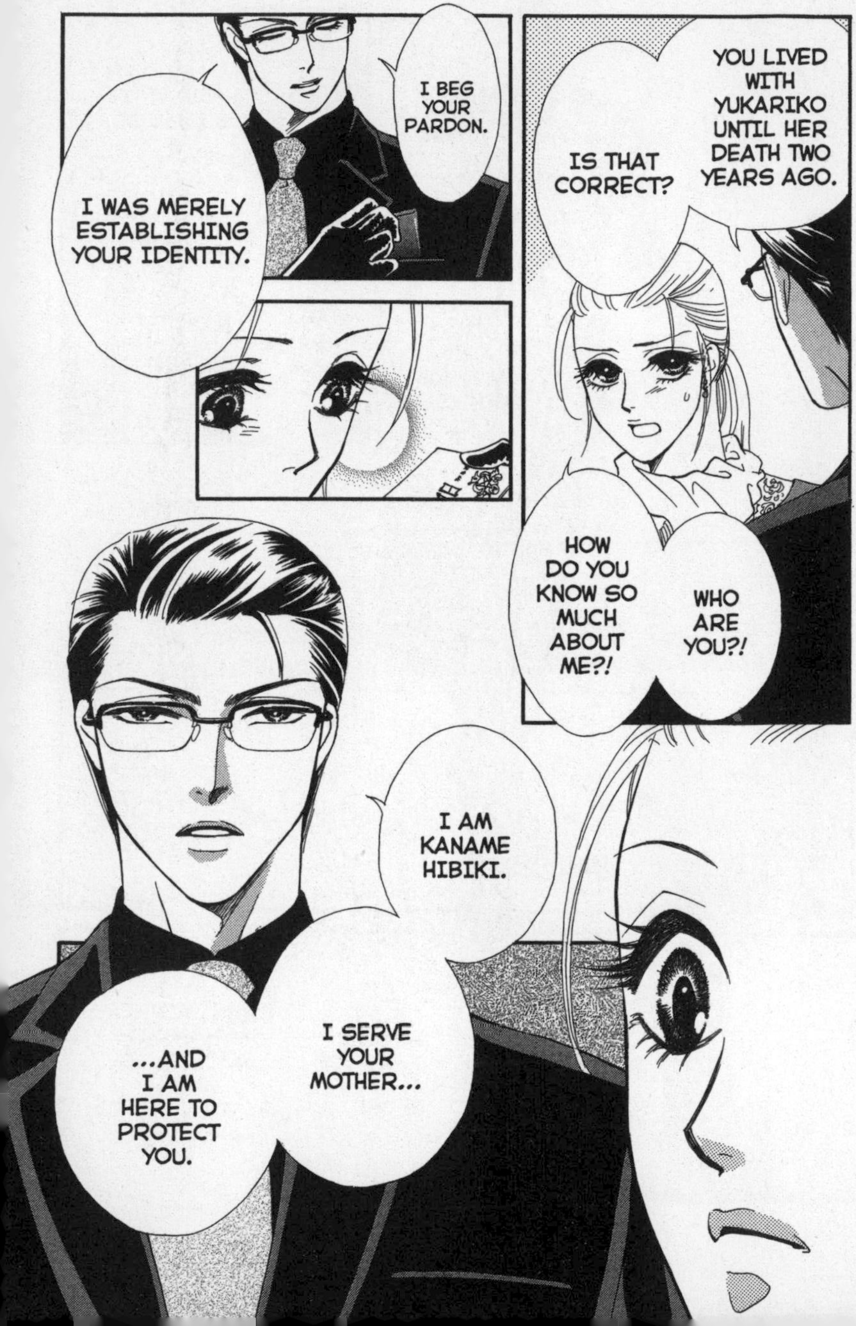
YOU LIVED WITH YUKARIKO UNTIL HER DEATH TWO YEARS AGO.
IS THAT CORRECT?
WHO ARE YOU?!
HOW DO YOU KNOW SO MUCH ABOUT ME?!
I BEG YOUR PARDON.
I WAS MERELY ESTABLISHING YOUR IDENTITY.
I AM KANAME HIBIKI.
I SERVE YOUR MOTHER...
...AND I AM HERE TO PROTECT YOU.

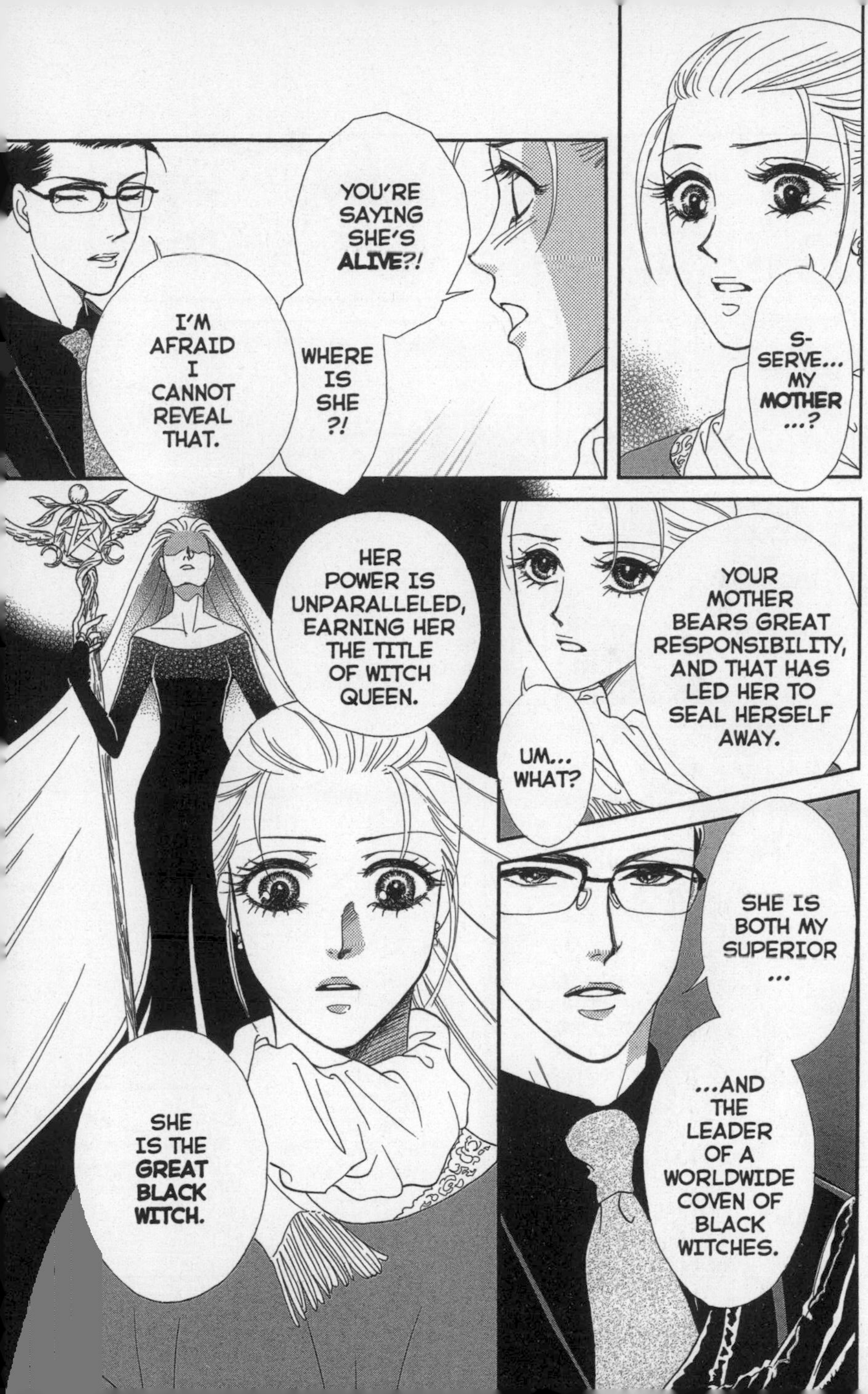
S-SERVE... MY **MOTHER** ...?
YOU'RE SAYING SHE'S **ALIVE**?!
WHERE IS SHE ?!
I'M AFRAID I CANNOT REVEAL THAT.
YOUR MOTHER BEARS GREAT RESPONSIBILITY, AND THAT HAS LED HER TO SEAL HERSELF AWAY.
UM... WHAT?
SHE IS BOTH MY SUPERIOR ...
...AND THE LEADER OF A WORLDWIDE COVEN OF BLACK WITCHES.
HER POWER IS UNPARALLELED, EARNING HER THE TITLE OF WITCH QUEEN.
SHE IS THE **GREAT BLACK WITCH.**

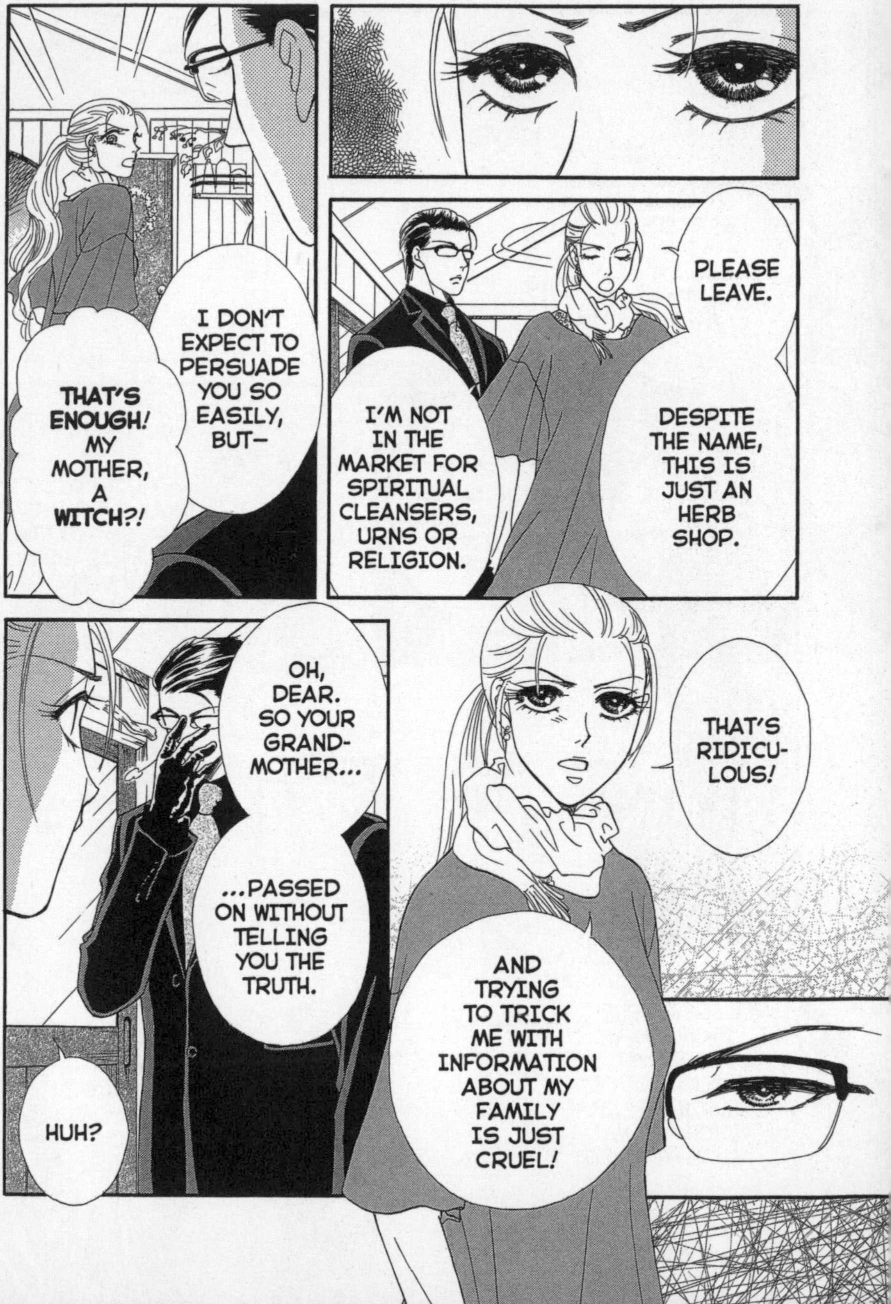
PLEASE LEAVE.
DESPITE THE NAME, THIS IS JUST AN HERB SHOP.
I'M NOT IN THE MARKET FOR SPIRITUAL CLEANSERS, URNS OR RELIGION.
I DON'T EXPECT TO PERSUADE YOU SO EASILY, BUT—
THAT'S ENOUGH! MY MOTHER, A WITCH?!
THAT'S RIDICU-LOUS!
AND TRYING TO TRICK ME WITH INFORMATION ABOUT MY FAMILY IS JUST CRUEL!
OH, DEAR. SO YOUR GRAND-MOTHER...
...PASSED ON WITHOUT TELLING YOU THE TRUTH.
HUH?

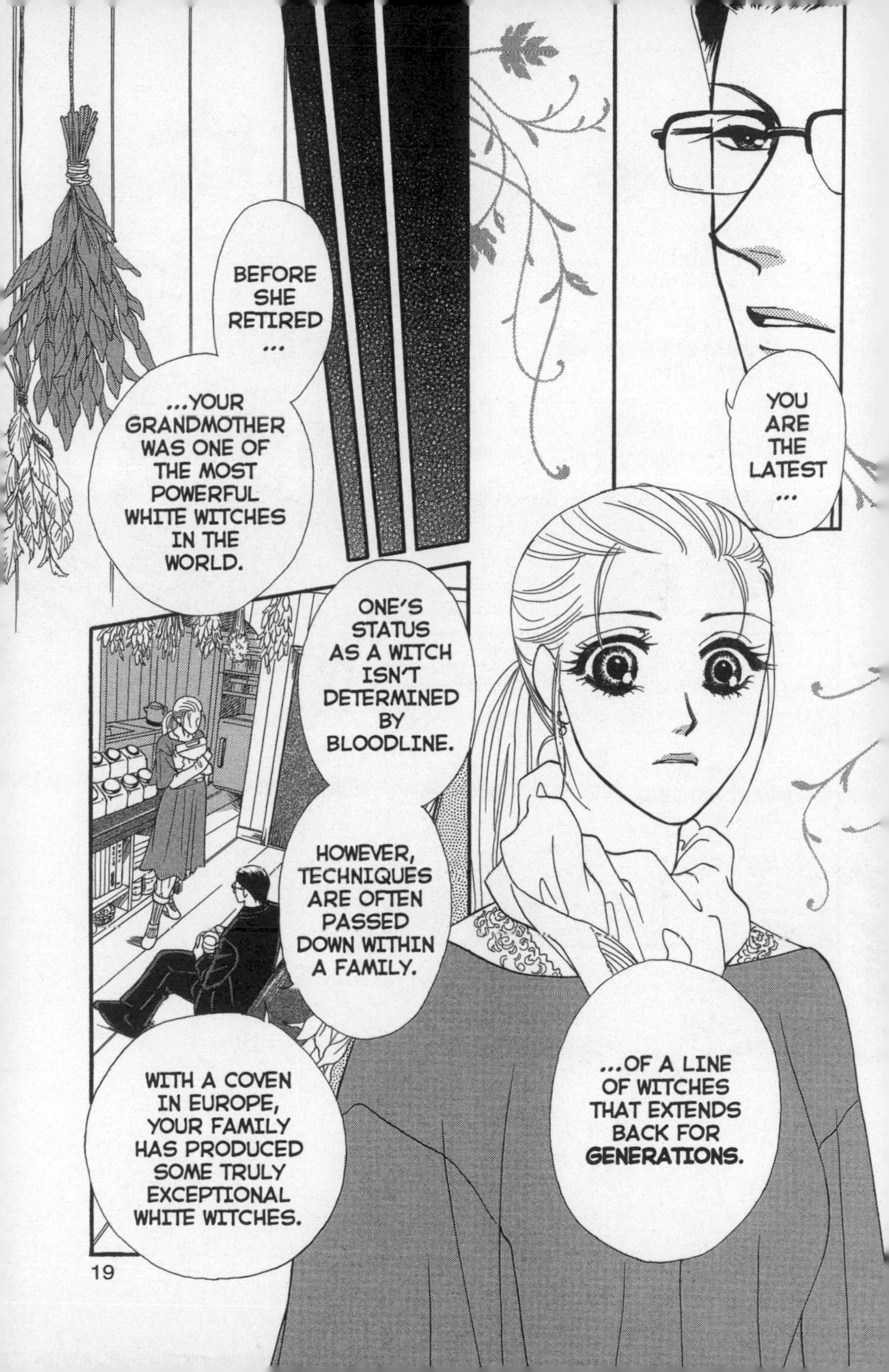
BEFORE SHE RETIRED ...
...YOUR GRANDMOTHER WAS ONE OF THE MOST POWERFUL WHITE WITCHES IN THE WORLD.
ONE'S STATUS AS A WITCH ISN'T DETERMINED BY BLOODLINE.
HOWEVER, TECHNIQUES ARE OFTEN PASSED DOWN WITHIN A FAMILY.
WITH A COVEN IN EUROPE, YOUR FAMILY HAS PRODUCED SOME TRULY EXCEPTIONAL WHITE WITCHES.
YOU ARE THE LATEST ...
...OF A LINE OF WITCHES THAT EXTENDS BACK FOR **GENERATIONS.**

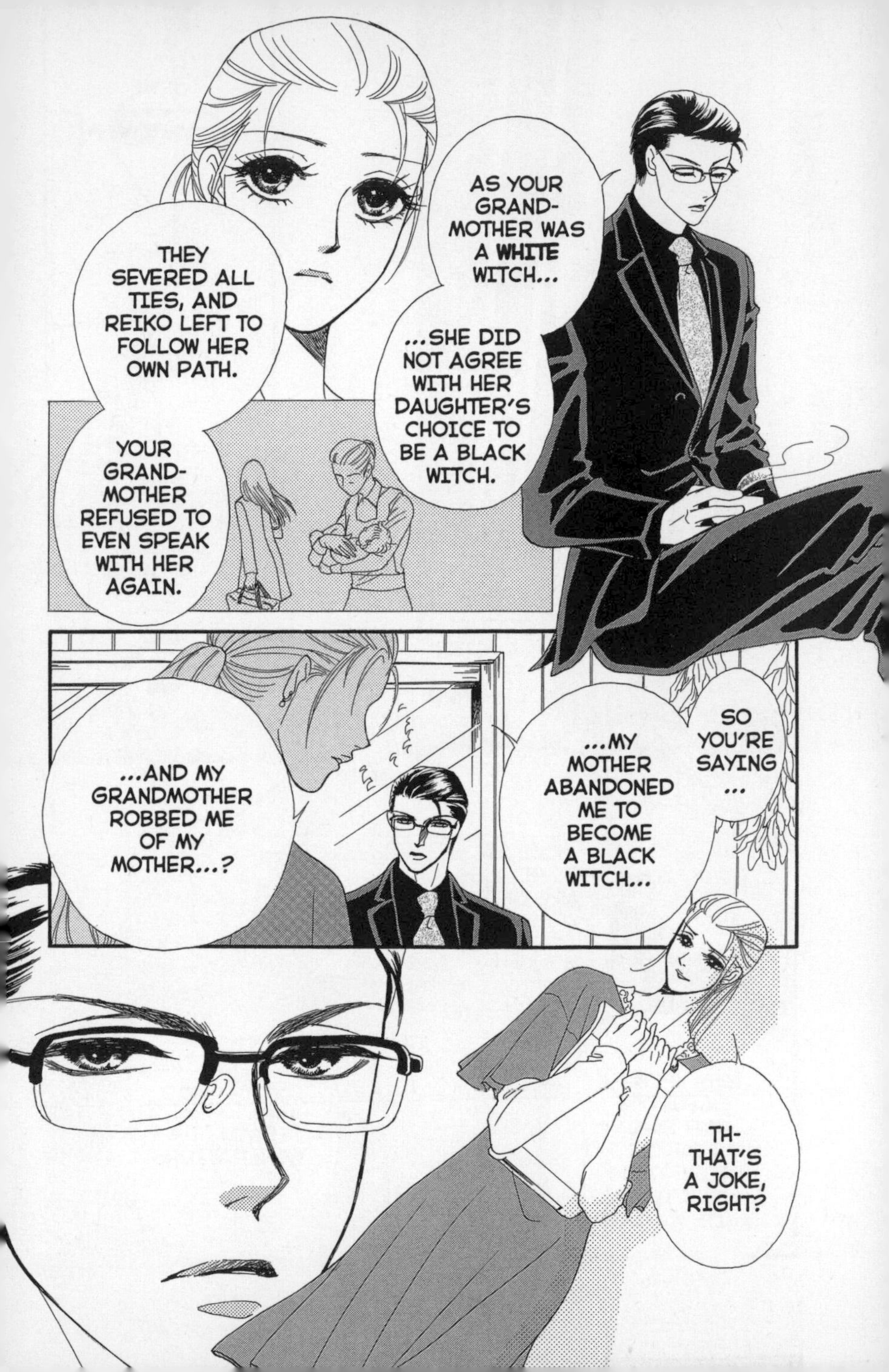
AS YOUR GRAND-MOTHER WAS A WHITE WITCH...
...SHE DID NOT AGREE WITH HER DAUGHTER'S CHOICE TO BE A BLACK WITCH.
THEY SEVERED ALL TIES, AND REIKO LEFT TO FOLLOW HER OWN PATH.
YOUR GRAND-MOTHER REFUSED TO EVEN SPEAK WITH HER AGAIN.
SO YOU'RE SAYING...
...MY MOTHER ABANDONED ME TO BECOME A BLACK WITCH...
...AND MY GRANDMOTHER ROBBED ME OF MY MOTHER...?
TH-THAT'S A JOKE, RIGHT?

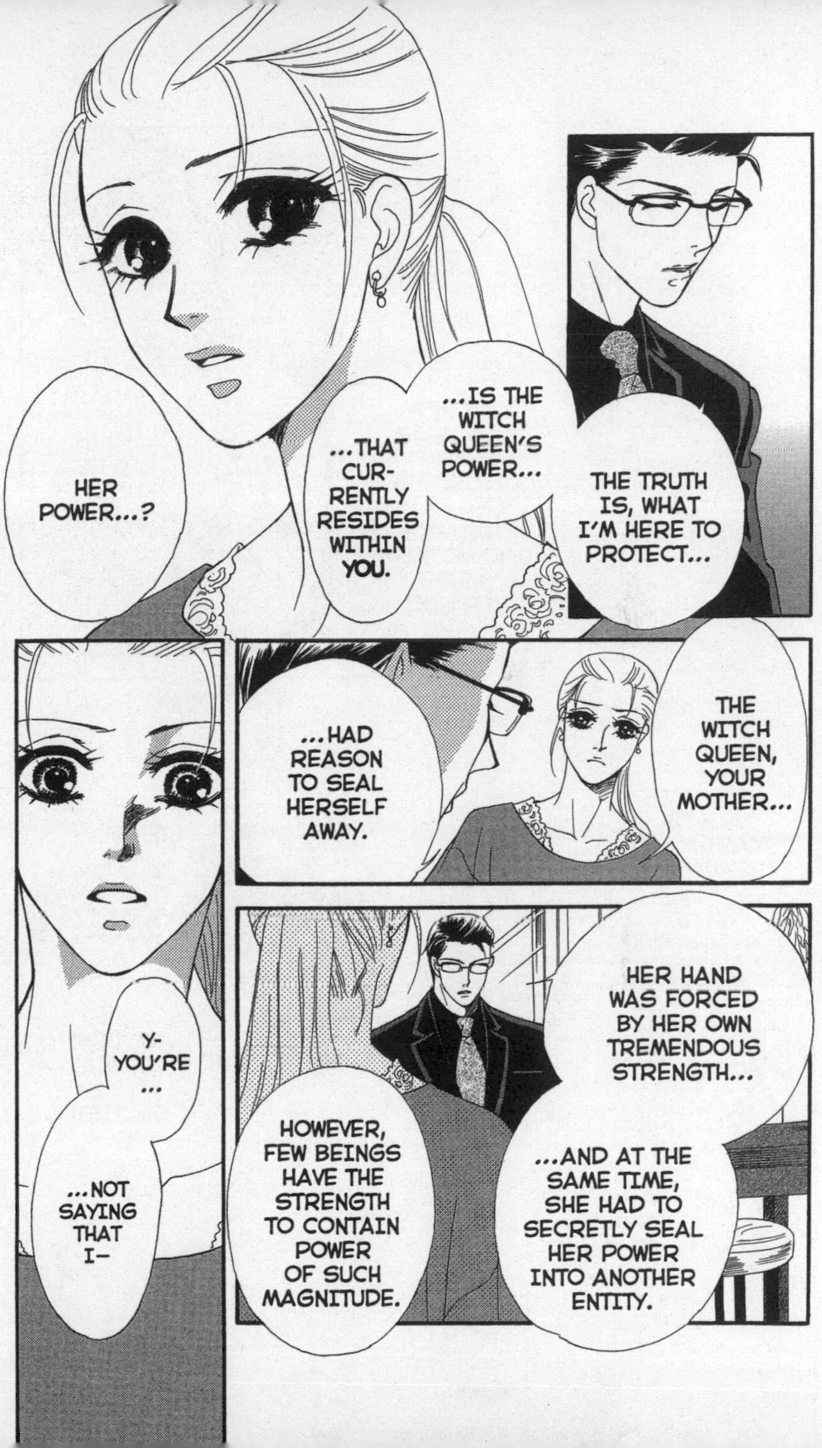
THE TRUTH IS, WHAT I'M HERE TO PROTECT...
...IS THE WITCH QUEEN'S POWER...
...THAT CURRENTLY RESIDES WITHIN YOU.
HER POWER...?
THE WITCH QUEEN, YOUR MOTHER...
...HAD REASON TO SEAL HERSELF AWAY.
HER HAND WAS FORCED BY HER OWN TREMENDOUS STRENGTH...
...AND AT THE SAME TIME, SHE HAD TO SECRETLY SEAL HER POWER INTO ANOTHER ENTITY.
HOWEVER, FEW BEINGS HAVE THE STRENGTH TO CONTAIN POWER OF SUCH MAGNITUDE.
Y-YOU'RE...
...NOT SAYING THAT I—

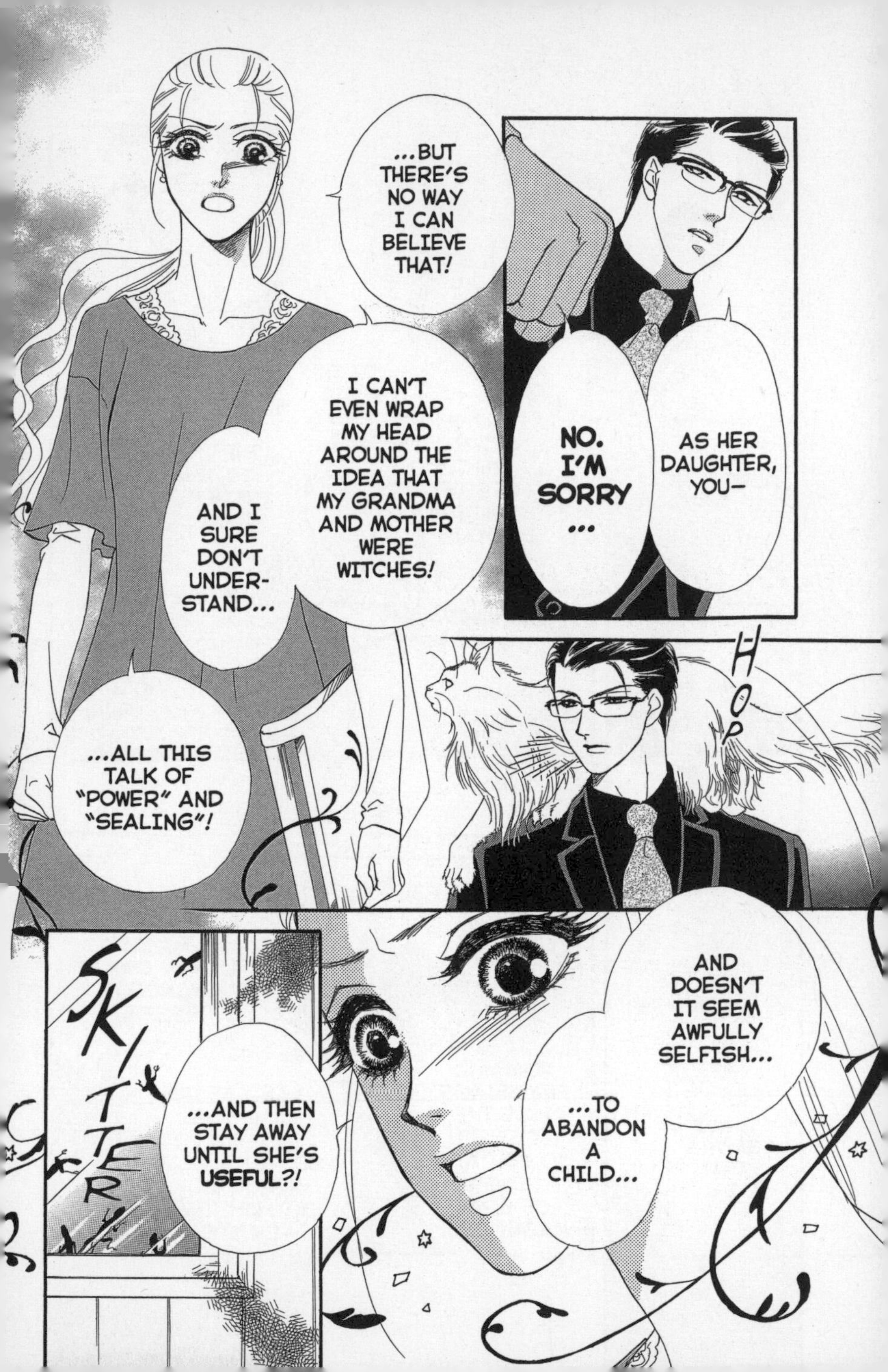
AS HER DAUGHTER, YOU–
NO. I'M SORRY...
HOP
...BUT THERE'S NO WAY I CAN BELIEVE THAT!
I CAN'T EVEN WRAP MY HEAD AROUND THE IDEA THAT MY GRANDMA AND MOTHER WERE WITCHES!
AND I SURE DON'T UNDERSTAND...
...ALL THIS TALK OF "POWER" AND "SEALING"!
AND DOESN'T IT SEEM AWFULLY SELFISH...
...TO ABANDON A CHILD...
...AND THEN STAY AWAY UNTIL SHE'S **USEFUL**?!
SKITTER

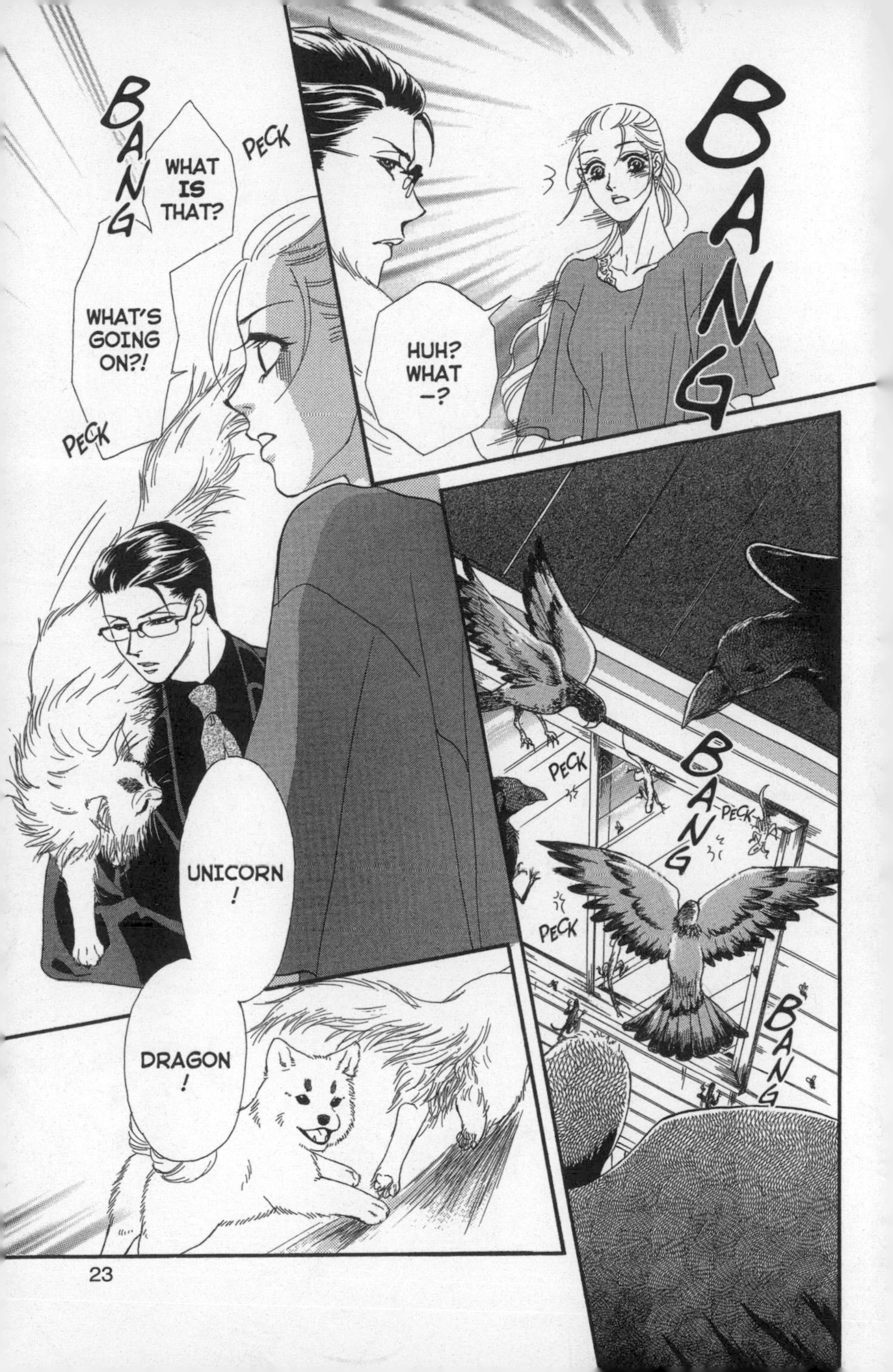
BANG
HUH? WHAT —?
BANG
WHAT IS THAT?
PECK
WHAT'S GOING ON?!
PECK
BANG
PECK
PECK
PECK
BANG
UNICORN!
DRAGON!

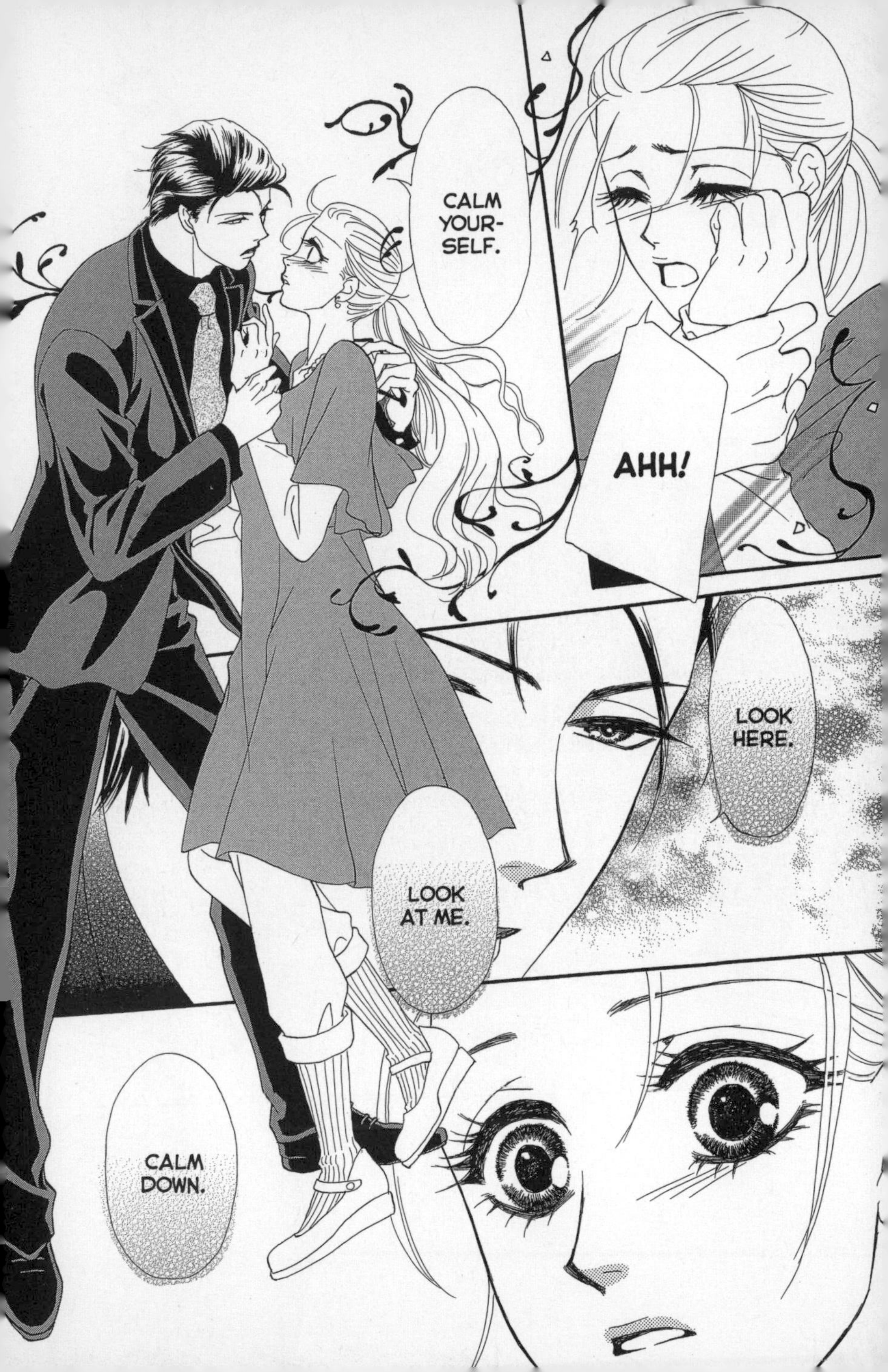
AHH!
CALM YOURSELF.
LOOK HERE.
LOOK AT ME.
CALM DOWN.

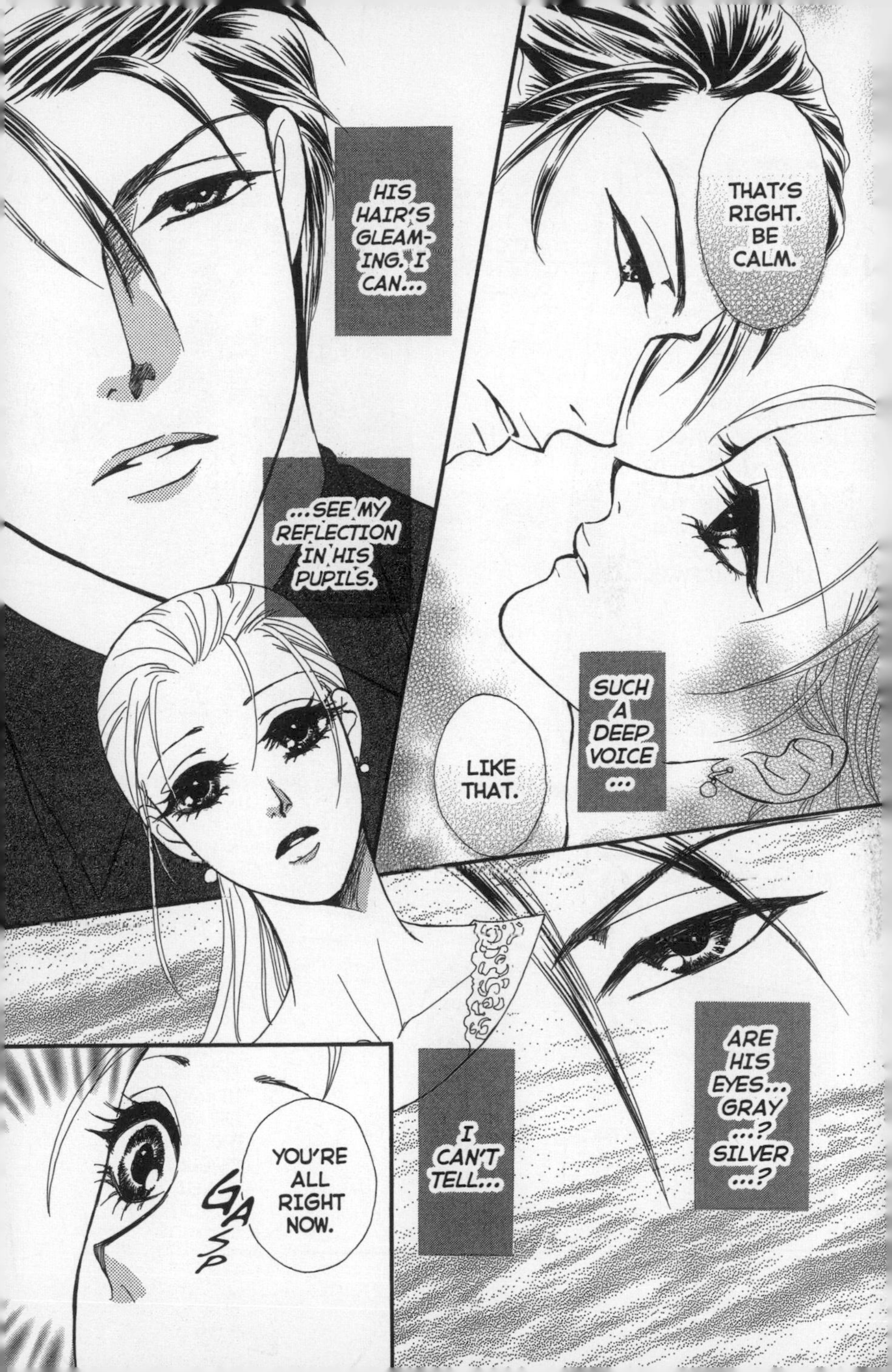
THAT'S RIGHT. BE CALM.
SUCH A DEEP VOICE...
LIKE THAT.
HIS HAIR'S GLEAM-ING. I CAN...
...SEE MY REFLECTION IN HIS PUPILS.
ARE HIS EYES... GRAY...? SILVER...?
I CAN'T TELL...
YOU'RE ALL RIGHT NOW.
GASP

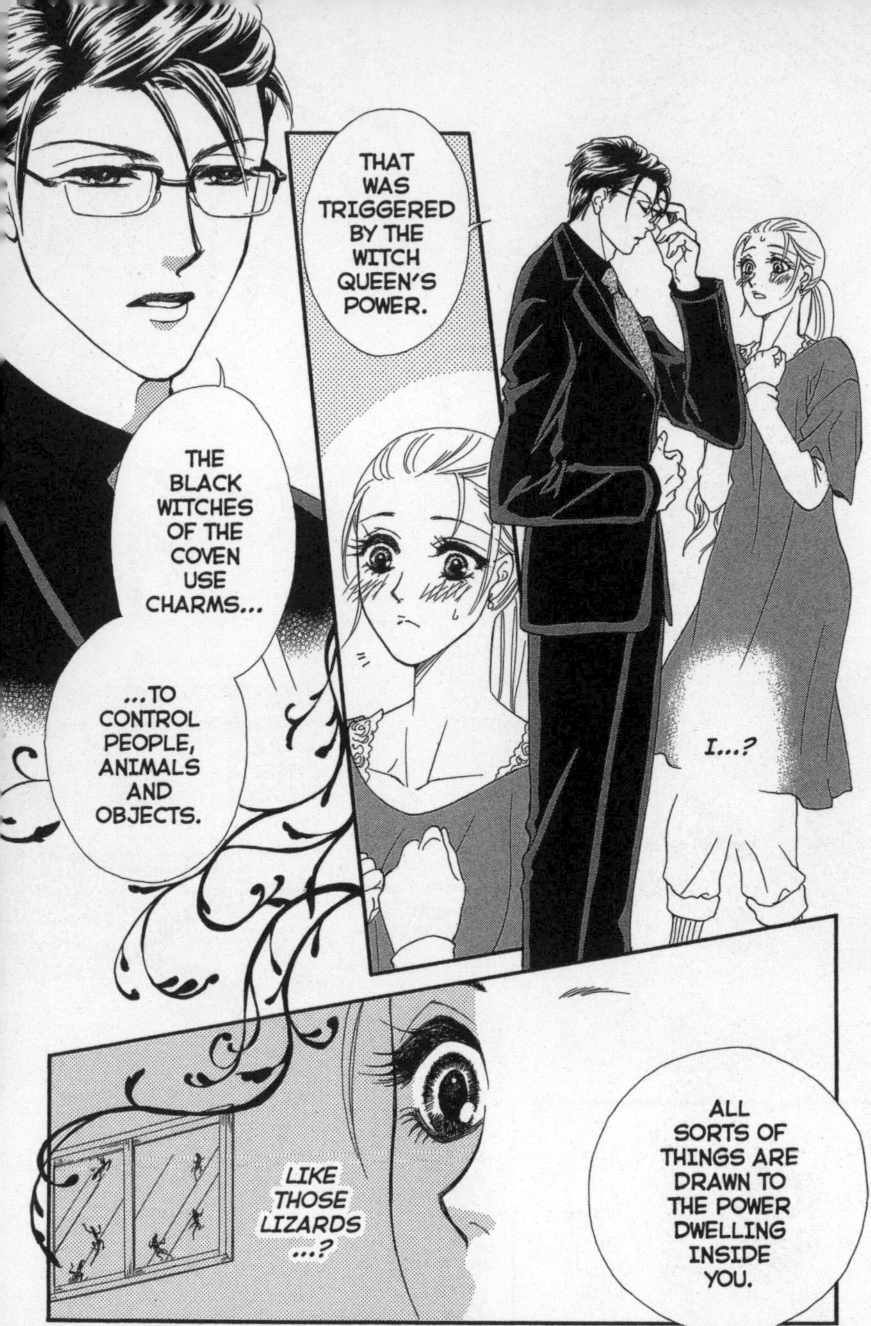
I...?
THAT WAS TRIGGERED BY THE WITCH QUEEN'S POWER.
THE BLACK WITCHES OF THE COVEN USE CHARMS...
...TO CONTROL PEOPLE, ANIMALS AND OBJECTS.
ALL SORTS OF THINGS ARE DRAWN TO THE POWER DWELLING INSIDE YOU.
LIKE THOSE LIZARDS ...?

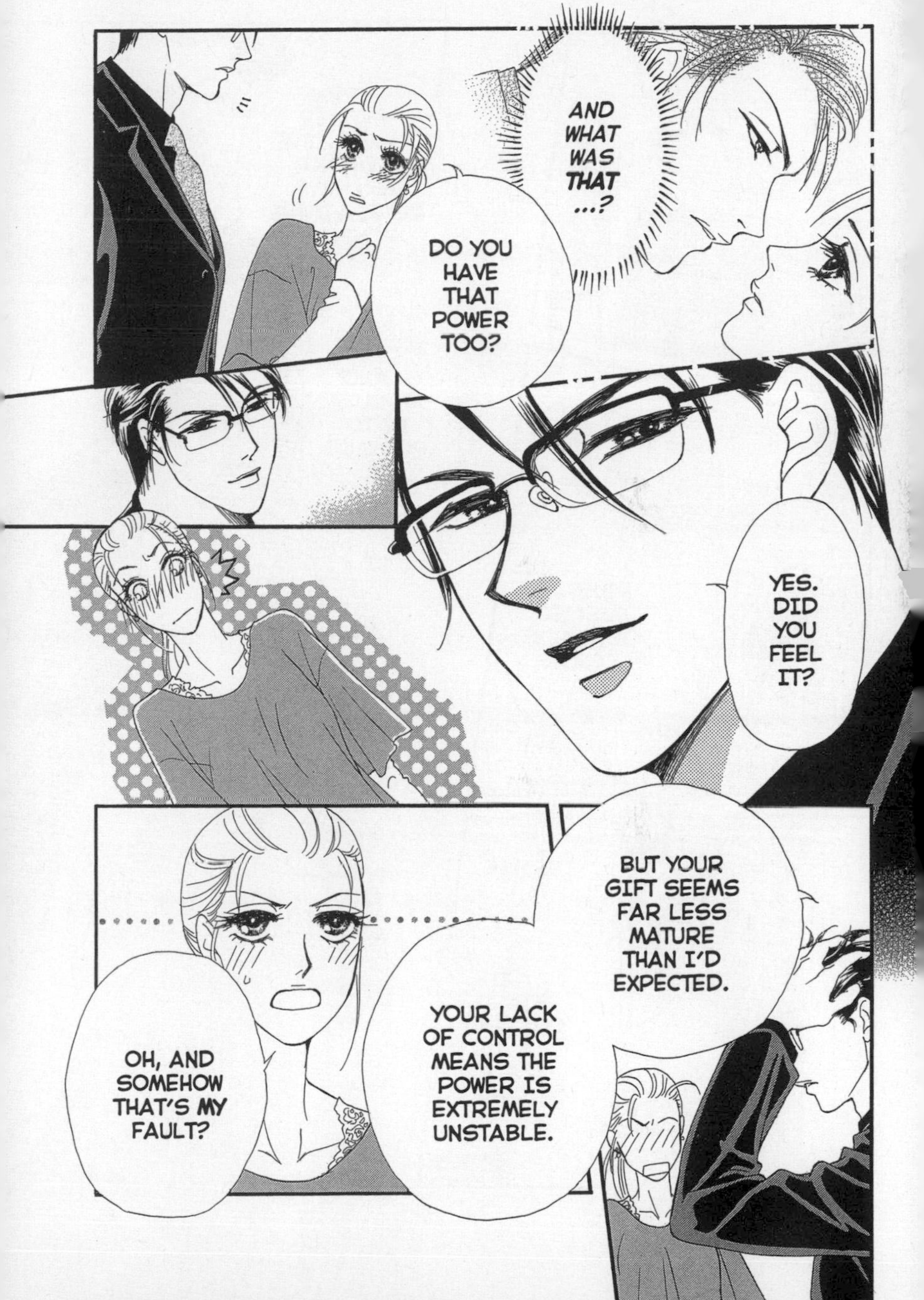
AND WHAT WAS THAT ...?
DO YOU HAVE THAT POWER TOO?
YES. DID YOU FEEL IT?
BUT YOUR GIFT SEEMS FAR LESS MATURE THAN I'D EXPECTED.
YOUR LACK OF CONTROL MEANS THE POWER IS EXTREMELY UNSTABLE.
OH, AND SOMEHOW THAT'S MY FAULT?

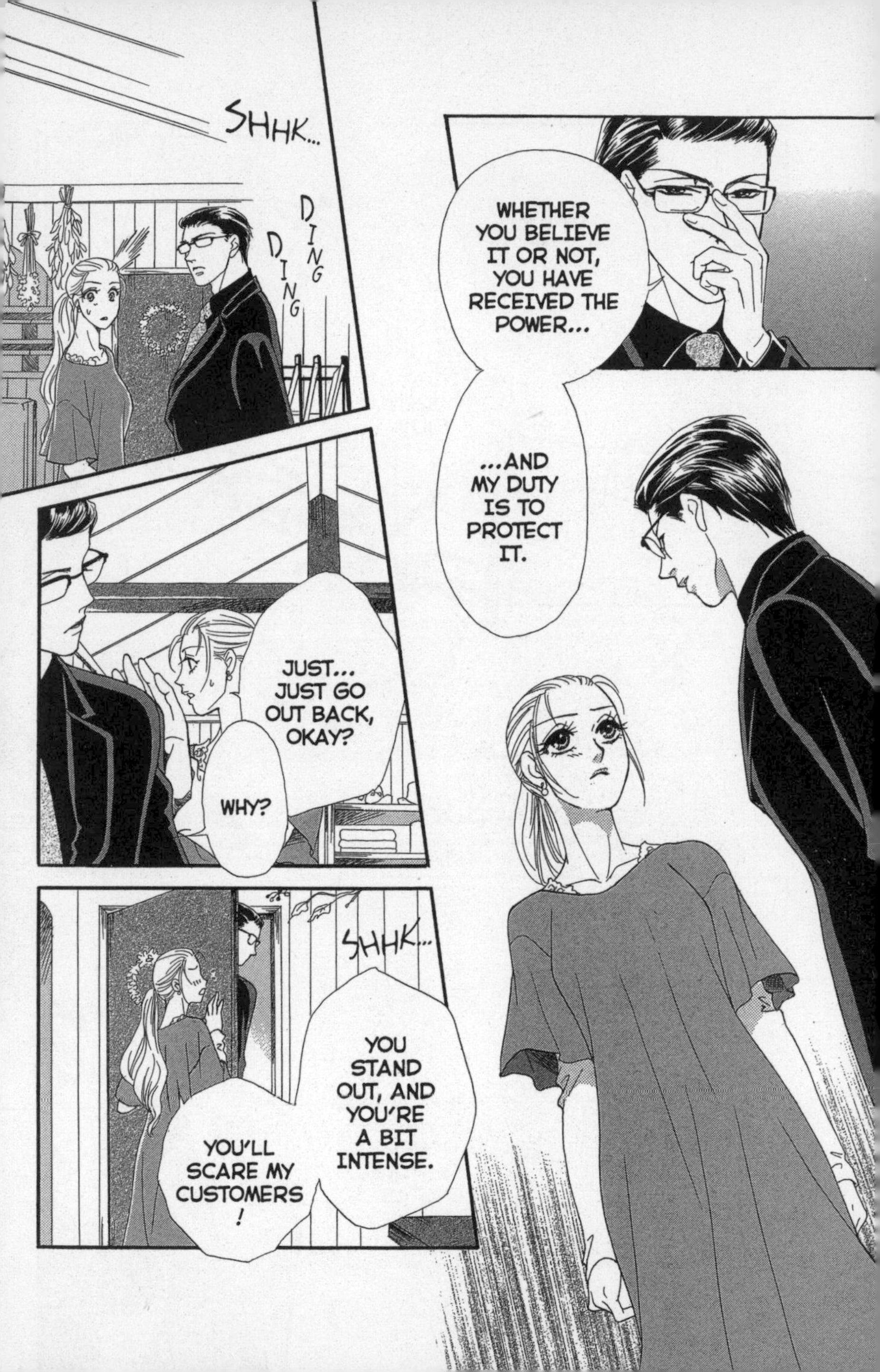
WHETHER YOU BELIEVE IT OR NOT, YOU HAVE RECEIVED THE POWER...
...AND MY DUTY IS TO PROTECT IT.
SHHK...
DING
DING
JUST... JUST GO OUT BACK, OKAY?
WHY?
SHHK...
YOU STAND OUT, AND YOU'RE A BIT INTENSE.
YOU'LL SCARE MY CUSTOMERS!

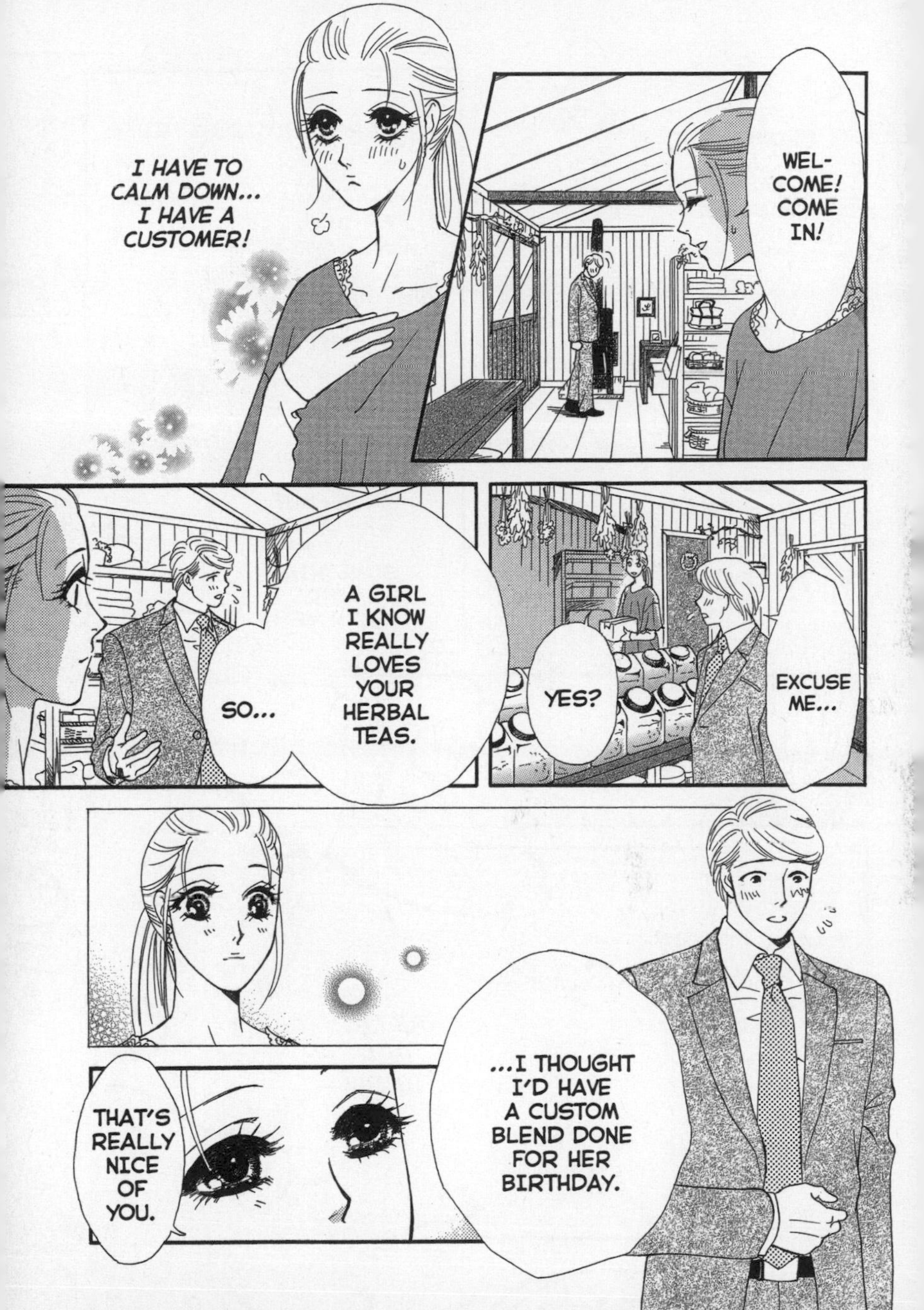
WELCOME! COME IN!
I HAVE TO CALM DOWN... I HAVE A CUSTOMER!
EXCUSE ME...
YES?
A GIRL I KNOW REALLY LOVES YOUR HERBAL TEAS.
SO...
...I THOUGHT I'D HAVE A CUSTOM BLEND DONE FOR HER BIRTHDAY.
THAT'S REALLY NICE OF YOU.

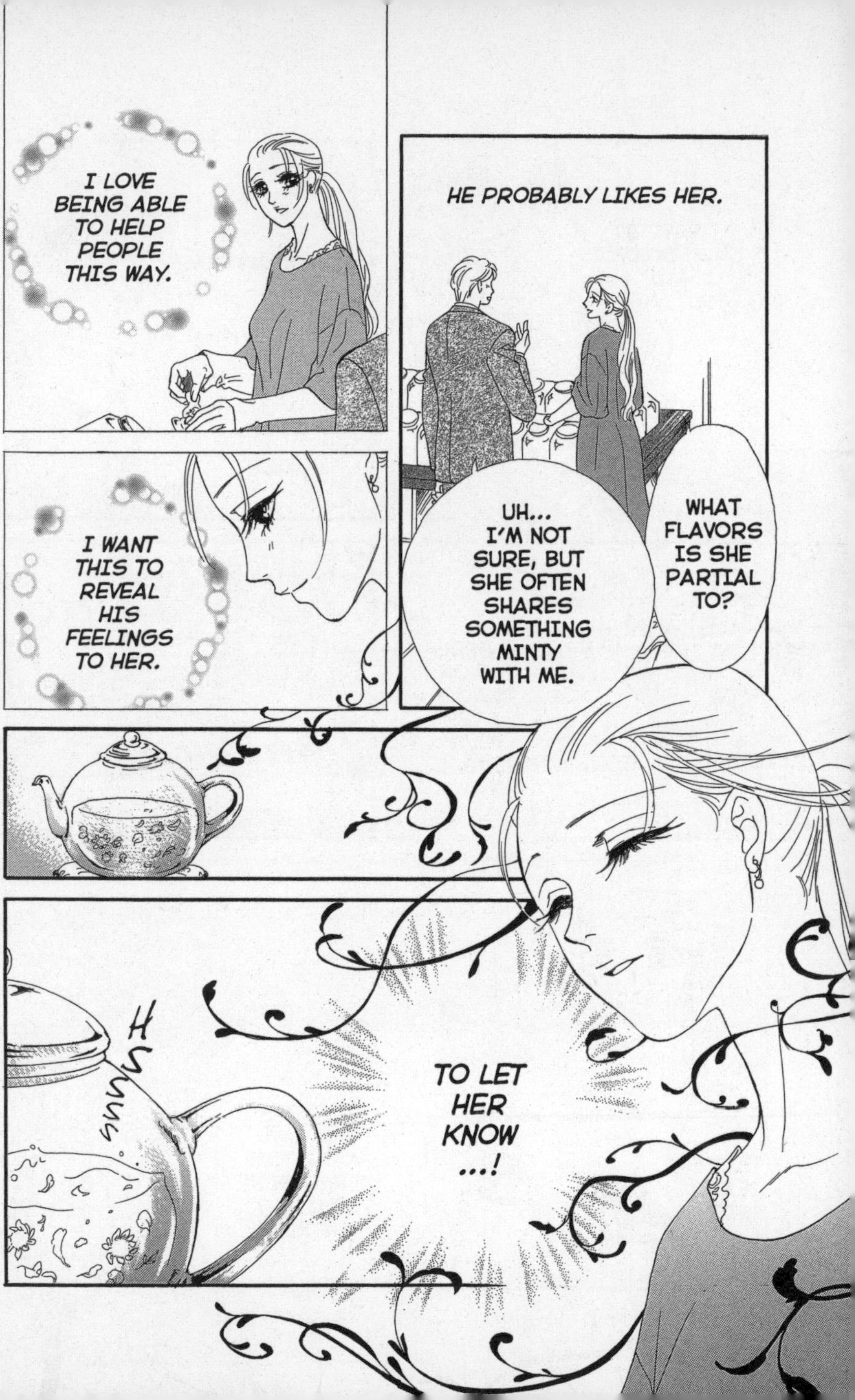
HE PROBABLY LIKES HER.
WHAT FLAVORS IS SHE PARTIAL TO?
UH... I'M NOT SURE, BUT SHE OFTEN SHARES SOMETHING MINTY WITH ME.
I LOVE BEING ABLE TO HELP PEOPLE THIS WAY.
I WANT THIS TO REVEAL HIS FEELINGS TO HER.
HSSSS
TO LET HER KNOW ...!

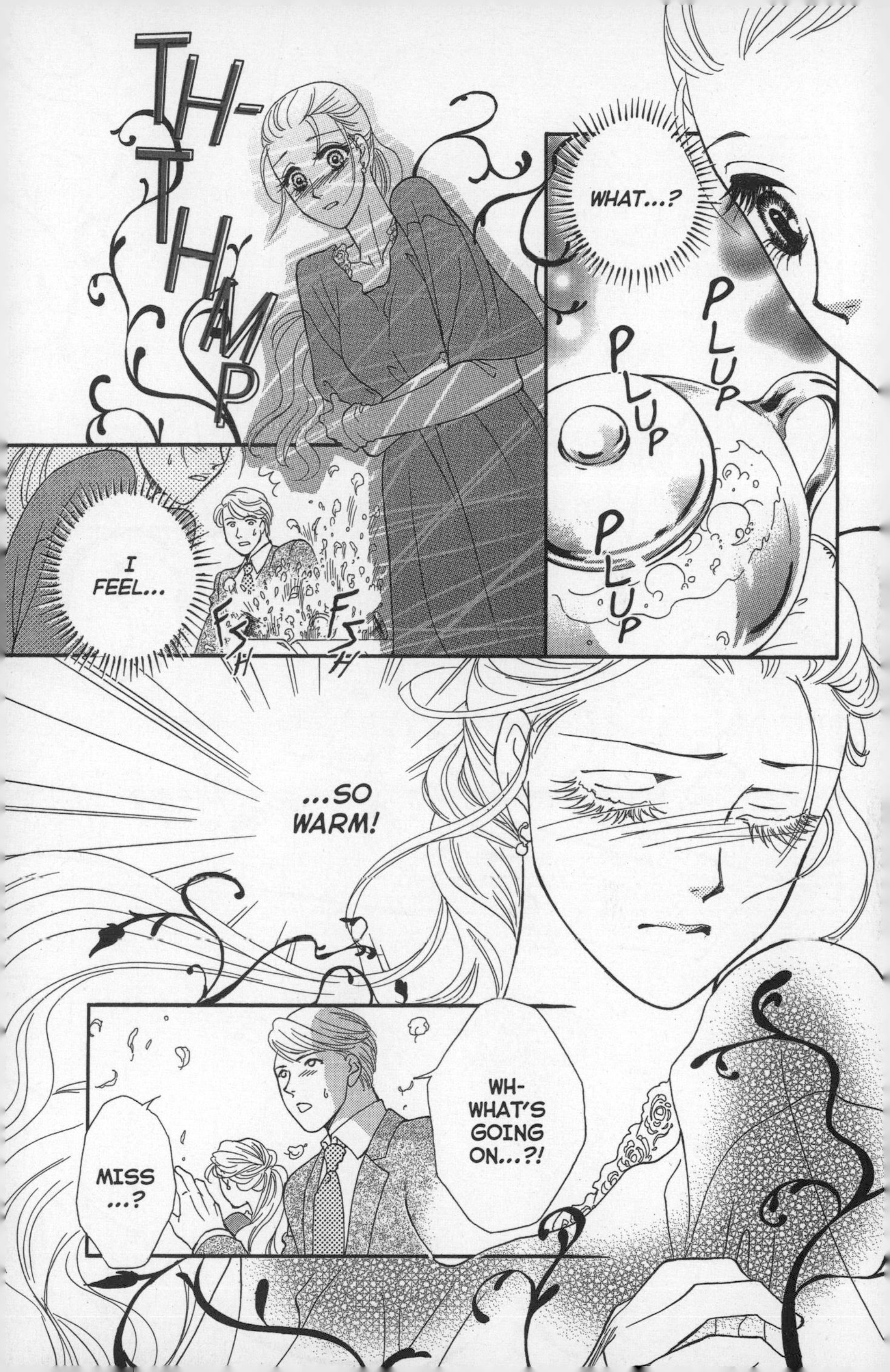
WHAT...?
PLUP
PLUP
PLUP
PLUP
TH-THAMP
I FEEL...
...SO WARM!
WH-WHAT'S GOING ON...?!
MISS...?

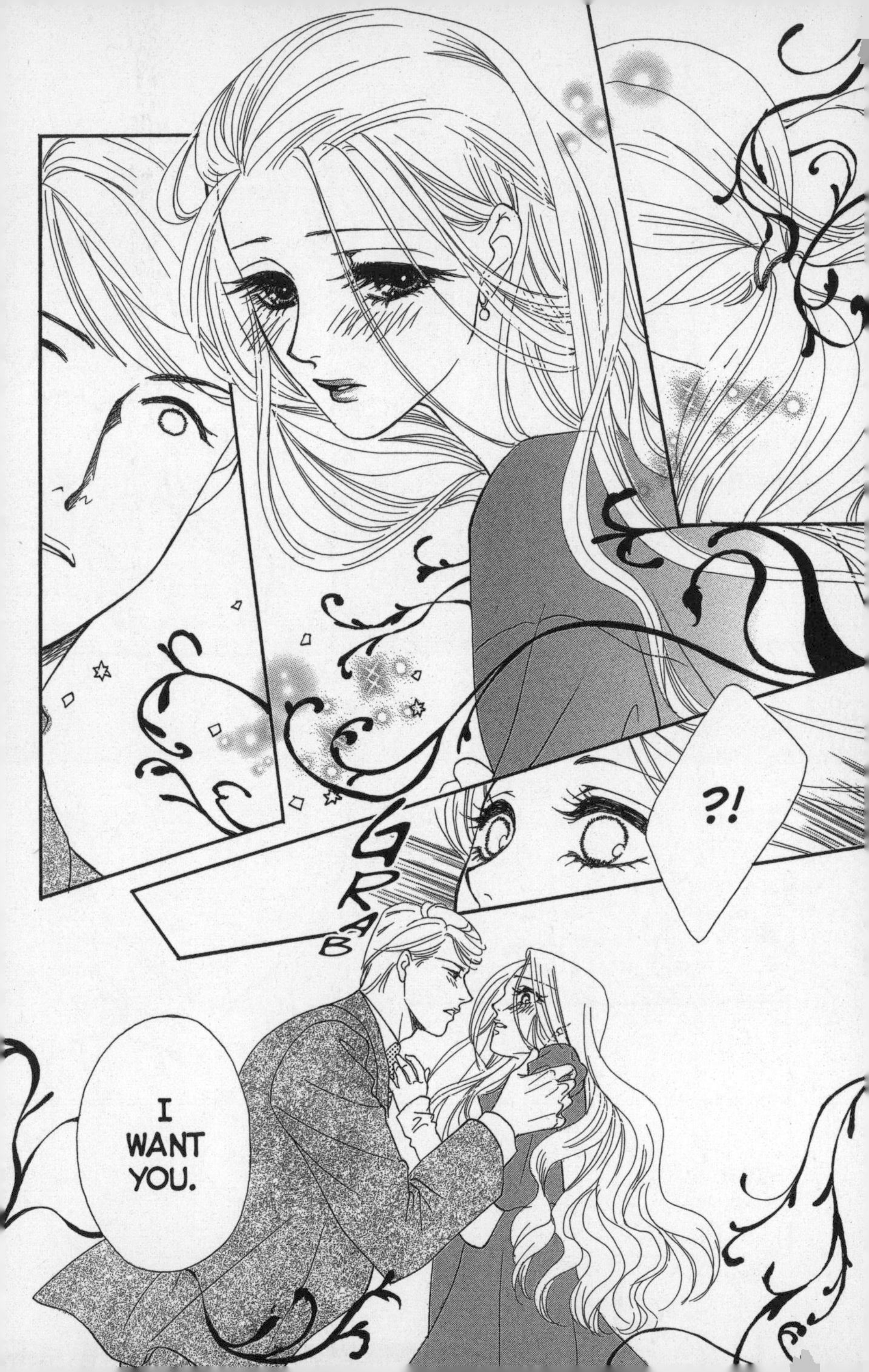

?!
GRAB
I WANT YOU.

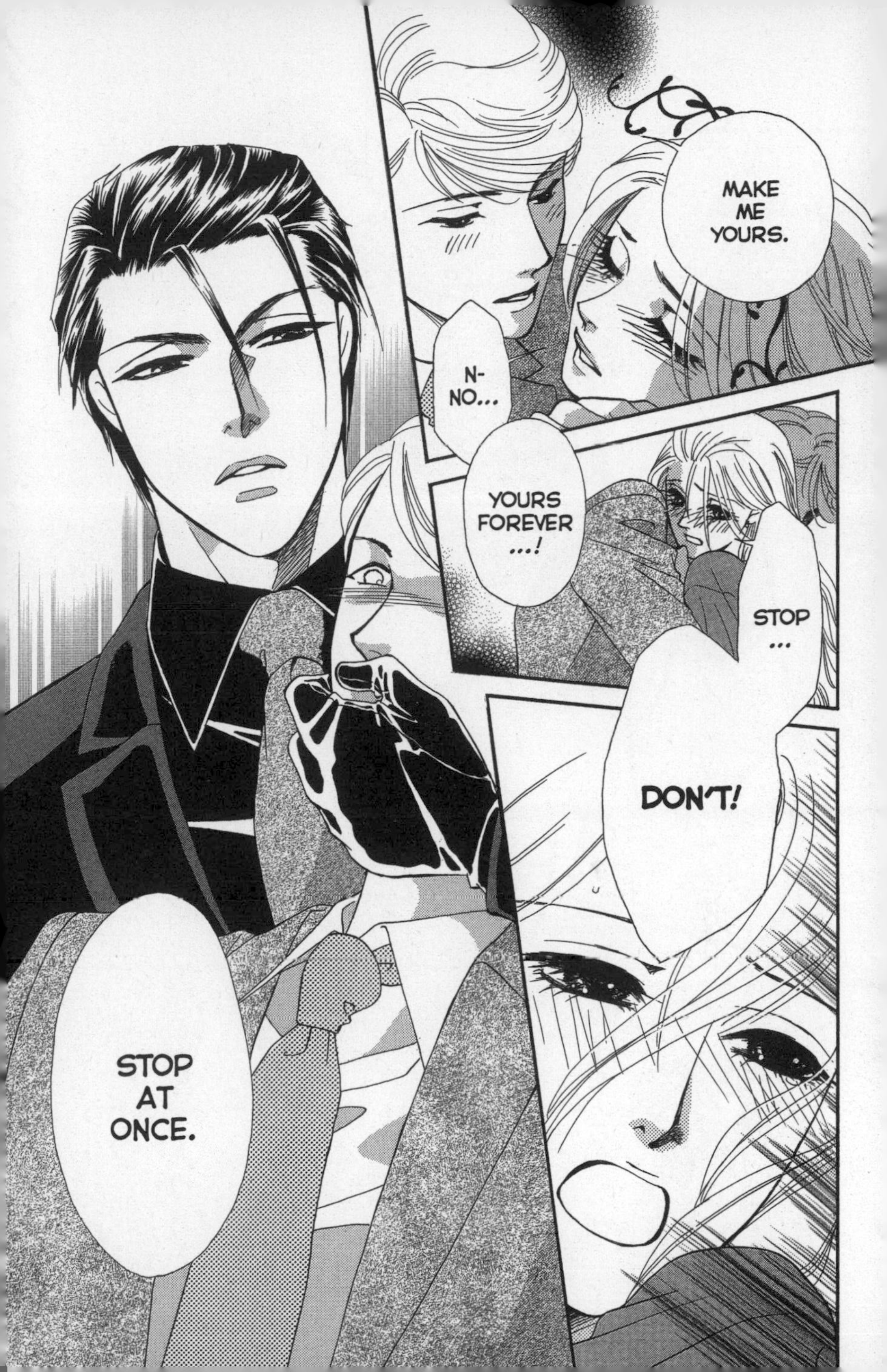
MAKE ME YOURS.
N-NO...
YOURS FOREVER ...!
STOP ...
DON'T!
STOP AT ONCE.

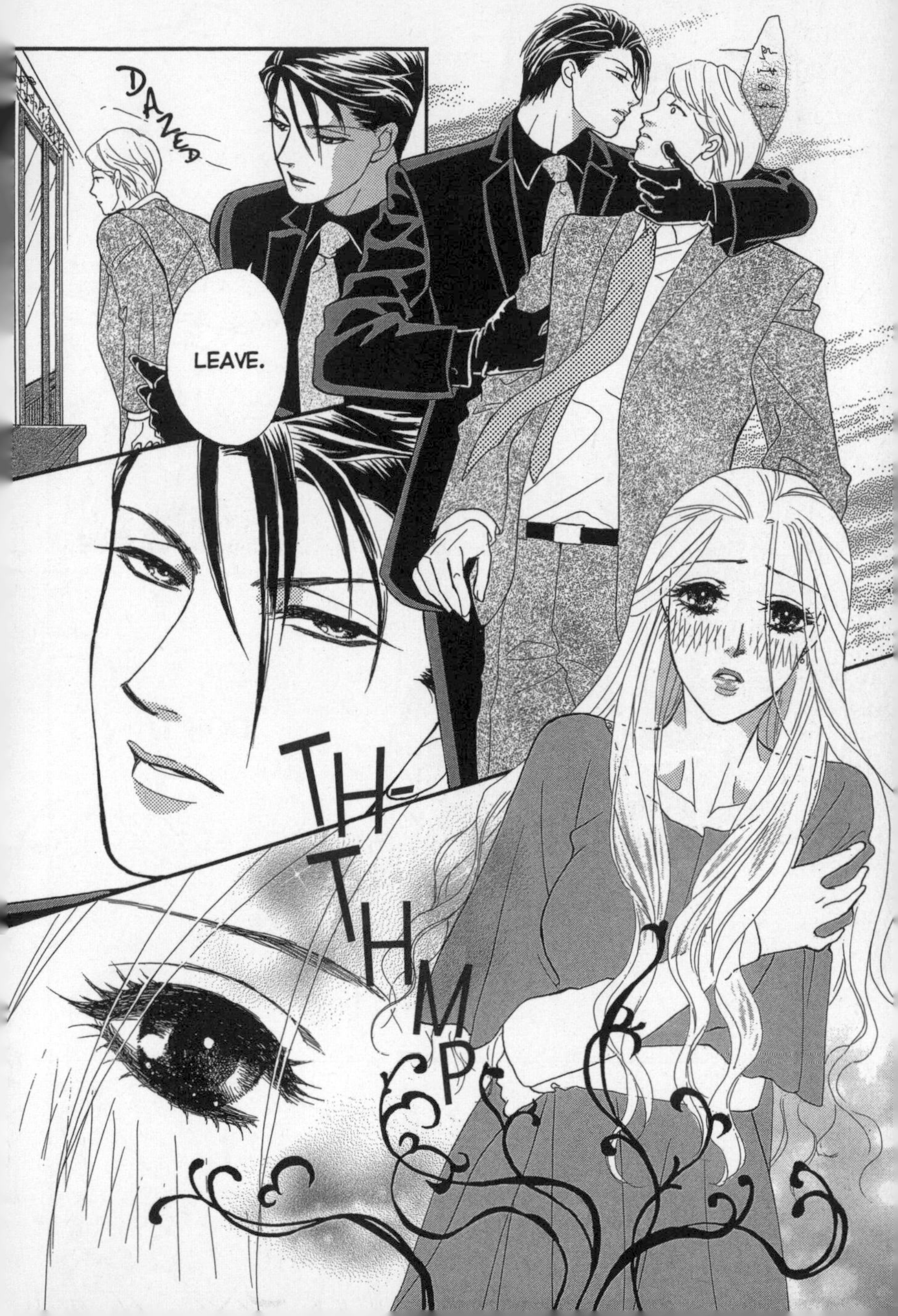
DAZED
LEAVE.
TH-THMP

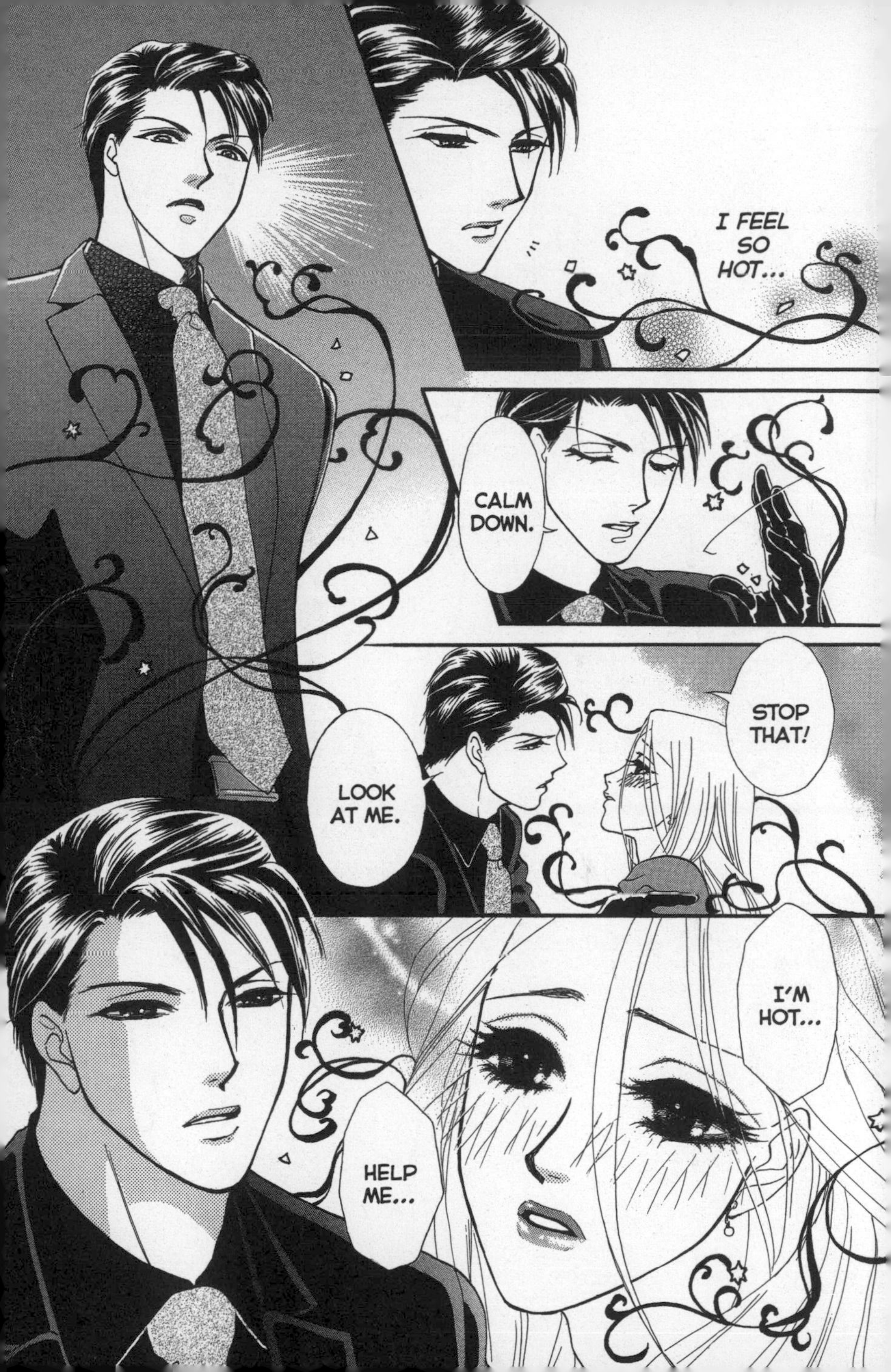
I FEEL SO HOT...
CALM DOWN.
STOP THAT!
LOOK AT ME.
I'M HOT...
HELP ME...

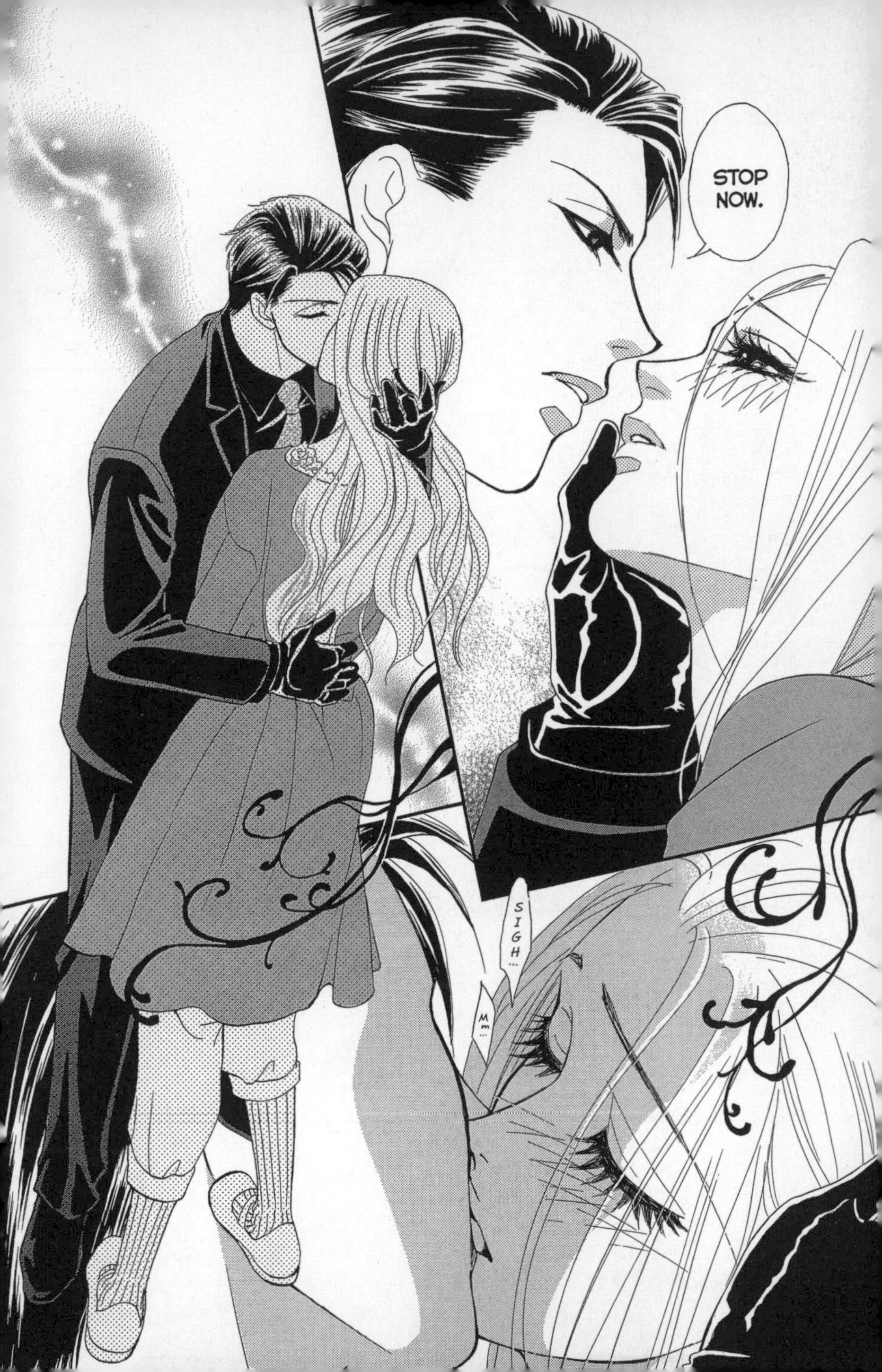
STOP NOW.
SIGH...
Mm...

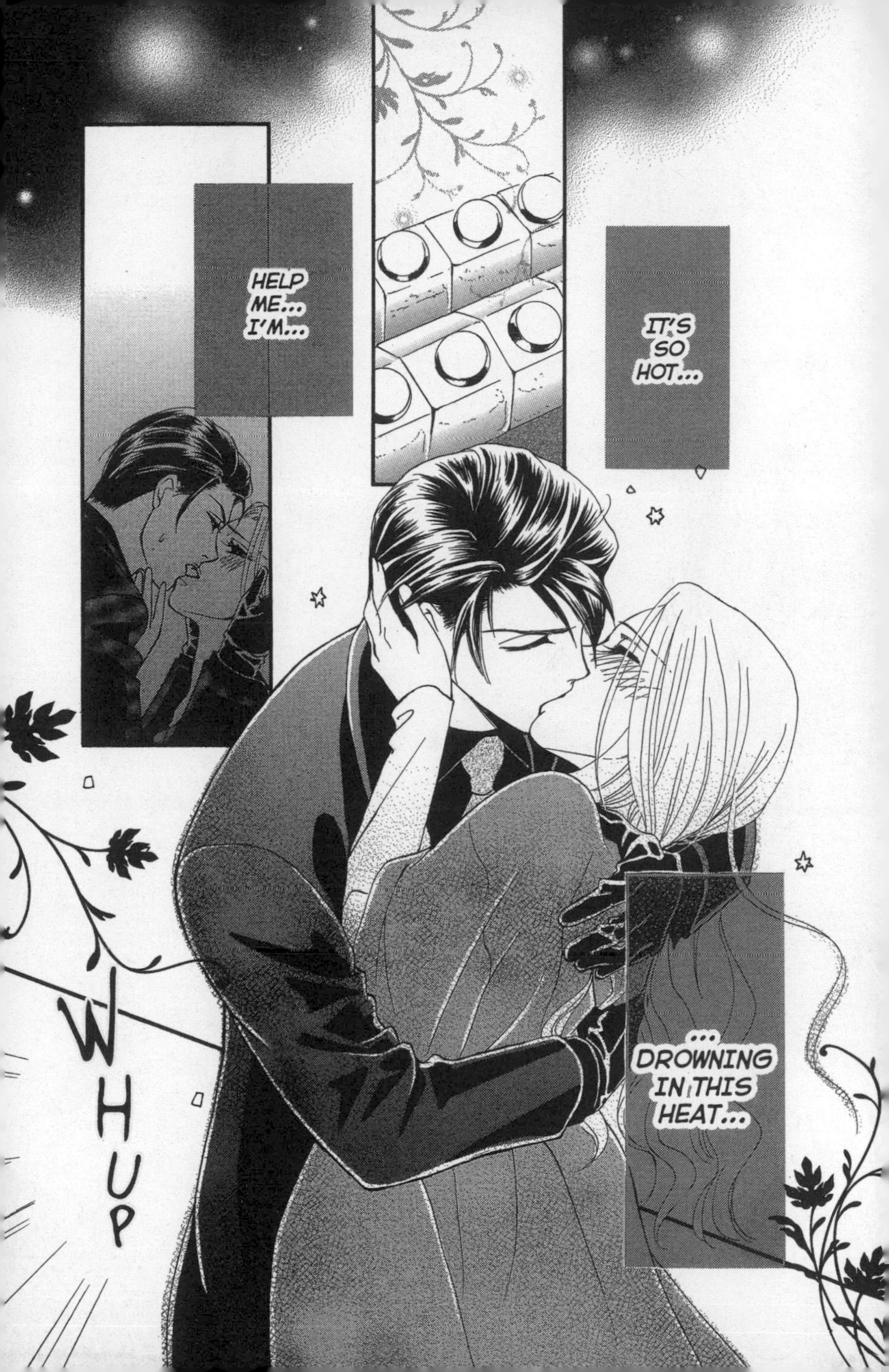
IT'S SO HOT...
HELP ME... I'M...
... DROWNING IN THIS HEAT...
WHUP

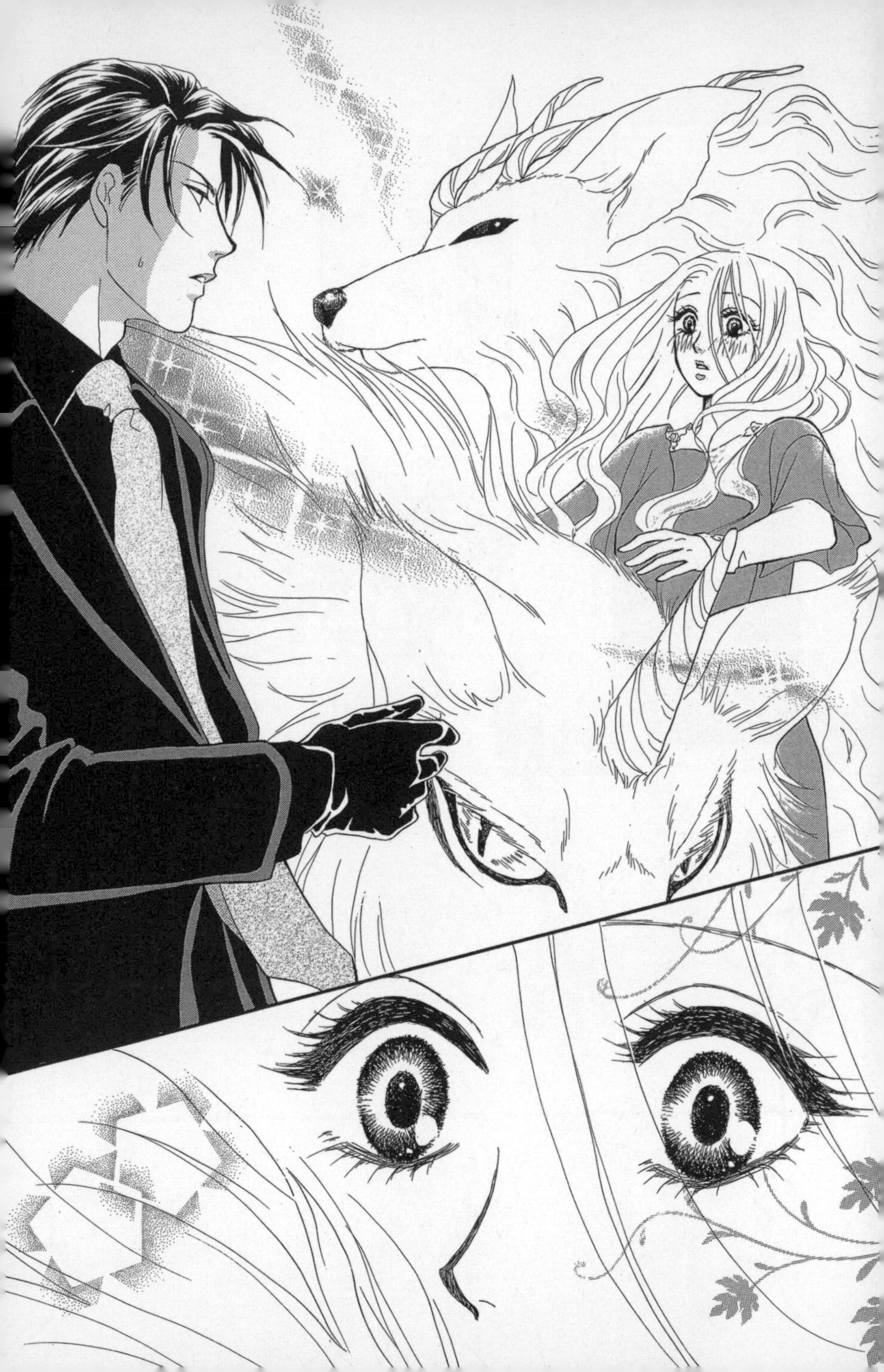

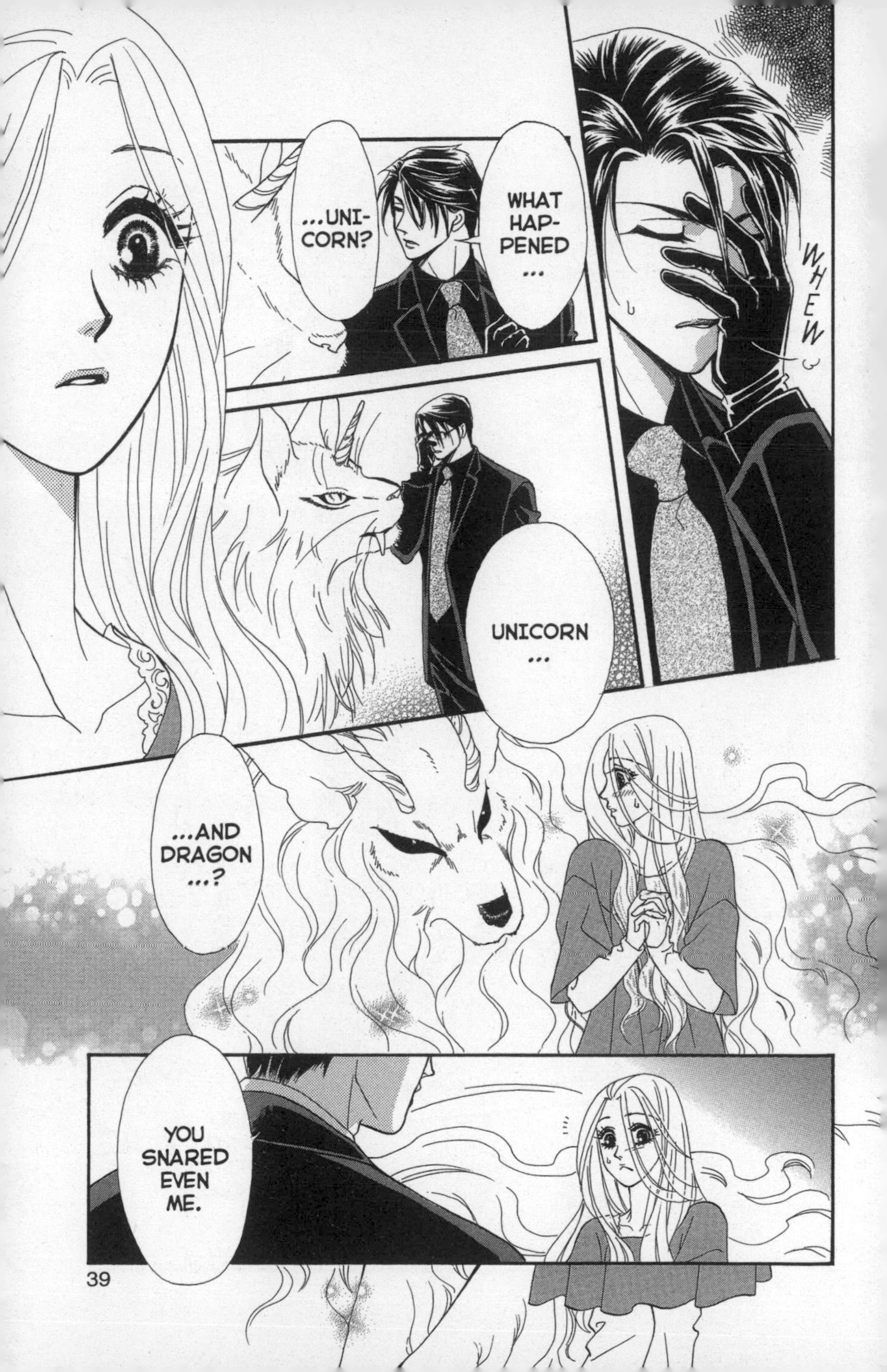
WHEW
WHAT HAP-PENED ...
...UNI-CORN?
UNICORN ...
...AND DRAGON ...?
YOU SNARED EVEN ME.

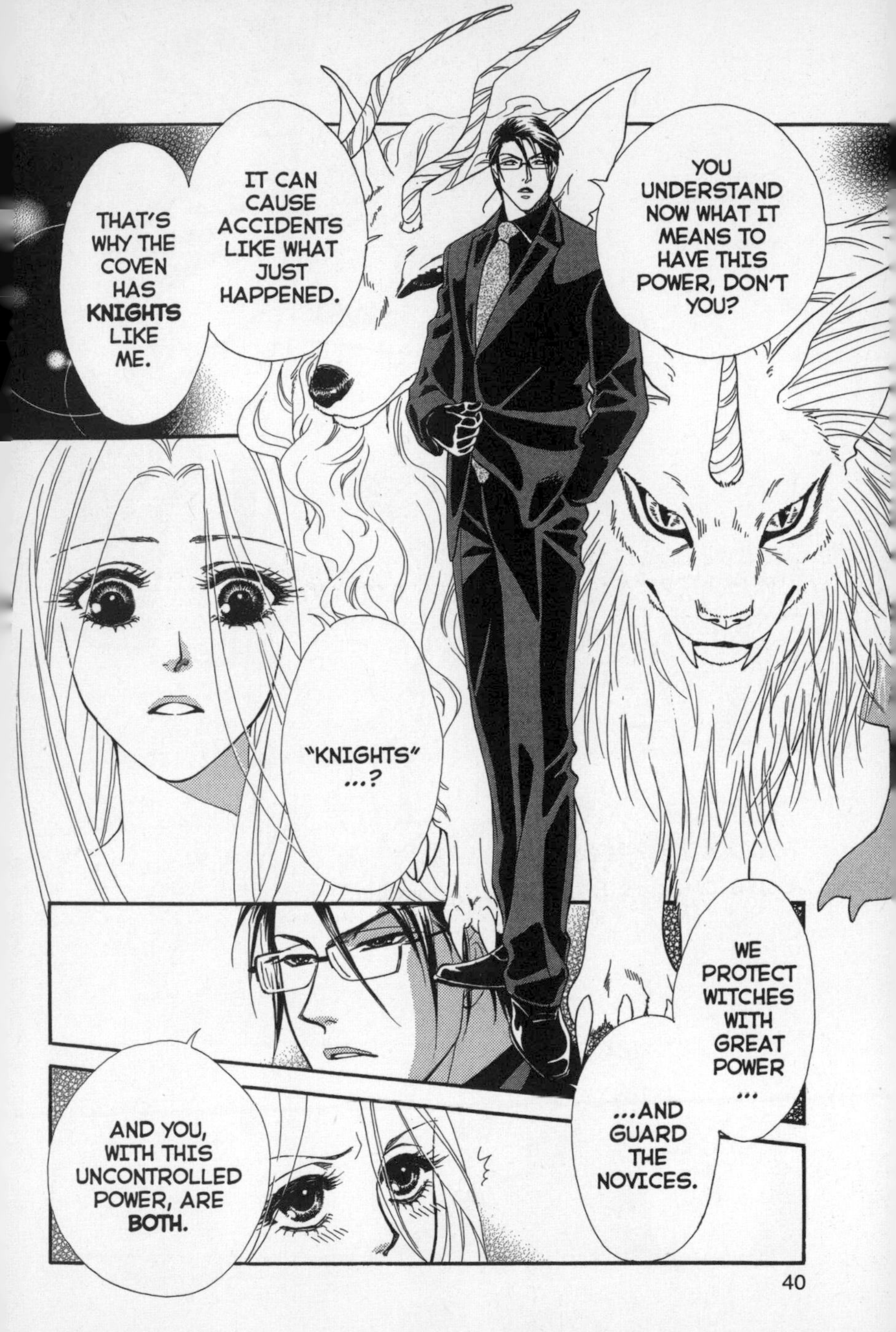
YOU UNDERSTAND NOW WHAT IT MEANS TO HAVE THIS POWER, DON'T YOU?
IT CAN CAUSE ACCIDENTS LIKE WHAT JUST HAPPENED.
THAT'S WHY THE COVEN HAS KNIGHTS LIKE ME.
"KNIGHTS" ...?
WE PROTECT WITCHES WITH GREAT POWER ...
...AND GUARD THE NOVICES.
AND YOU, WITH THIS UNCONTROLLED POWER, ARE BOTH.

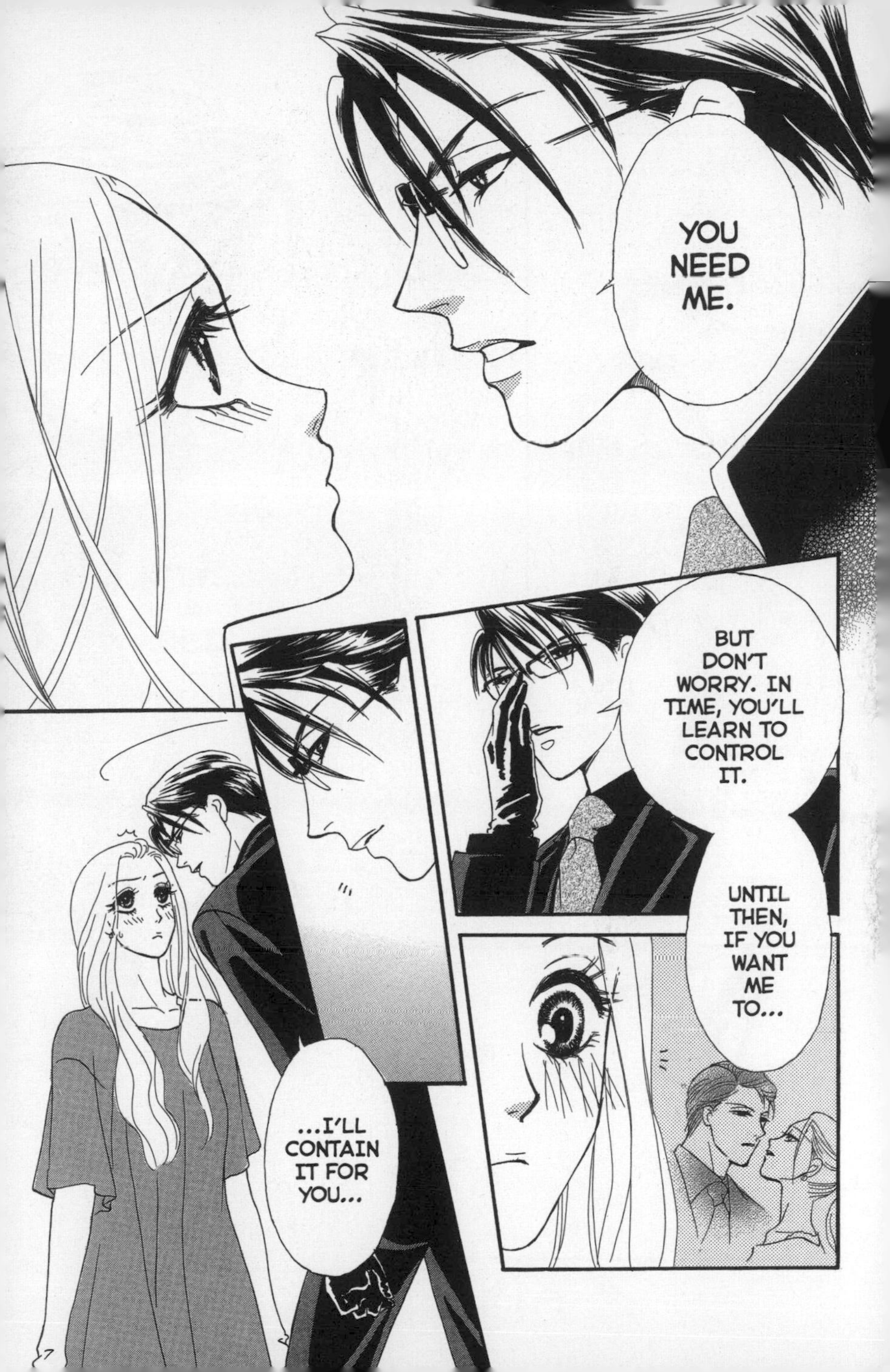
YOU NEED ME.
BUT DON'T WORRY. IN TIME, YOU'LL LEARN TO CONTROL IT.
UNTIL THEN, IF YOU WANT ME TO...
...I'LL CONTAIN IT FOR YOU...

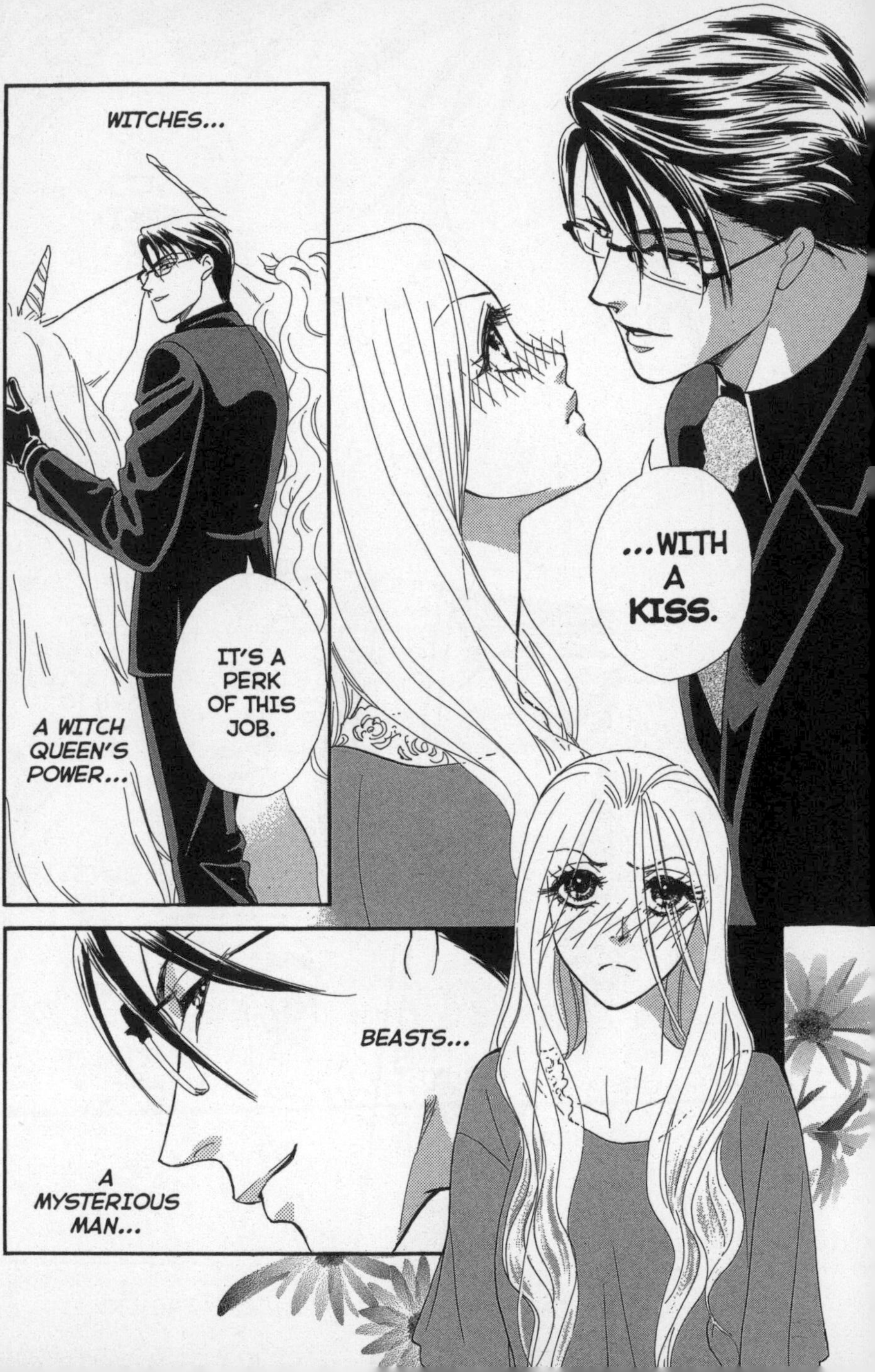
...WITH A KISS.
WITCHES...
IT'S A PERK OF THIS JOB.
A WITCH QUEEN'S POWER...
BEASTS...
A MYSTERIOUS MAN...

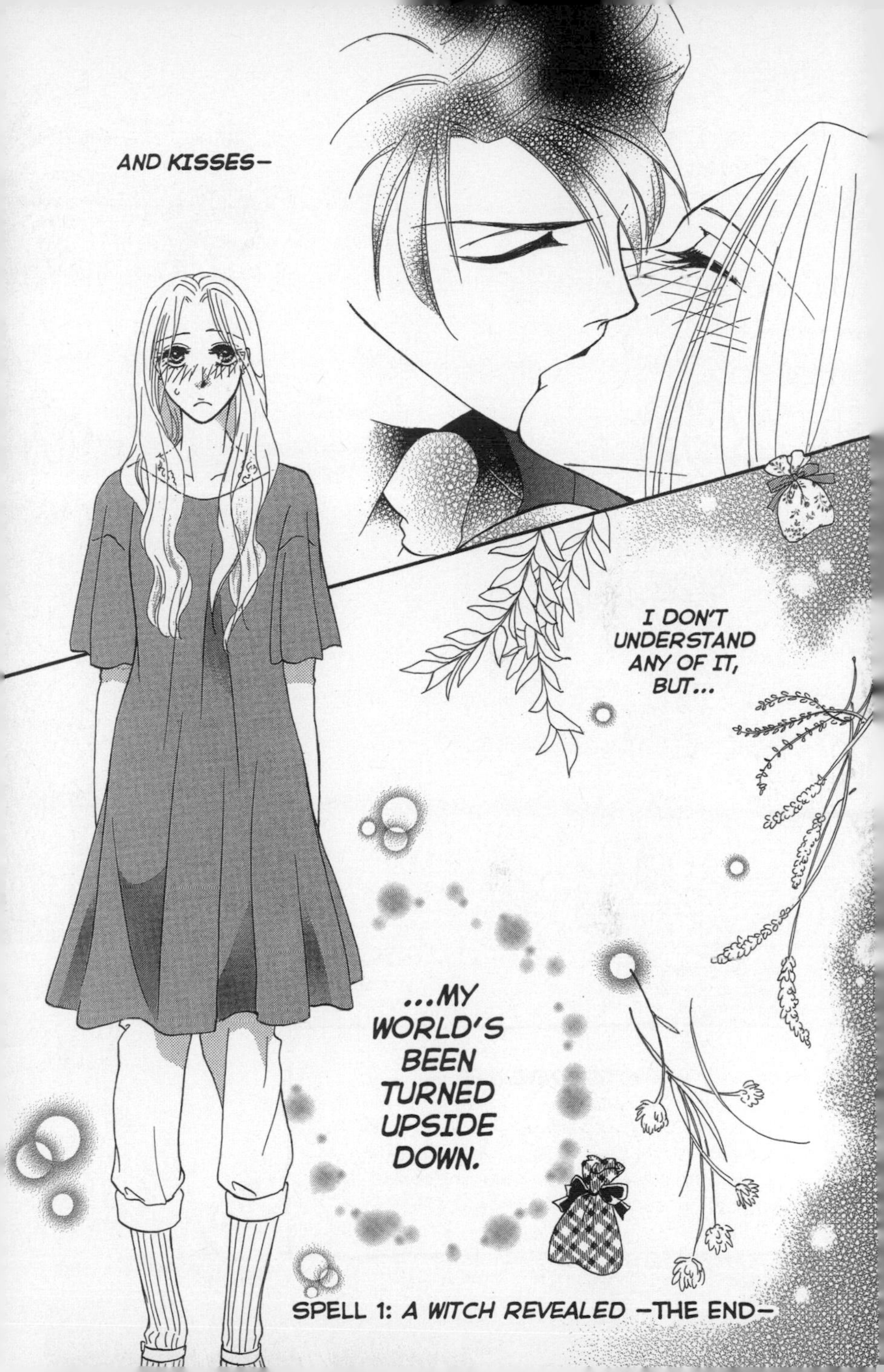
AND KISSES—
I DON'T UNDERSTAND ANY OF IT, BUT...
...MY WORLD'S BEEN TURNED UPSIDE DOWN.
SPELL 1: A WITCH REVEALED —THE END—

— A WITCH REVEALED —

Kaname dresses entirely in black, so it takes a long time to draw him properly. He practically reduces my assistants to tears. (Wry smile)

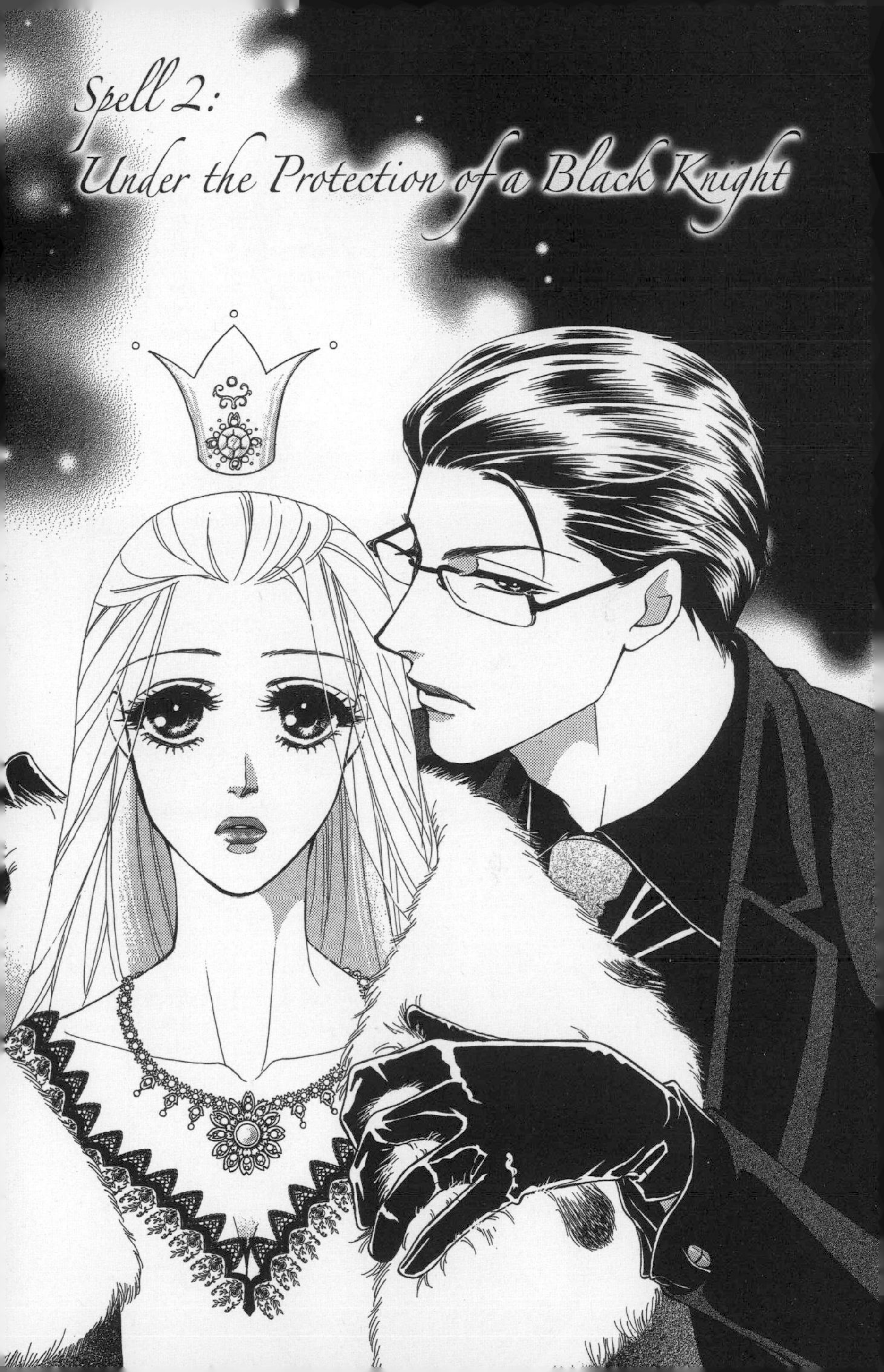
Spell 2:
Under the Protection of a Black Knight

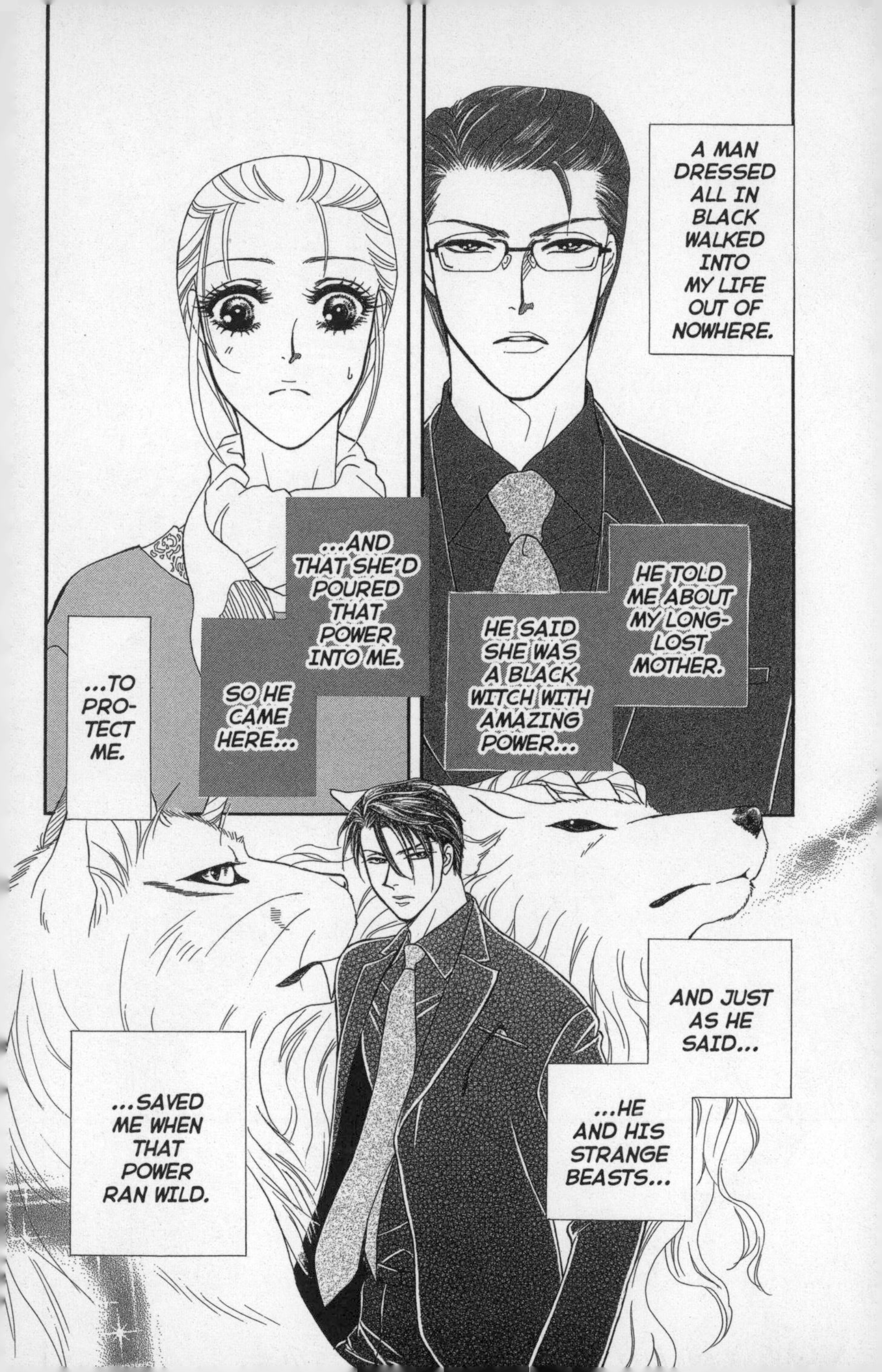
A MAN DRESSED ALL IN BLACK WALKED INTO MY LIFE OUT OF NOWHERE.
HE TOLD ME ABOUT MY LONG-LOST MOTHER.
HE SAID SHE WAS A BLACK WITCH WITH AMAZING POWER...
...AND THAT SHE'D POURED THAT POWER INTO ME.
SO HE CAME HERE...
...TO PROTECT ME.
AND JUST AS HE SAID...
...HE AND HIS STRANGE BEASTS...
...SAVED ME WHEN THAT POWER RAN WILD.

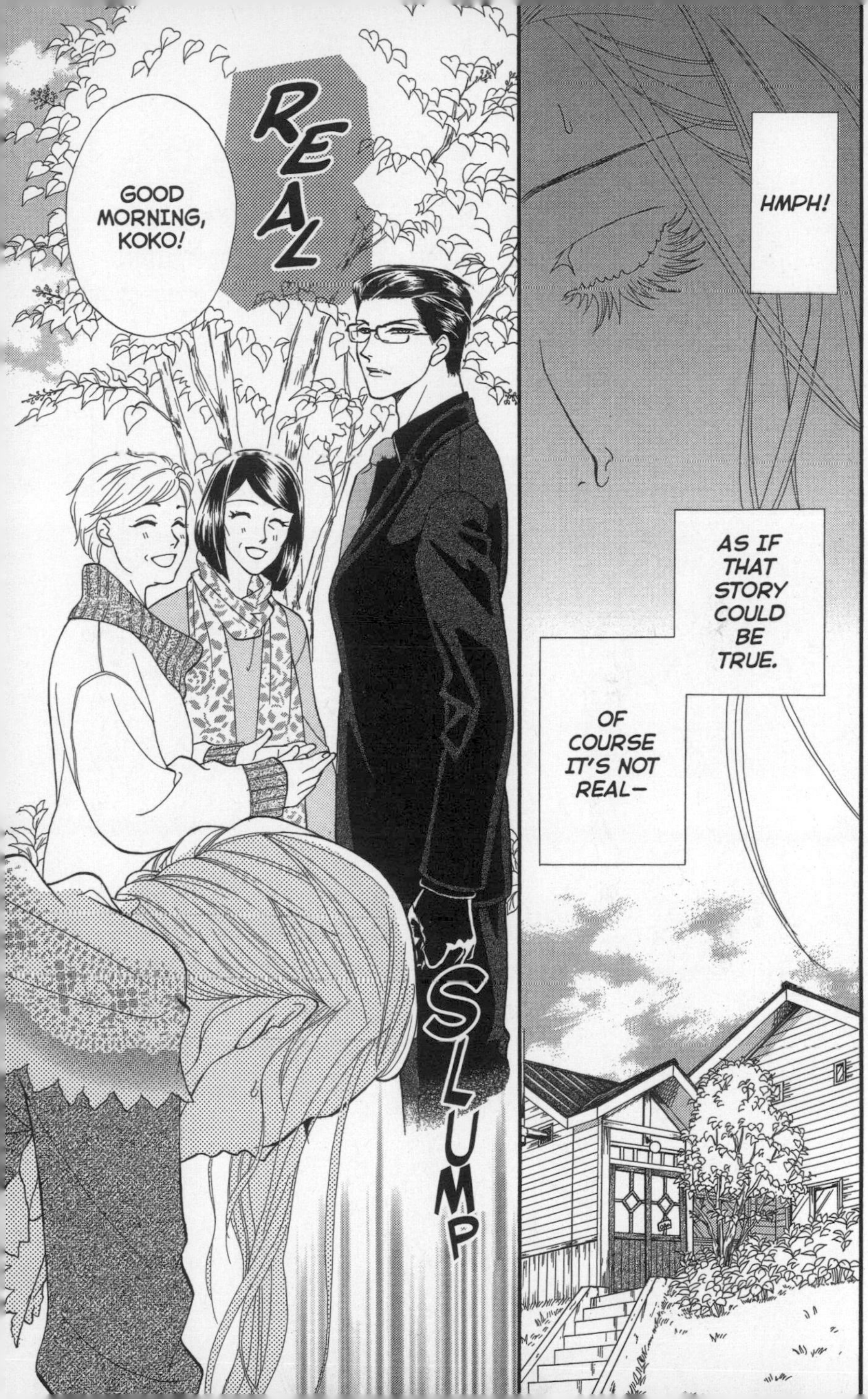
HMPH!
AS IF THAT STORY COULD BE TRUE.
OF COURSE IT'S NOT REAL—
REAL
GOOD MORNING, KOKO!
SLUMP

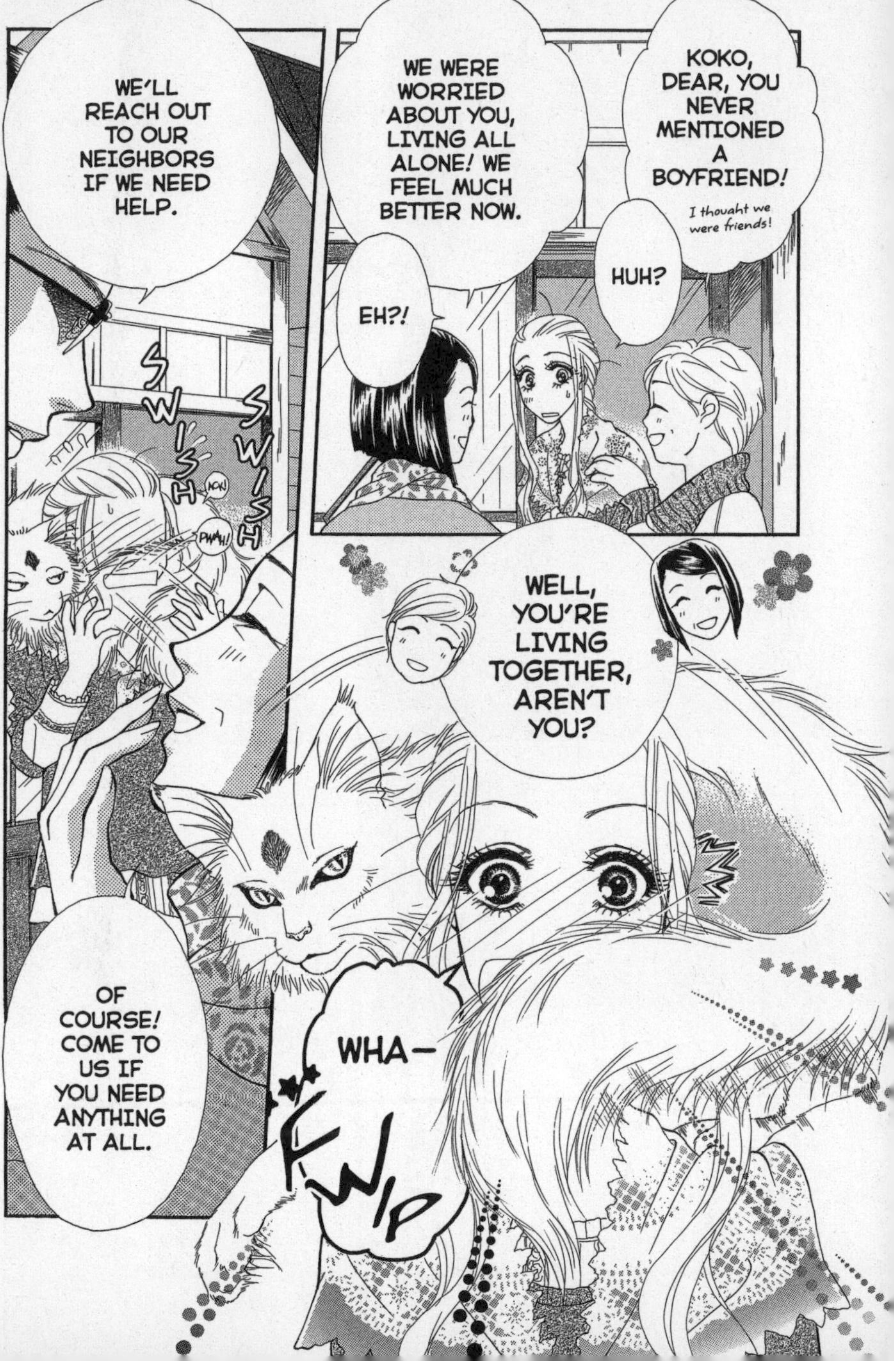
KOKO, DEAR, YOU NEVER MENTIONED A BOYFRIEND!
I thought we were friends!
WE WERE WORRIED ABOUT YOU, LIVING ALL ALONE! WE FEEL MUCH BETTER NOW.
HUH?
EH?!
WELL, YOU'RE LIVING TOGETHER, AREN'T YOU?
WHA-
FWIP
WE'LL REACH OUT TO OUR NEIGHBORS IF WE NEED HELP.
SWISH
SWISH
ACK!
PWAH!
OF COURSE! COME TO US IF YOU NEED ANYTHING AT ALL.

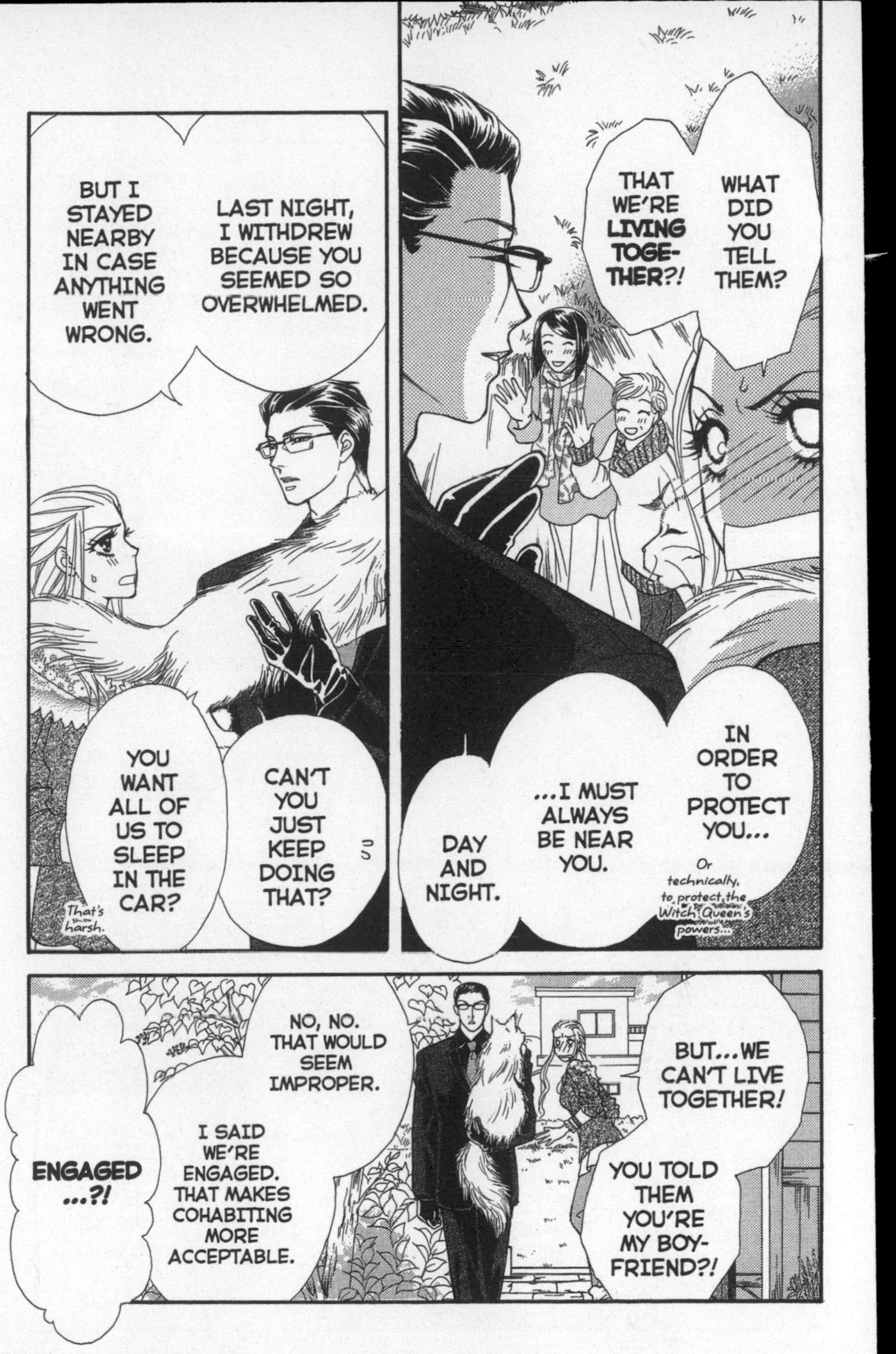
WHAT DID YOU TELL THEM?
THAT WE'RE LIVING TOGE-THER?!
IN ORDER TO PROTECT YOU...
...I MUST ALWAYS BE NEAR YOU.
DAY AND NIGHT.
Or technically, to protect the Witch Queen's powers...
LAST NIGHT, I WITHDREW BECAUSE YOU SEEMED SO OVERWHELMED.
BUT I STAYED NEARBY IN CASE ANYTHING WENT WRONG.
CAN'T YOU JUST KEEP DOING THAT?
YOU WANT ALL OF US TO SLEEP IN THE CAR?
That's harsh.
BUT...WE CAN'T LIVE TOGETHER!
YOU TOLD THEM YOU'RE MY BOY-FRIEND?!
NO, NO. THAT WOULD SEEM IMPROPER.
I SAID WE'RE ENGAGED. THAT MAKES COHABITING MORE ACCEPTABLE.
ENGAGED ...?!

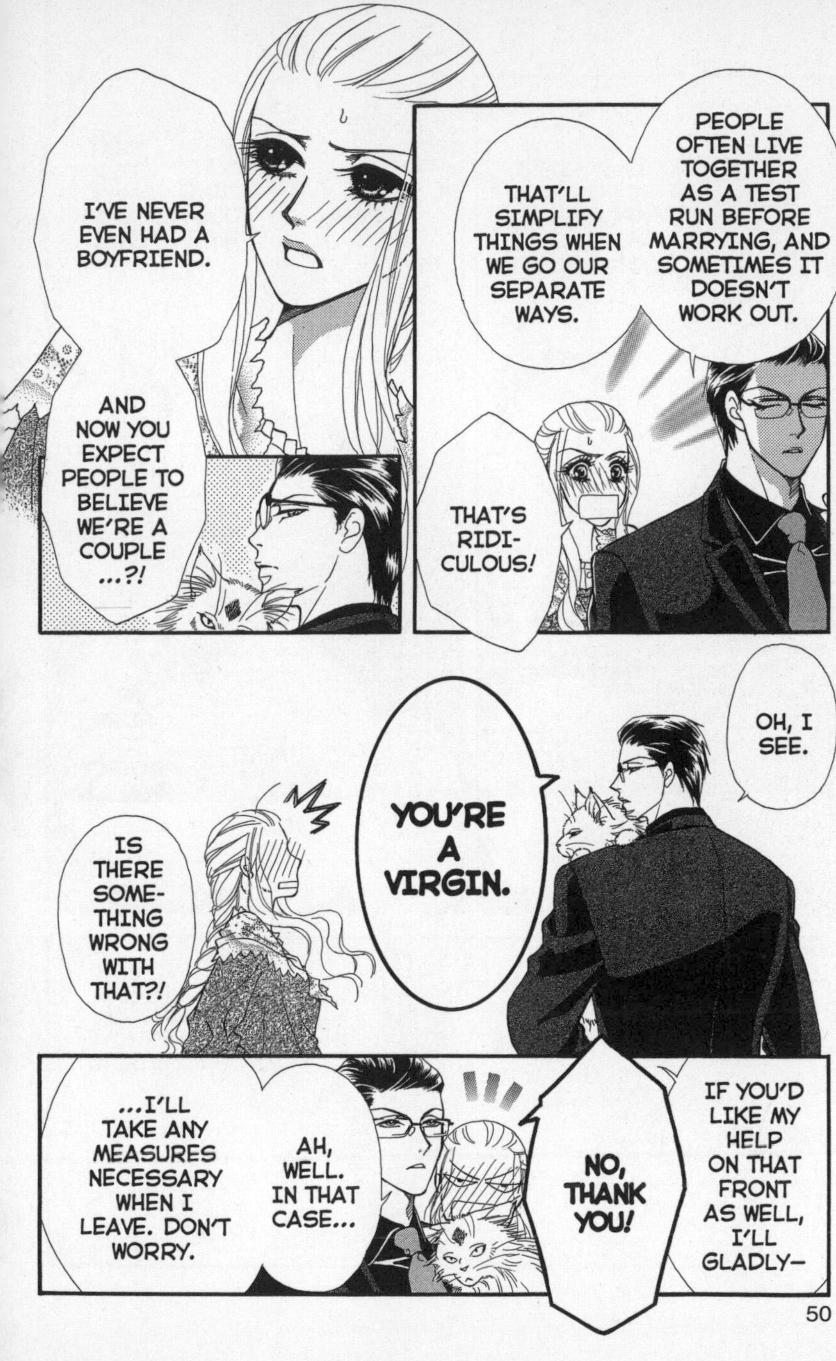
PEOPLE OFTEN LIVE TOGETHER AS A TEST RUN BEFORE MARRYING, AND SOMETIMES IT DOESN'T WORK OUT.
THAT'LL SIMPLIFY THINGS WHEN WE GO OUR SEPARATE WAYS.
THAT'S RIDI-CULOUS!
I'VE NEVER EVEN HAD A BOYFRIEND.
AND NOW YOU EXPECT PEOPLE TO BELIEVE WE'RE A COUPLE ...?!
OH, I SEE.
YOU'RE A VIRGIN.
IS THERE SOME-THING WRONG WITH THAT?!
IF YOU'D LIKE MY HELP ON THAT FRONT AS WELL, I'LL GLADLY–
NO, THANK YOU!
AH, WELL. IN THAT CASE...
...I'LL TAKE ANY MEASURES NECESSARY WHEN I LEAVE. DON'T WORRY.

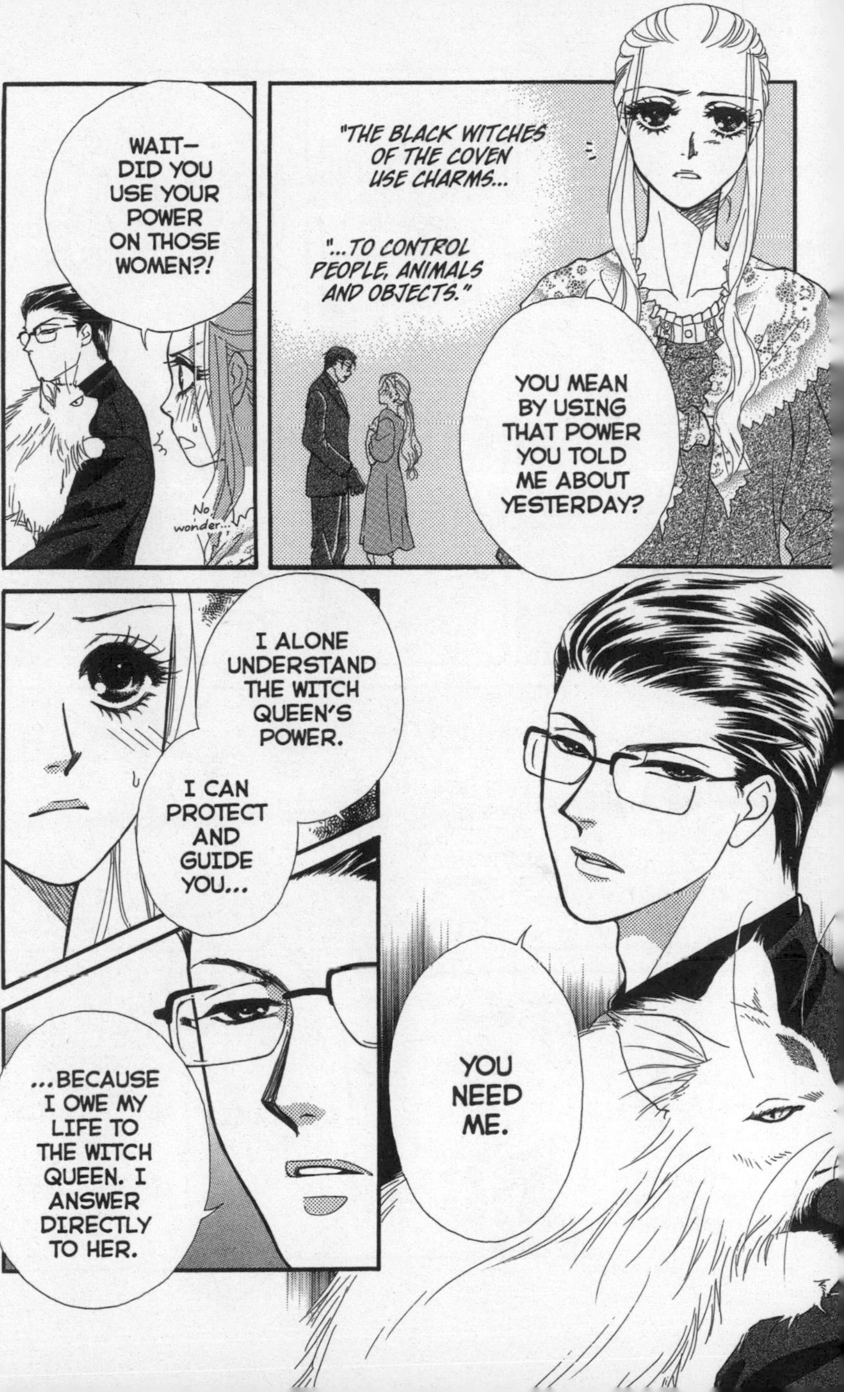
"THE BLACK WITCHES OF THE COVEN USE CHARMS...
"...TO CONTROL PEOPLE, ANIMALS AND OBJECTS."
YOU MEAN BY USING THAT POWER YOU TOLD ME ABOUT YESTERDAY?
WAIT— DID YOU USE YOUR POWER ON THOSE WOMEN?!
No wonder...
YOU NEED ME.
I ALONE UNDERSTAND THE WITCH QUEEN'S POWER.
I CAN PROTECT AND GUIDE YOU...
...BECAUSE I OWE MY LIFE TO THE WITCH QUEEN. I ANSWER DIRECTLY TO HER.

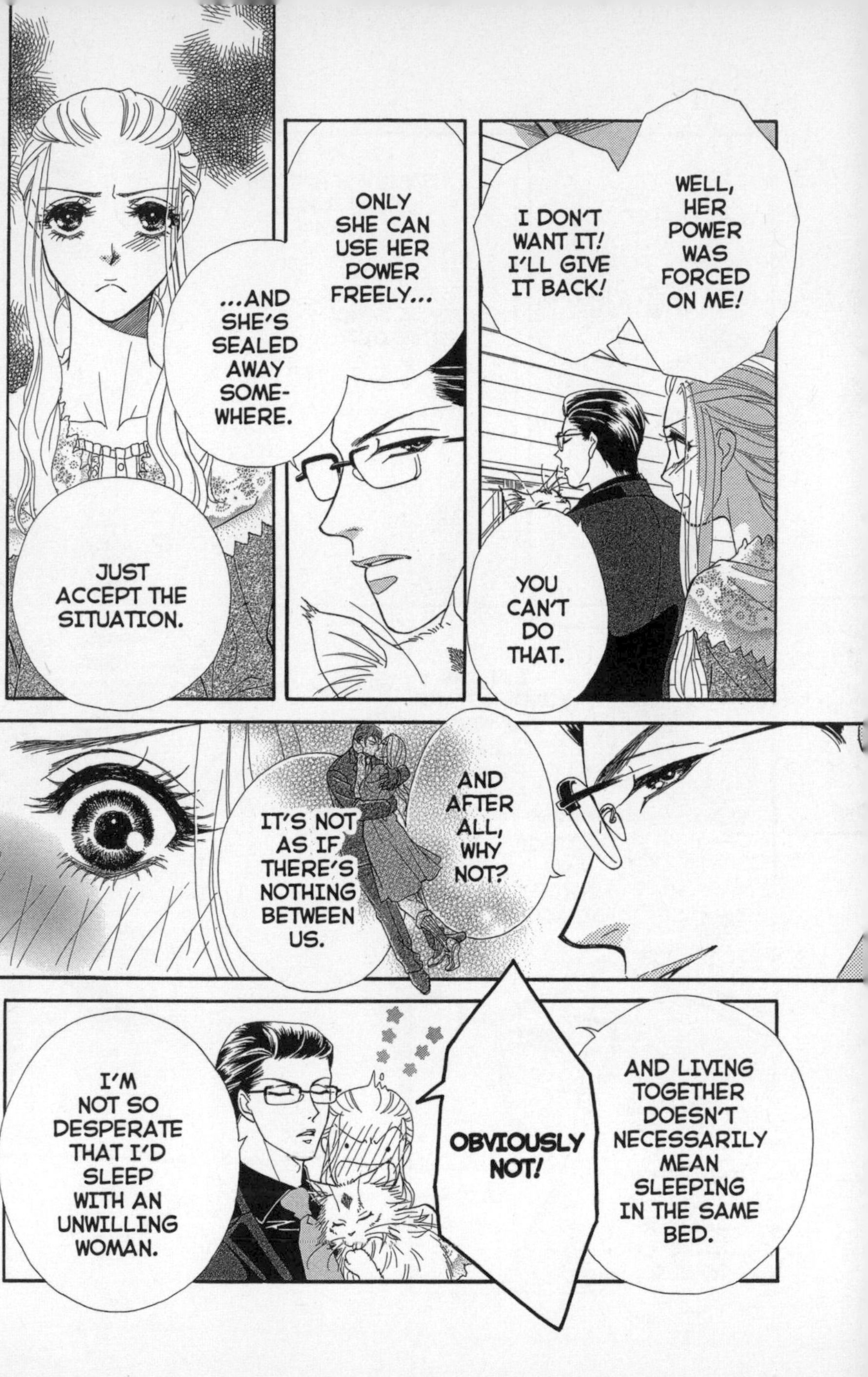
WELL, HER POWER WAS FORCED ON ME!
I DON'T WANT IT! I'LL GIVE IT BACK!
YOU CAN'T DO THAT.
ONLY SHE CAN USE HER POWER FREELY...
...AND SHE'S SEALED AWAY SOME-WHERE.
JUST ACCEPT THE SITUATION.
AND AFTER ALL, WHY NOT?
IT'S NOT AS IF THERE'S NOTHING BETWEEN US.
AND LIVING TOGETHER DOESN'T NECESSARILY MEAN SLEEPING IN THE SAME BED.
OBVIOUSLY NOT!
I'M NOT SO DESPERATE THAT I'D SLEEP WITH AN UNWILLING WOMAN.

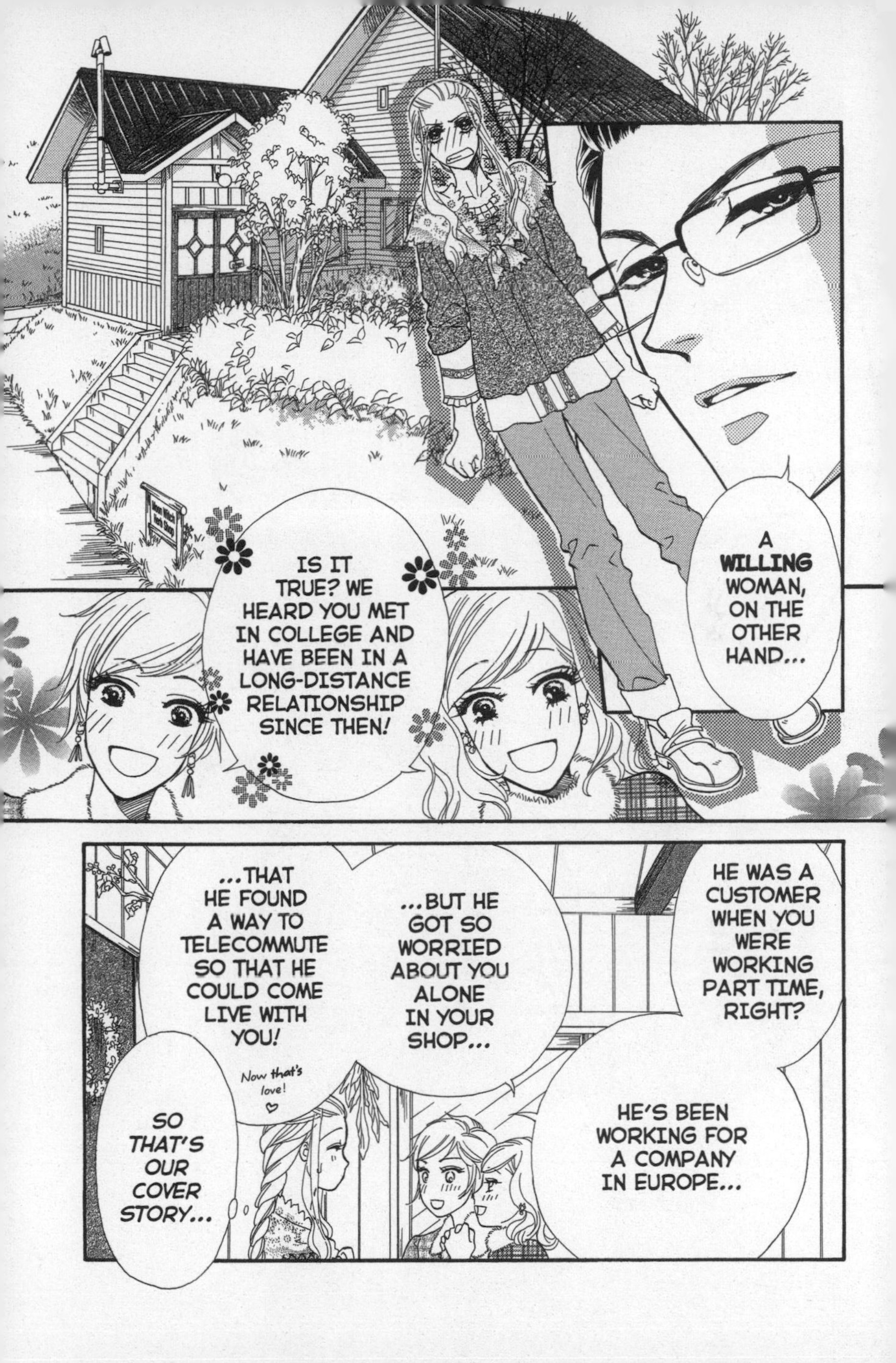
A **WILLING** WOMAN, ON THE OTHER HAND...
Moon Witch Herb Shop
IS IT TRUE? WE HEARD YOU MET IN COLLEGE AND HAVE BEEN IN A LONG-DISTANCE RELATIONSHIP SINCE THEN!
HE WAS A CUSTOMER WHEN YOU WERE WORKING PART TIME, RIGHT?
HE'S BEEN WORKING FOR A COMPANY IN EUROPE...
...BUT HE GOT SO WORRIED ABOUT YOU ALONE IN YOUR SHOP...
...THAT HE FOUND A WAY TO TELECOMMUTE SO THAT HE COULD COME LIVE WITH YOU!
Now that's love! ♡
SO THAT'S OUR COVER STORY...

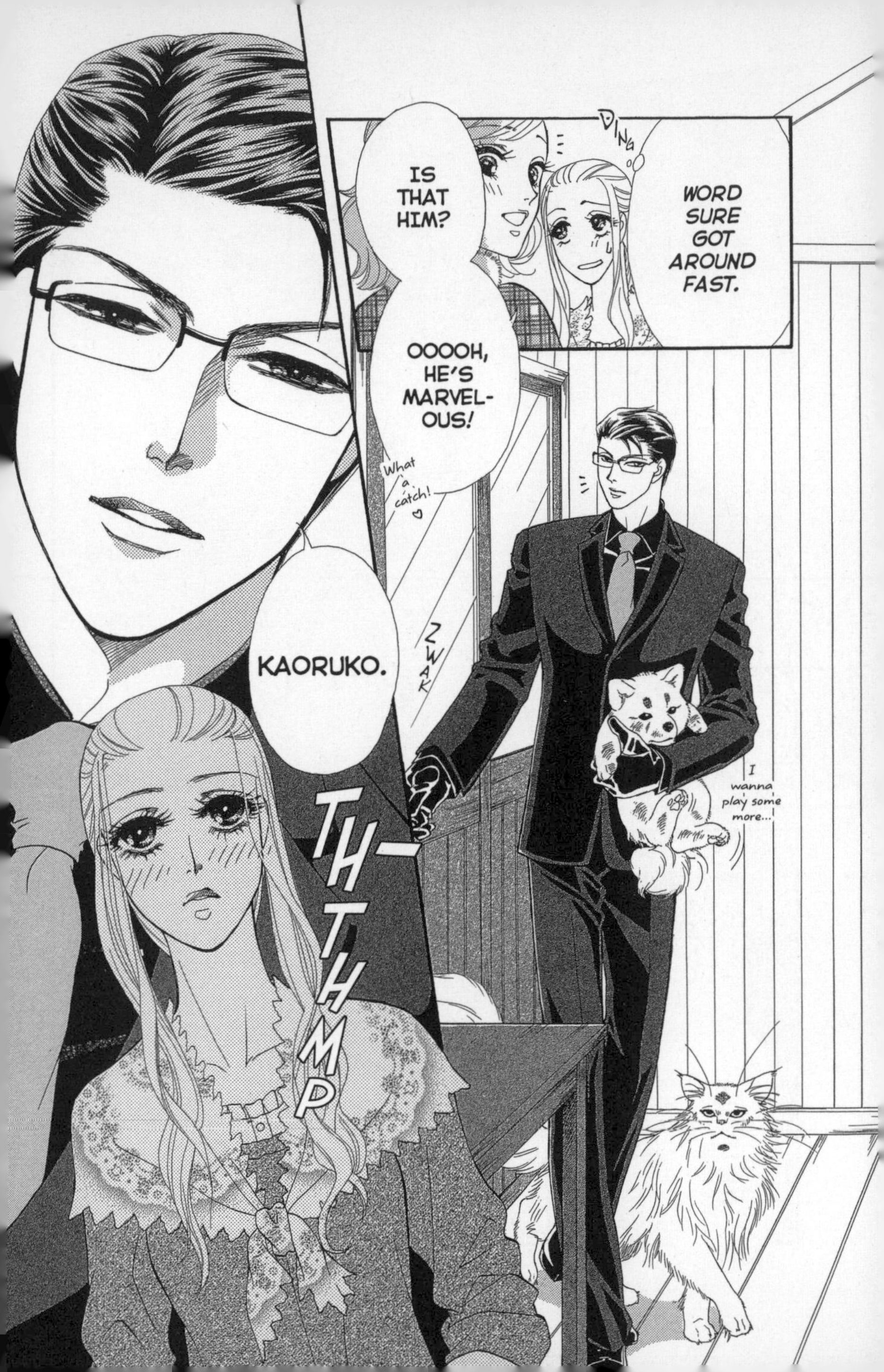
DING
WORD SURE GOT AROUND FAST.
IS THAT HIM?
OOOOH, HE'S MARVEL-OUS!
What a catch! ♡
ZWAK
I wanna play some more...
KAORUKO.
TH-THTHMP

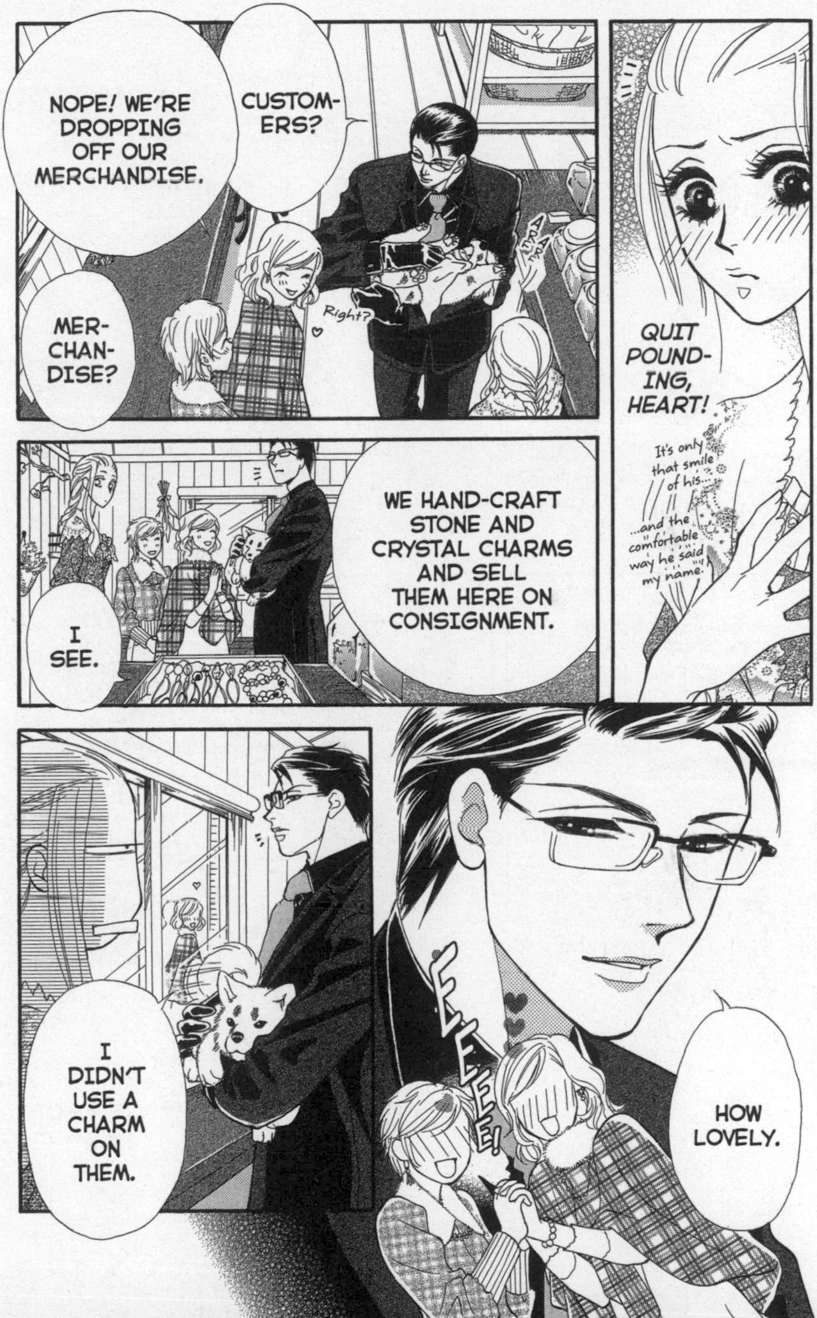
QUIT POUNDING, HEART!
It's only that smile of his...
...and the comfortable way he said my name.
CUSTOMERS?
NOPE! WE'RE DROPPING OFF OUR MERCHANDISE.
ARF ARF
Right? ♡
MERCHANDISE?
WE HAND-CRAFT STONE AND CRYSTAL CHARMS AND SELL THEM HERE ON CONSIGNMENT.
I SEE.
HOW LOVELY.
EEEEE!
I DIDN'T USE A CHARM ON THEM.

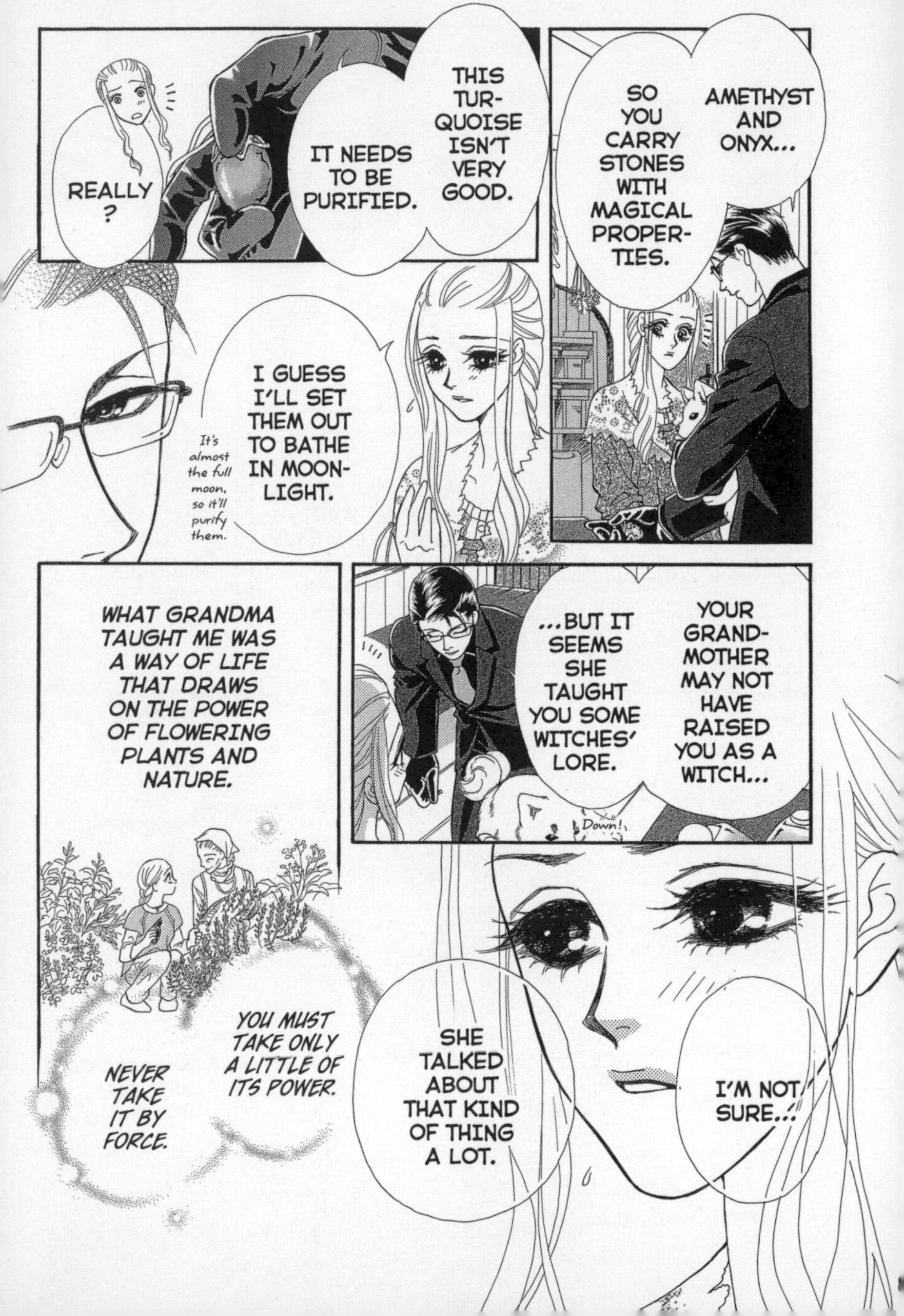
AMETHYST AND ONYX...
SO YOU CARRY STONES WITH MAGICAL PROPERTIES.
THIS TURQUOISE ISN'T VERY GOOD.
IT NEEDS TO BE PURIFIED.
REALLY?
I GUESS I'LL SET THEM OUT TO BATHE IN MOONLIGHT.
It's almost the full moon, so it'll purify them.
YOUR GRANDMOTHER MAY NOT HAVE RAISED YOU AS A WITCH...
...BUT IT SEEMS SHE TAUGHT YOU SOME WITCHES' LORE.
Down!
WHAT GRANDMA TAUGHT ME WAS A WAY OF LIFE THAT DRAWS ON THE POWER OF FLOWERING PLANTS AND NATURE.
I'M NOT SURE...
SHE TALKED ABOUT THAT KIND OF THING A LOT.
YOU MUST TAKE ONLY A LITTLE OF ITS POWER.
NEVER TAKE IT BY FORCE.

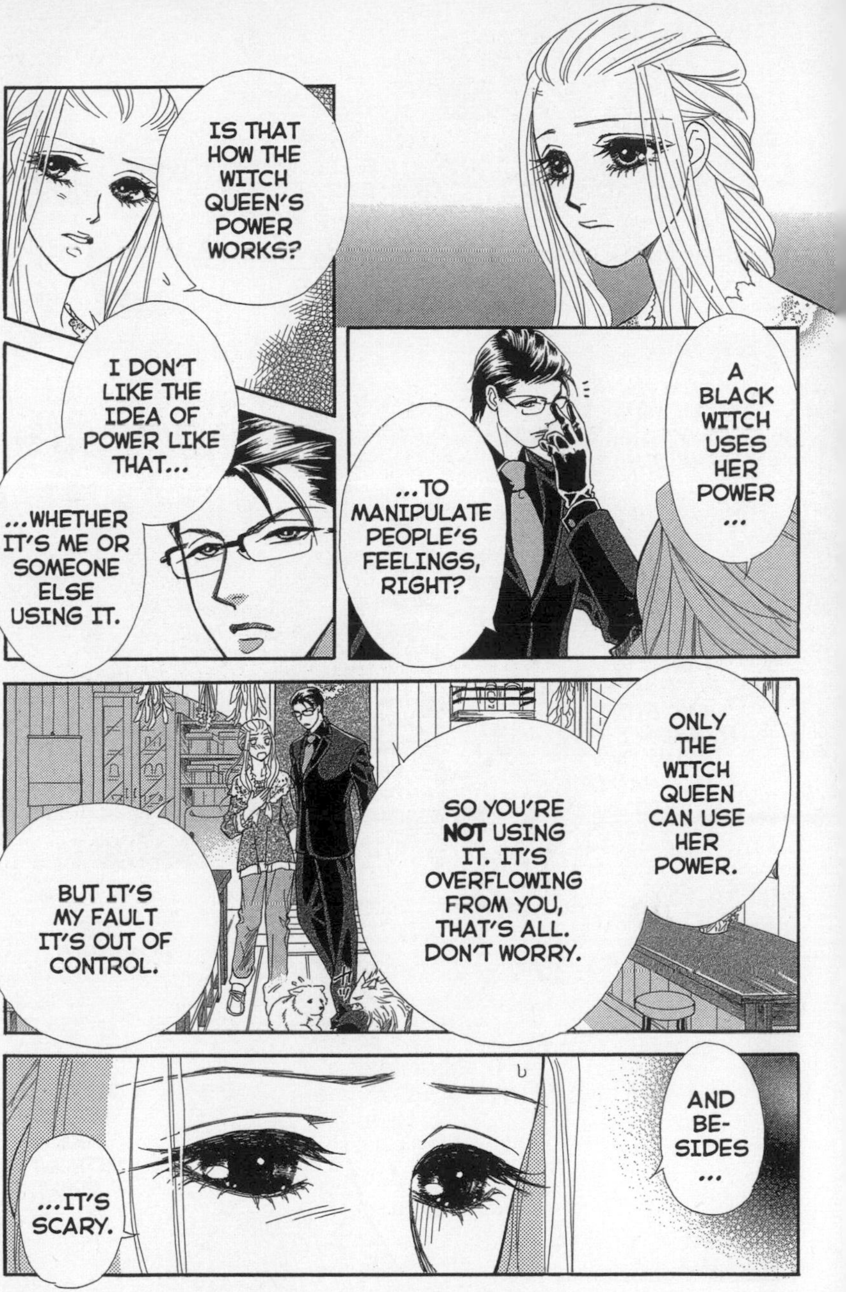
IS THAT HOW THE WITCH QUEEN'S POWER WORKS?
A BLACK WITCH USES HER POWER...
...TO MANIPULATE PEOPLE'S FEELINGS, RIGHT?
I DON'T LIKE THE IDEA OF POWER LIKE THAT...
...WHETHER IT'S ME OR SOMEONE ELSE USING IT.
ONLY THE WITCH QUEEN CAN USE HER POWER.
SO YOU'RE **NOT** USING IT. IT'S OVERFLOWING FROM YOU, THAT'S ALL. DON'T WORRY.
BUT IT'S MY FAULT IT'S OUT OF CONTROL.
AND BE-SIDES...
...IT'S SCARY.

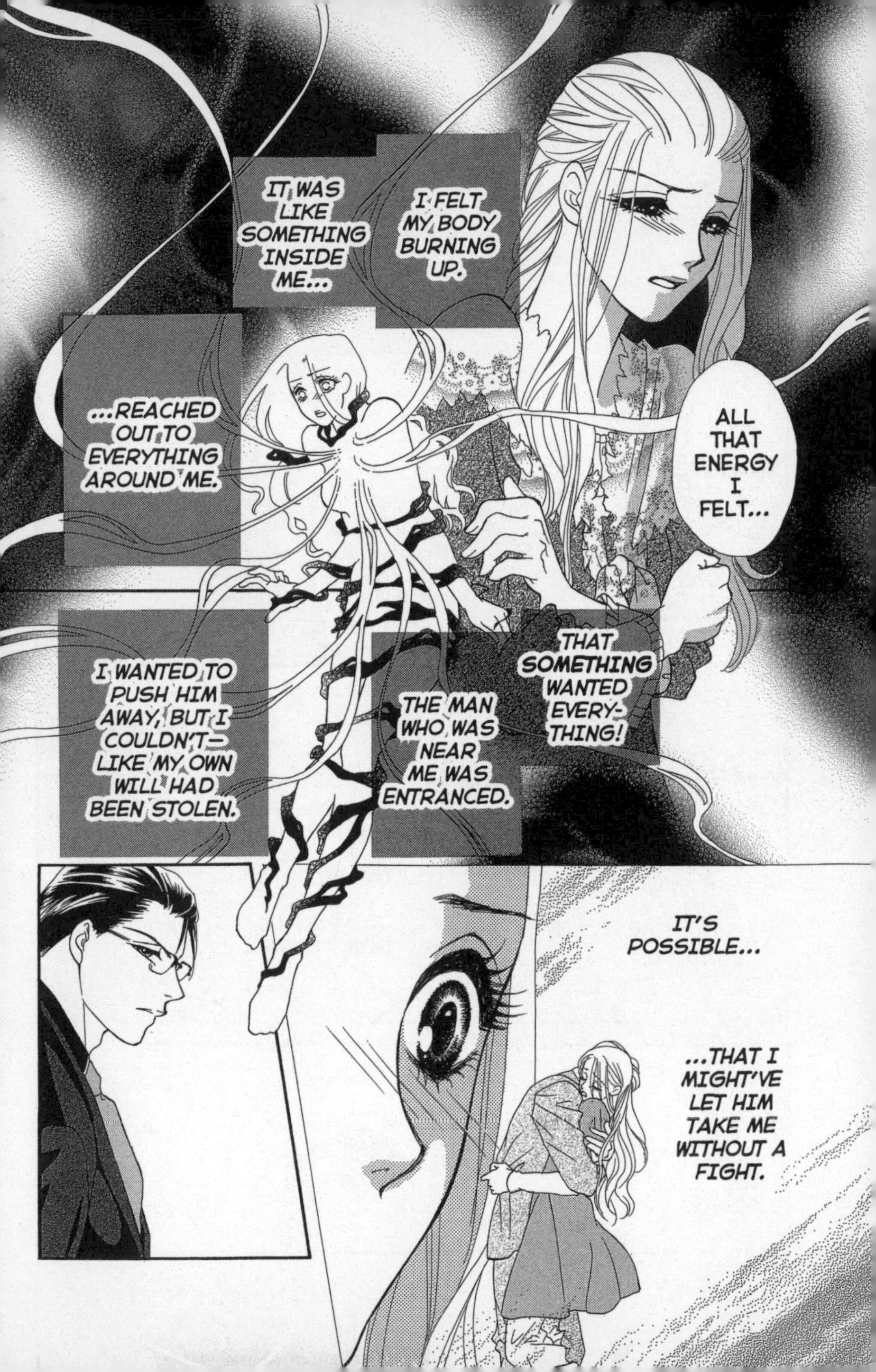
I FELT MY BODY BURNING UP.
IT WAS LIKE SOMETHING INSIDE ME...
...REACHED OUT TO EVERYTHING AROUND ME.
ALL THAT ENERGY I FELT...
THAT SOMETHING WANTED EVERY-THING!
THE MAN WHO WAS NEAR ME WAS ENTRANCED.
I WANTED TO PUSH HIM AWAY, BUT I COULDN'T—LIKE MY OWN WILL HAD BEEN STOLEN.
IT'S POSSIBLE...
...THAT I MIGHT'VE LET HIM TAKE ME WITHOUT A FIGHT.

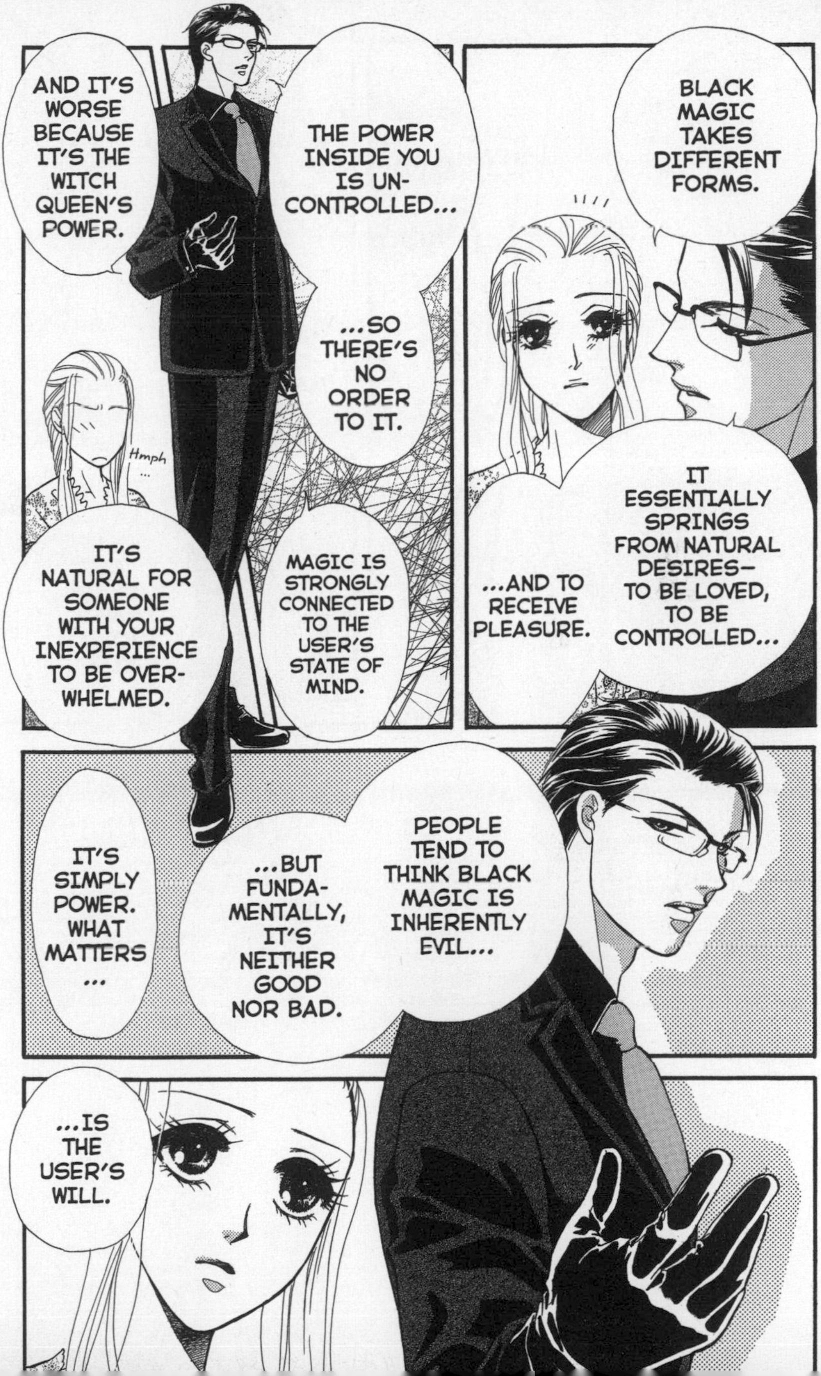
BLACK MAGIC TAKES DIFFERENT FORMS.
IT ESSENTIALLY SPRINGS FROM NATURAL DESIRES— TO BE LOVED, TO BE CONTROLLED...
...AND TO RECEIVE PLEASURE.
THE POWER INSIDE YOU IS UN-CONTROLLED...
...SO THERE'S NO ORDER TO IT.
AND IT'S WORSE BECAUSE IT'S THE WITCH QUEEN'S POWER.
Hmph...
MAGIC IS STRONGLY CONNECTED TO THE USER'S STATE OF MIND.
IT'S NATURAL FOR SOMEONE WITH YOUR INEXPERIENCE TO BE OVER-WHELMED.
PEOPLE TEND TO THINK BLACK MAGIC IS INHERENTLY EVIL...
...BUT FUNDA-MENTALLY, IT'S NEITHER GOOD NOR BAD.
IT'S SIMPLY POWER. WHAT MATTERS...
...IS THE USER'S WILL.

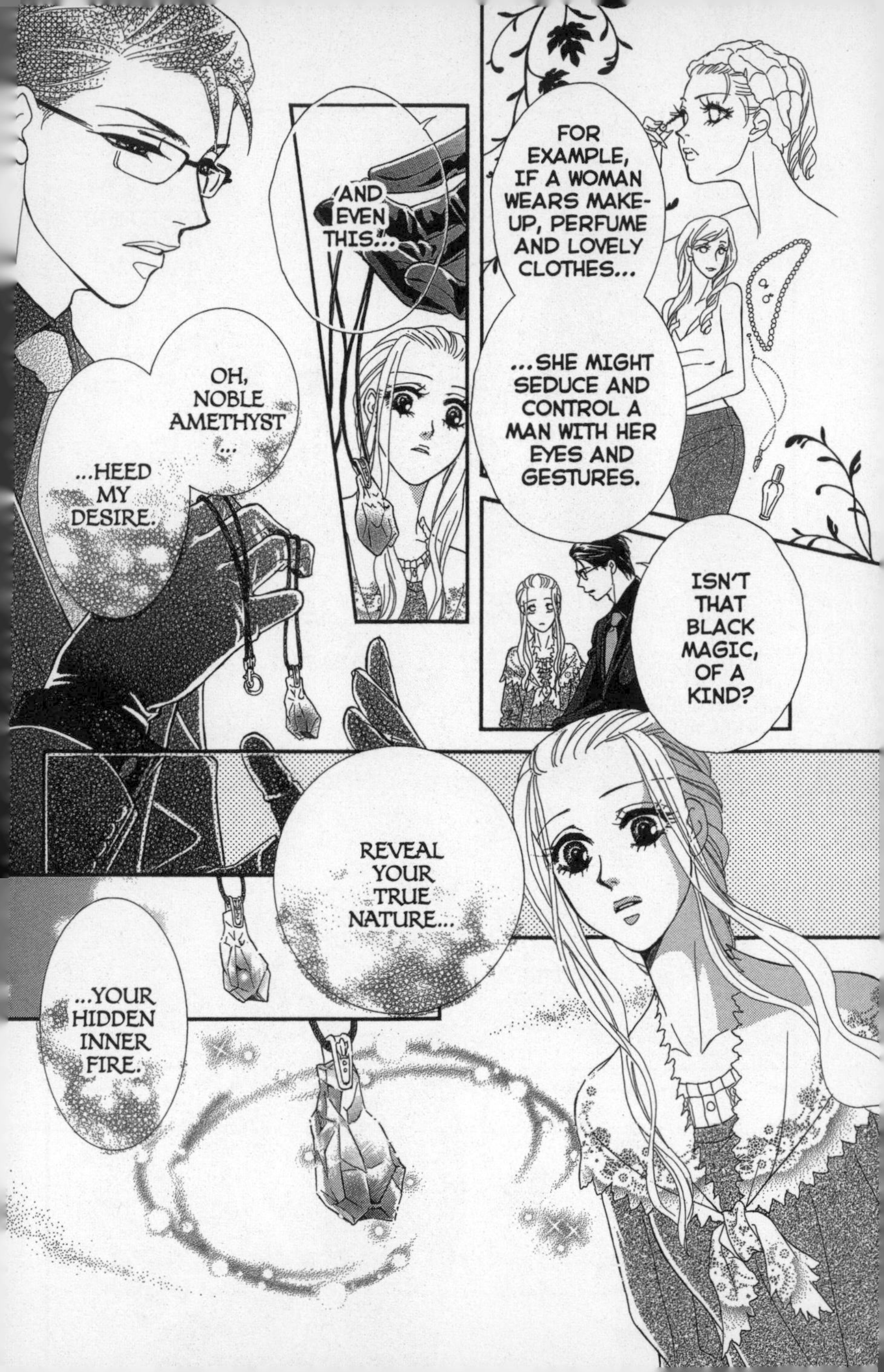
FOR EXAMPLE, IF A WOMAN WEARS MAKE-UP, PERFUME AND LOVELY CLOTHES...
...SHE MIGHT SEDUCE AND CONTROL A MAN WITH HER EYES AND GESTURES.
ISN'T THAT BLACK MAGIC, OF A KIND?
AND EVEN THIS...
OH, NOBLE AMETHYST...
...HEED MY DESIRE.
REVEAL YOUR TRUE NATURE...
...YOUR HIDDEN INNER FIRE.

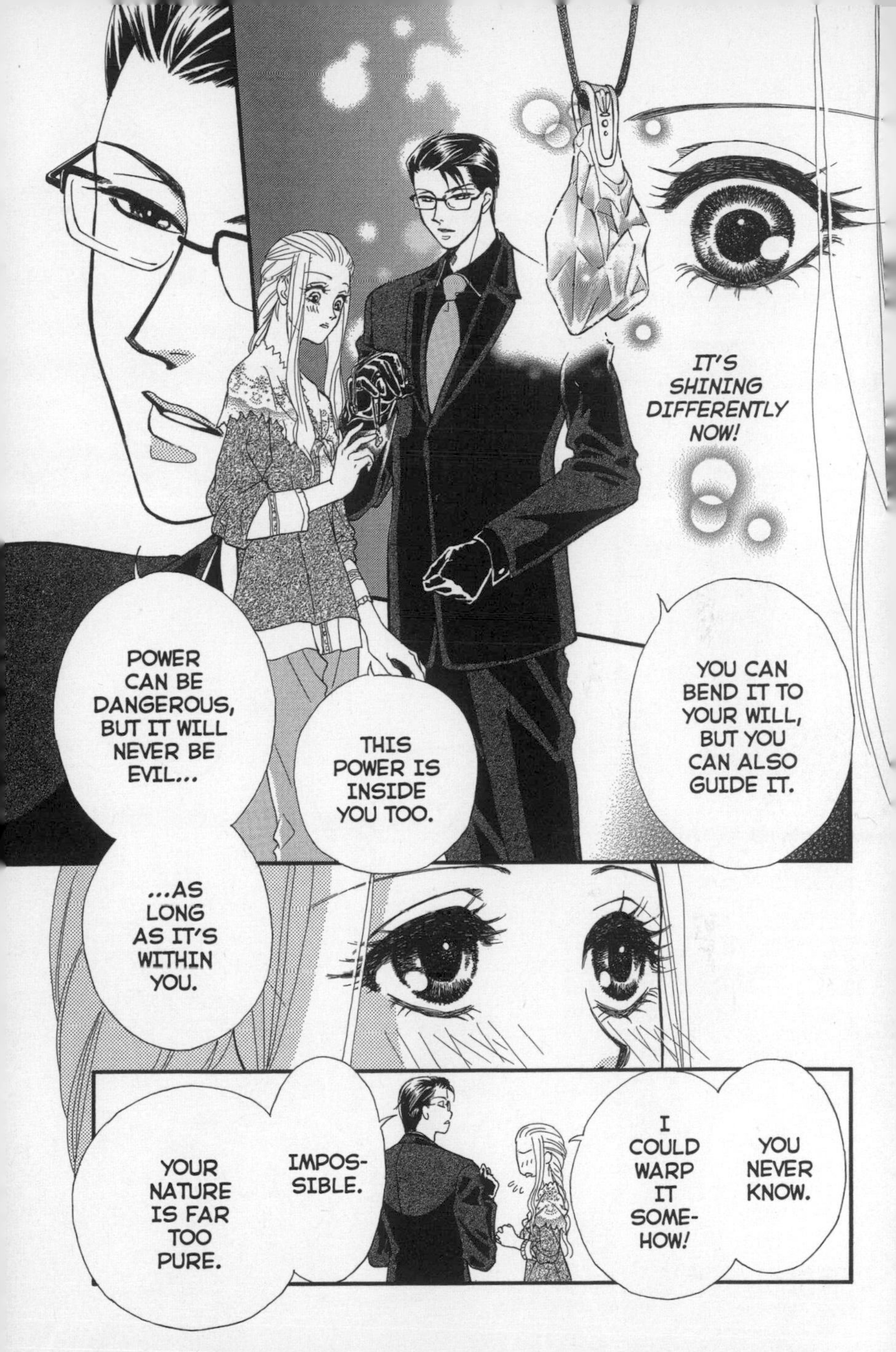
IT'S SHINING DIFFERENTLY NOW!
YOU CAN BEND IT TO YOUR WILL, BUT YOU CAN ALSO GUIDE IT.
THIS POWER IS INSIDE YOU TOO.
POWER CAN BE DANGEROUS, BUT IT WILL NEVER BE EVIL...
...AS LONG AS IT'S WITHIN YOU.
YOU NEVER KNOW.
I COULD WARP IT SOMEHOW!
IMPOS-SIBLE.
YOUR NATURE IS FAR TOO PURE.

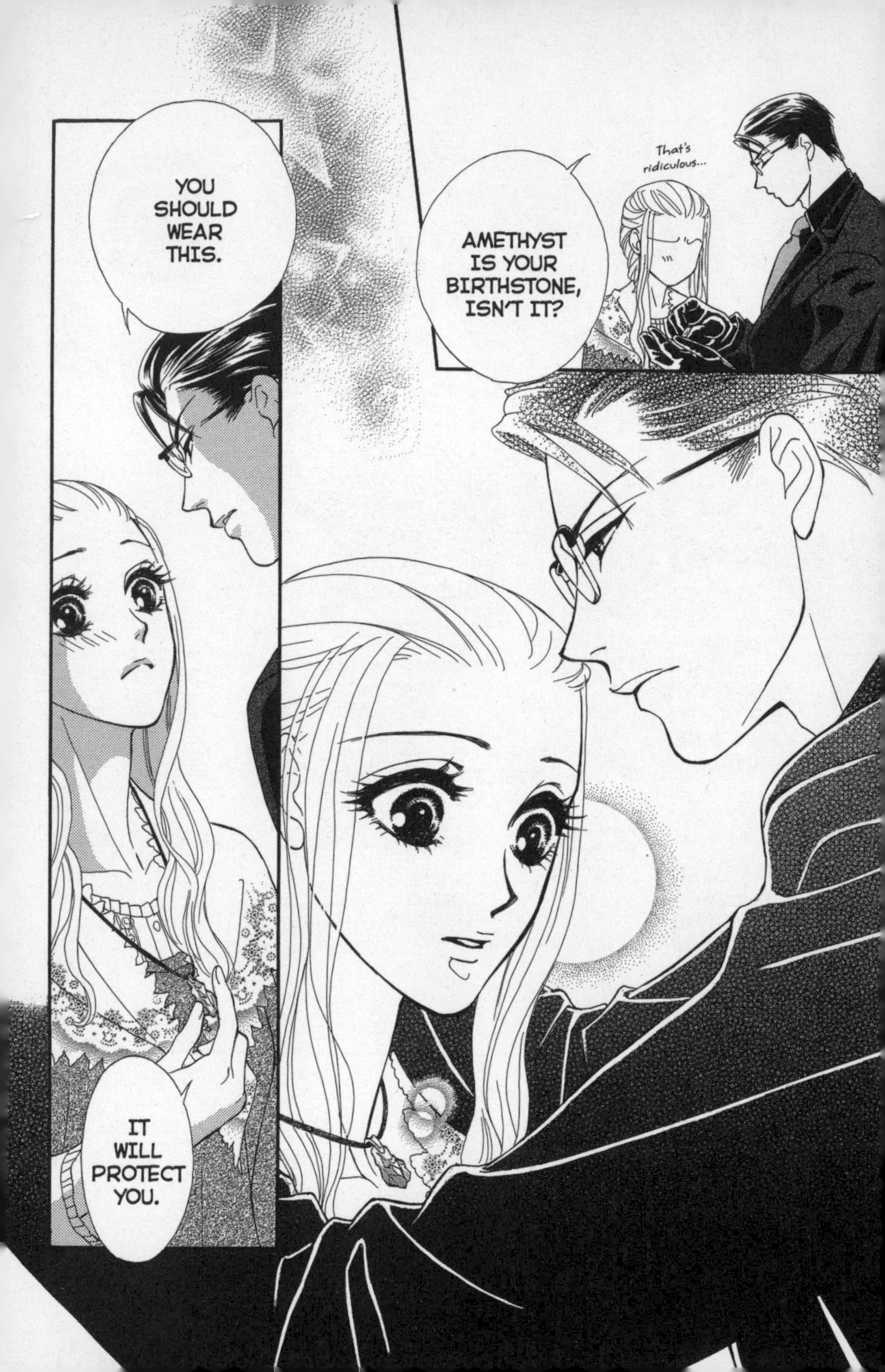
That's ridiculous...
AMETHYST IS YOUR BIRTHSTONE, ISN'T IT?
YOU SHOULD WEAR THIS.
IT WILL PROTECT YOU.

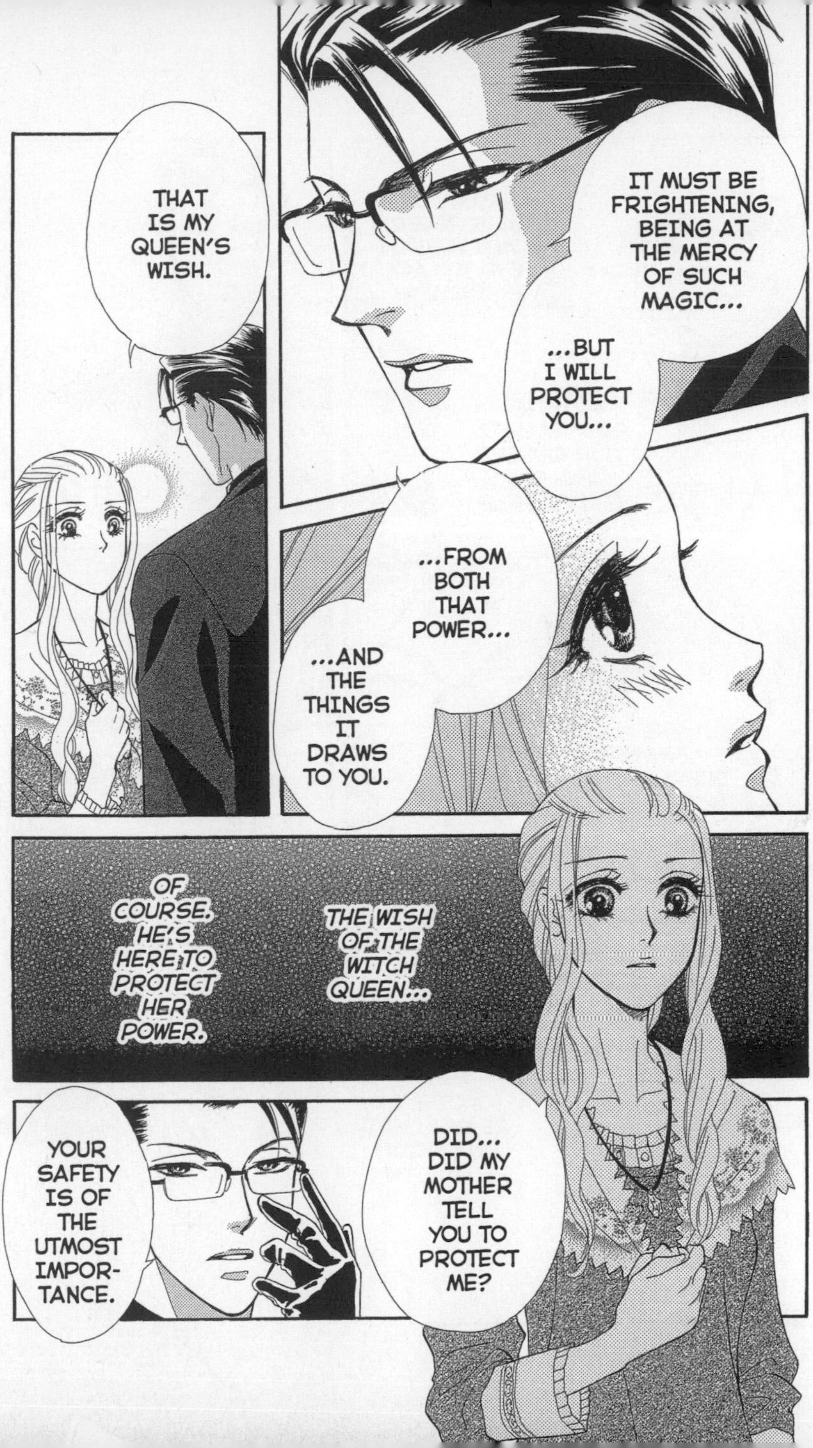
IT MUST BE FRIGHTENING, BEING AT THE MERCY OF SUCH MAGIC...
...BUT I WILL PROTECT YOU...
...FROM BOTH THAT POWER...
...AND THE THINGS IT DRAWS TO YOU.
THAT IS MY QUEEN'S WISH.
THE WISH OF THE WITCH QUEEN...
OF COURSE. HE'S HERE TO PROTECT HER POWER.
DID... DID MY MOTHER TELL YOU TO PROTECT ME?
YOUR SAFETY IS OF THE UTMOST IMPOR-TANCE.

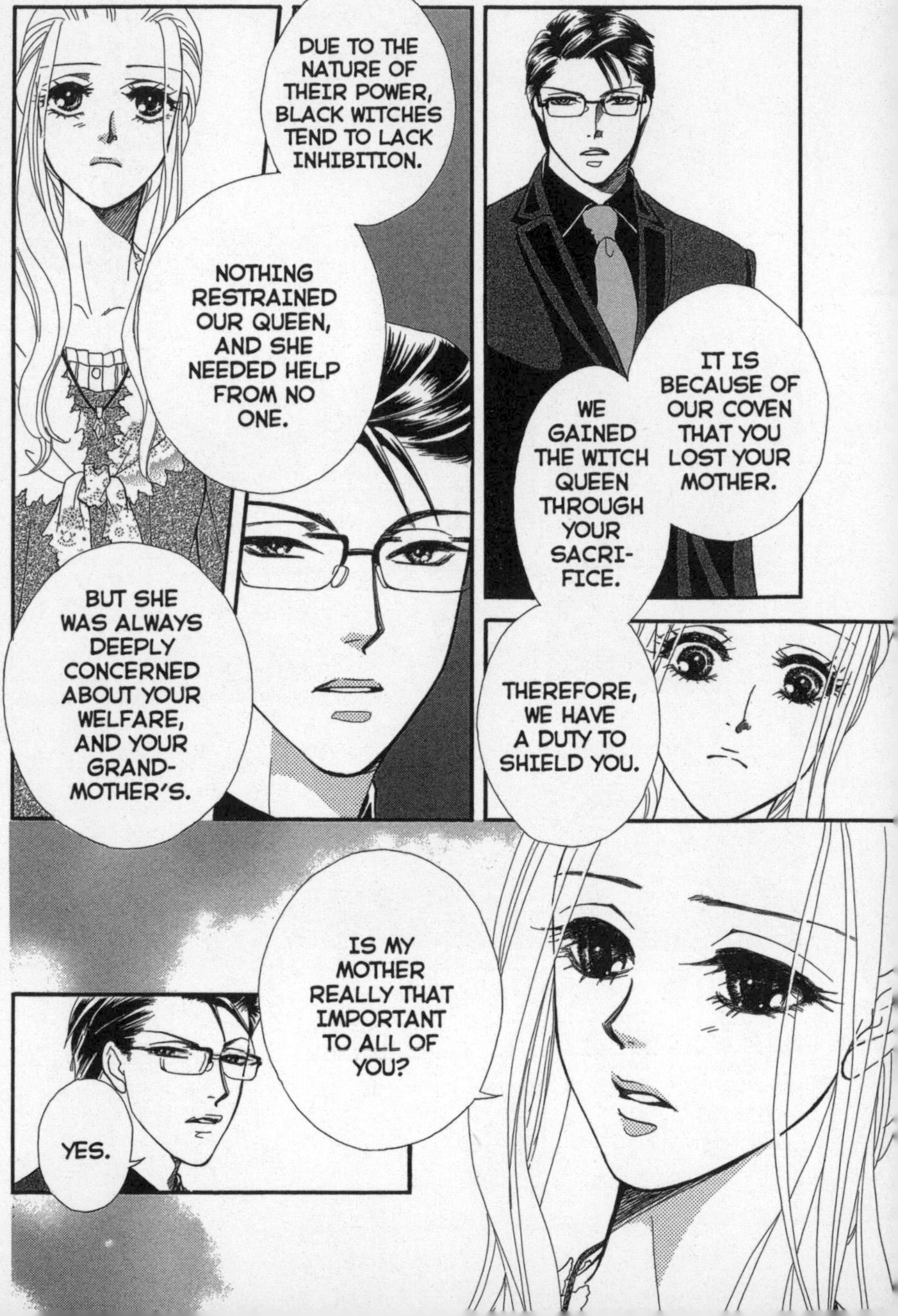
IT IS BECAUSE OF OUR COVEN THAT YOU LOST YOUR MOTHER.
WE GAINED THE WITCH QUEEN THROUGH YOUR SACRI-FICE.
THEREFORE, WE HAVE A DUTY TO SHIELD YOU.
DUE TO THE NATURE OF THEIR POWER, BLACK WITCHES TEND TO LACK INHIBITION.
NOTHING RESTRAINED OUR QUEEN, AND SHE NEEDED HELP FROM NO ONE.
BUT SHE WAS ALWAYS DEEPLY CONCERNED ABOUT YOUR WELFARE, AND YOUR GRAND-MOTHER'S.
IS MY MOTHER REALLY THAT IMPORTANT TO ALL OF YOU?
YES.

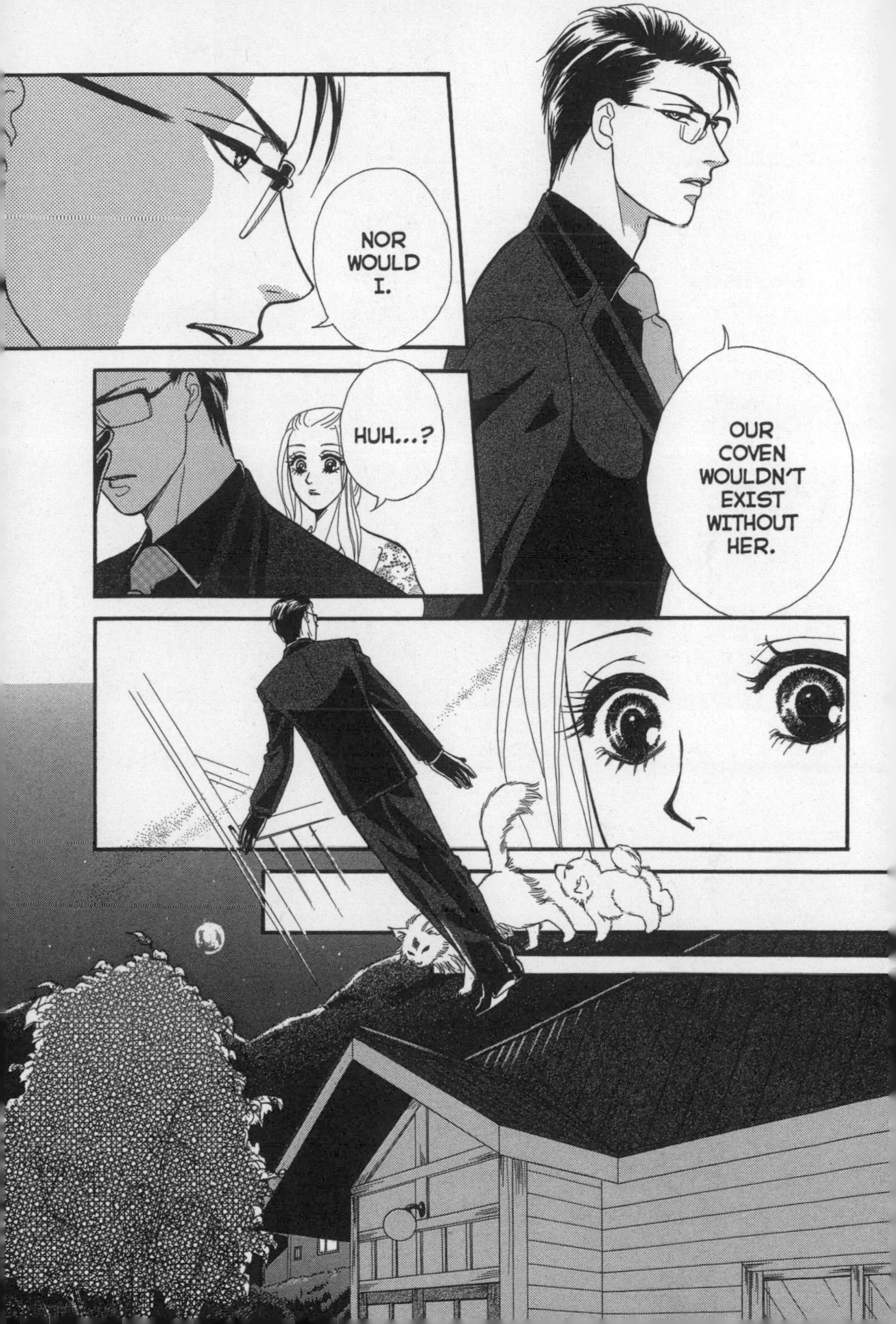
OUR COVEN WOULDN'T EXIST WITHOUT HER.
NOR WOULD I.
HUH...?

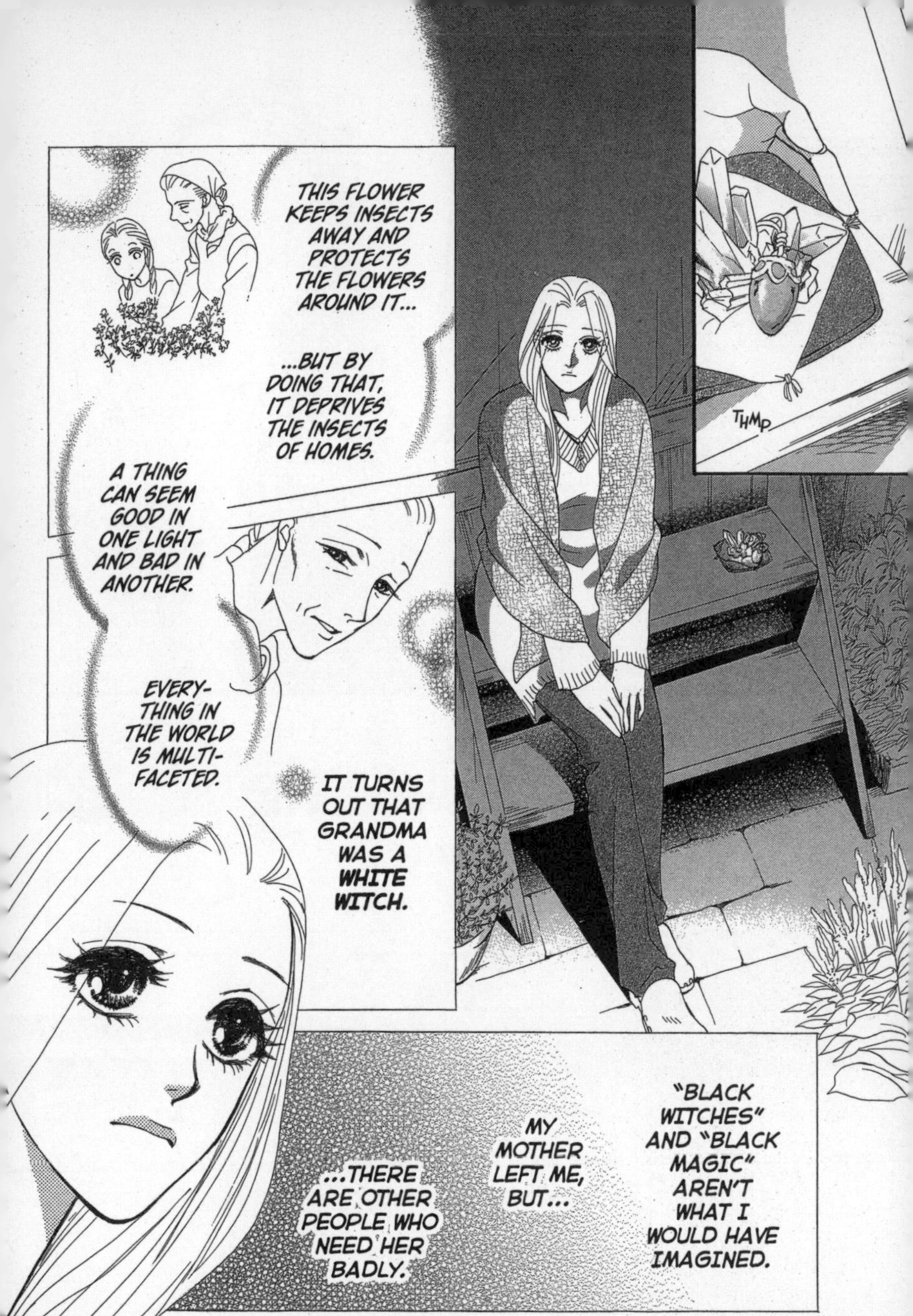
THMP
THIS FLOWER KEEPS INSECTS AWAY AND PROTECTS THE FLOWERS AROUND IT...
...BUT BY DOING THAT, IT DEPRIVES THE INSECTS OF HOMES.
A THING CAN SEEM GOOD IN ONE LIGHT AND BAD IN ANOTHER.
EVERY-THING IN THE WORLD IS MULTI-FACETED.
IT TURNS OUT THAT GRANDMA WAS A WHITE WITCH.
"BLACK WITCHES" AND "BLACK MAGIC" AREN'T WHAT I WOULD HAVE IMAGINED.
MY MOTHER LEFT ME, BUT...
...THERE ARE OTHER PEOPLE WHO NEED HER BADLY.

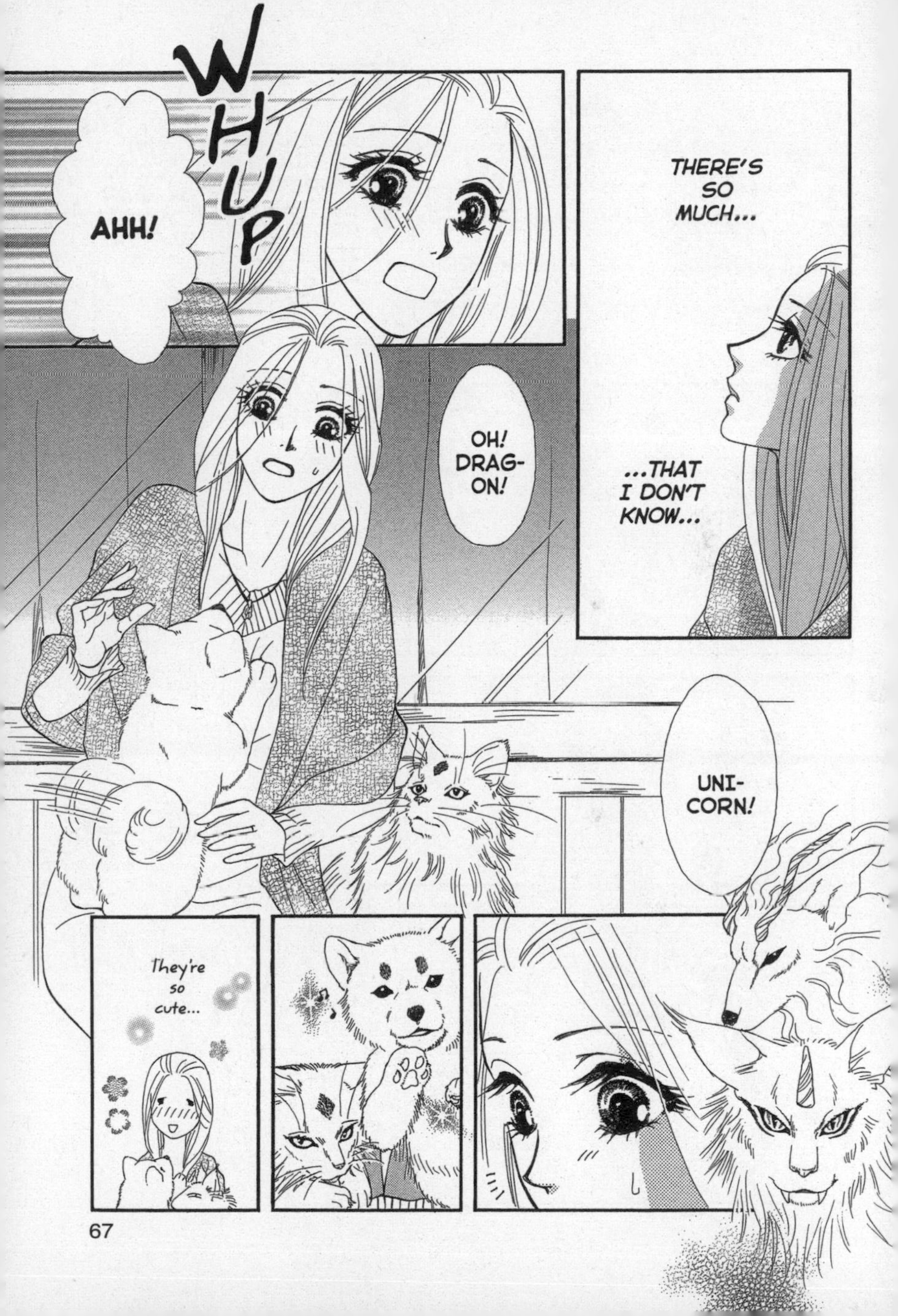
THERE'S SO MUCH...
...THAT I DON'T KNOW...
WHUP
AHH!
OH! DRAG-ON!
UNI-CORN!
They're so cute...

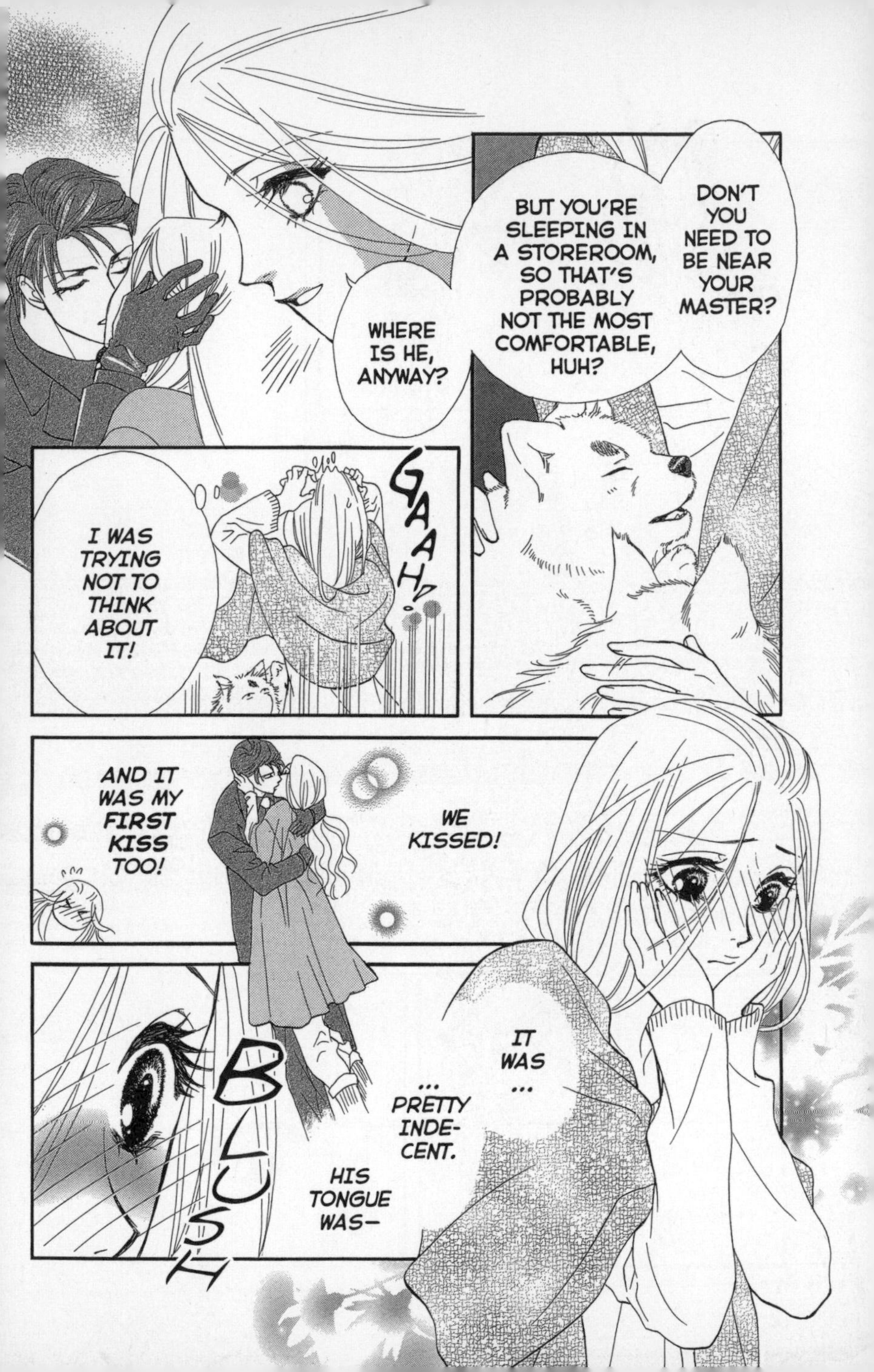
DON'T YOU NEED TO BE NEAR YOUR MASTER?
BUT YOU'RE SLEEPING IN A STOREROOM, SO THAT'S PROBABLY NOT THE MOST COMFORTABLE, HUH?
WHERE IS HE, ANYWAY?
GAAAH!?
I WAS TRYING NOT TO THINK ABOUT IT!
WE KISSED!
AND IT WAS MY FIRST KISS TOO!
IT WAS ...
... PRETTY INDE-CENT.
HIS TONGUE WAS—
BLUSH

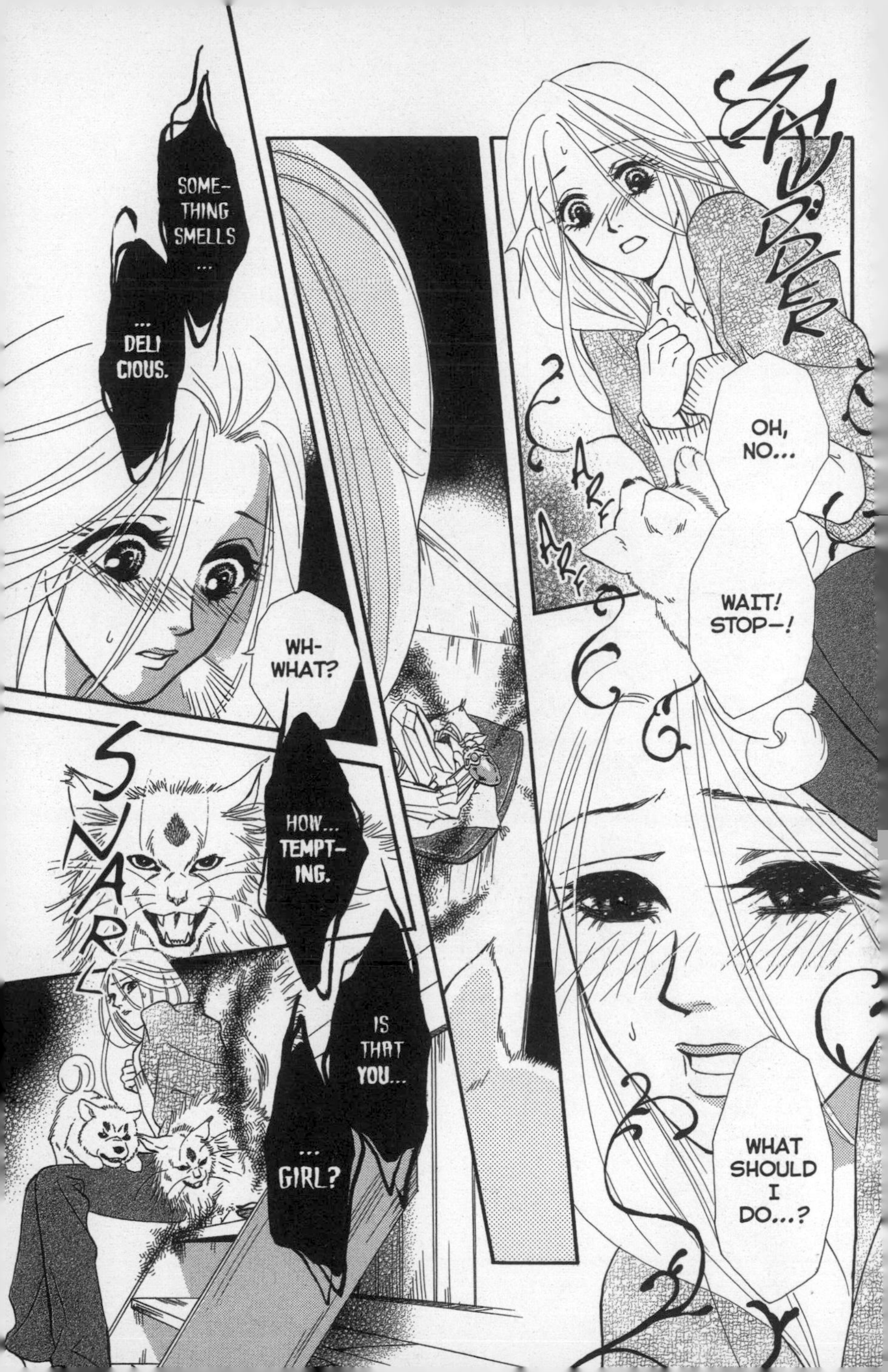
SHUDDER
OH, NO...
ARF ARF
WAIT! STOP—!
SOME-THING SMELLS...
...DELICIOUS.
WH-WHAT?
WHAT SHOULD I DO...?
SNARL
HOW... TEMPT-ING.
IS THAT YOU...
...GIRL?

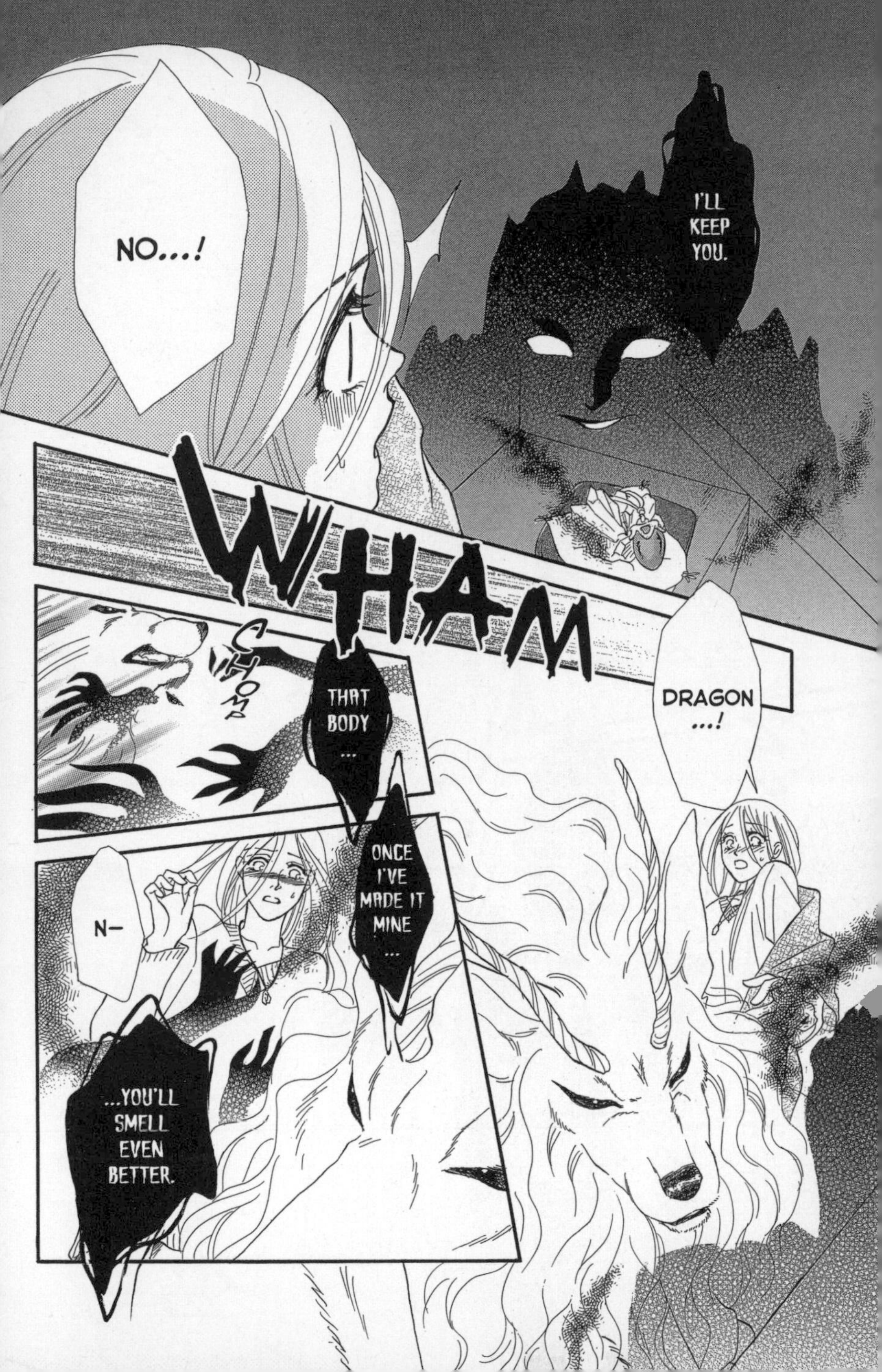
I'LL KEEP YOU.
NO...!
WHAM
DRAGON ...!
CHOMP
THAT BODY ...
N–
ONCE I'VE MADE IT MINE ...
...YOU'LL SMELL EVEN BETTER.

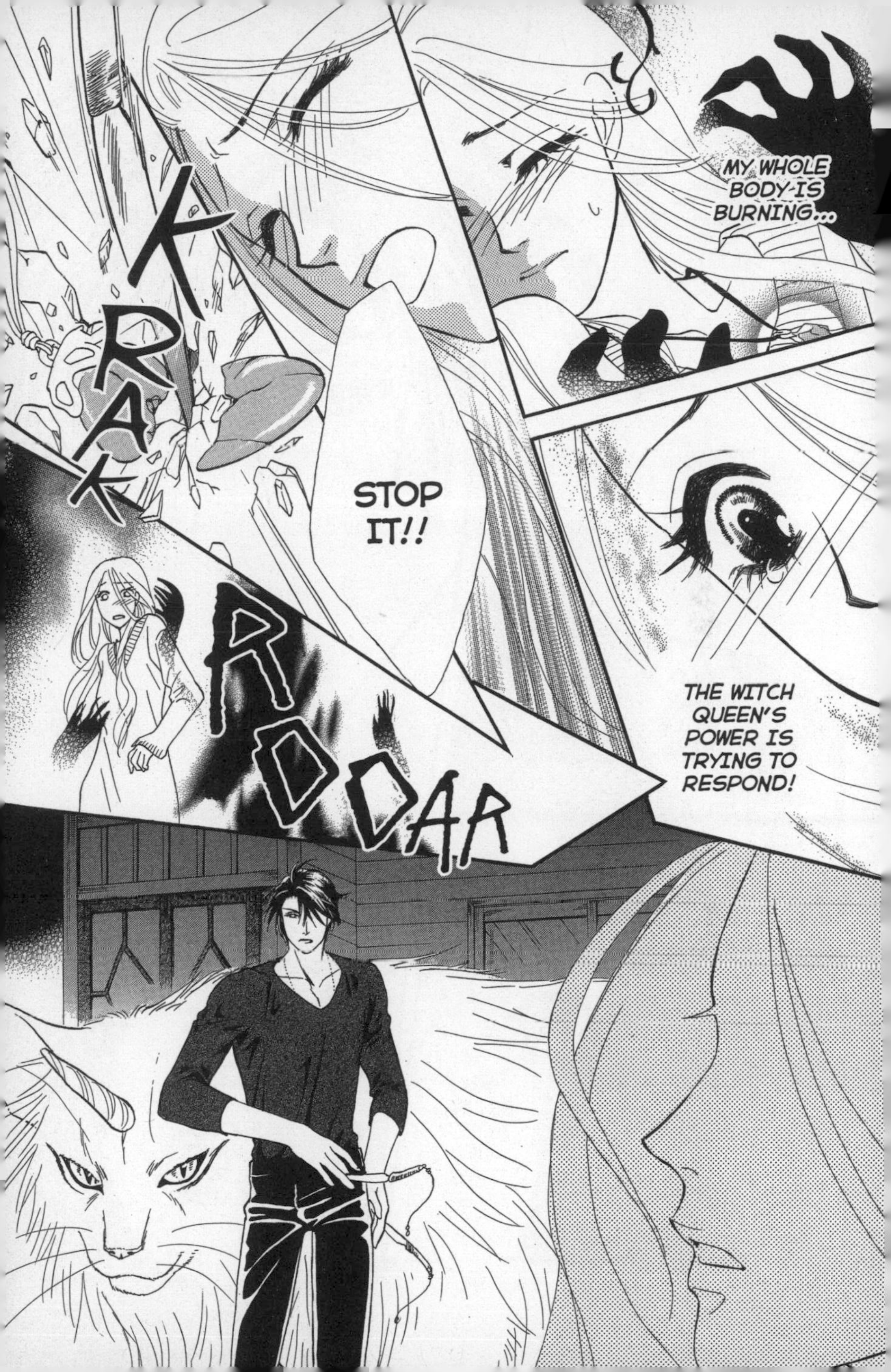

MY WHOLE BODY IS BURNING...
KRAK
THE WITCH QUEEN'S POWER IS TRYING TO RESPOND!
STOP IT!!
ROOAR

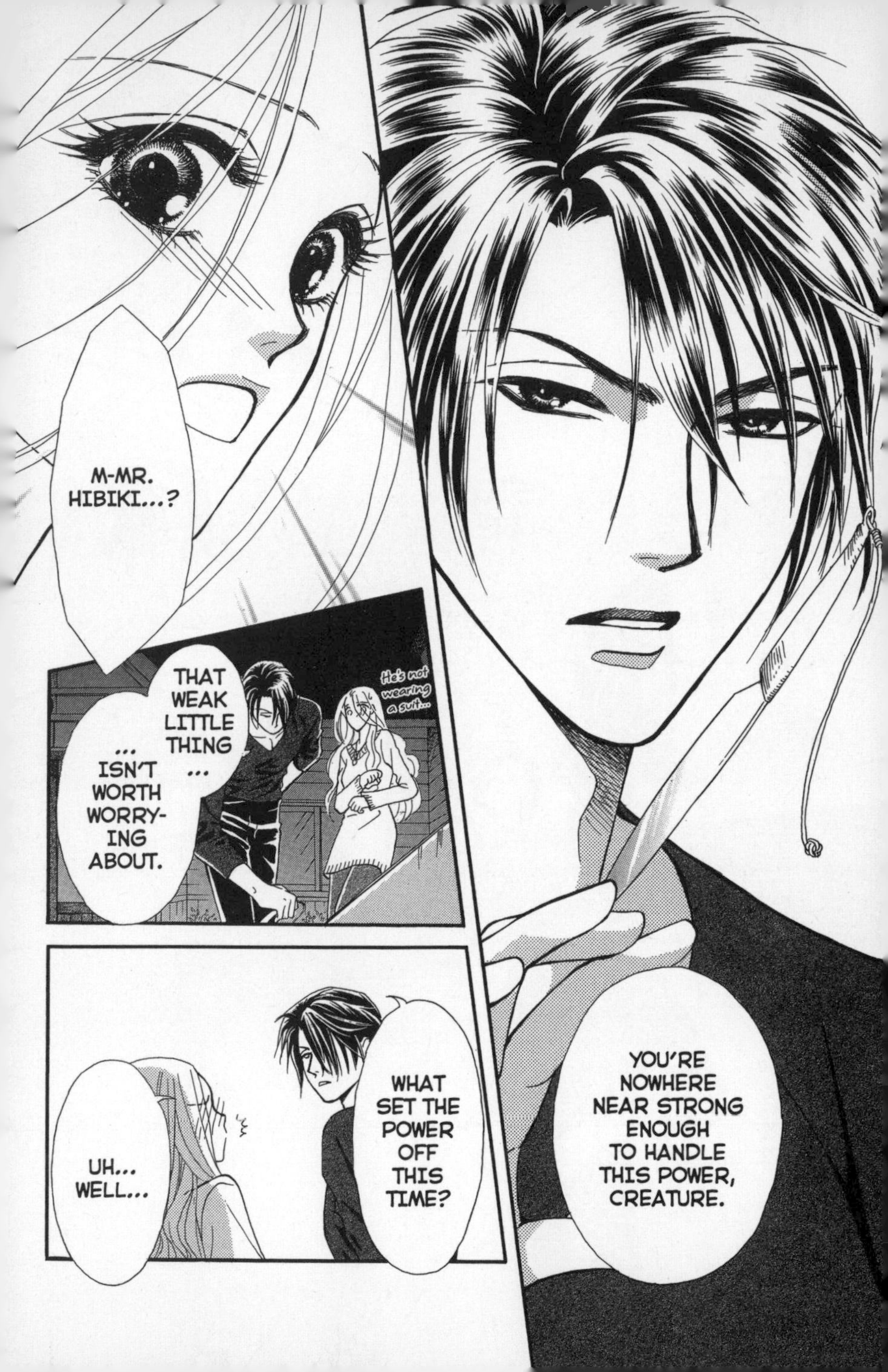
YOU'RE NOWHERE NEAR STRONG ENOUGH TO HANDLE THIS POWER, CREATURE.
M-MR. HIBIKI...?
THAT WEAK LITTLE THING ...
... ISN'T WORTH WORRYING ABOUT.
He's not wearing a suit...
WHAT SET THE POWER OFF THIS TIME?
UH... WELL...

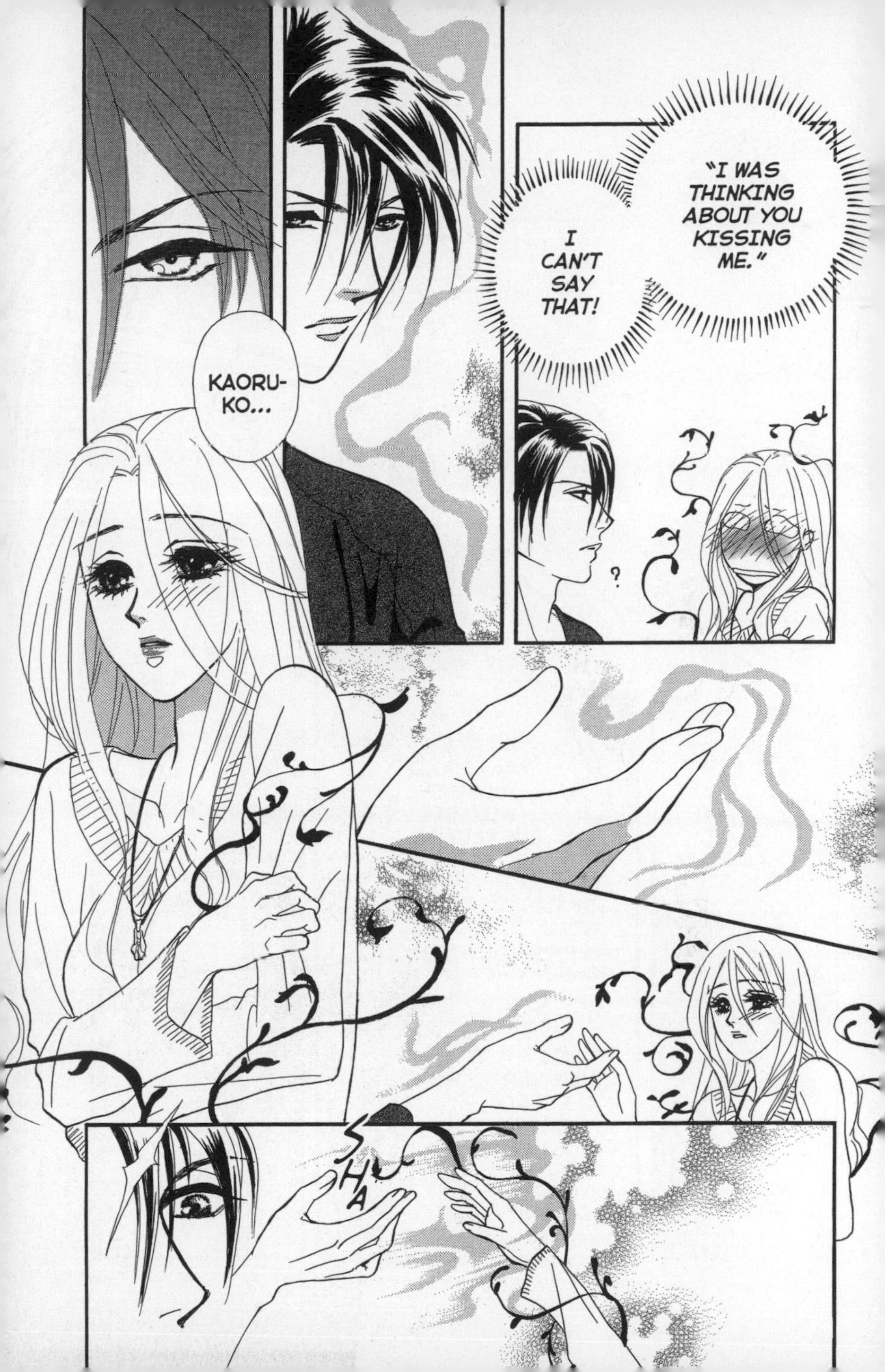
"I WAS THINKING ABOUT YOU KISSING ME."
I CAN'T SAY THAT!
KAORU-KO...
SHA

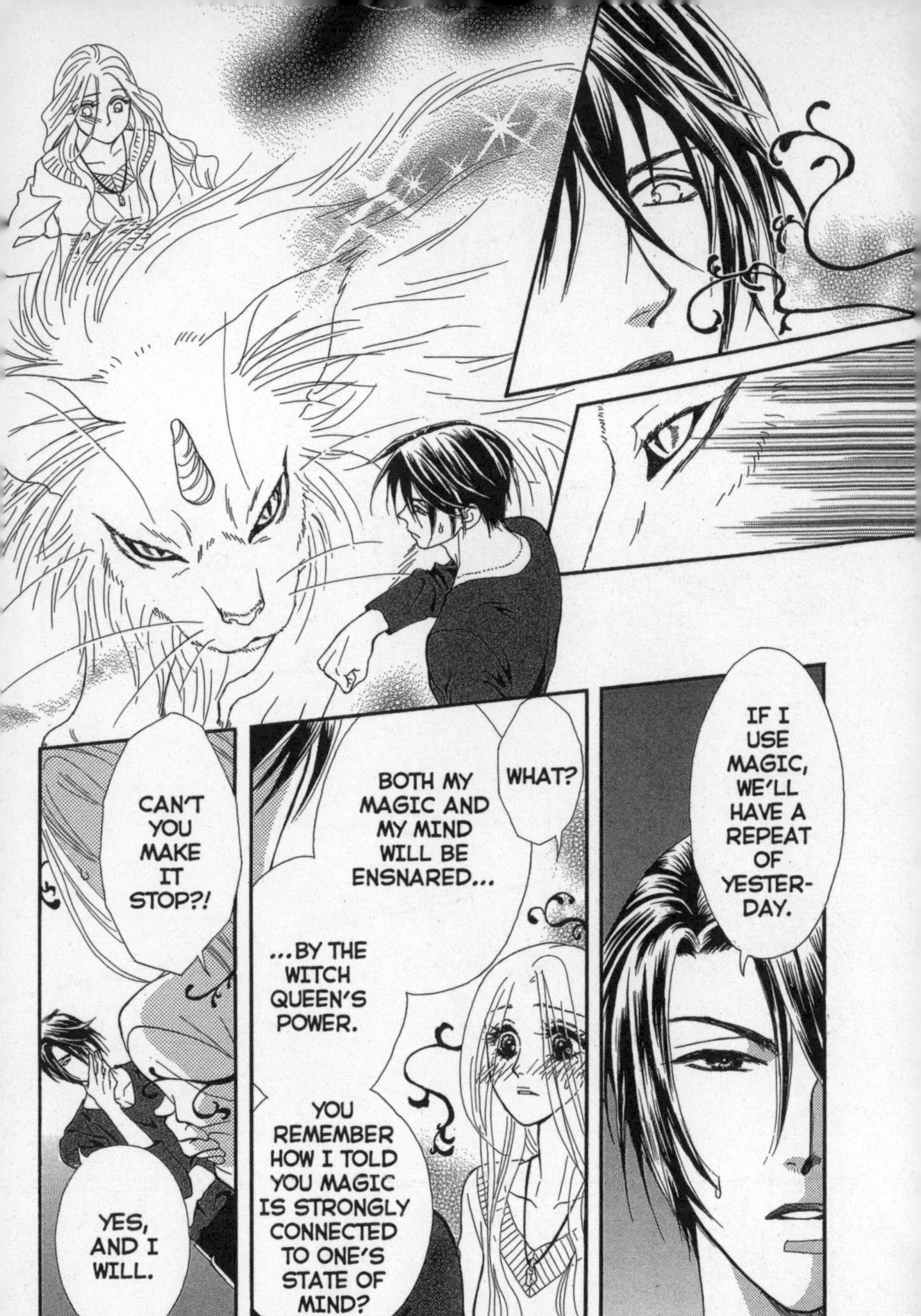
IF I USE MAGIC, WE'LL HAVE A REPEAT OF YESTER-DAY.
WHAT?
BOTH MY MAGIC AND MY MIND WILL BE ENSNARED...
...BY THE WITCH QUEEN'S POWER.
YOU REMEMBER HOW I TOLD YOU MAGIC IS STRONGLY CONNECTED TO ONE'S STATE OF MIND?
CAN'T YOU MAKE IT STOP?!
YES, AND I WILL.

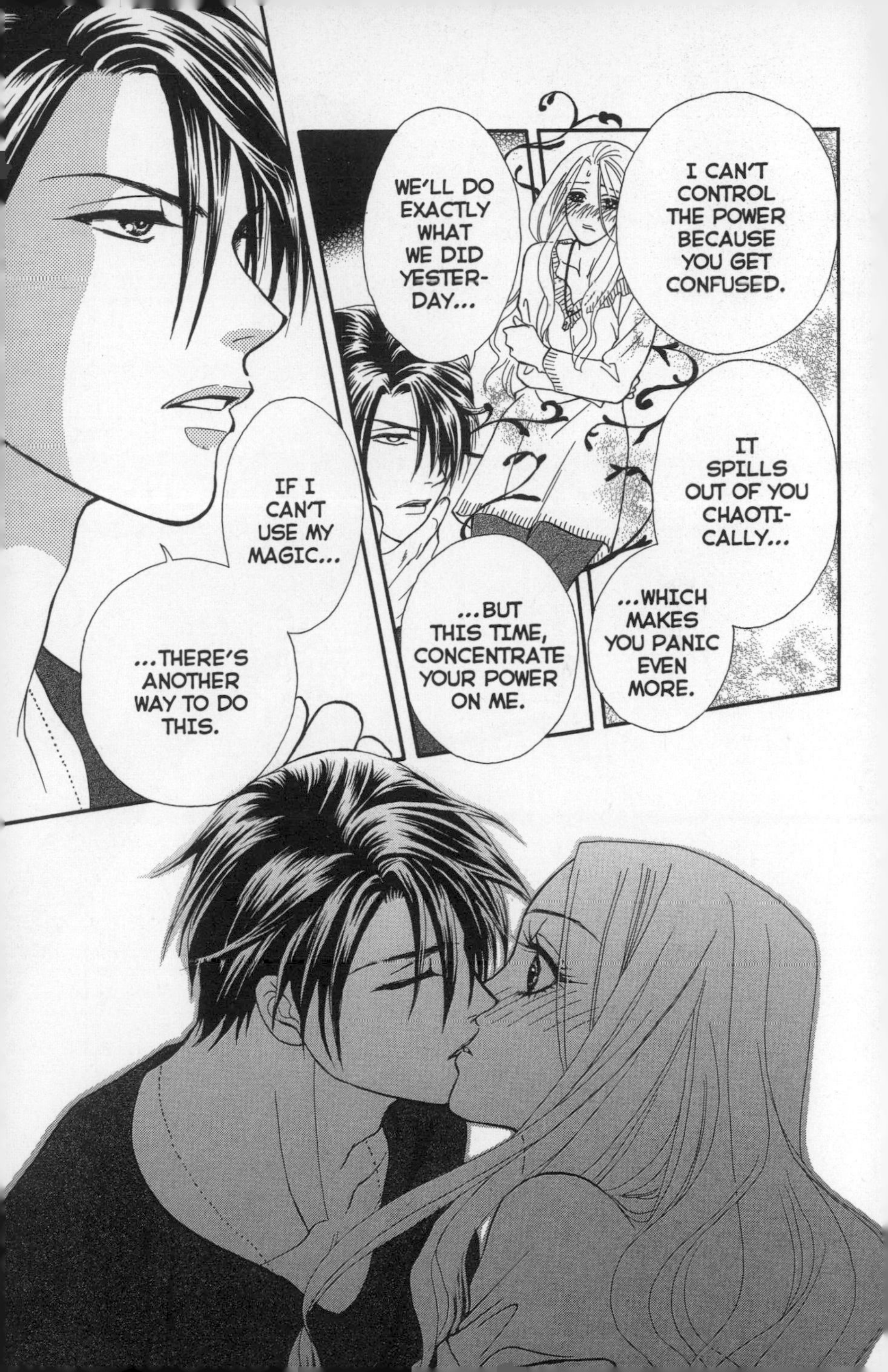
I CAN'T CONTROL THE POWER BECAUSE YOU GET CONFUSED.
IT SPILLS OUT OF YOU CHAOTI-CALLY...
...WHICH MAKES YOU PANIC EVEN MORE.
WE'LL DO EXACTLY WHAT WE DID YESTER-DAY...
...BUT THIS TIME, CONCENTRATE YOUR POWER ON ME.
IF I CAN'T USE MY MAGIC...
...THERE'S ANOTHER WAY TO DO THIS.

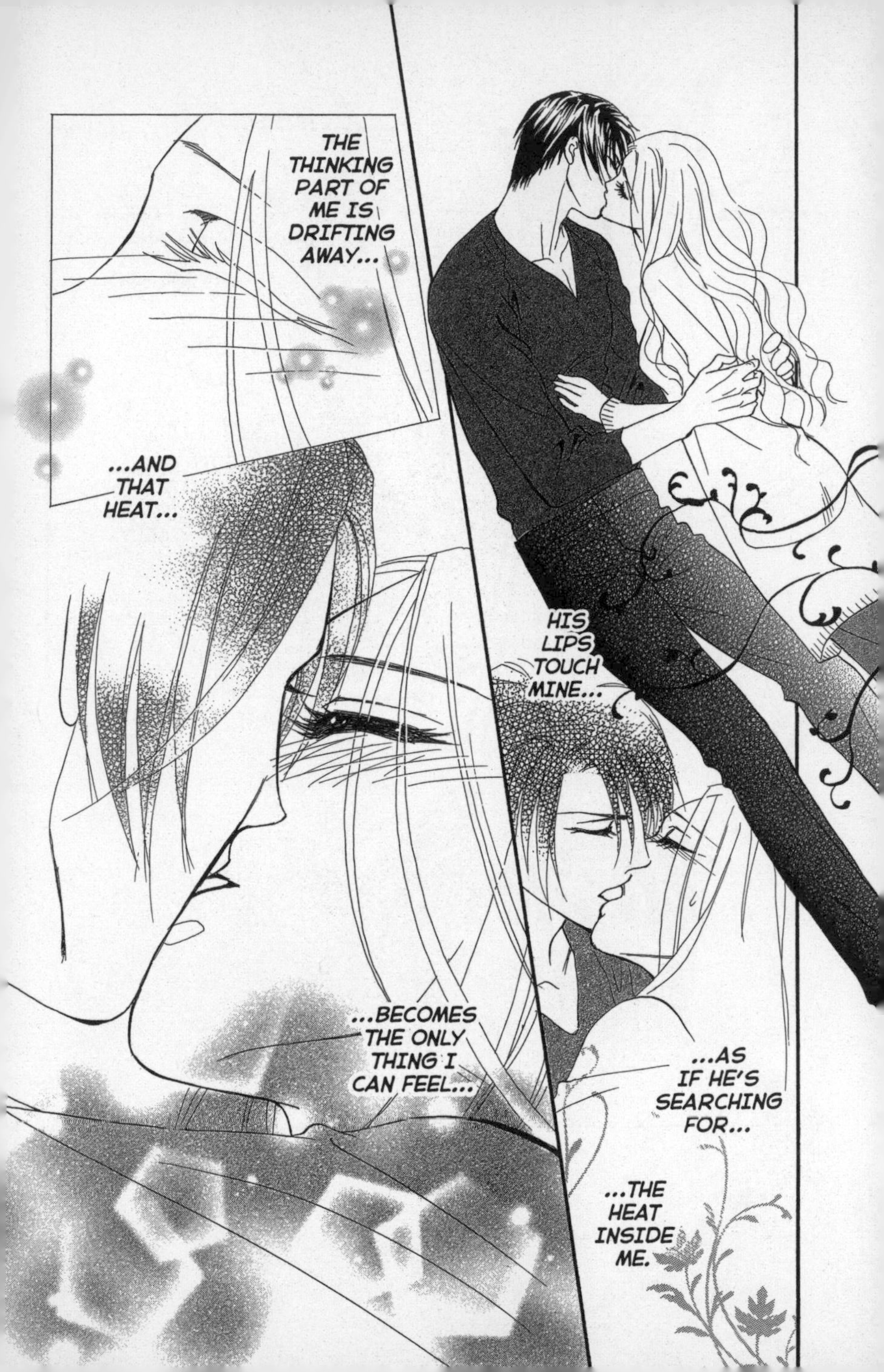
HIS LIPS TOUCH MINE...
...AS IF HE'S SEARCHING FOR...
...THE HEAT INSIDE ME.
THE THINKING PART OF ME IS DRIFTING AWAY...
...AND THAT HEAT...
...BECOMES THE ONLY THING I CAN FEEL...

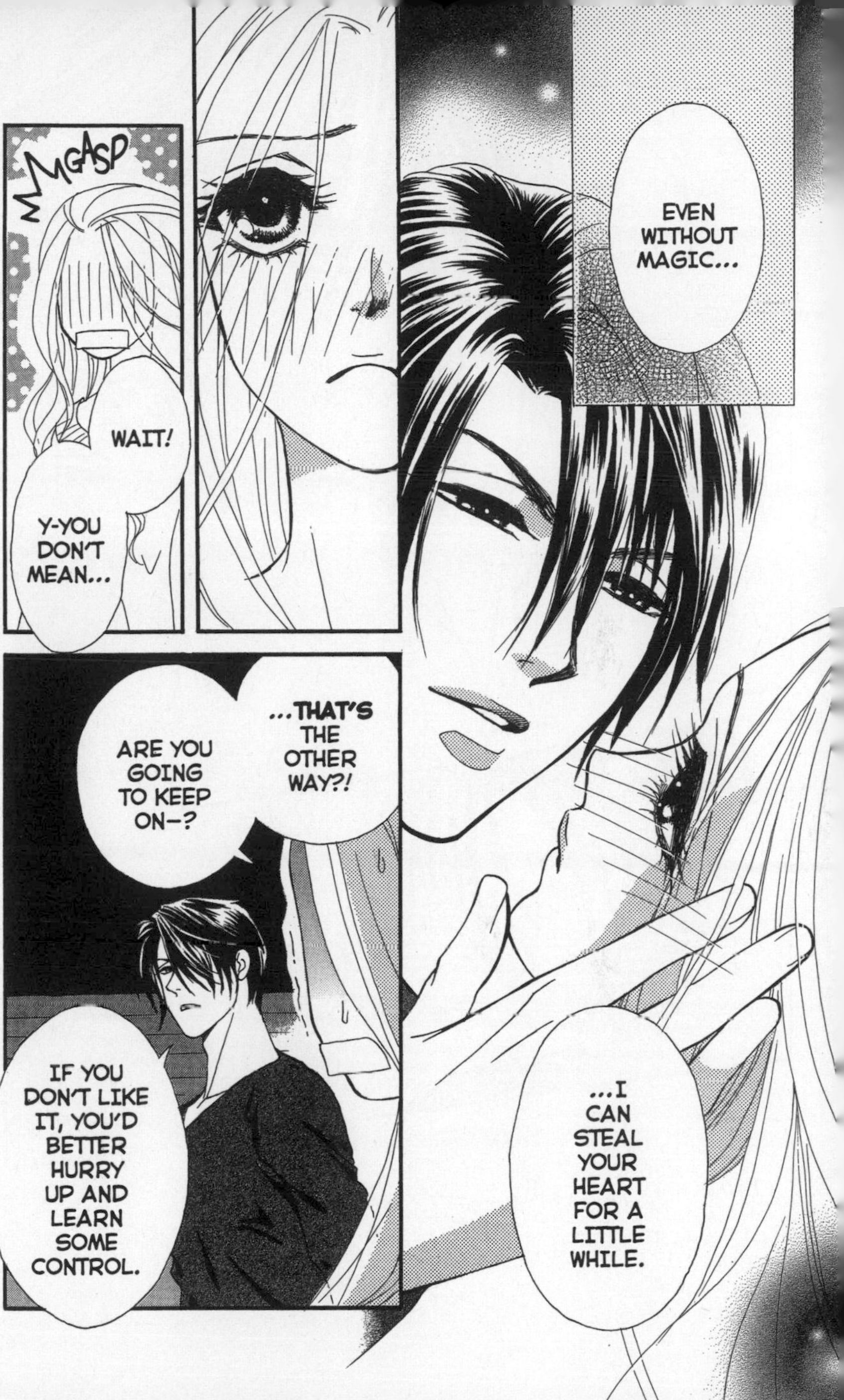
EVEN WITHOUT MAGIC...
...I CAN STEAL YOUR HEART FOR A LITTLE WHILE.
GASP
WAIT!
Y-YOU DON'T MEAN...
...THAT'S THE OTHER WAY?!
ARE YOU GOING TO KEEP ON–?
IF YOU DON'T LIKE IT, YOU'D BETTER HURRY UP AND LEARN SOME CONTROL.

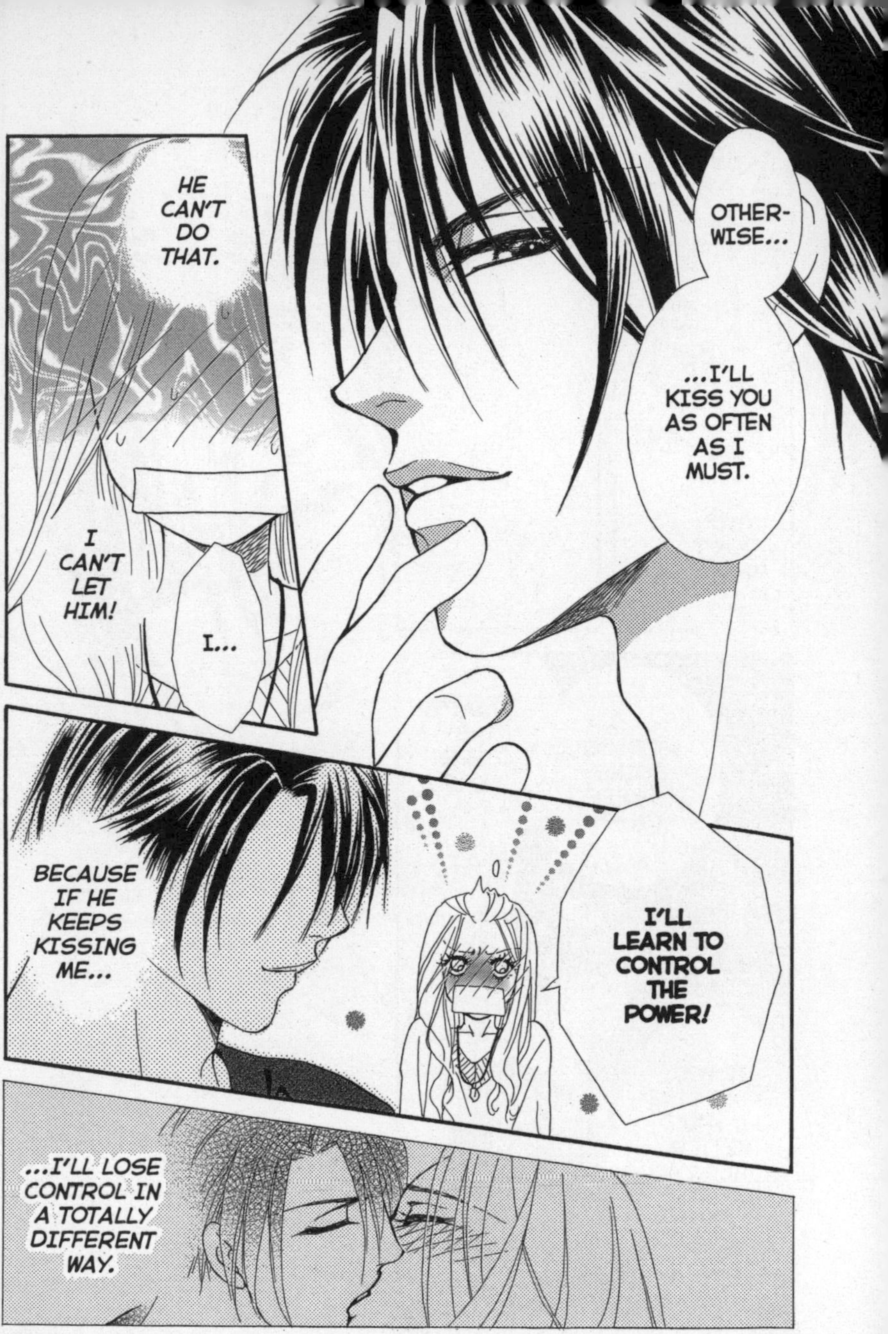
OTHER-WISE...
...I'LL KISS YOU AS OFTEN AS I MUST.
HE CAN'T DO THAT.
I...
I CAN'T LET HIM!
I'LL LEARN TO CONTROL THE POWER!
BECAUSE IF HE KEEPS KISSING ME...
...I'LL LOSE CONTROL IN A TOTALLY DIFFERENT WAY.

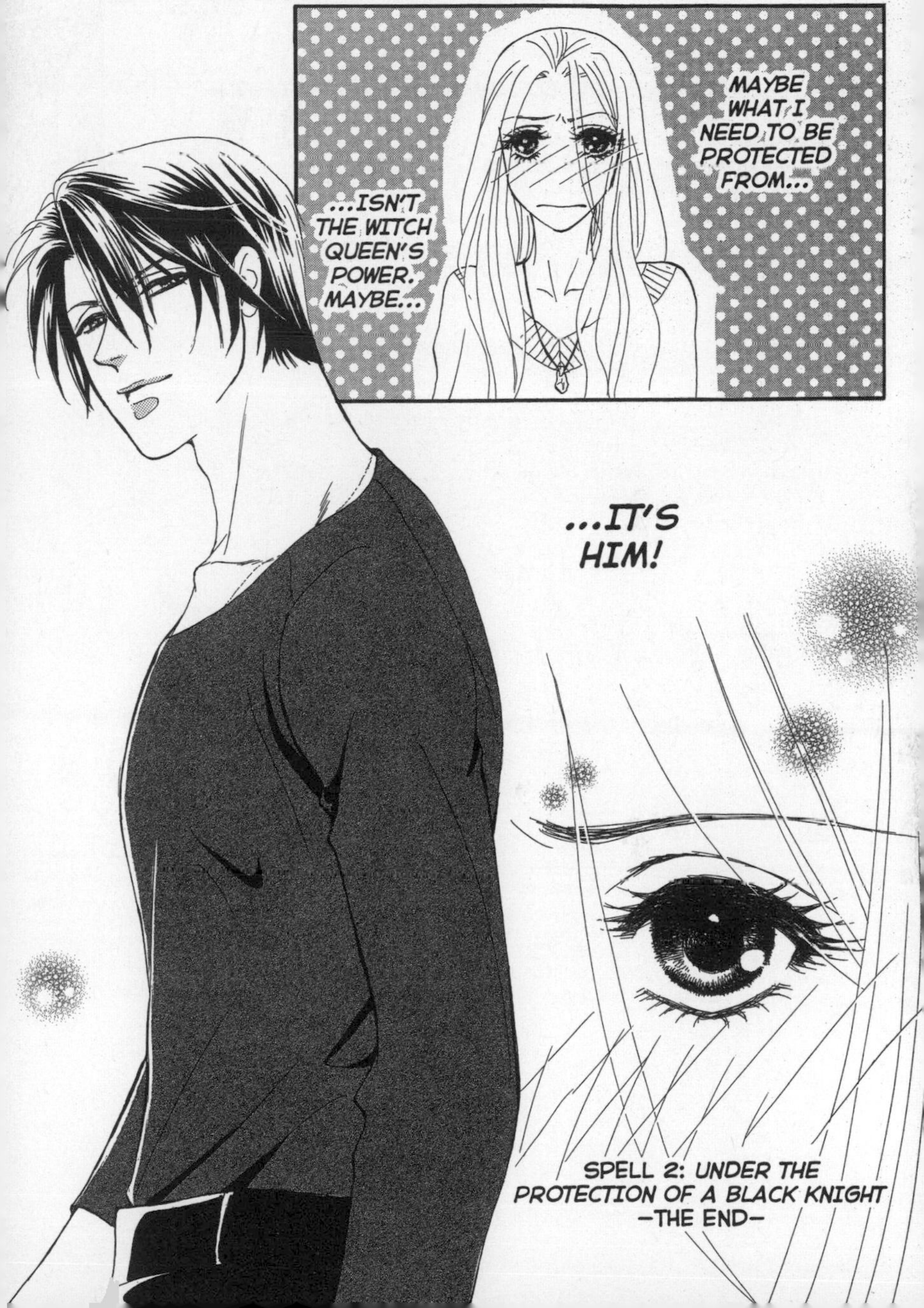
MAYBE WHAT I NEED TO BE PROTECTED FROM...
...ISN'T THE WITCH QUEEN'S POWER. MAYBE...
...IT'S HIM!
SPELL 2: UNDER THE PROTECTION OF A BLACK KNIGHT
-THE END-

– UNDER THE PROTECTION OF A BLACK KNIGHT –

I have a confession to make! This series has both a unicorn and a dragon! (Smile)
But I guess you knew that, didn't you?

Unicorn and Dragon strike Koko as being very strange creatures, but she seems to have accepted them because they're so cute.♡

I like drawing them BIG, too!
(Smile)

But I think it would be a little scary if such huge beasts really appeared out of nowhere...

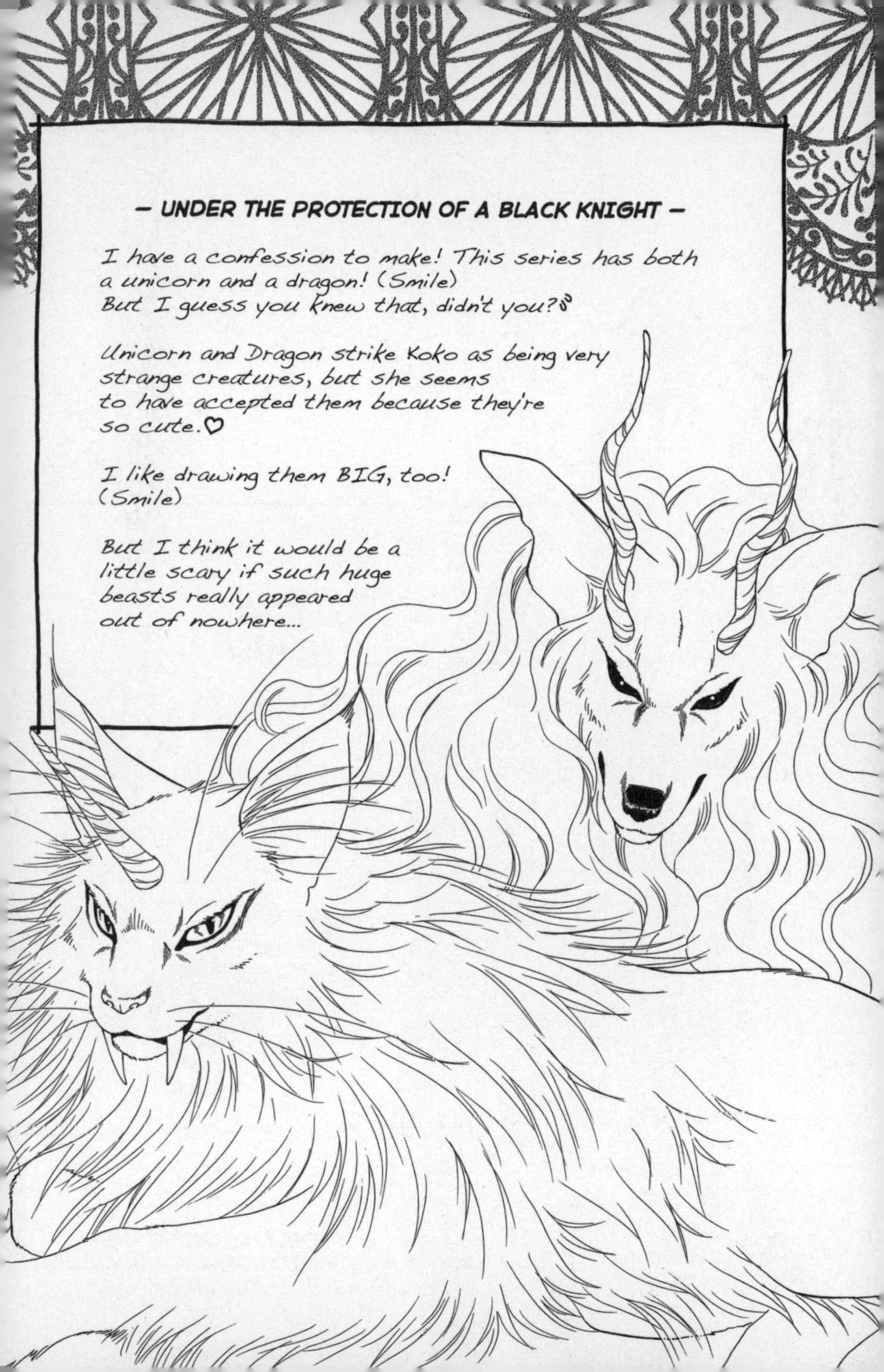

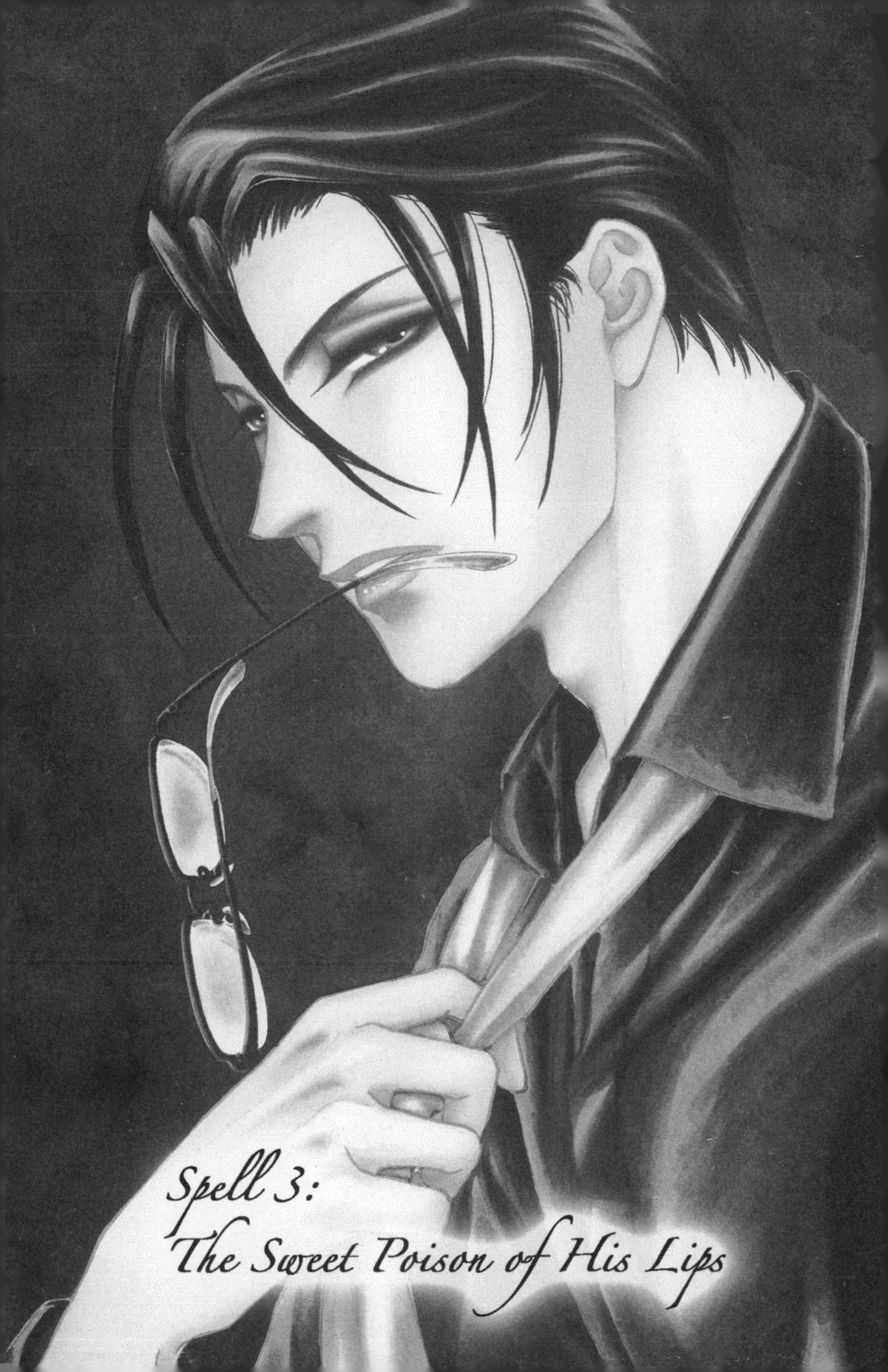
Spell 3:
The Sweet Poison of His Lips

Kaname is always holding Unicorn and Dragon even though he wears a black suit. I wonder how he keeps from getting covered in fur?

My suit repels the fur of beasts.

No way!

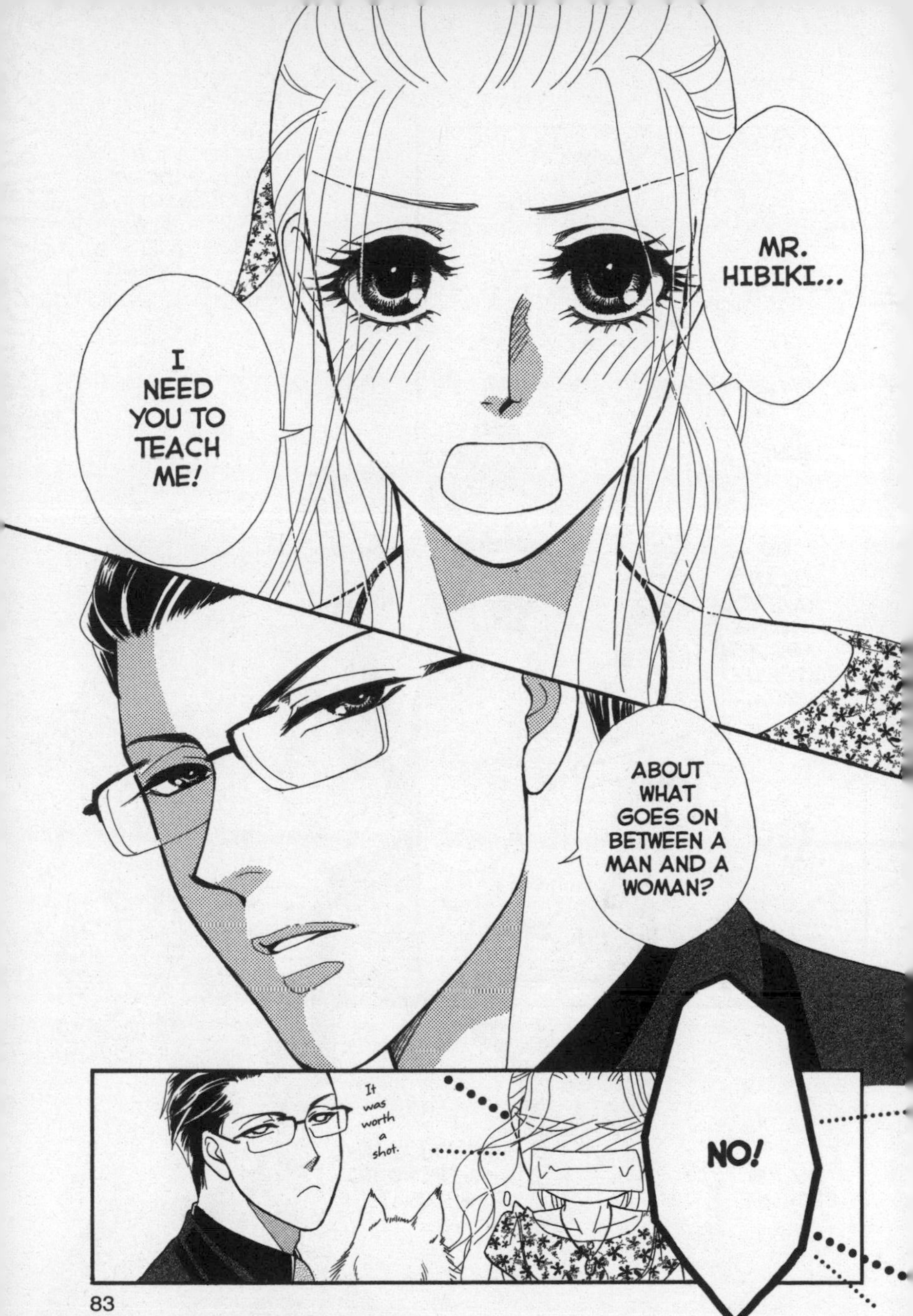
MR. HIBIKI...
I NEED YOU TO TEACH ME!
ABOUT WHAT GOES ON BETWEEN A MAN AND A WOMAN?
NO!
It was worth a shot.

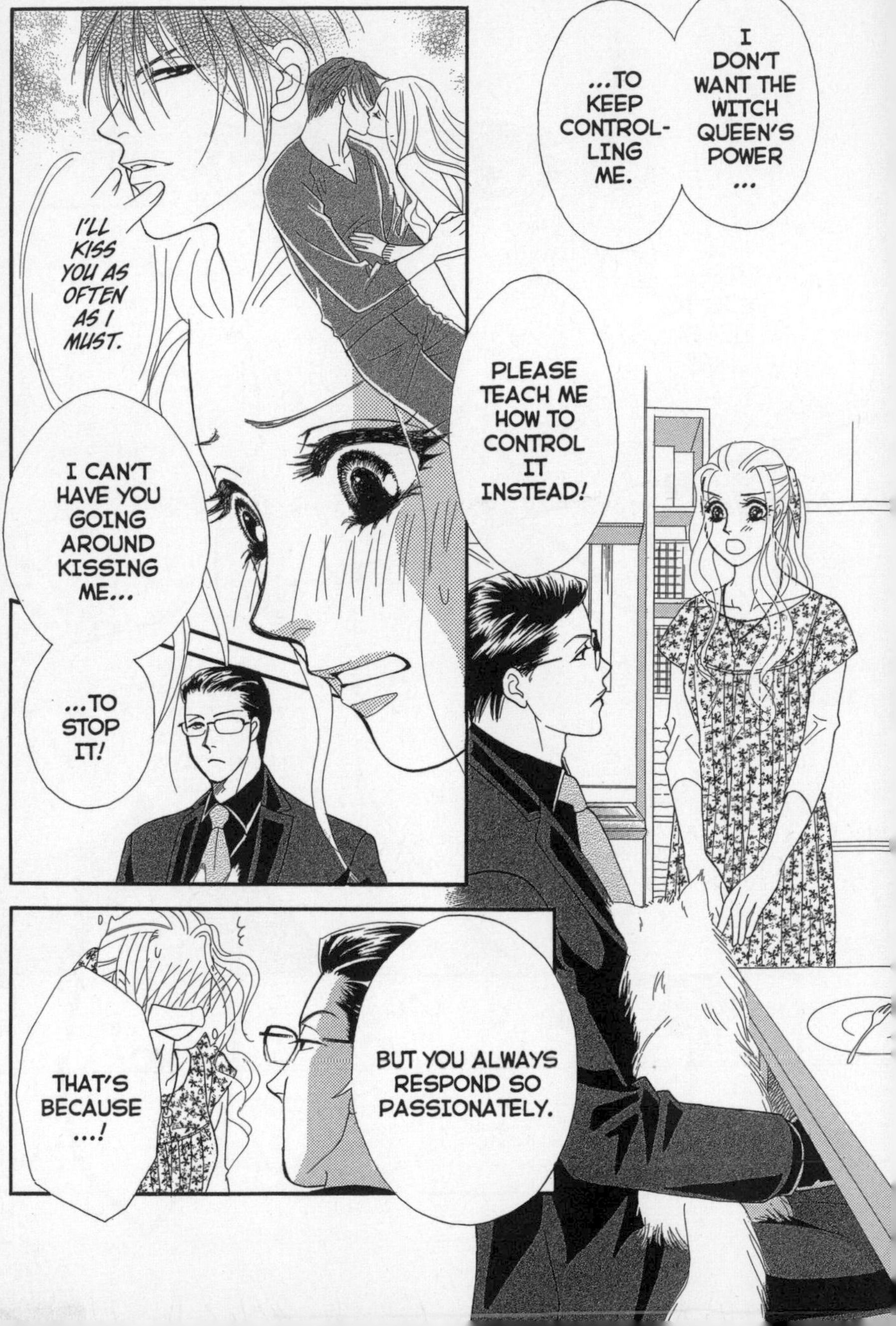
I DON'T WANT THE WITCH QUEEN'S POWER...
...TO KEEP CONTROL-LING ME.
PLEASE TEACH ME HOW TO CONTROL IT INSTEAD!
I'LL KISS YOU AS OFTEN AS I MUST.
I CAN'T HAVE YOU GOING AROUND KISSING ME...
...TO STOP IT!
BUT YOU ALWAYS RESPOND SO PASSIONATELY.
THAT'S BECAUSE...!

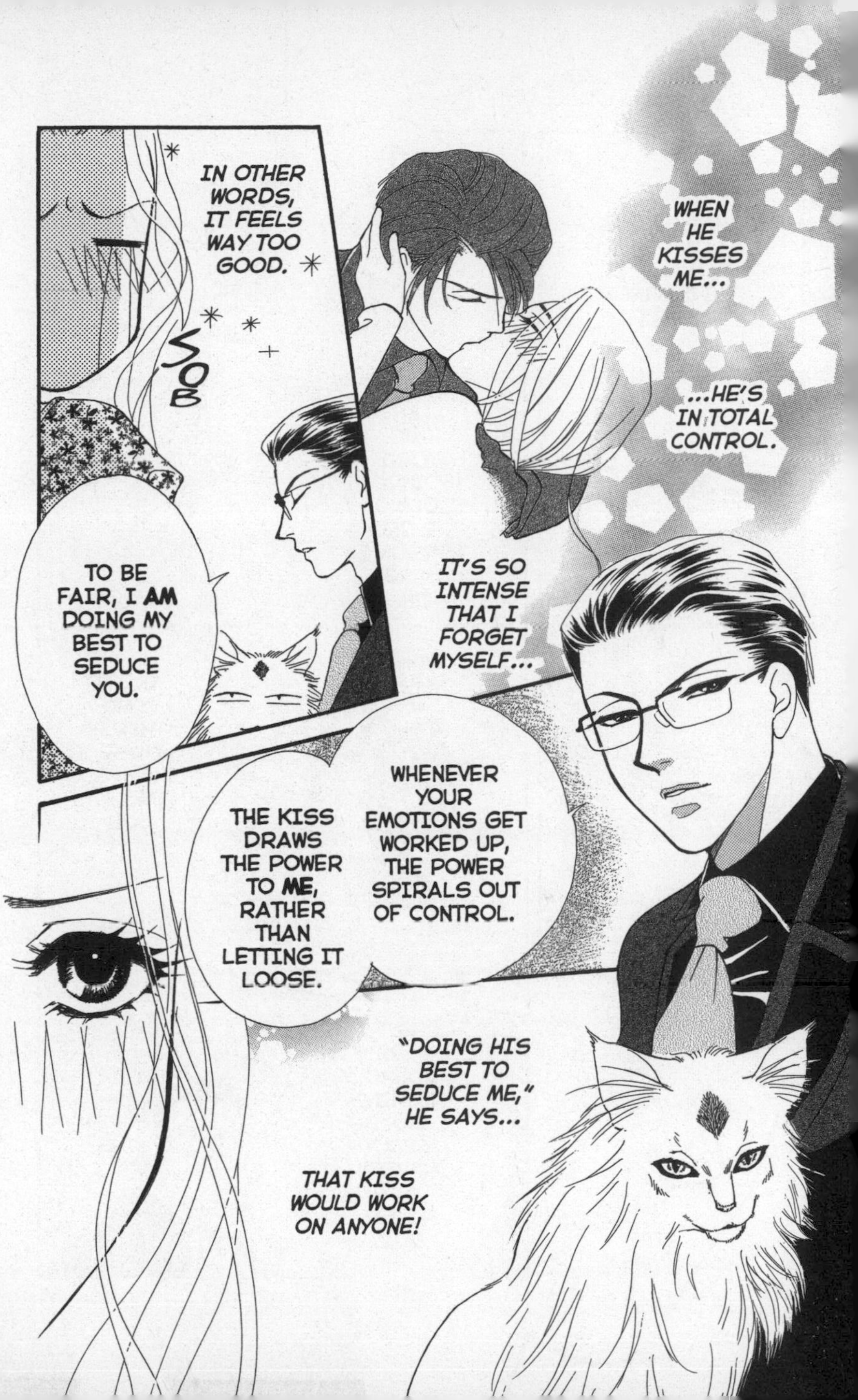
WHEN HE KISSES ME...
...HE'S IN TOTAL CONTROL.
IT'S SO INTENSE THAT I FORGET MYSELF...
IN OTHER WORDS, IT FEELS WAY TOO GOOD.
SOB
TO BE FAIR, I **AM** DOING MY BEST TO SEDUCE YOU.
WHENEVER YOUR EMOTIONS GET WORKED UP, THE POWER SPIRALS OUT OF CONTROL.
THE KISS DRAWS THE POWER TO **ME**, RATHER THAN LETTING IT LOOSE.
"DOING HIS BEST TO SEDUCE ME," HE SAYS...
THAT KISS WOULD WORK ON ANYONE!

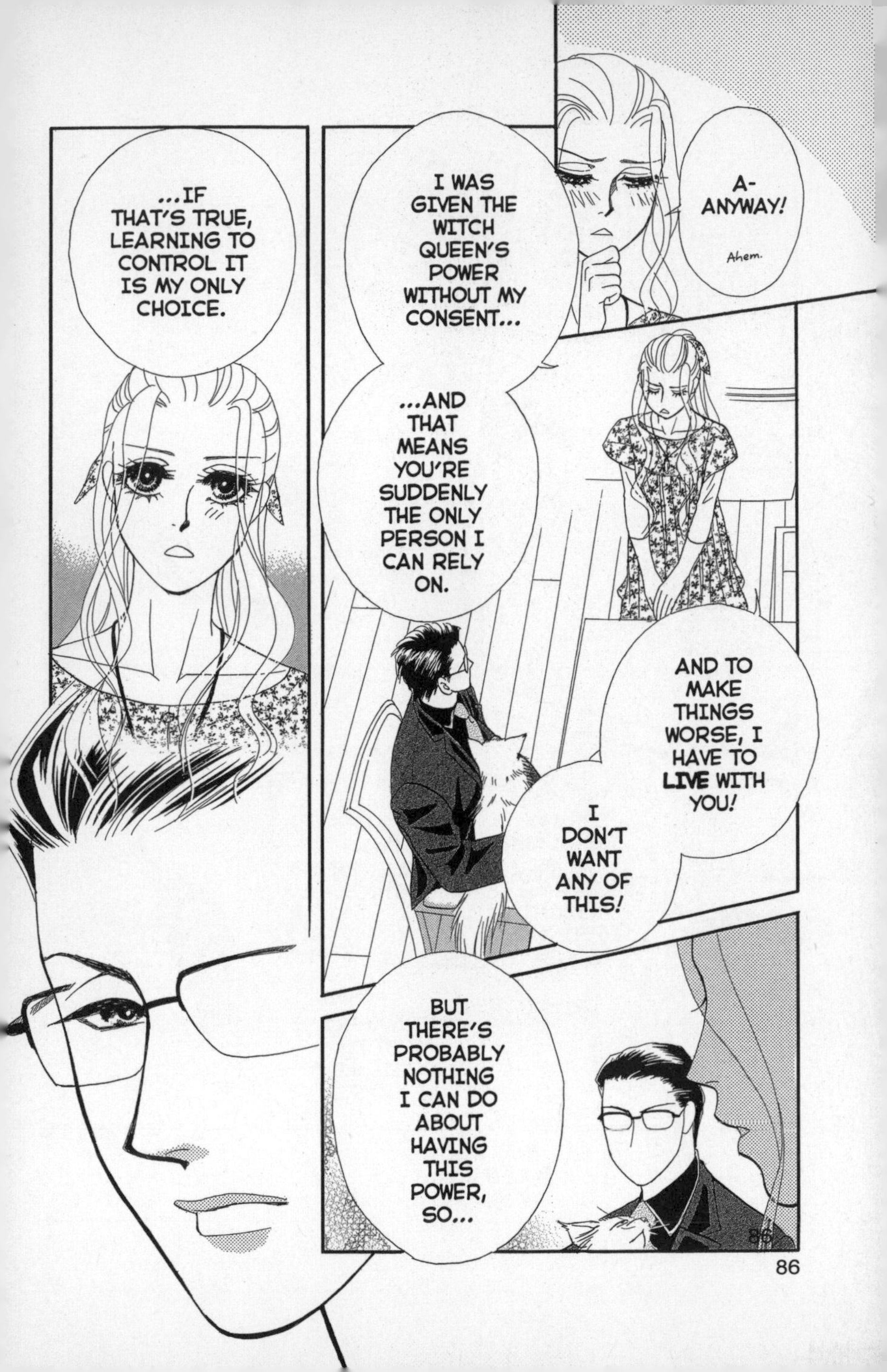
A- ANYWAY!
Ahem.
I WAS GIVEN THE WITCH QUEEN'S POWER WITHOUT MY CONSENT...
...AND THAT MEANS YOU'RE SUDDENLY THE ONLY PERSON I CAN RELY ON.
AND TO MAKE THINGS WORSE, I HAVE TO **LIVE** WITH YOU!
I DON'T WANT ANY OF THIS!
BUT THERE'S PROBABLY NOTHING I CAN DO ABOUT HAVING THIS POWER, SO...
...IF THAT'S TRUE, LEARNING TO CONTROL IT IS MY ONLY CHOICE.

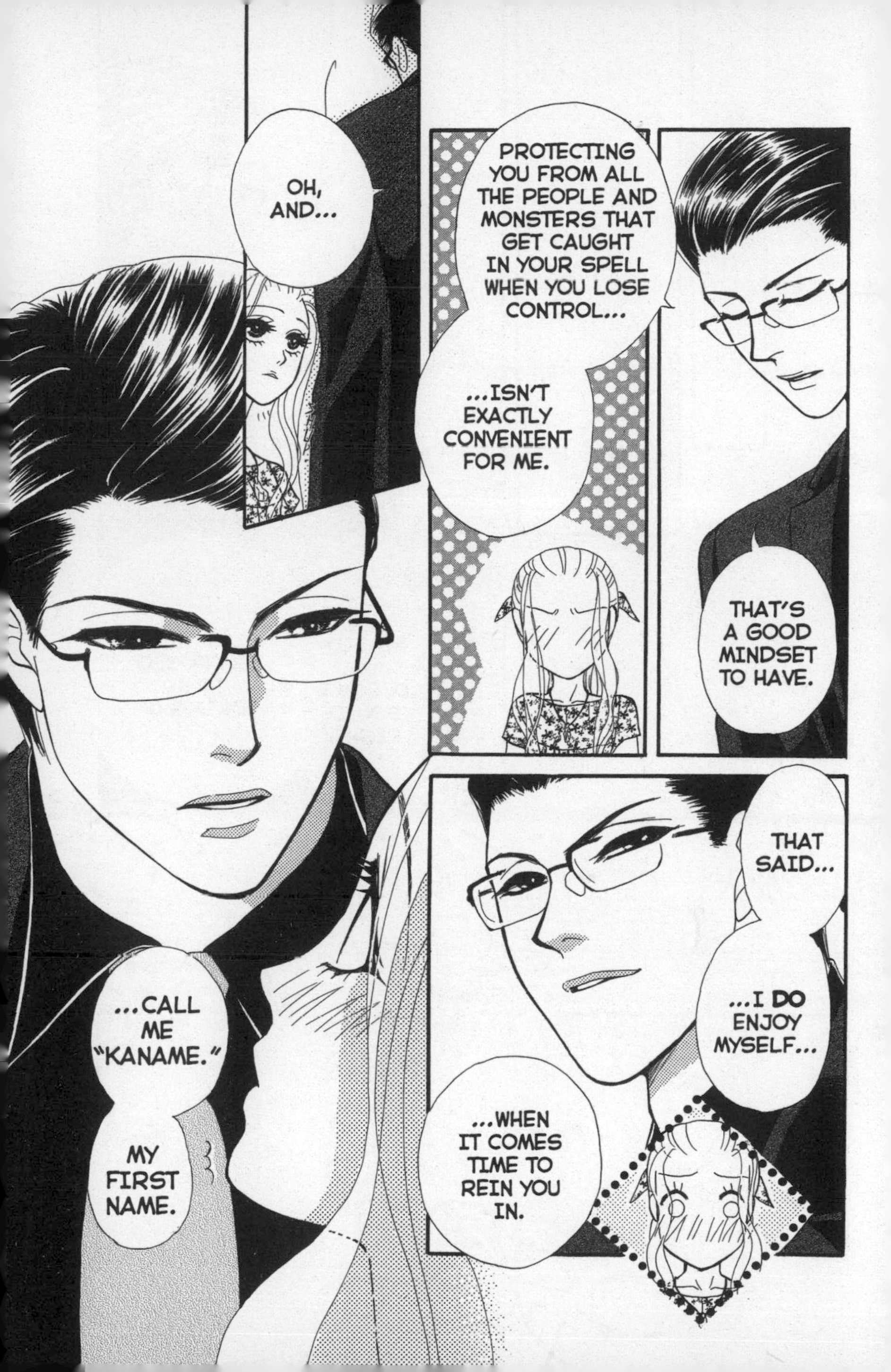
THAT'S A GOOD MINDSET TO HAVE.
PROTECTING YOU FROM ALL THE PEOPLE AND MONSTERS THAT GET CAUGHT IN YOUR SPELL WHEN YOU LOSE CONTROL...
...ISN'T EXACTLY CONVENIENT FOR ME.
THAT SAID...
...I DO ENJOY MYSELF...
...WHEN IT COMES TIME TO REIN YOU IN.
OH, AND...
...CALL ME "KANAME."
MY FIRST NAME.

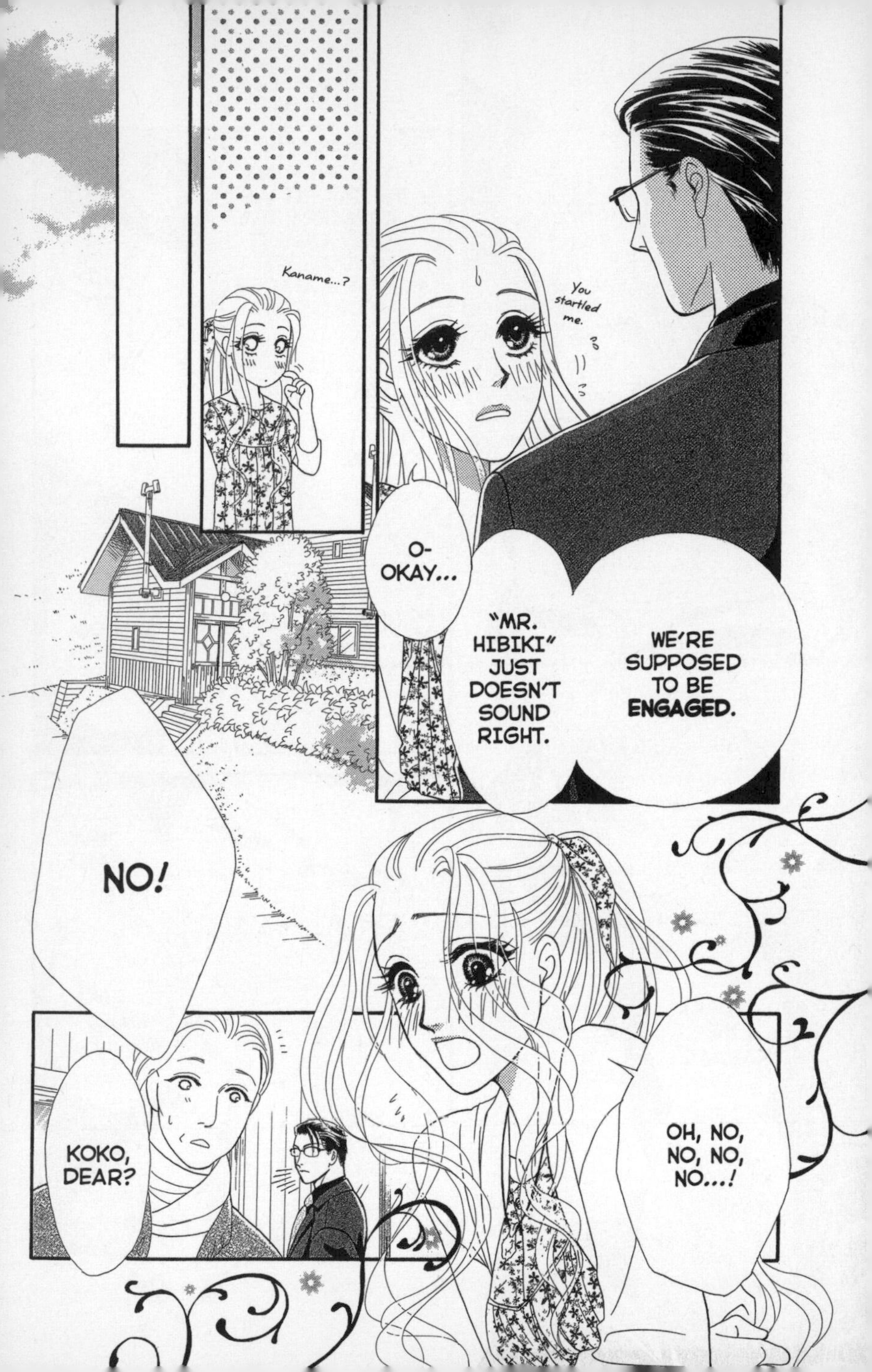
You startled me.
WE'RE SUPPOSED TO BE ENGAGED.
"MR. HIBIKI" JUST DOESN'T SOUND RIGHT.
O-OKAY...
Kaname...?
OH, NO, NO, NO, NO...!
NO!
KOKO, DEAR?

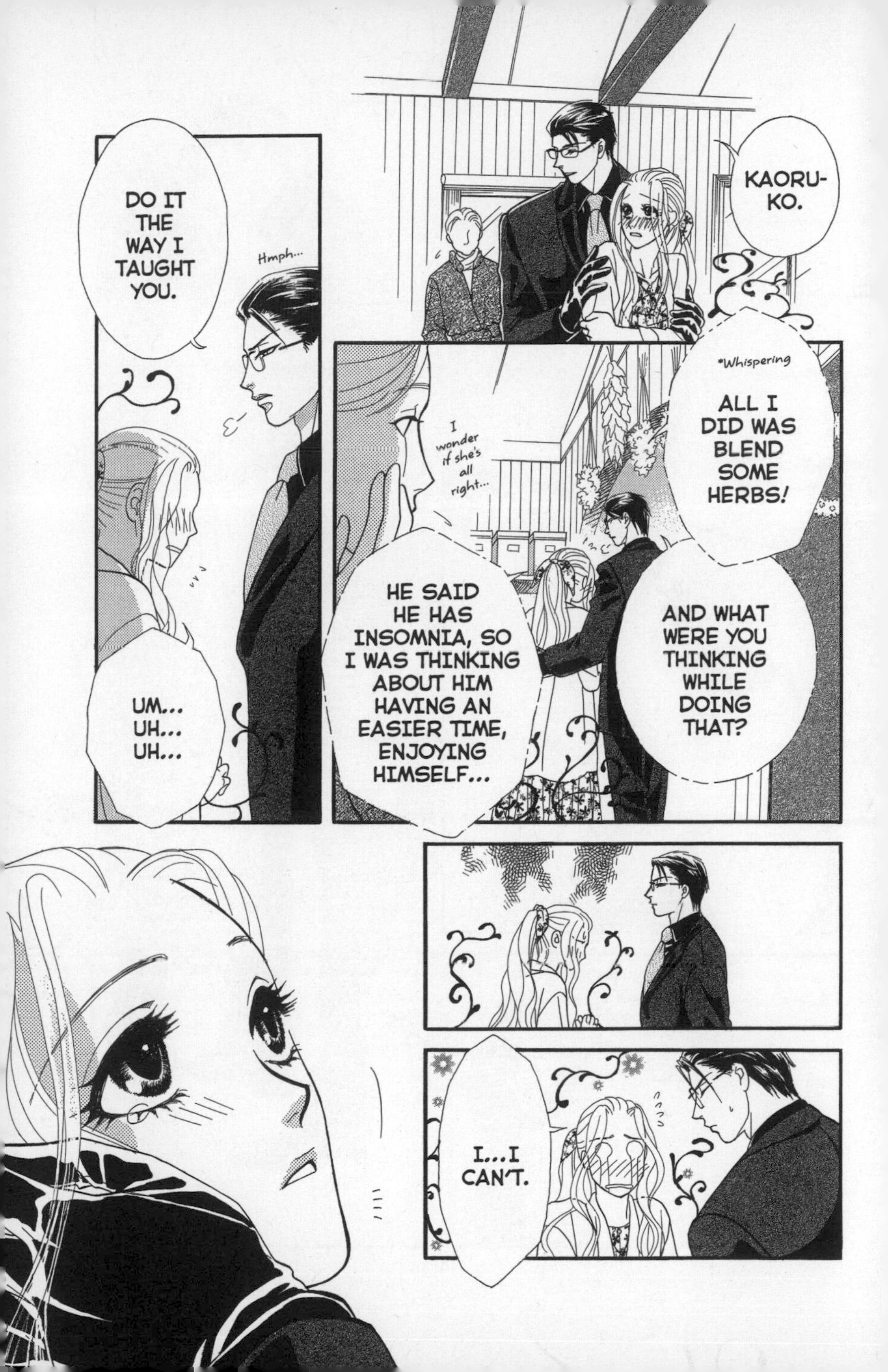
KAORU-KO.
*Whispering
ALL I DID WAS BLEND SOME HERBS!
I wonder if she's all right...
AND WHAT WERE YOU THINKING WHILE DOING THAT?
HE SAID HE HAS INSOMNIA, SO I WAS THINKING ABOUT HIM HAVING AN EASIER TIME, ENJOYING HIMSELF...
DO IT THE WAY I TAUGHT YOU.
Hmph...
UM... UH... UH...
I...I CAN'T.

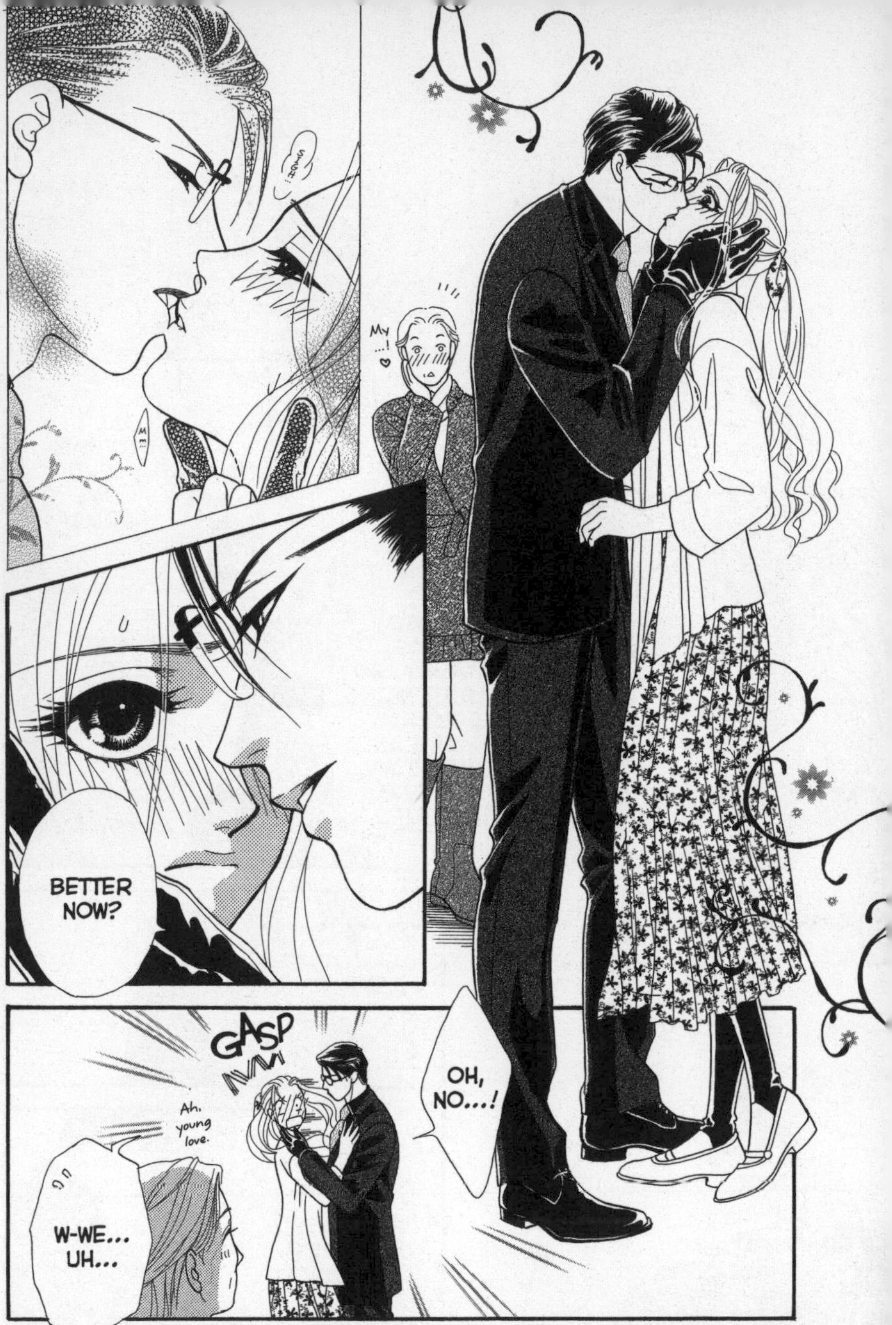
My ...!
OH, NO...!
SIGH!!
Mm...
BETTER NOW?
GASP
Ah, young love.
W-WE... UH...

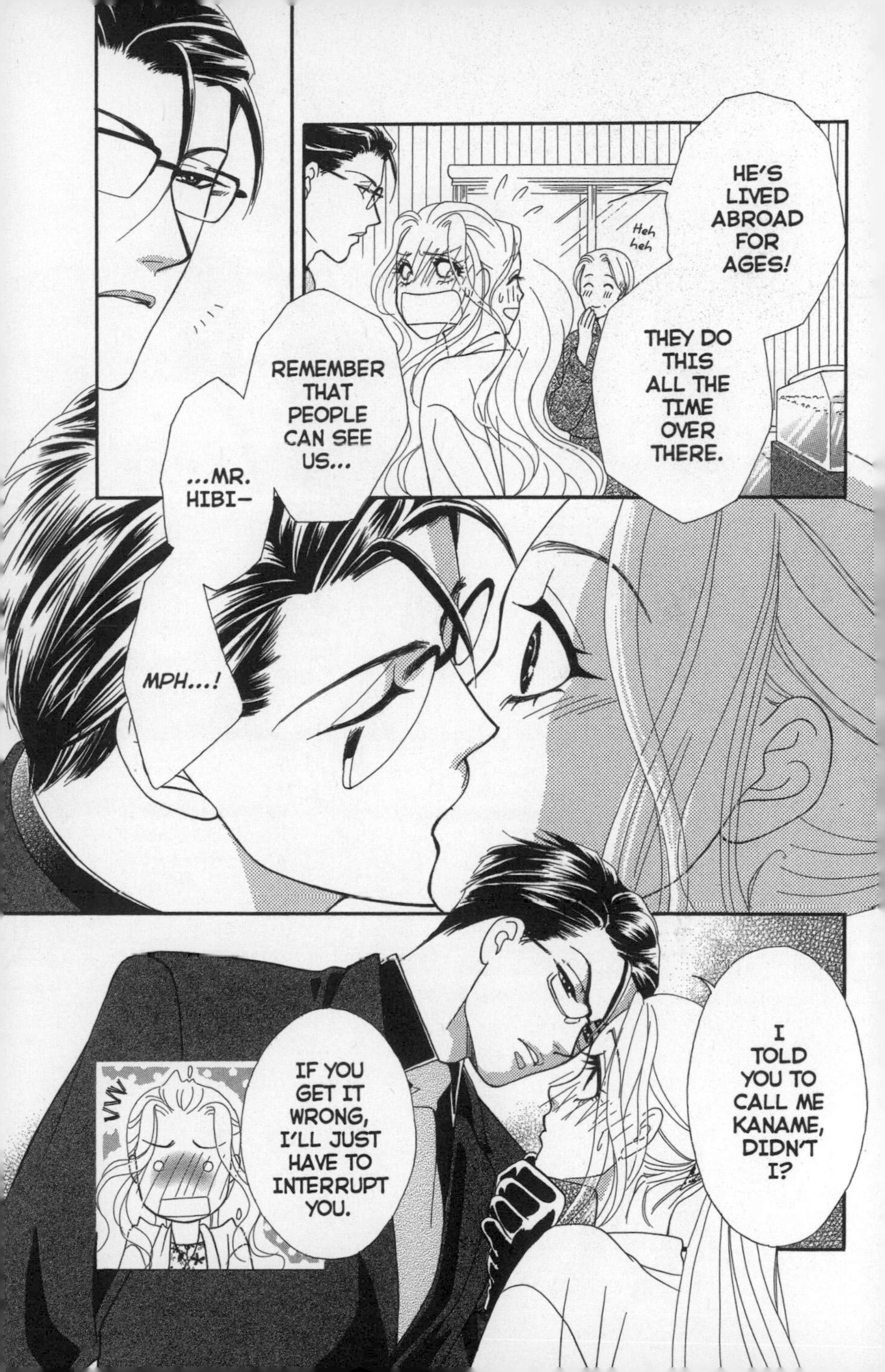
HE'S LIVED ABROAD FOR AGES!
Heh heh
THEY DO THIS ALL THE TIME OVER THERE.
REMEMBER THAT PEOPLE CAN SEE US...
...MR. HIBI-
MPH...!
I TOLD YOU TO CALL ME KANAME, DIDN'T I?
IF YOU GET IT WRONG, I'LL JUST HAVE TO INTERRUPT YOU.

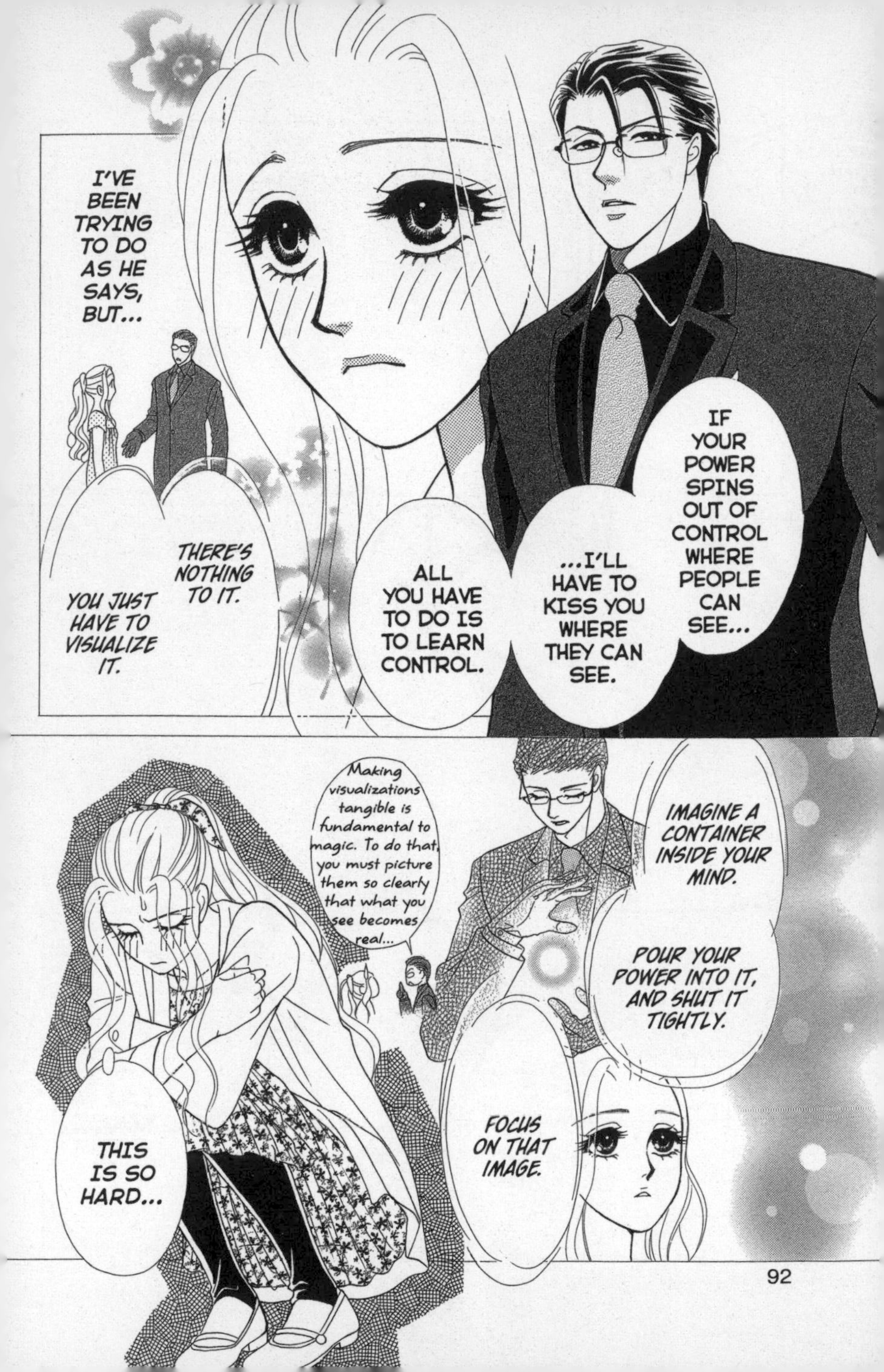
IF YOUR POWER SPINS OUT OF CONTROL WHERE PEOPLE CAN SEE...
...I'LL HAVE TO KISS YOU WHERE THEY CAN SEE.
ALL YOU HAVE TO DO IS TO LEARN CONTROL.
I'VE BEEN TRYING TO DO AS HE SAYS, BUT...
THERE'S NOTHING TO IT.
YOU JUST HAVE TO VISUALIZE IT.
IMAGINE A CONTAINER INSIDE YOUR MIND.
Making visualizations tangible is fundamental to magic. To do that, you must picture them so clearly that what you see becomes real...
POUR YOUR POWER INTO IT, AND SHUT IT TIGHTLY.
FOCUS ON THAT IMAGE.
THIS IS SO HARD...

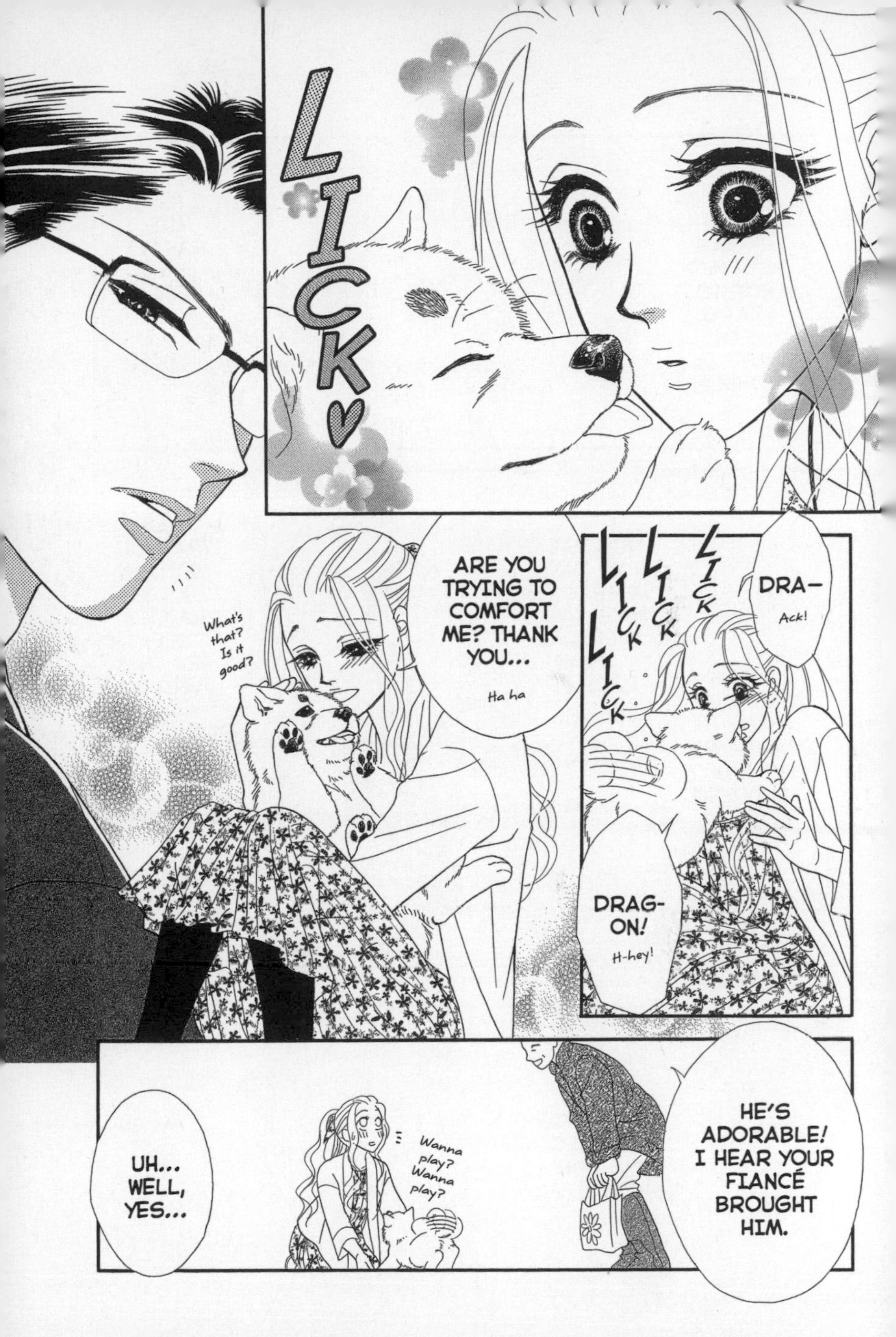
LICK♥
LICK LICK LICK
DRA—
Ack!
DRAG-ON!
H-hey!
ARE YOU TRYING TO COMFORT ME? THANK YOU...
Ha ha
What's that? Is it good?
HE'S ADORABLE! I HEAR YOUR FIANCÉ BROUGHT HIM.
Wanna play? Wanna play?
UH... WELL, YES...

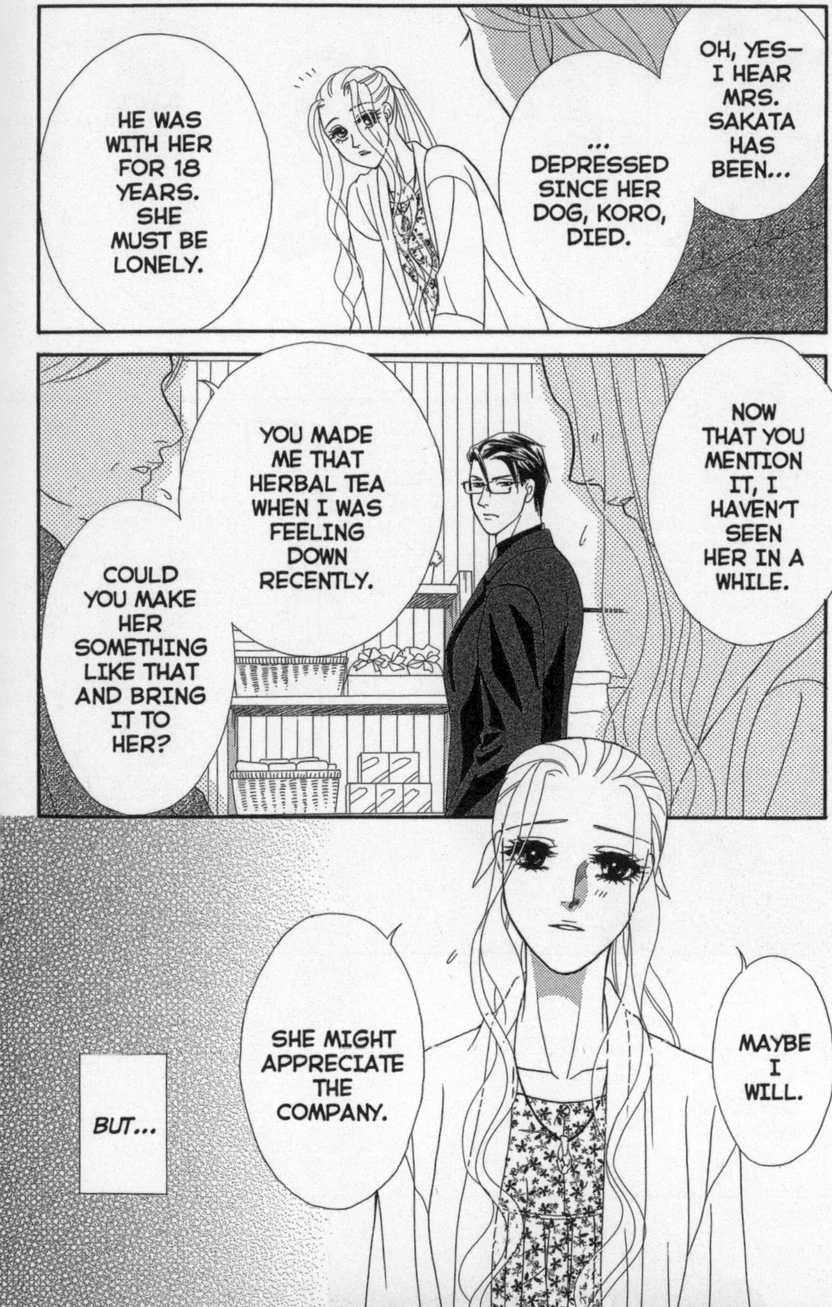
OH, YES— I HEAR MRS. SAKATA HAS BEEN...
... DEPRESSED SINCE HER DOG, KORO, DIED.
HE WAS WITH HER FOR 18 YEARS. SHE MUST BE LONELY.
NOW THAT YOU MENTION IT, I HAVEN'T SEEN HER IN A WHILE.
YOU MADE ME THAT HERBAL TEA WHEN I WAS FEELING DOWN RECENTLY.
COULD YOU MAKE HER SOMETHING LIKE THAT AND BRING IT TO HER?
MAYBE I WILL.
SHE MIGHT APPRECIATE THE COMPANY.
BUT...

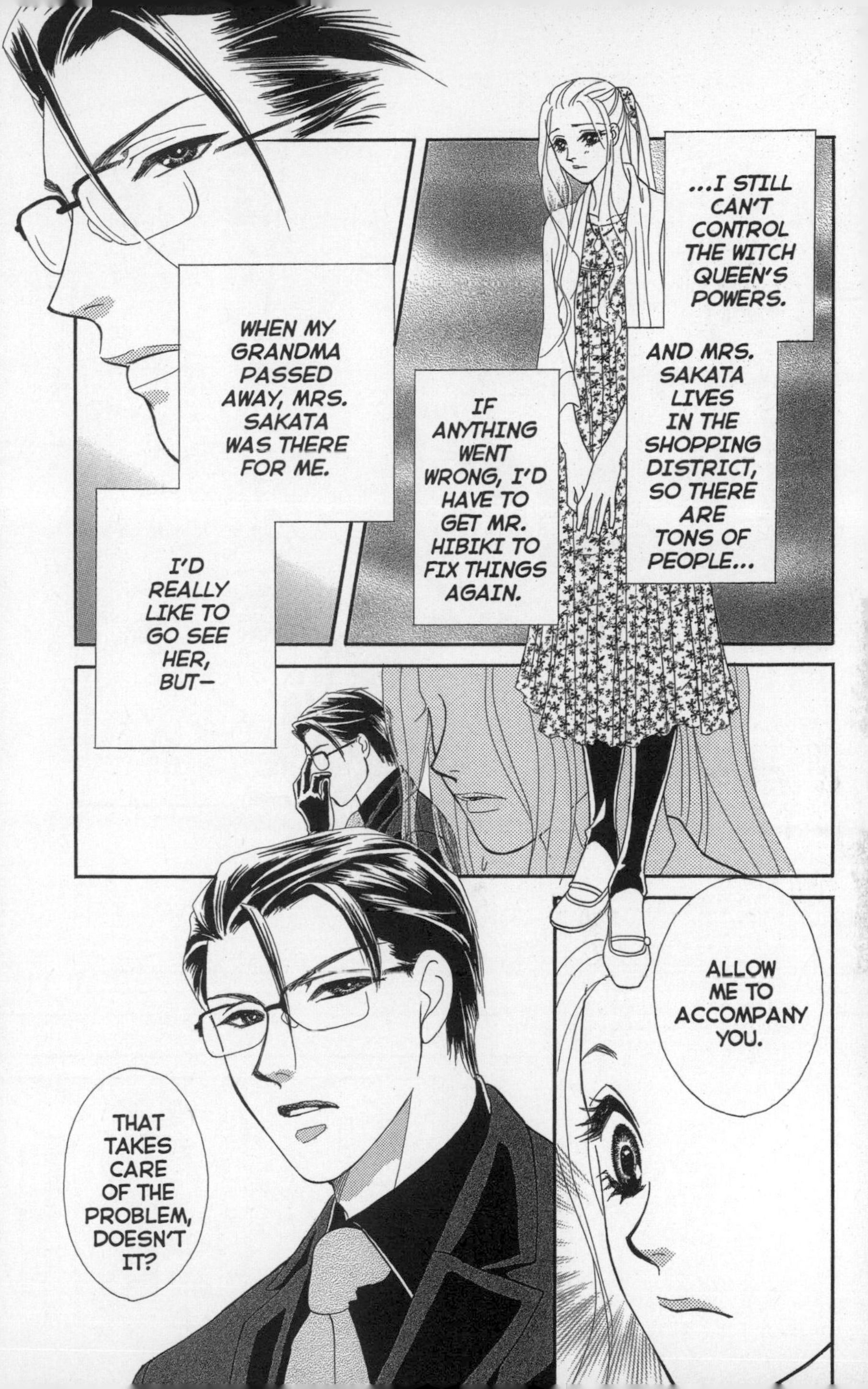
...I STILL CAN'T CONTROL THE WITCH QUEEN'S POWERS.
AND MRS. SAKATA LIVES IN THE SHOPPING DISTRICT, SO THERE ARE TONS OF PEOPLE...
IF ANYTHING WENT WRONG, I'D HAVE TO GET MR. HIBIKI TO FIX THINGS AGAIN.
WHEN MY GRANDMA PASSED AWAY, MRS. SAKATA WAS THERE FOR ME.
I'D REALLY LIKE TO GO SEE HER, BUT—
ALLOW ME TO ACCOMPANY YOU.
THAT TAKES CARE OF THE PROBLEM, DOESN'T IT?

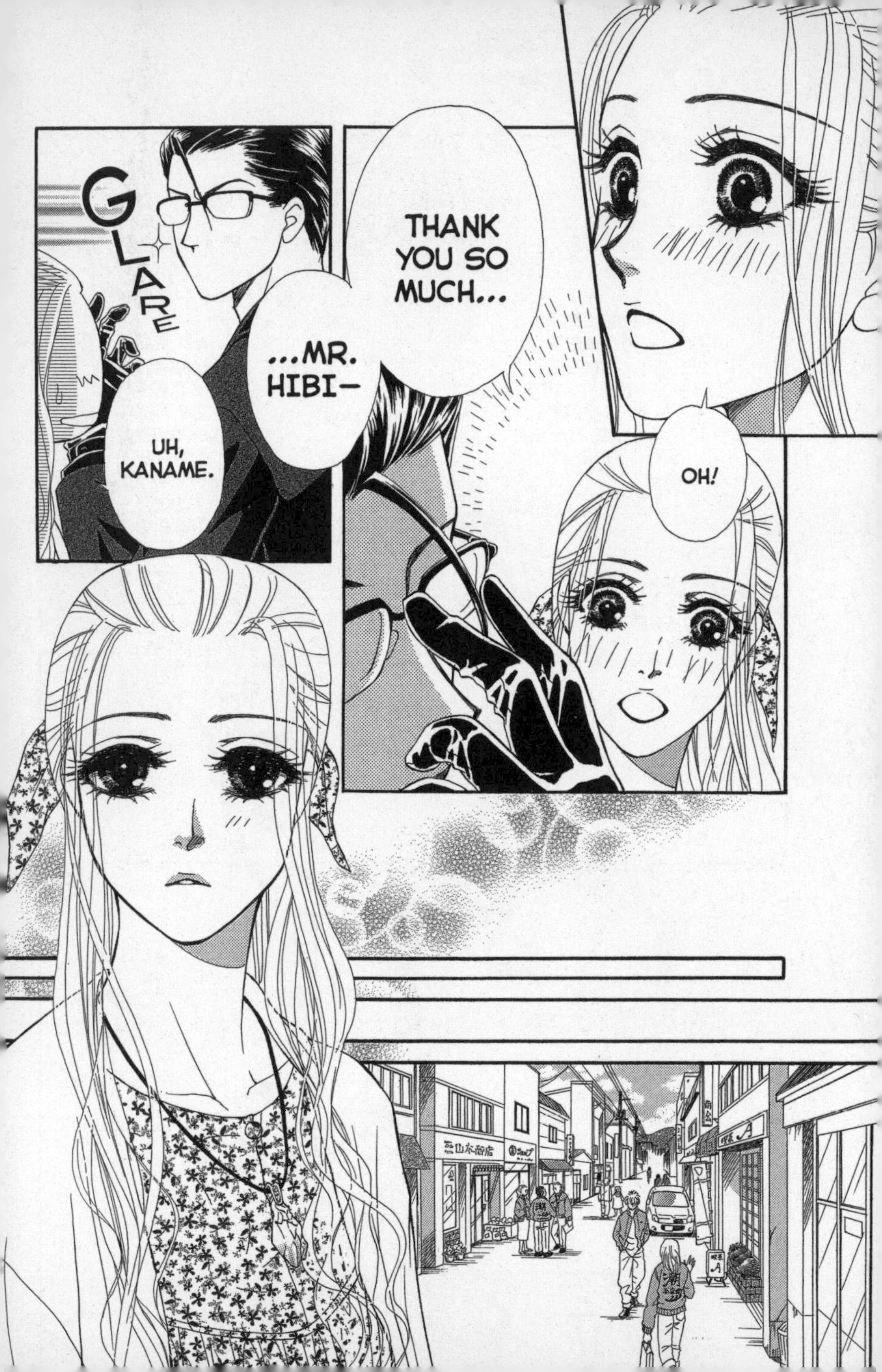
THANK YOU SO MUCH...
...MR. HIBI—
GLARE
UH, KANAME.
OH!

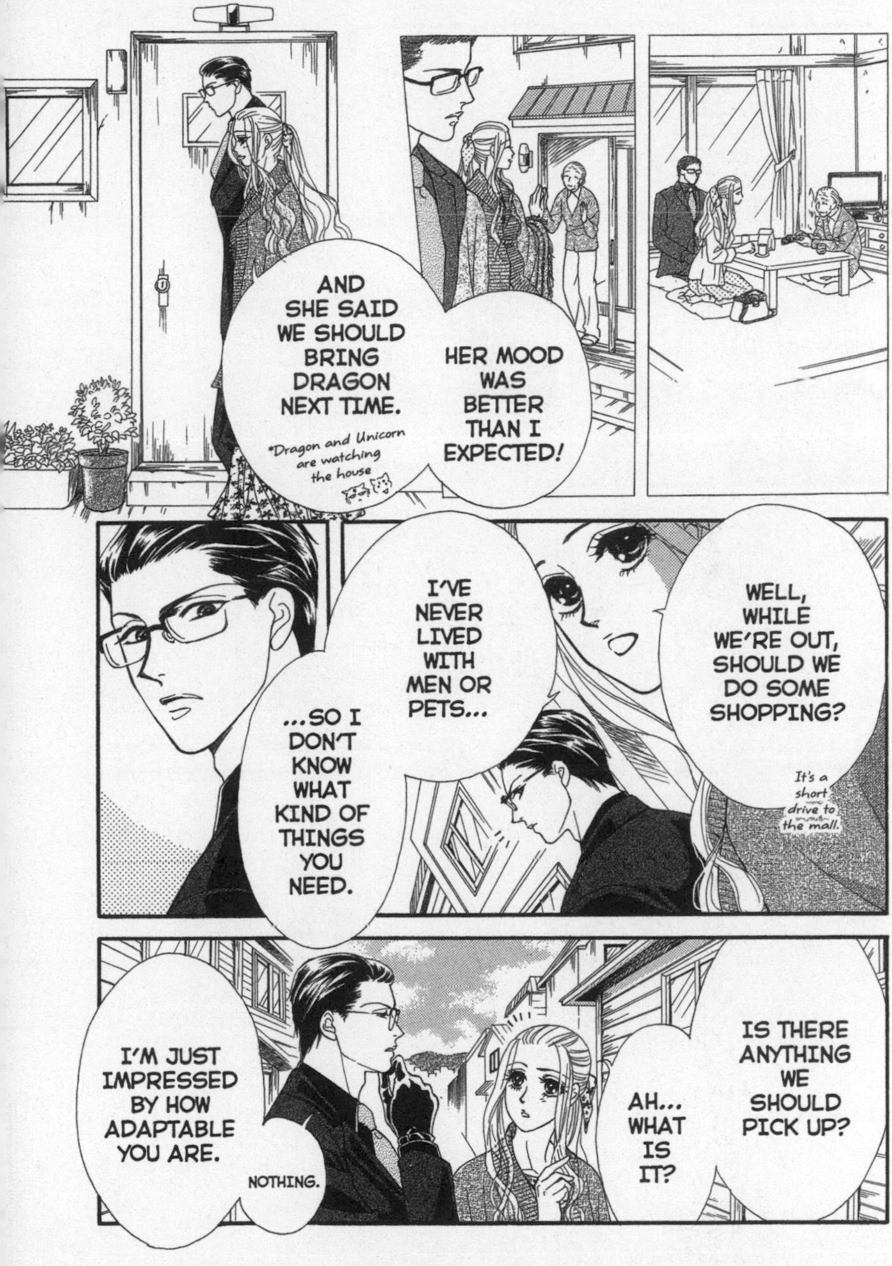
HER MOOD WAS BETTER THAN I EXPECTED!
AND SHE SAID WE SHOULD BRING DRAGON NEXT TIME.
*Dragon and Unicorn are watching the house
WELL, WHILE WE'RE OUT, SHOULD WE DO SOME SHOPPING?
It's a short drive to the mall.
I'VE NEVER LIVED WITH MEN OR PETS...
...SO I DON'T KNOW WHAT KIND OF THINGS YOU NEED.
IS THERE ANYTHING WE SHOULD PICK UP?
AH... WHAT IS IT?
NOTHING.
I'M JUST IMPRESSED BY HOW ADAPTABLE YOU ARE.

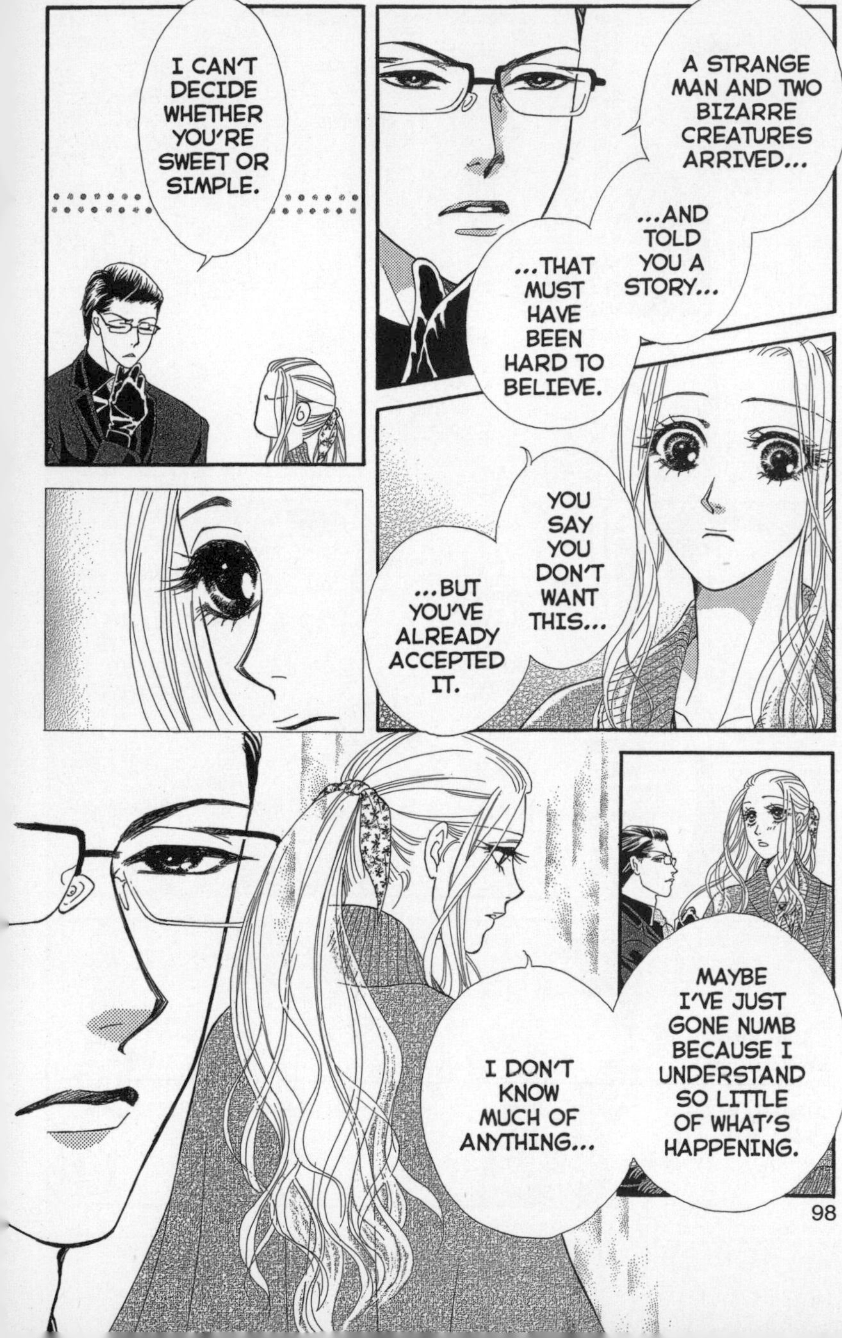
A STRANGE MAN AND TWO BIZARRE CREATURES ARRIVED...
...AND TOLD YOU A STORY...
...THAT MUST HAVE BEEN HARD TO BELIEVE.
I CAN'T DECIDE WHETHER YOU'RE SWEET OR SIMPLE.
YOU SAY YOU DON'T WANT THIS...
...BUT YOU'VE ALREADY ACCEPTED IT.
MAYBE I'VE JUST GONE NUMB BECAUSE I UNDERSTAND SO LITTLE OF WHAT'S HAPPENING.
I DON'T KNOW MUCH OF ANYTHING...

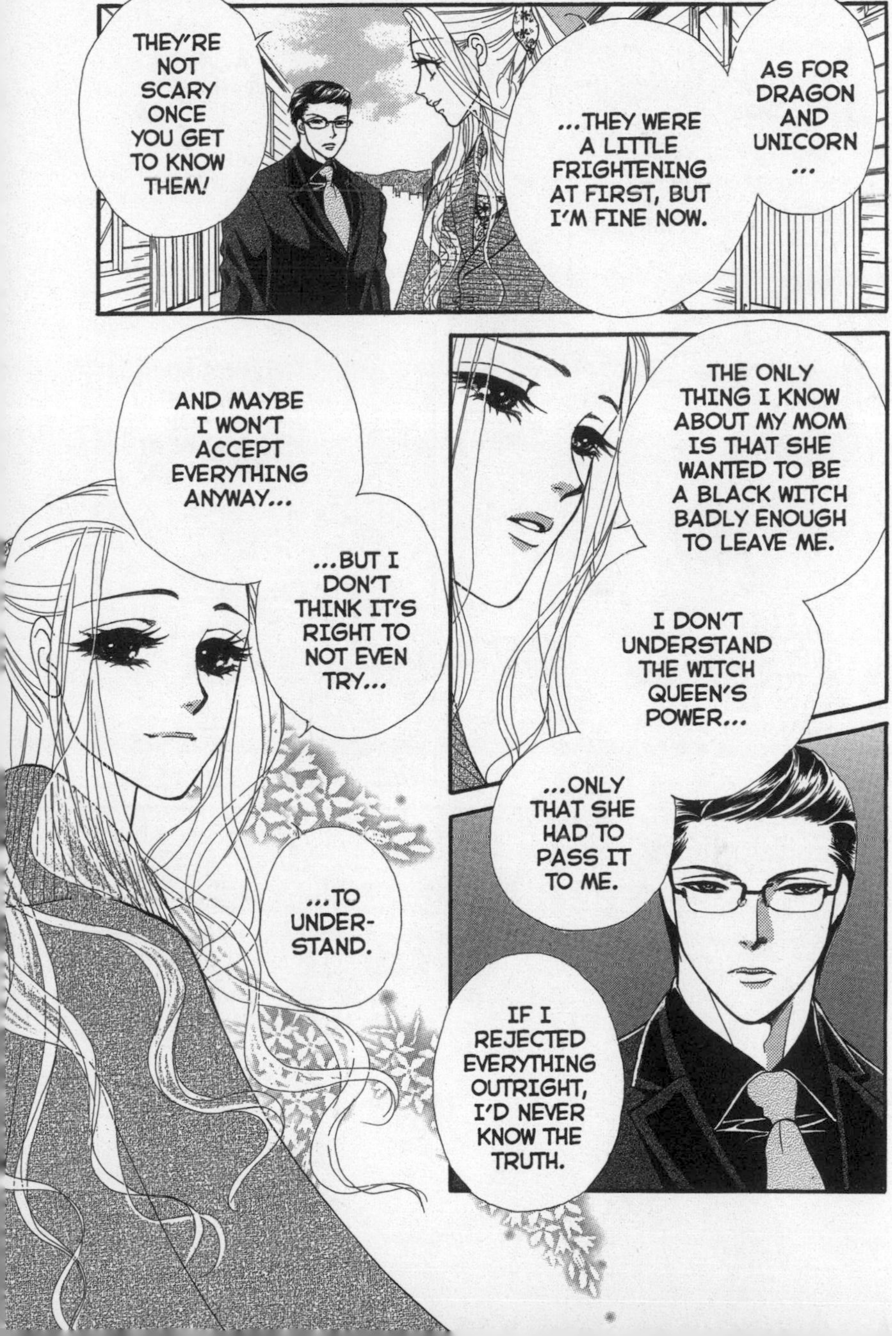
AS FOR DRAGON AND UNICORN...
...THEY WERE A LITTLE FRIGHTENING AT FIRST, BUT I'M FINE NOW.
THEY'RE NOT SCARY ONCE YOU GET TO KNOW THEM!
THE ONLY THING I KNOW ABOUT MY MOM IS THAT SHE WANTED TO BE A BLACK WITCH BADLY ENOUGH TO LEAVE ME.
I DON'T UNDERSTAND THE WITCH QUEEN'S POWER...
...ONLY THAT SHE HAD TO PASS IT TO ME.
IF I REJECTED EVERYTHING OUTRIGHT, I'D NEVER KNOW THE TRUTH.
AND MAYBE I WON'T ACCEPT EVERYTHING ANYWAY...
...BUT I DON'T THINK IT'S RIGHT TO NOT EVEN TRY...
...TO UNDERSTAND.

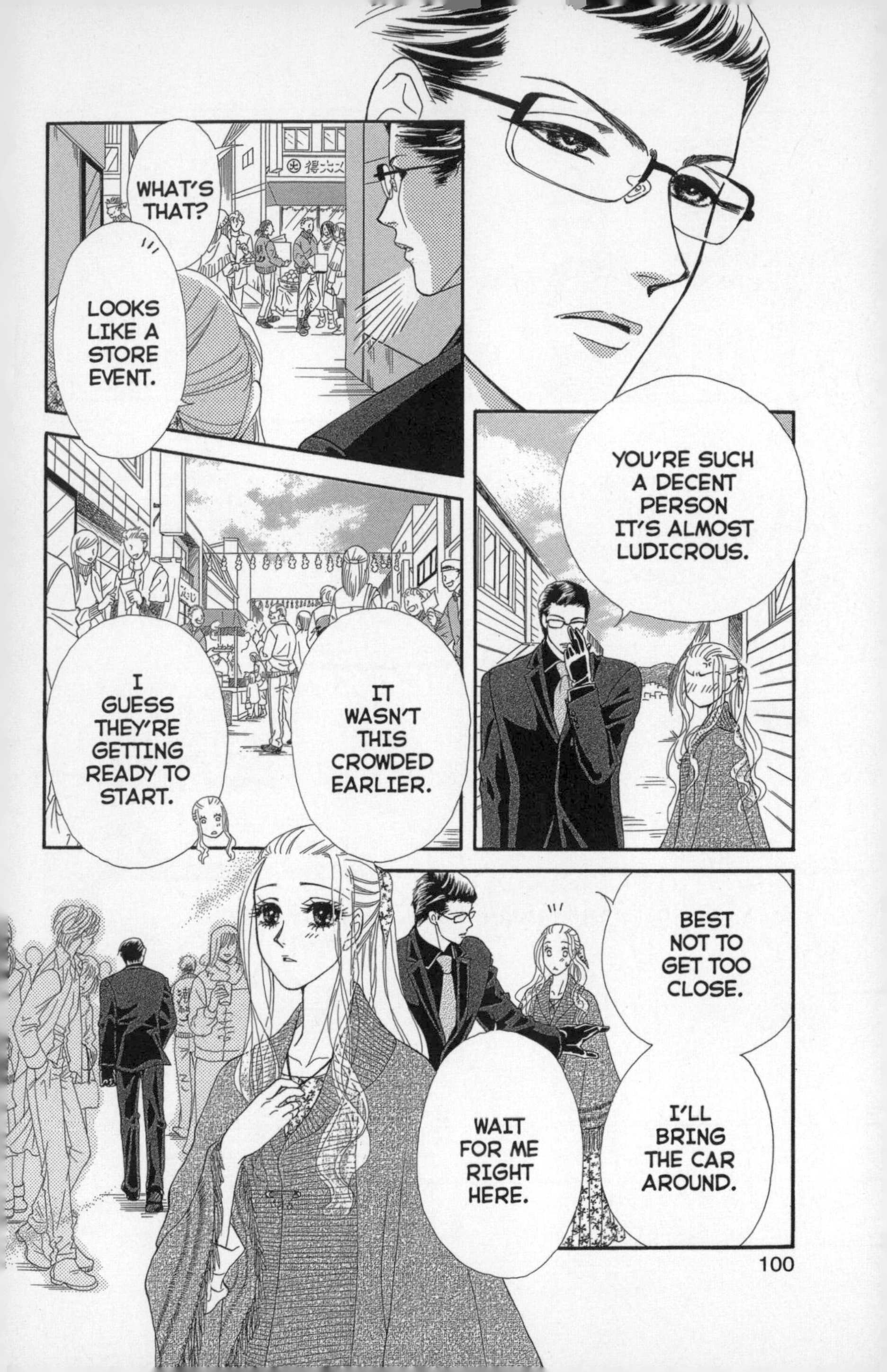
WHAT'S THAT?
LOOKS LIKE A STORE EVENT.
YOU'RE SUCH A DECENT PERSON IT'S ALMOST LUDICROUS.
IT WASN'T THIS CROWDED EARLIER.
I GUESS THEY'RE GETTING READY TO START.
BEST NOT TO GET TOO CLOSE.
I'LL BRING THE CAR AROUND.
WAIT FOR ME RIGHT HERE.

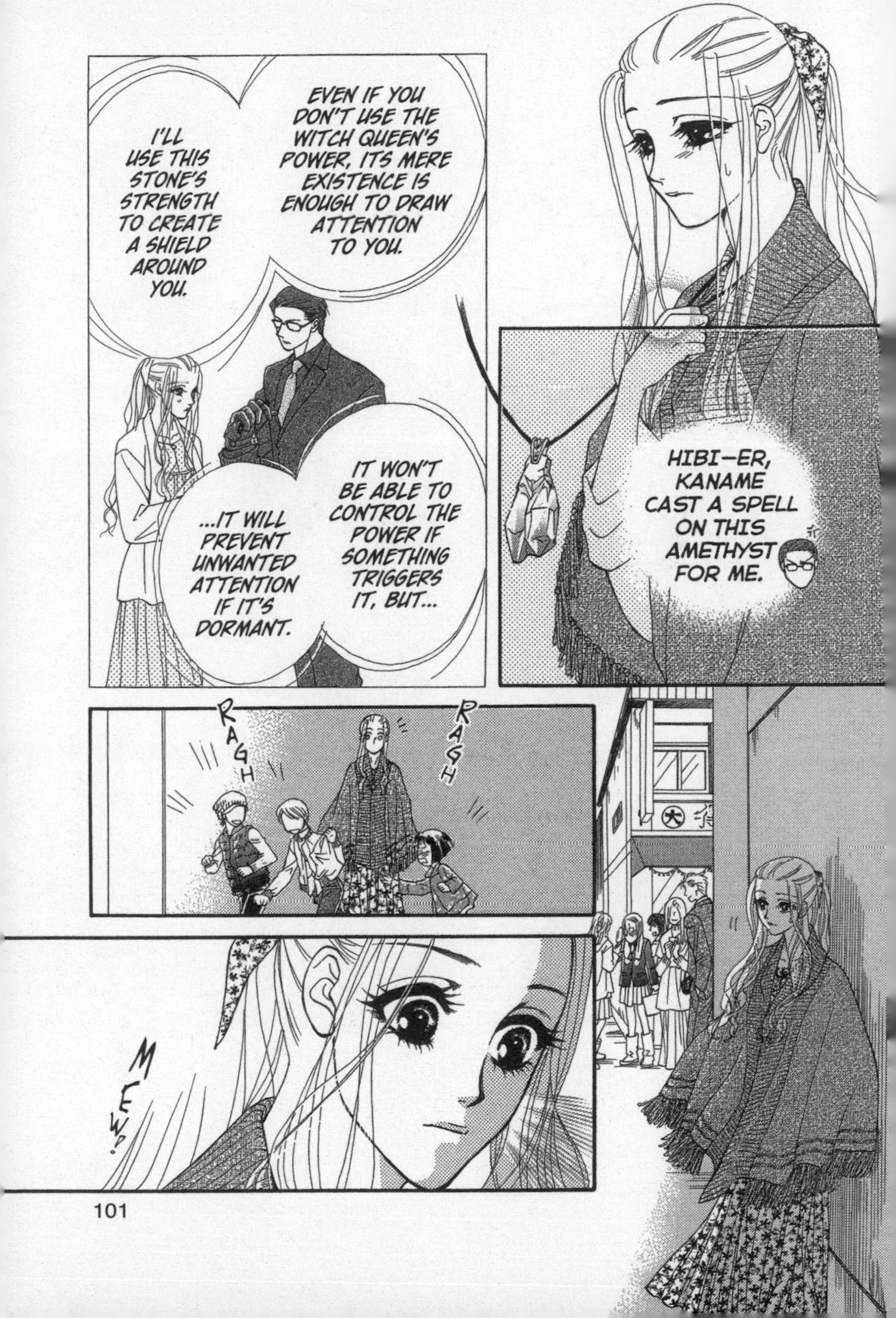
HIBI—ER, KANAME CAST A SPELL ON THIS AMETHYST FOR ME.
EVEN IF YOU DON'T USE THE WITCH QUEEN'S POWER, ITS MERE EXISTENCE IS ENOUGH TO DRAW ATTENTION TO YOU.
I'LL USE THIS STONE'S STRENGTH TO CREATE A SHIELD AROUND YOU.
IT WON'T BE ABLE TO CONTROL THE POWER IF SOMETHING TRIGGERS IT, BUT...
...IT WILL PREVENT UNWANTED ATTENTION IF IT'S DORMANT.
RAGH
RAGH
MEW?

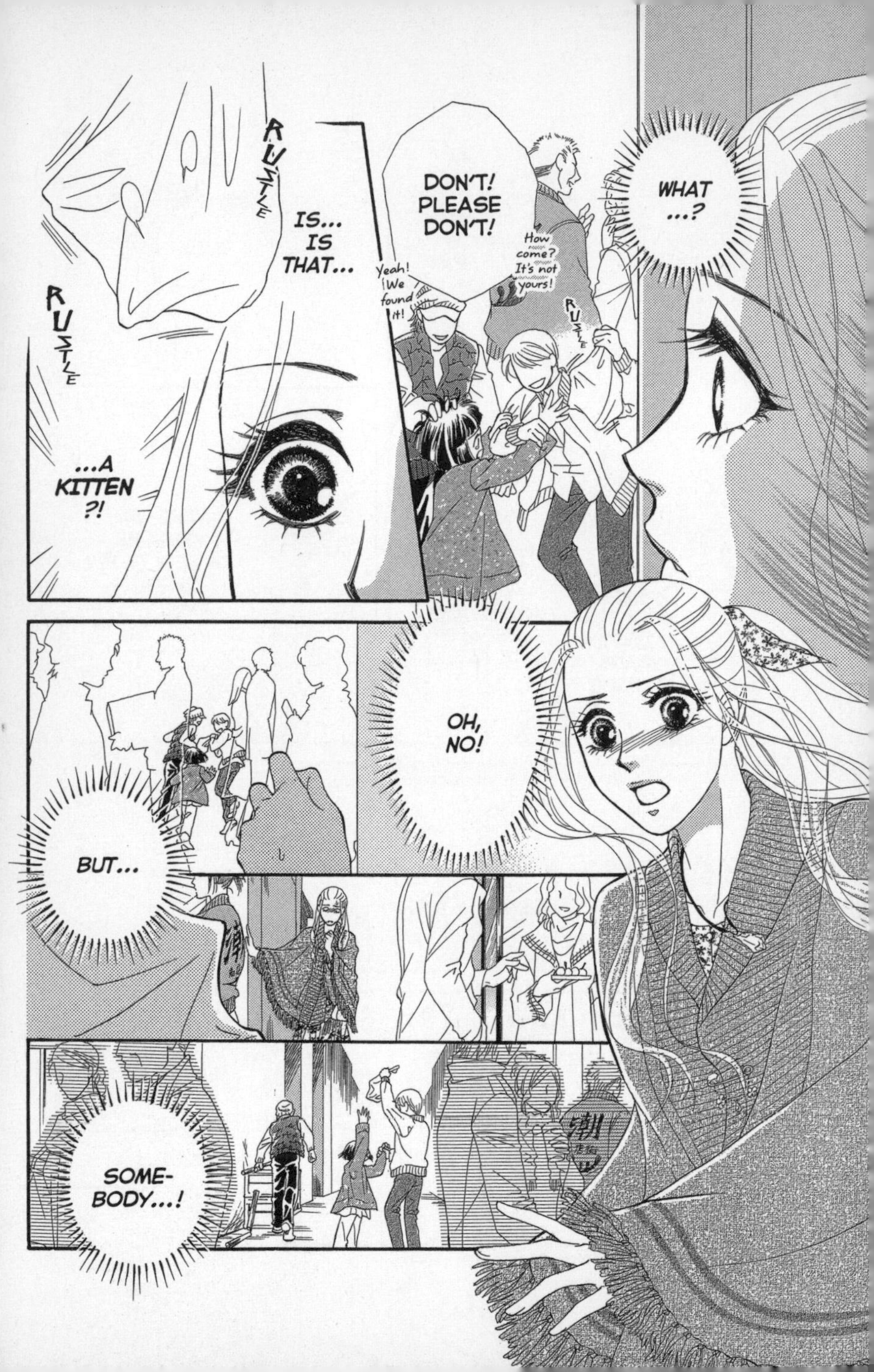
WHAT ...?
DON'T! PLEASE DON'T!
How come? It's not yours!
Yeah! We found it!
RUSTLE
RUSTLE
IS... IS THAT...
RUSTLE
...A KITTEN ?!
OH, NO!
BUT...
SOME-BODY...!

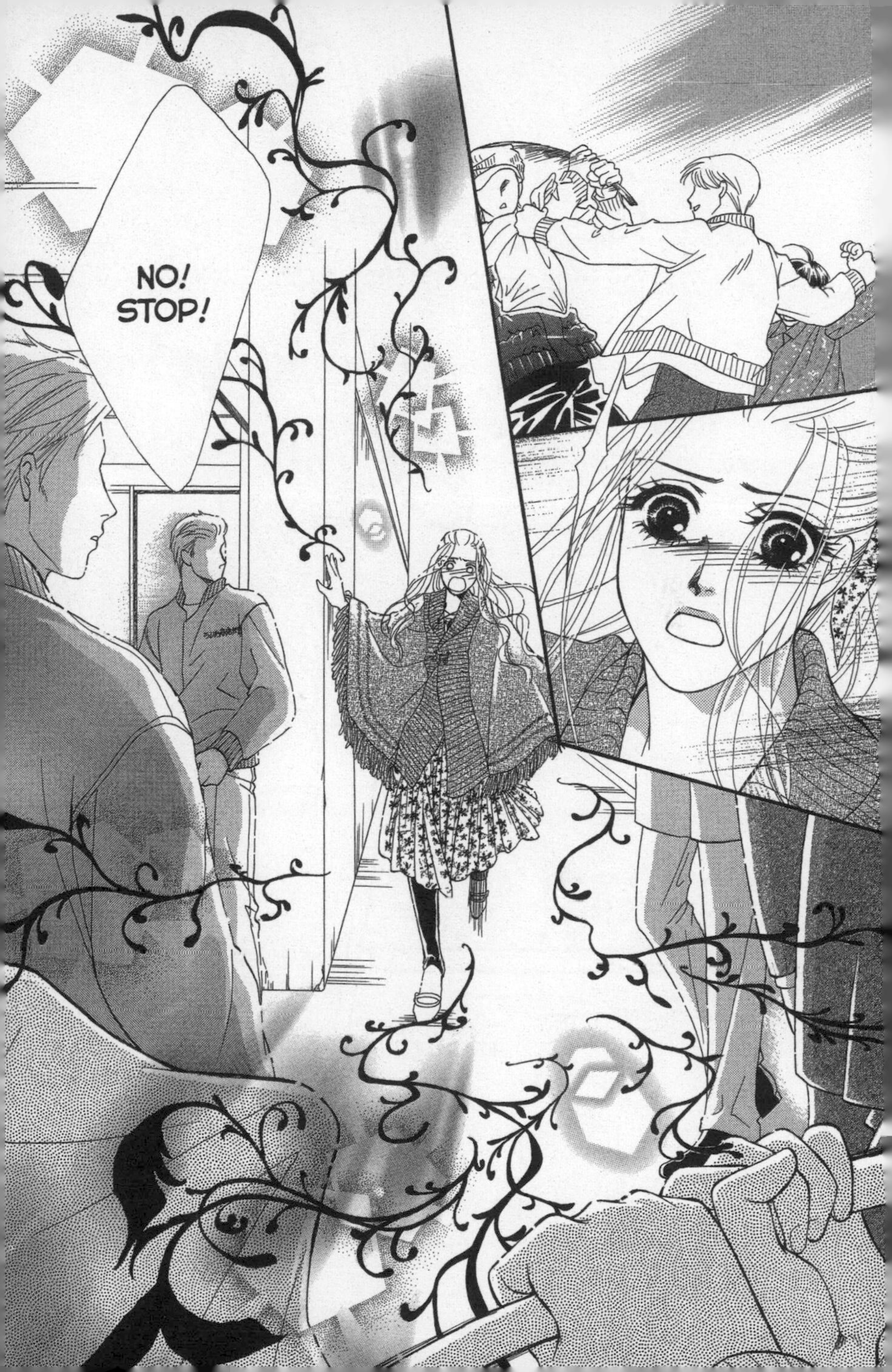
NO! STOP!

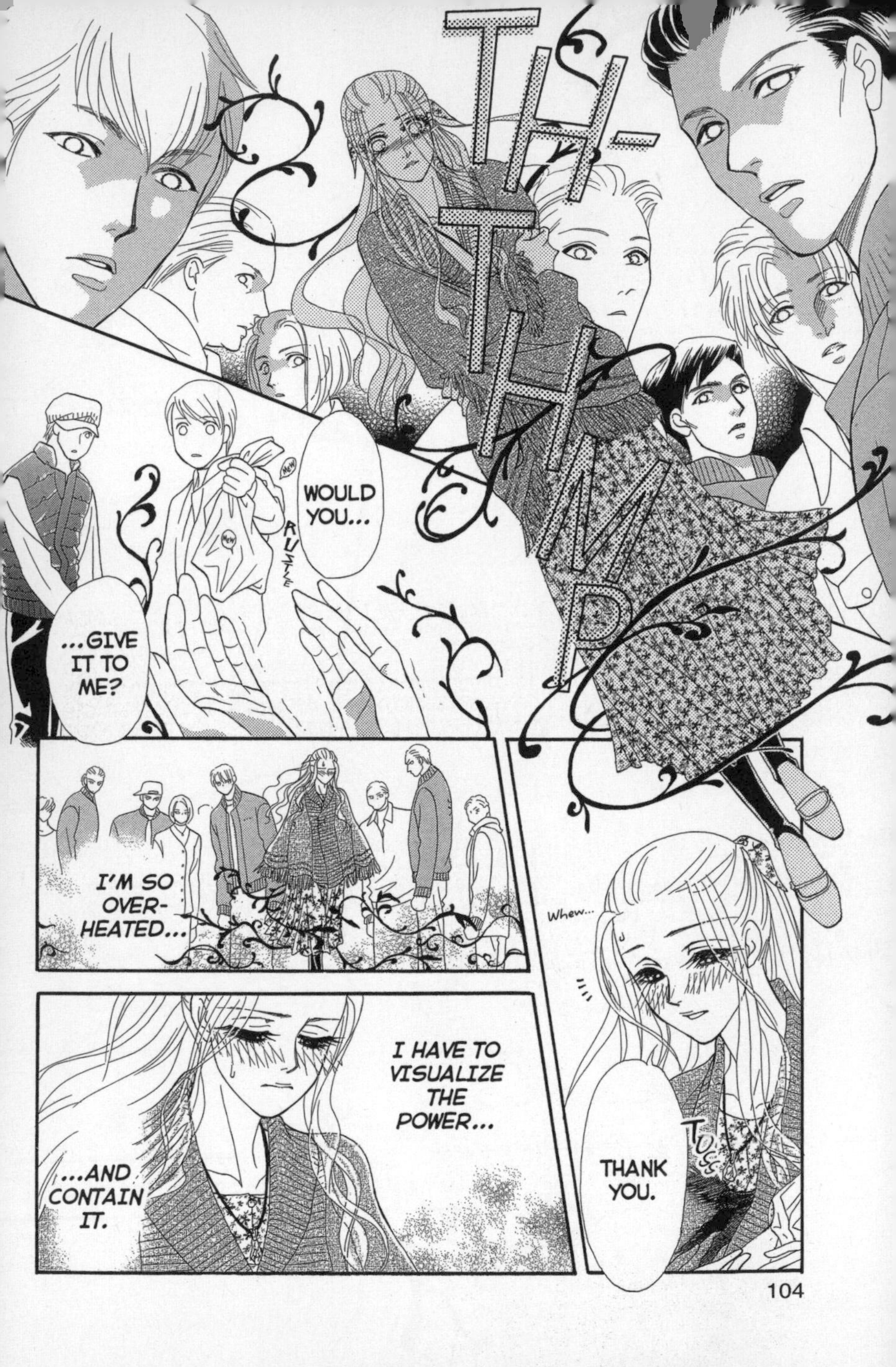
TH-THMP
WOULD YOU...
MEW
MEW
RUSTLE
...GIVE IT TO ME?
Whew...
THANK YOU.
TOSS
I'M SO OVER-HEATED...
I HAVE TO VISUALIZE THE POWER...
...AND CONTAIN IT.

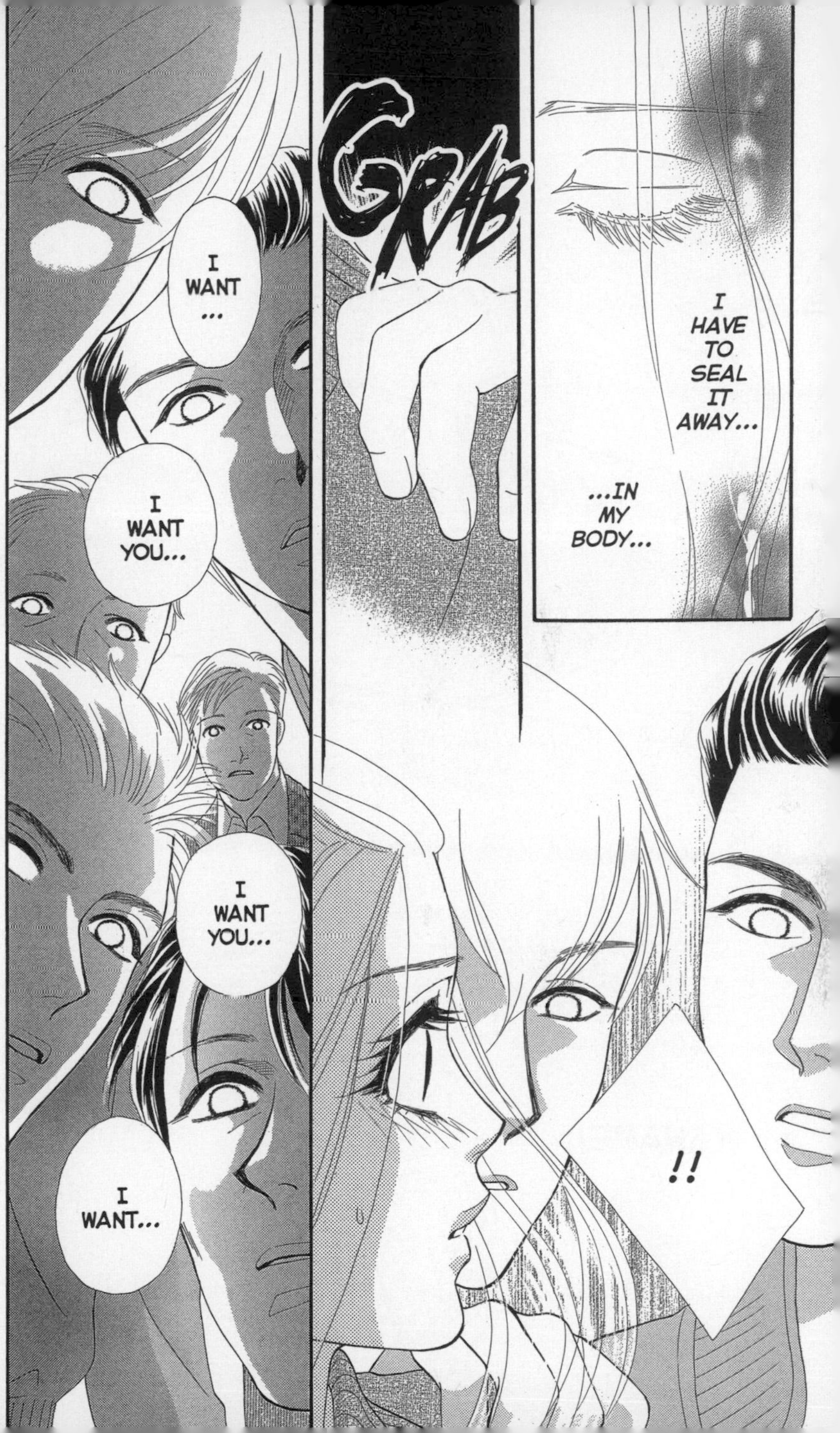
I HAVE TO SEAL IT AWAY...
...IN MY BODY...
GRAB
!!
I WANT...
I WANT YOU...
I WANT YOU...
I WANT...

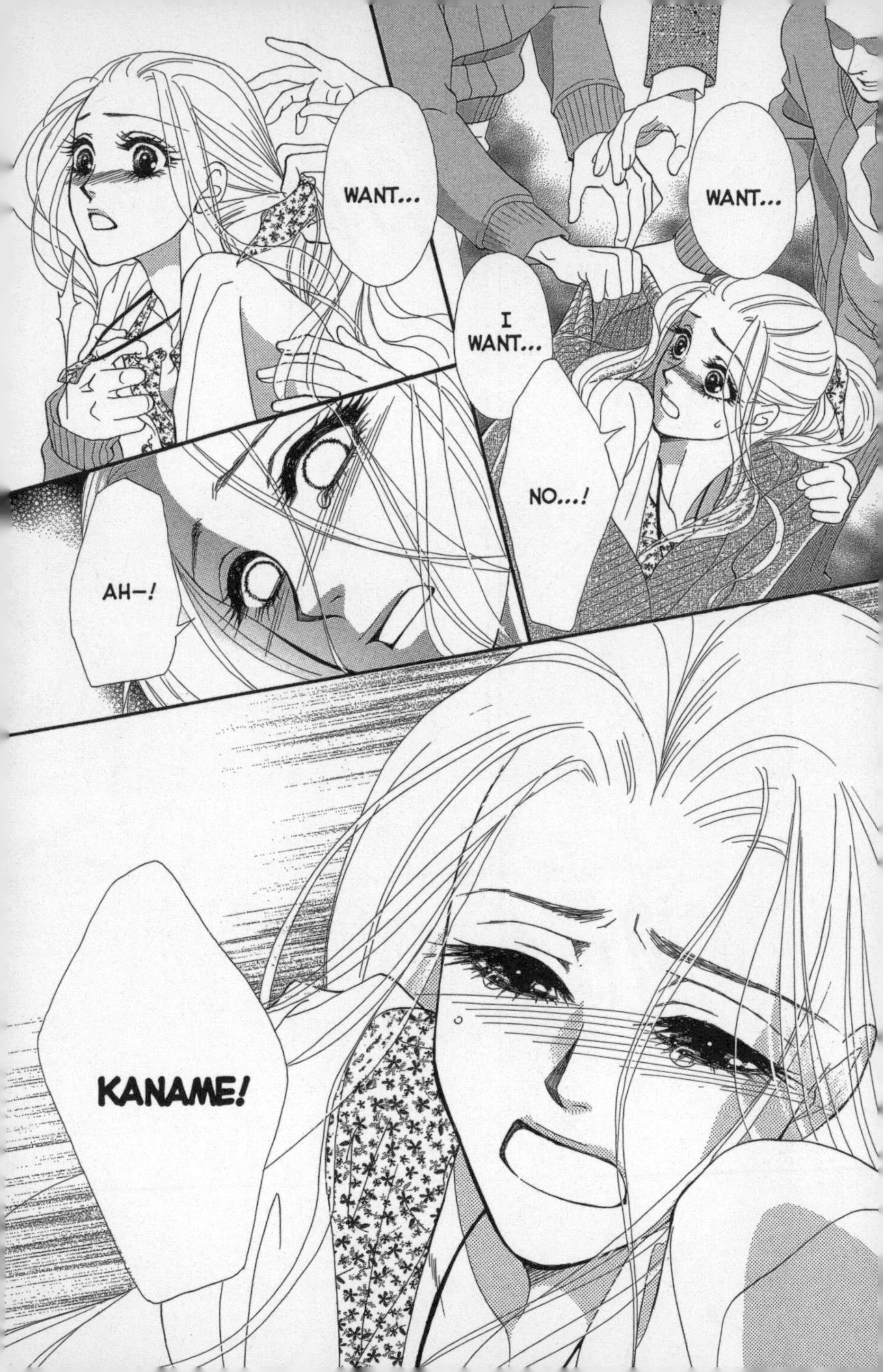

WANT...
I WANT...
NO...!
WANT...
AH-!
KANAME!

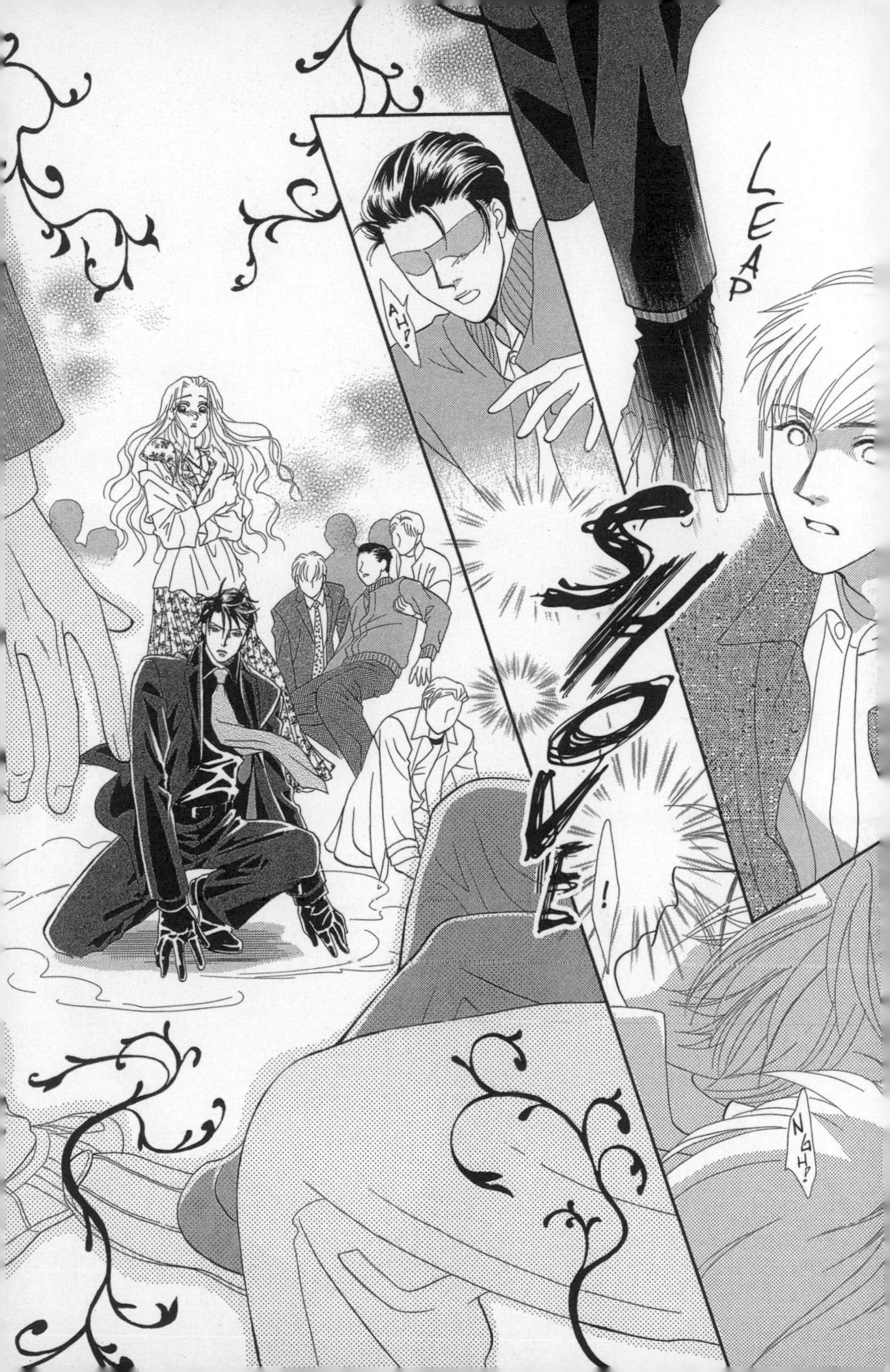
LEAP
AH!
SHOVE
!
NGH!

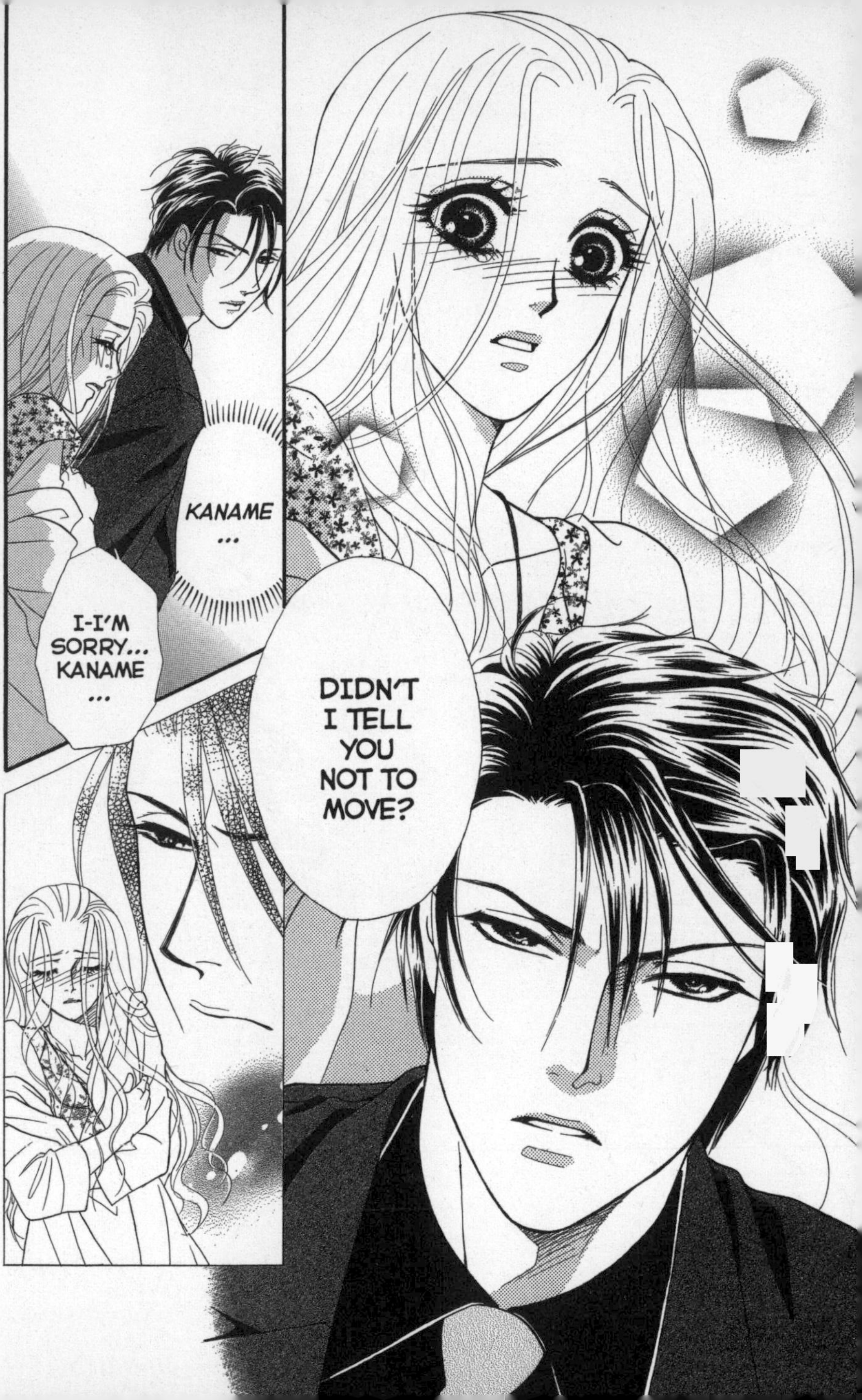
DIDN'T I TELL YOU NOT TO MOVE?
KANAME ...
I-I'M SORRY... KANAME ...

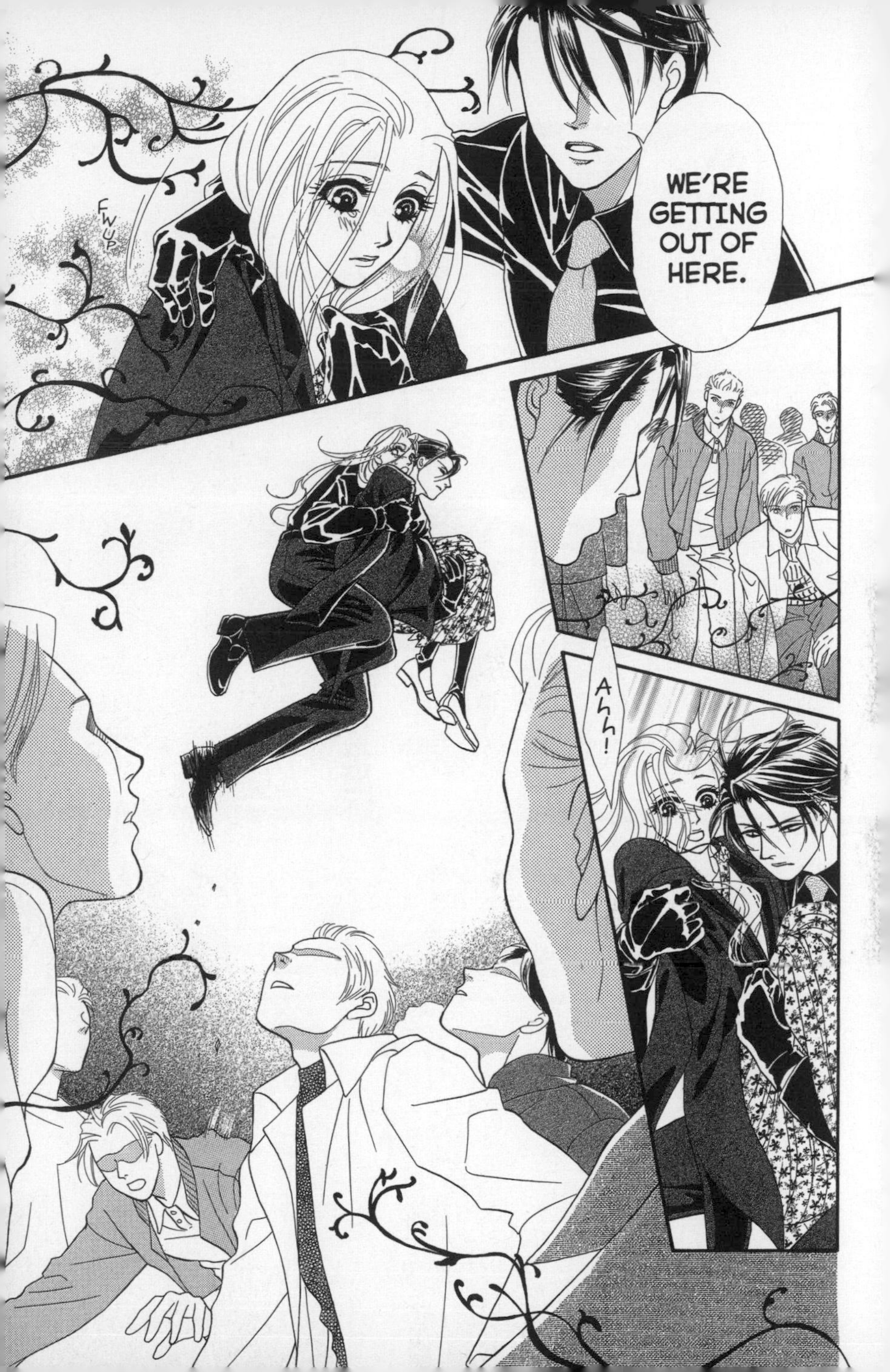
WE'RE GETTING OUT OF HERE.
FWUP
AHH!

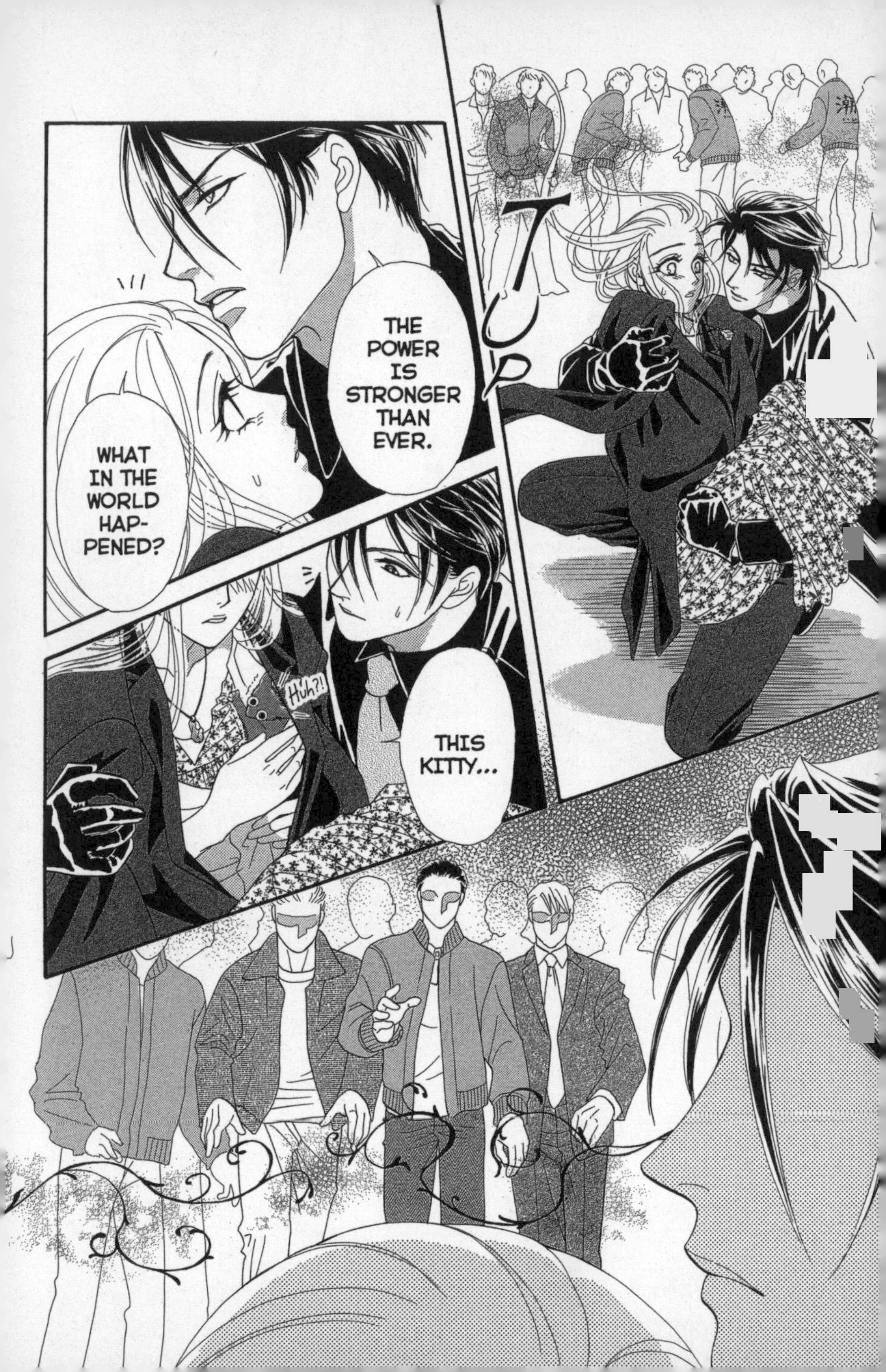
TUP
THE POWER IS STRONGER THAN EVER.
WHAT IN THE WORLD HAP-PENED?
THIS KITTY...
Huh?!

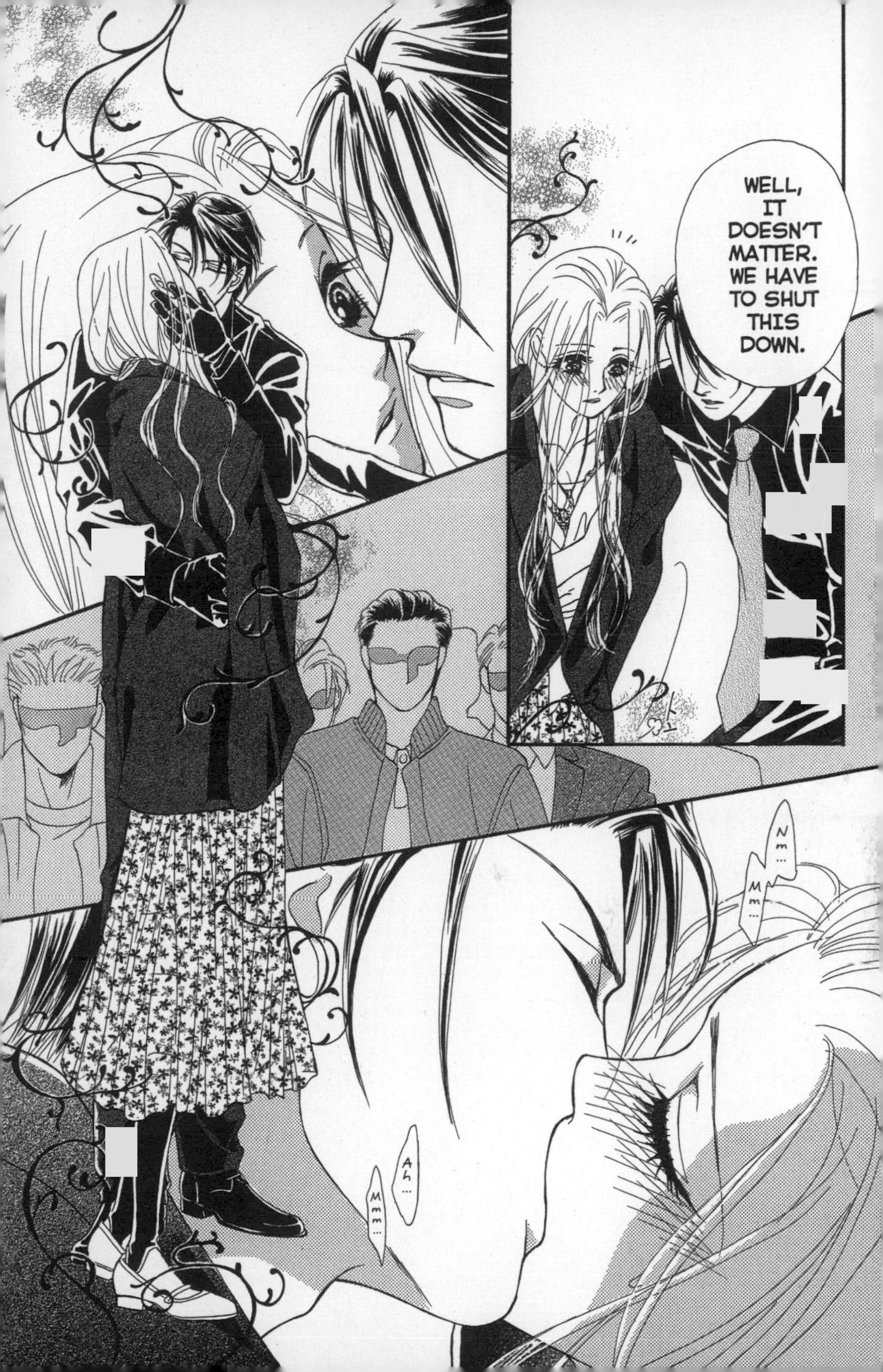
WELL, IT DOESN'T MATTER. WE HAVE TO SHUT THIS DOWN.
Nm... Mm...
Ah...
Mmm...

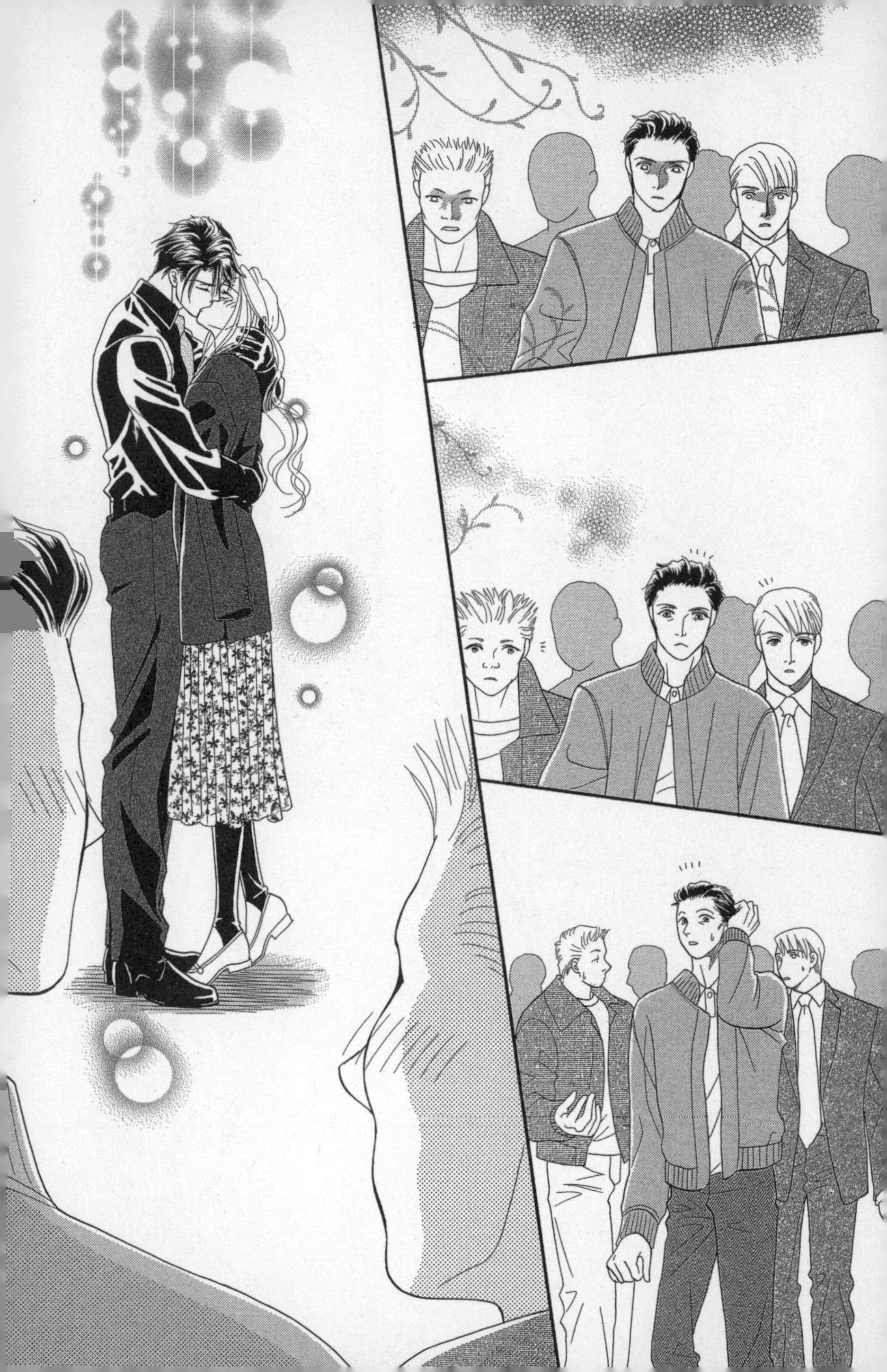

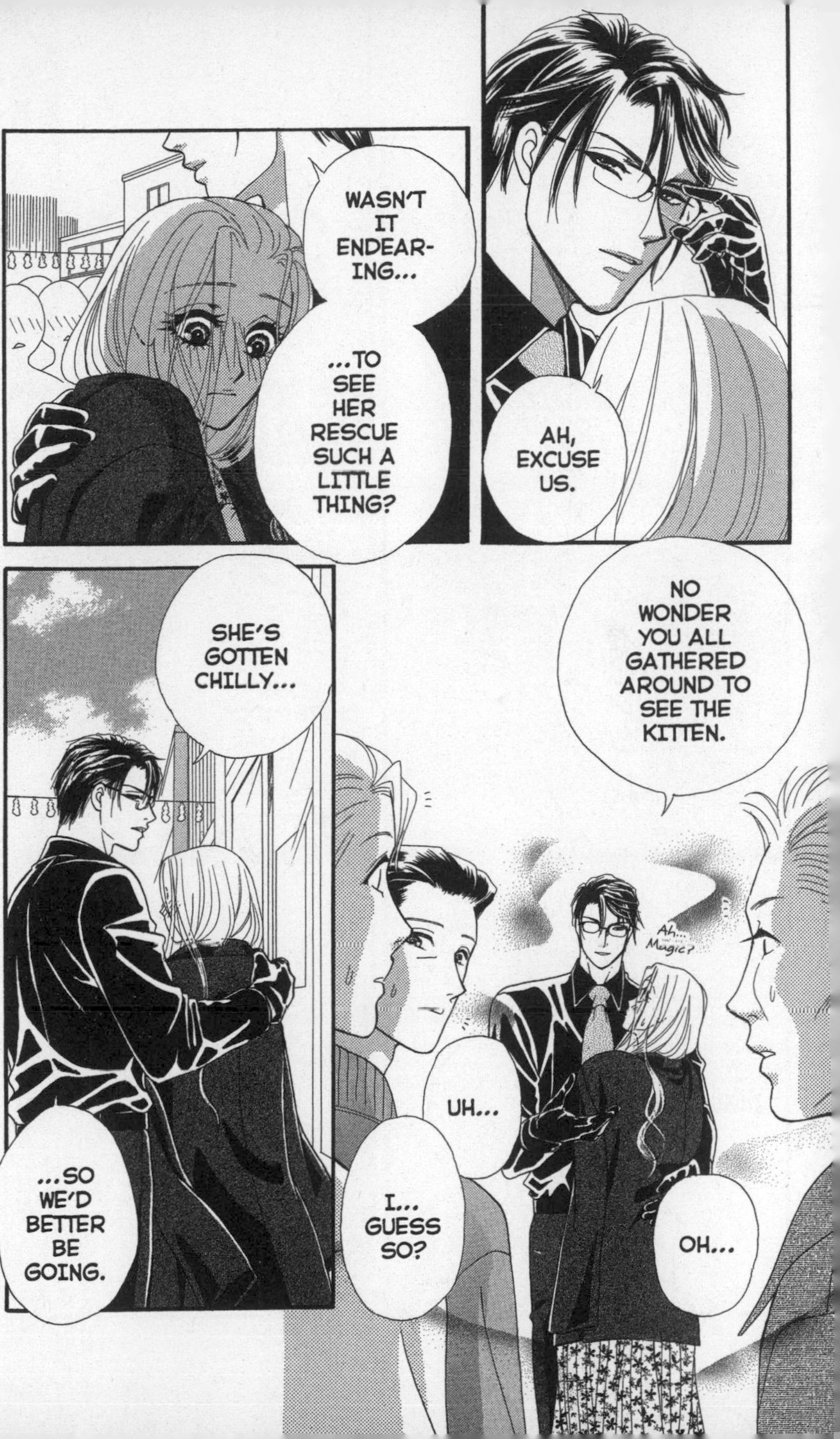
AH, EXCUSE US.
WASN'T IT ENDEARING...
...TO SEE HER RESCUE SUCH A LITTLE THING?
NO WONDER YOU ALL GATHERED AROUND TO SEE THE KITTEN.
Ah... Magic?
UH...
OH...
I... GUESS SO?
SHE'S GOTTEN CHILLY...
...SO WE'D BETTER BE GOING.

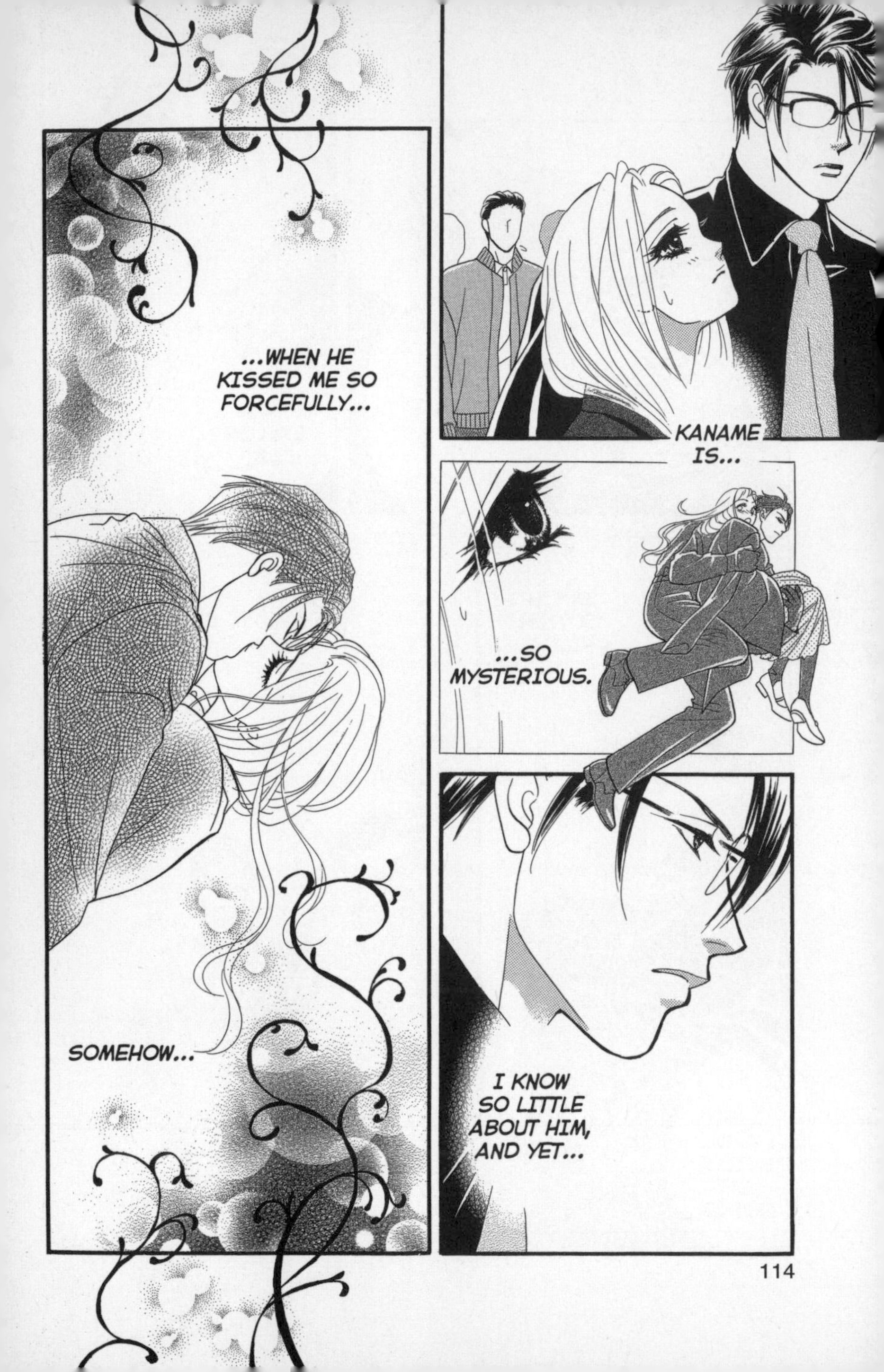
KANAME IS...
...SO MYSTERIOUS.
I KNOW SO LITTLE ABOUT HIM, AND YET...
...WHEN HE KISSED ME SO FORCEFULLY...
SOMEHOW...

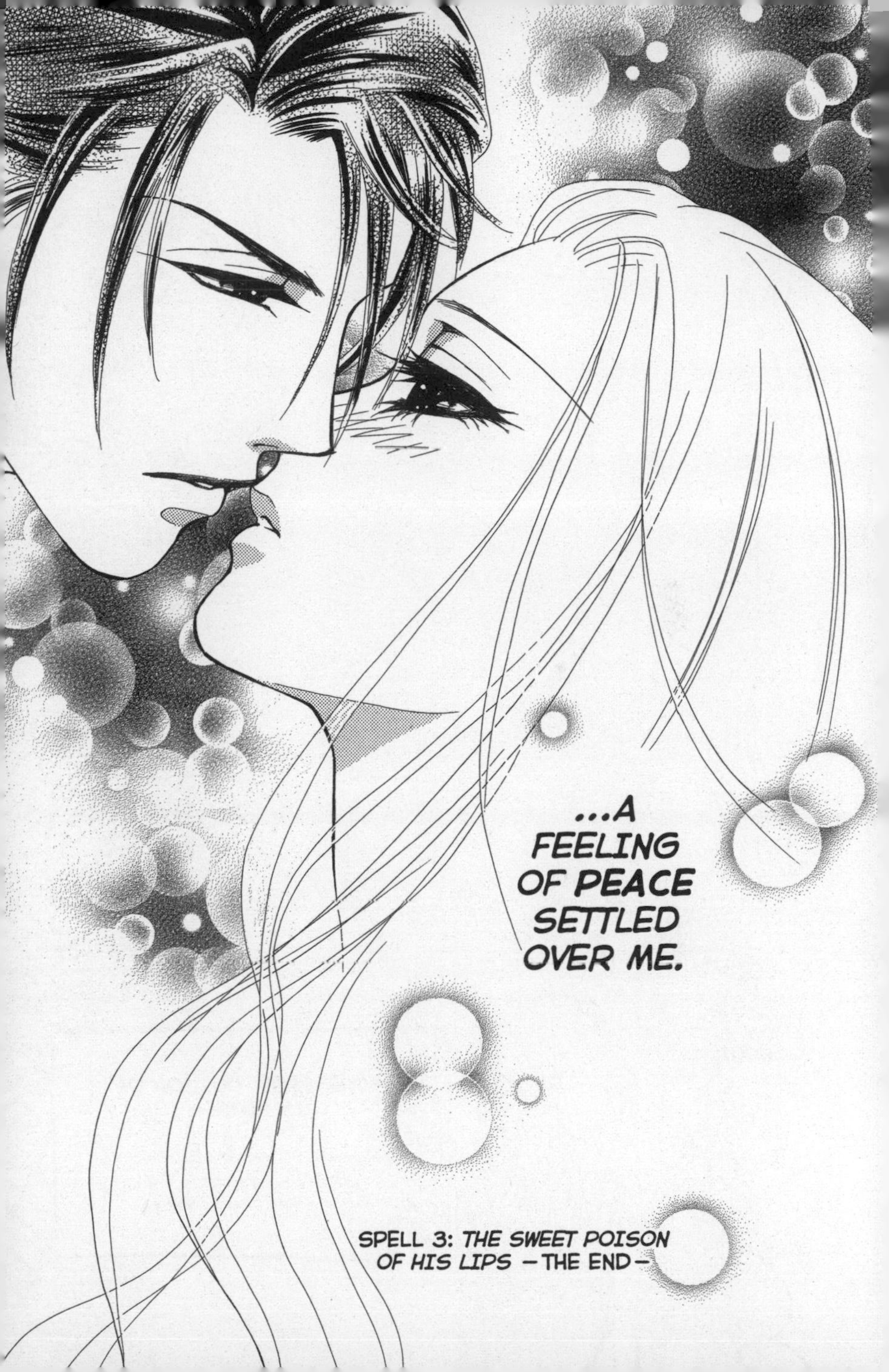
...A FEELING OF PEACE SETTLED OVER ME.
SPELL 3: THE SWEET POISON OF HIS LIPS —THE END—

– THE SWEET POISON OF HIS LIPS –

Kaname is a knight, but he's also like a ninja! He's a ninja knight! (Wry smile)

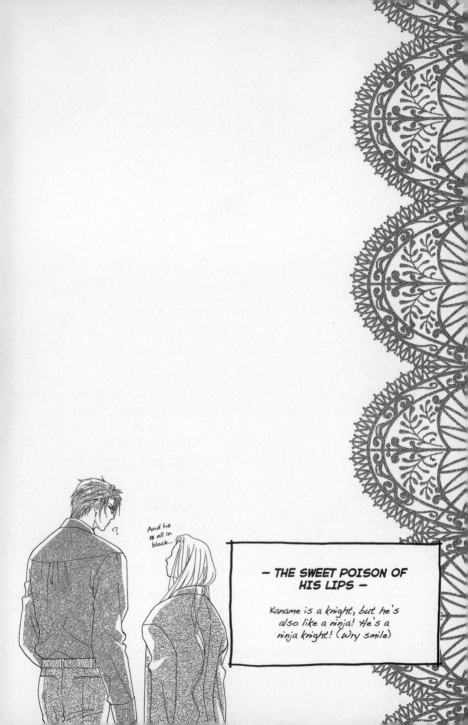

?
And he is all in black...

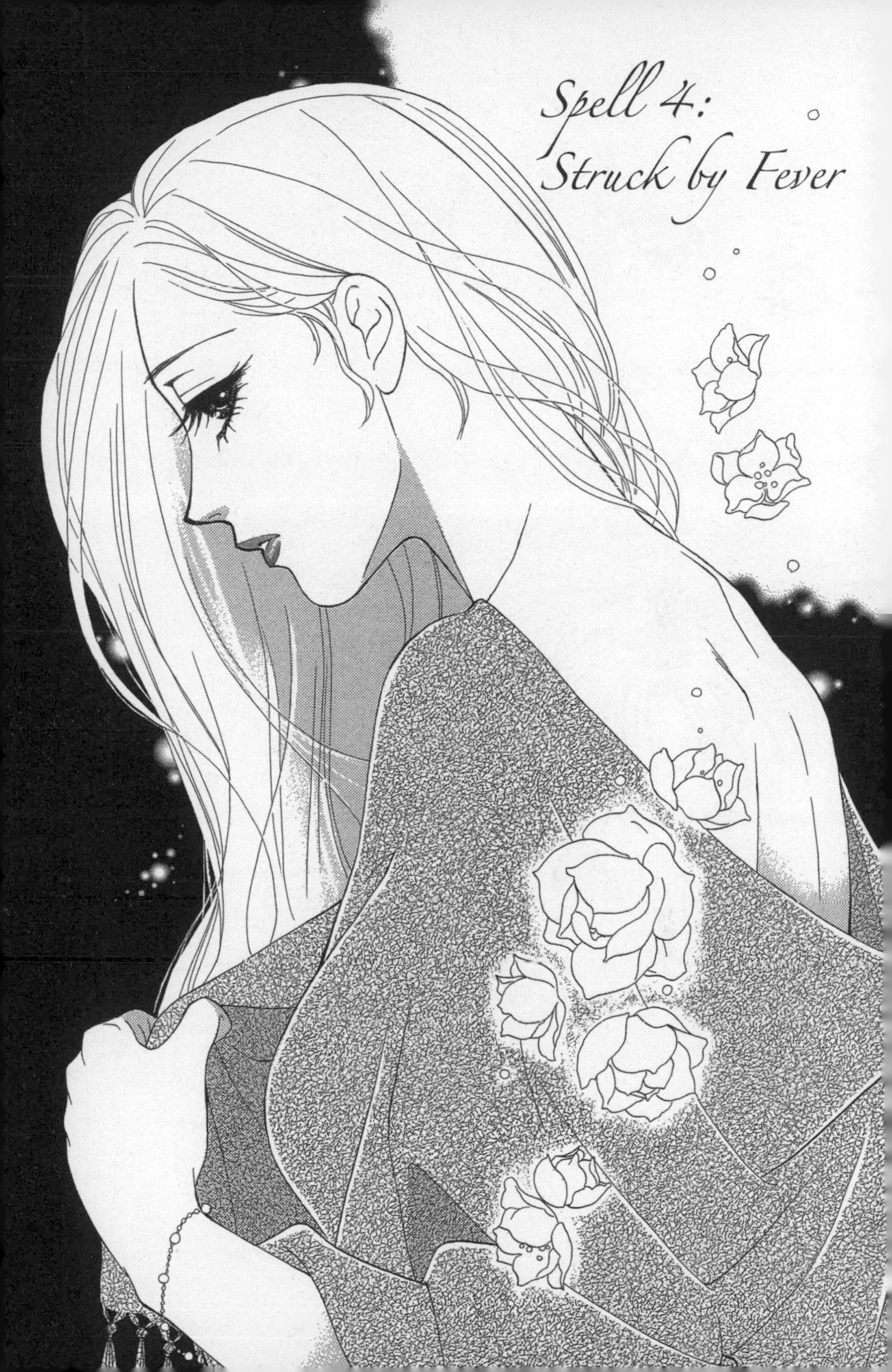
Spell 4:
Struck by Fever

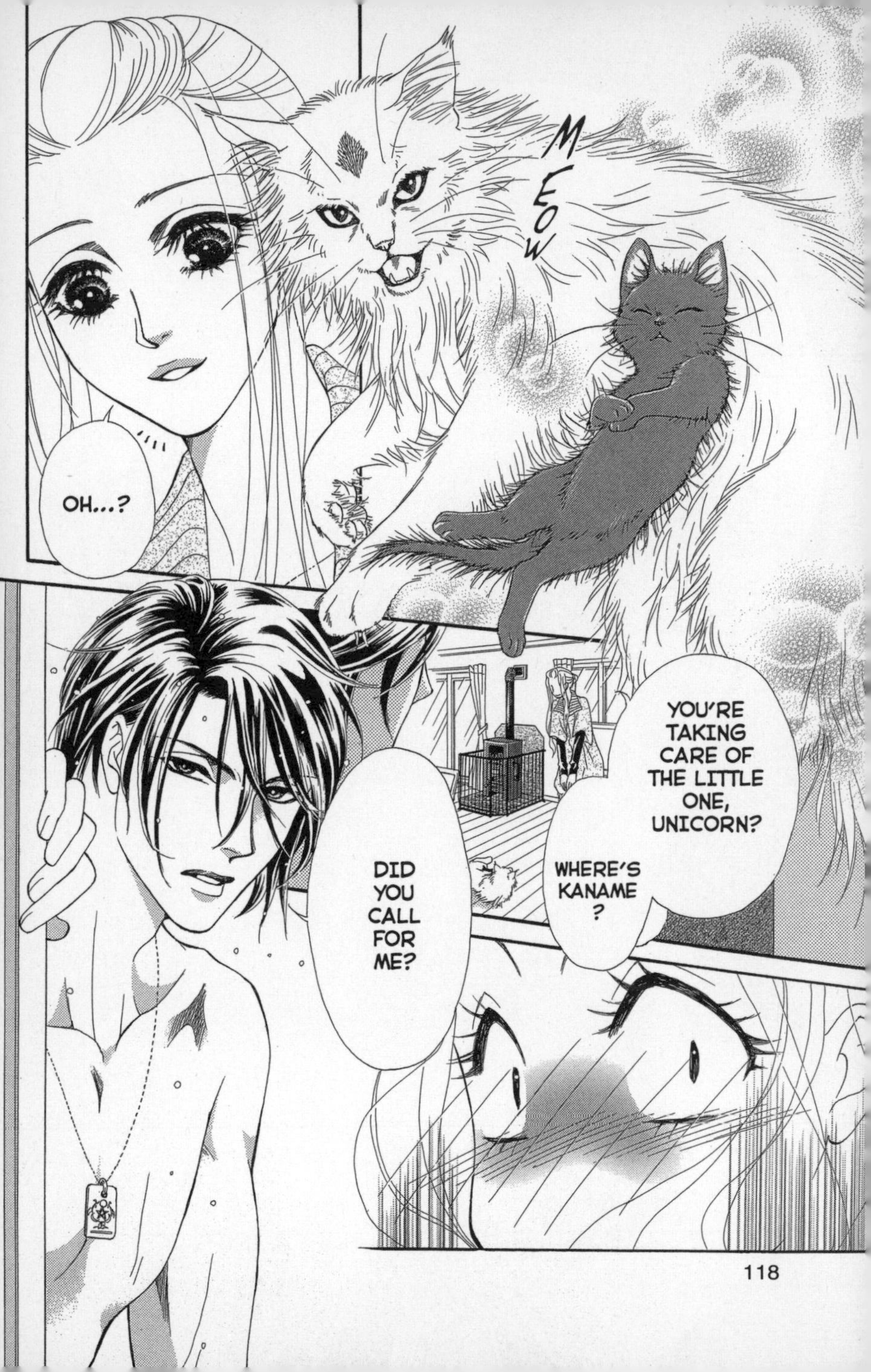
MEOW
OH...?
YOU'RE TAKING CARE OF THE LITTLE ONE, UNICORN?
WHERE'S KANAME?
DID YOU CALL FOR ME?

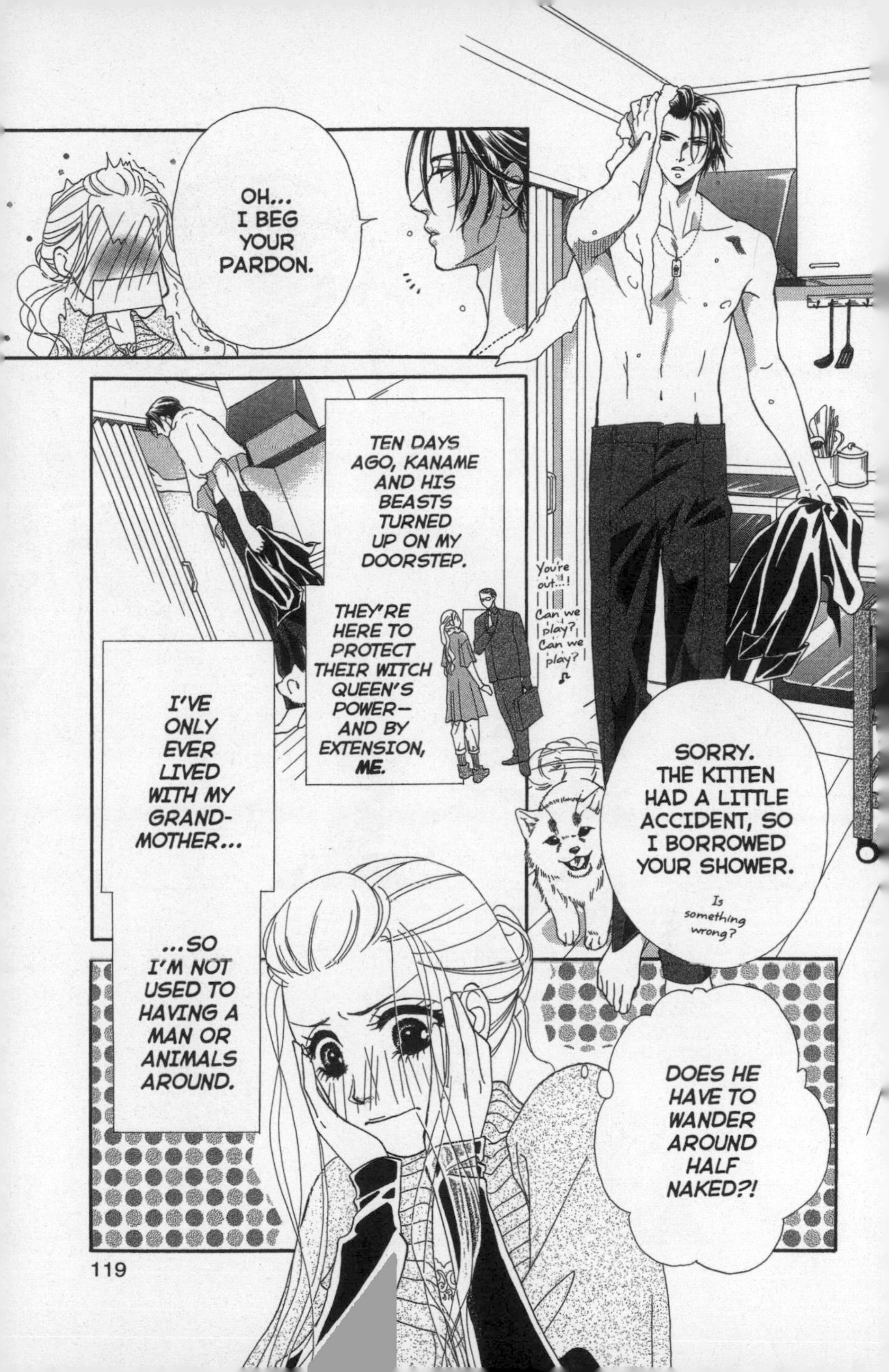
SORRY. THE KITTEN HAD A LITTLE ACCIDENT, SO I BORROWED YOUR SHOWER.
Is something wrong?
OH... I BEG YOUR PARDON.
TEN DAYS AGO, KANAME AND HIS BEASTS TURNED UP ON MY DOORSTEP.
THEY'RE HERE TO PROTECT THEIR WITCH QUEEN'S POWER—AND BY EXTENSION, ME.
You're out...! Can we play? Can we play? ♪
I'VE ONLY EVER LIVED WITH MY GRAND-MOTHER...
...SO I'M NOT USED TO HAVING A MAN OR ANIMALS AROUND.
DOES HE HAVE TO WANDER AROUND HALF NAKED?!

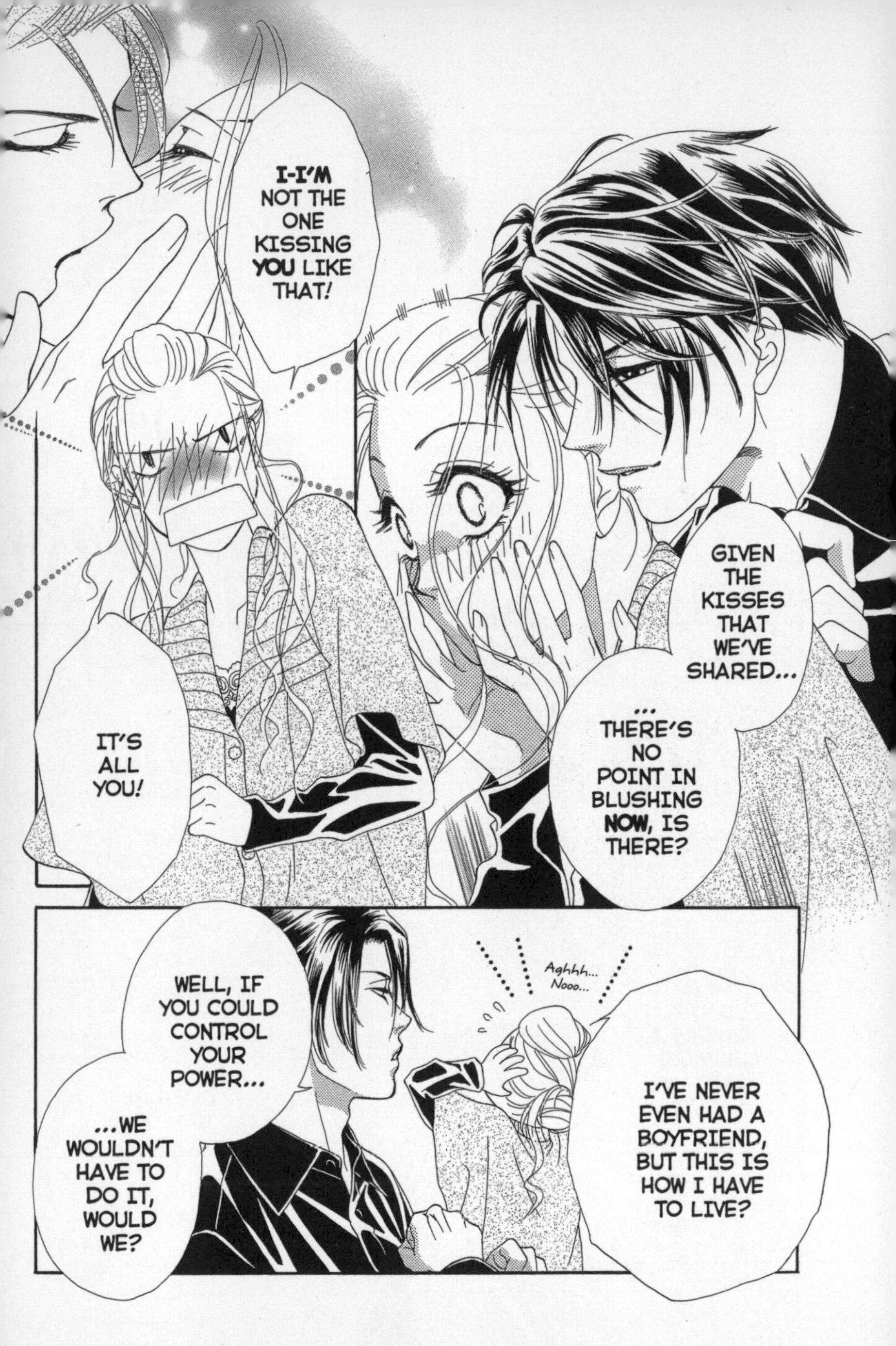
GIVEN THE KISSES THAT WE'VE SHARED...
...THERE'S NO POINT IN BLUSHING NOW, IS THERE?
I-I'M NOT THE ONE KISSING YOU LIKE THAT!
IT'S ALL YOU!
Aghhh... Nooo...
I'VE NEVER EVEN HAD A BOYFRIEND, BUT THIS IS HOW I HAVE TO LIVE?
WELL, IF YOU COULD CONTROL YOUR POWER...
...WE WOULDN'T HAVE TO DO IT, WOULD WE?

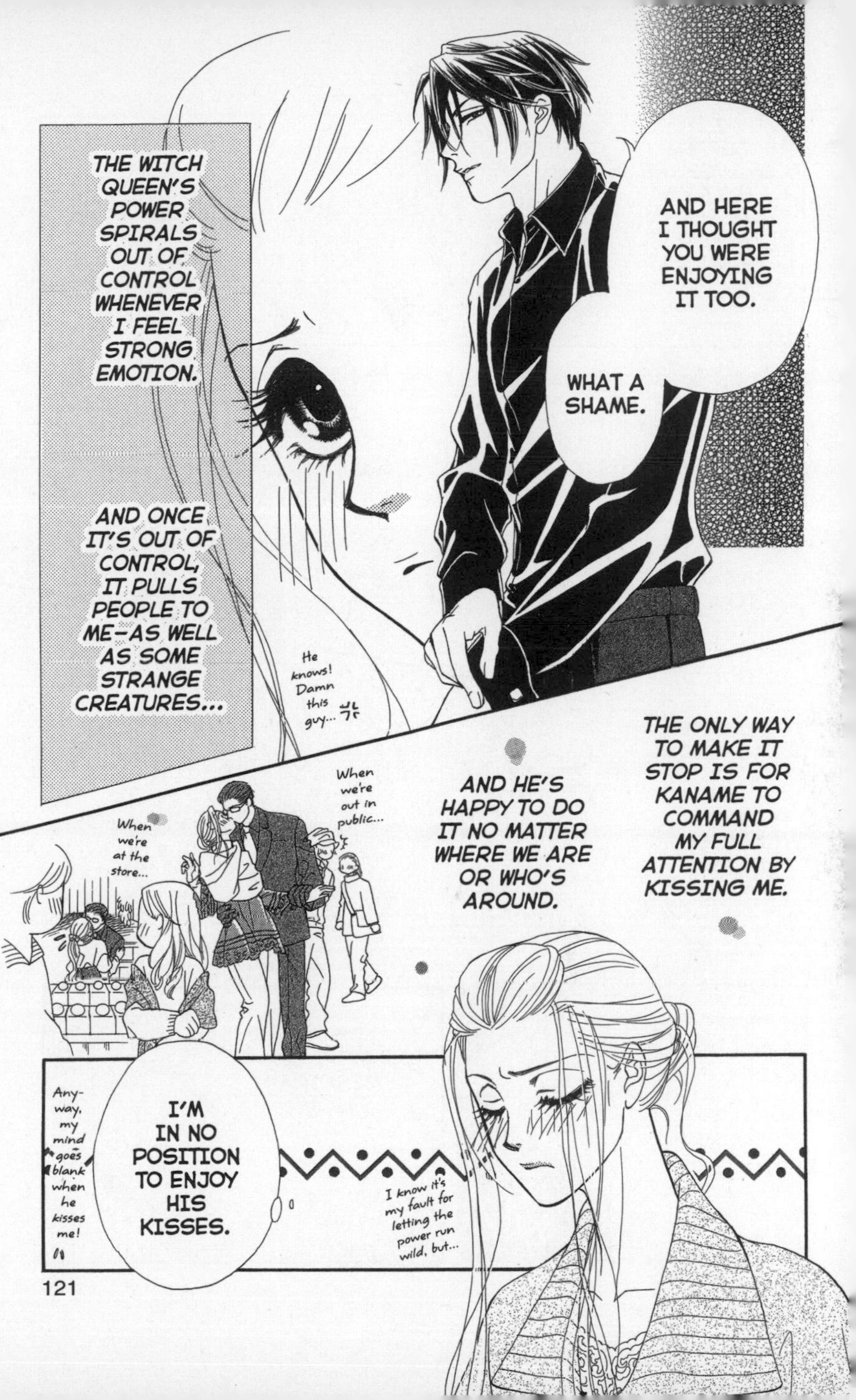

AND HERE I THOUGHT YOU WERE ENJOYING IT TOO.
WHAT A SHAME.
He knows! Damn this guy...
THE WITCH QUEEN'S POWER SPIRALS OUT OF CONTROL WHENEVER I FEEL STRONG EMOTION.
AND ONCE IT'S OUT OF CONTROL, IT PULLS PEOPLE TO ME—AS WELL AS SOME STRANGE CREATURES...
THE ONLY WAY TO MAKE IT STOP IS FOR KANAME TO COMMAND MY FULL ATTENTION BY KISSING ME.
AND HE'S HAPPY TO DO IT NO MATTER WHERE WE ARE OR WHO'S AROUND.
When we're out in public...
When we're at the store...
I know it's my fault for letting the power run wild, but...
I'M IN NO POSITION TO ENJOY HIS KISSES.
Any-way, my mind goes blank when he kisses me!

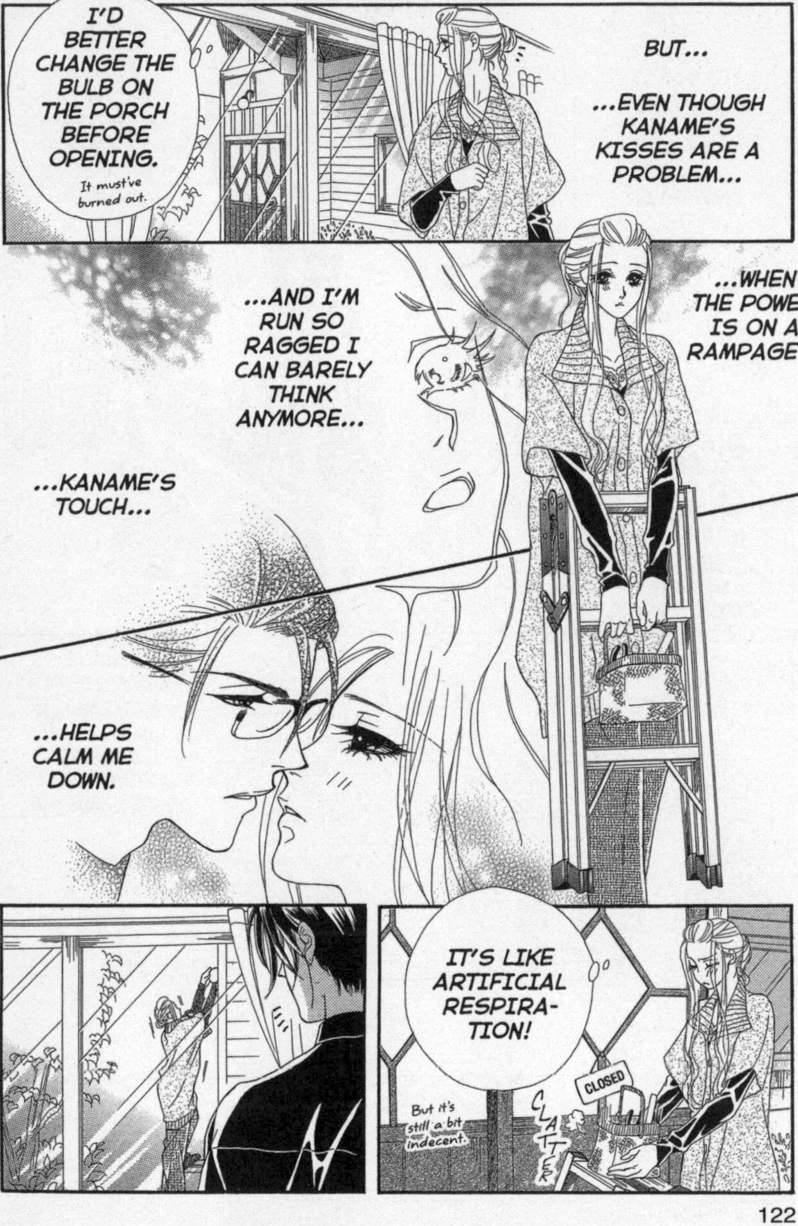
BUT...
...EVEN THOUGH KANAME'S KISSES ARE A PROBLEM...
I'D BETTER CHANGE THE BULB ON THE PORCH BEFORE OPENING.
It must've burned out.
...WHEN THE POWER IS ON A RAMPAGE...
...AND I'M RUN SO RAGGED I CAN BARELY THINK ANYMORE...
...KANAME'S TOUCH...
...HELPS CALM ME DOWN.
IT'S LIKE ARTIFICIAL RESPIRA-TION!
CLOSED
CLATTER
But it's still a bit indecent.

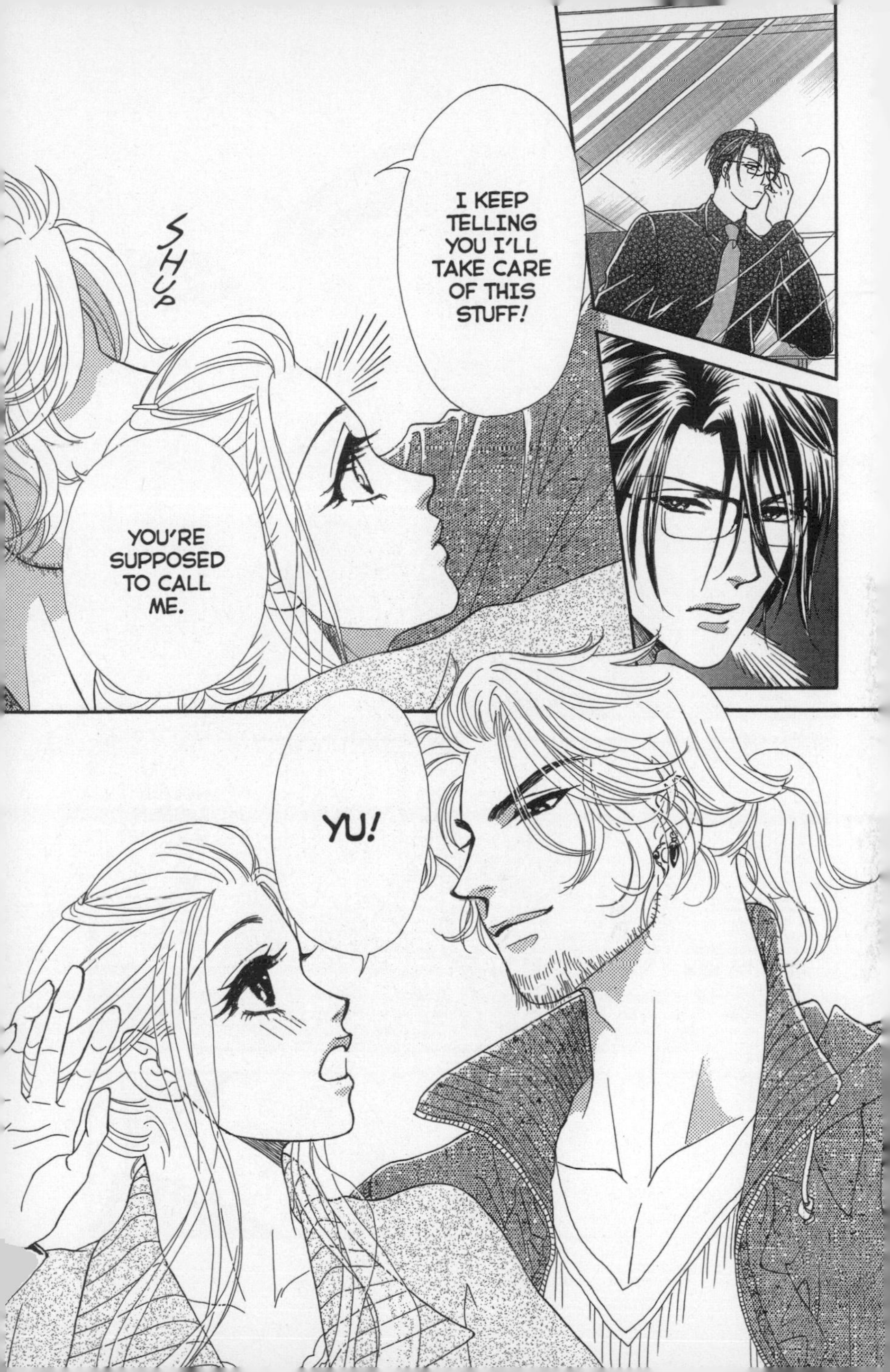
I KEEP TELLING YOU I'LL TAKE CARE OF THIS STUFF!
SHUP
YOU'RE SUPPOSED TO CALL ME.
YU!

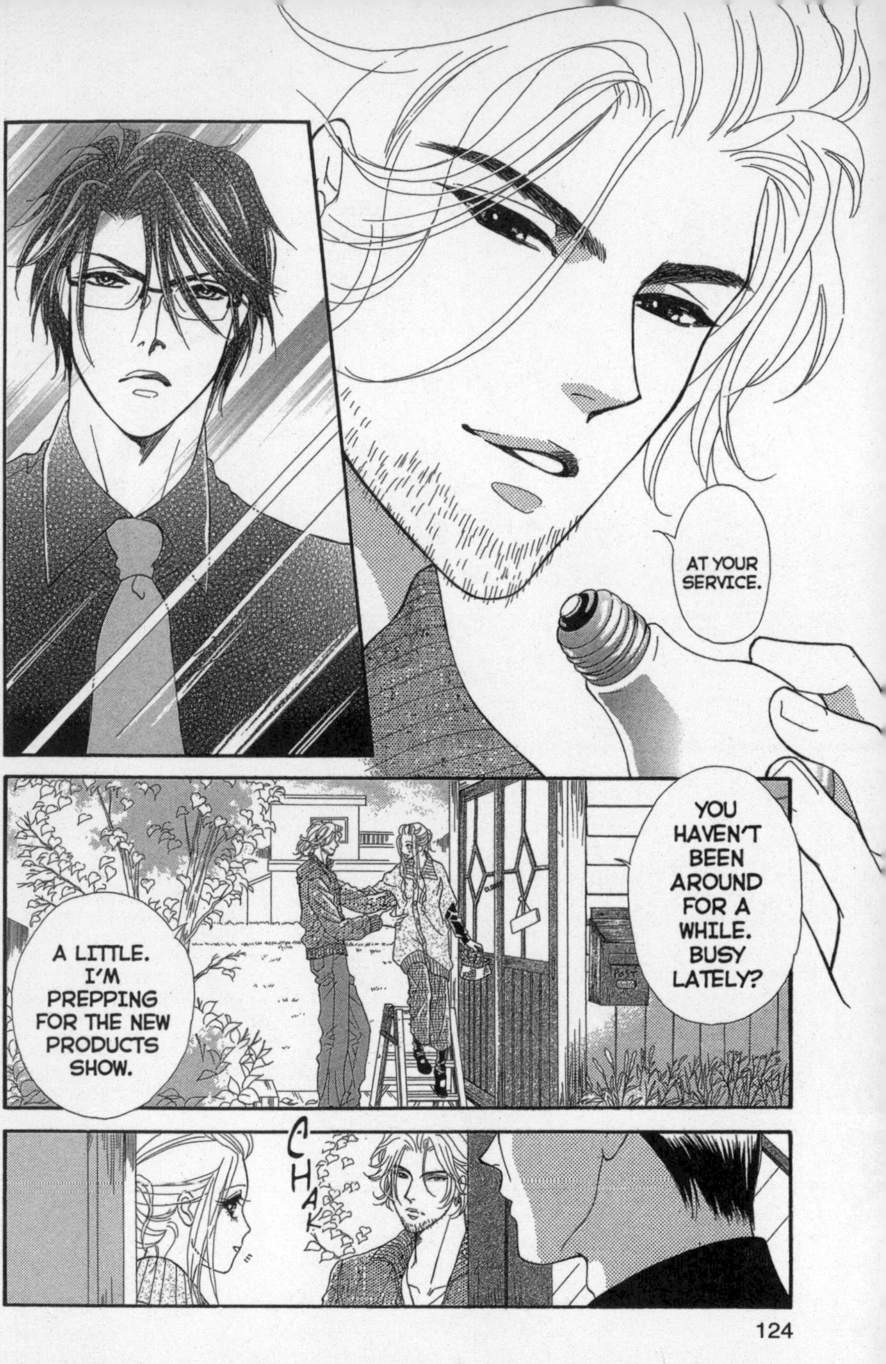
AT YOUR SERVICE.
YOU HAVEN'T BEEN AROUND FOR A WHILE. BUSY LATELY?
A LITTLE. I'M PREPPING FOR THE NEW PRODUCTS SHOW.
CHAK

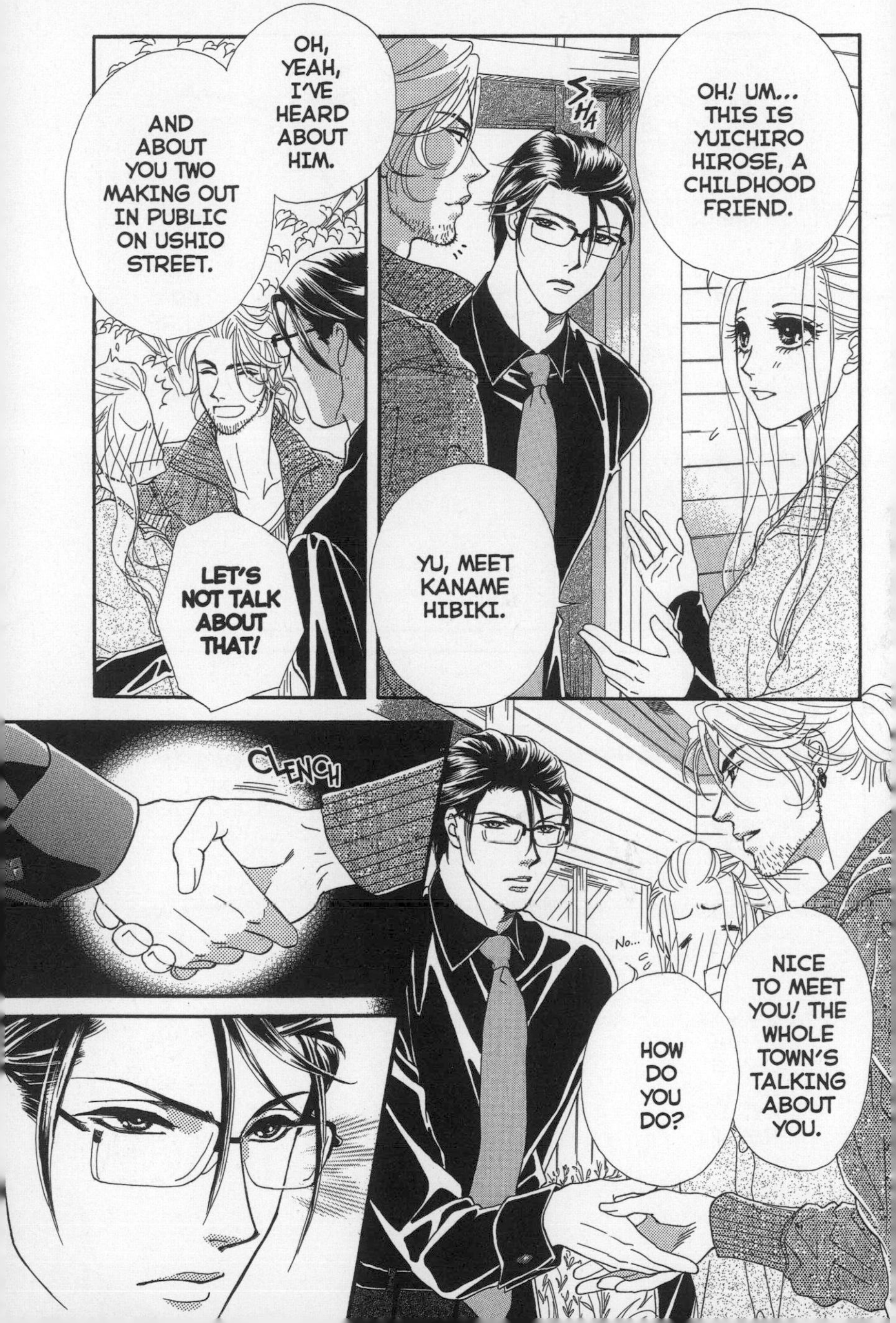
SHA
OH! UM... THIS IS YUICHIRO HIROSE, A CHILDHOOD FRIEND.
YU, MEET KANAME HIBIKI.
OH, YEAH, I'VE HEARD ABOUT HIM.
AND ABOUT YOU TWO MAKING OUT IN PUBLIC ON USHIO STREET.
LET'S NOT TALK ABOUT THAT!
NICE TO MEET YOU! THE WHOLE TOWN'S TALKING ABOUT YOU.
No...
HOW DO YOU DO?
CLENCH

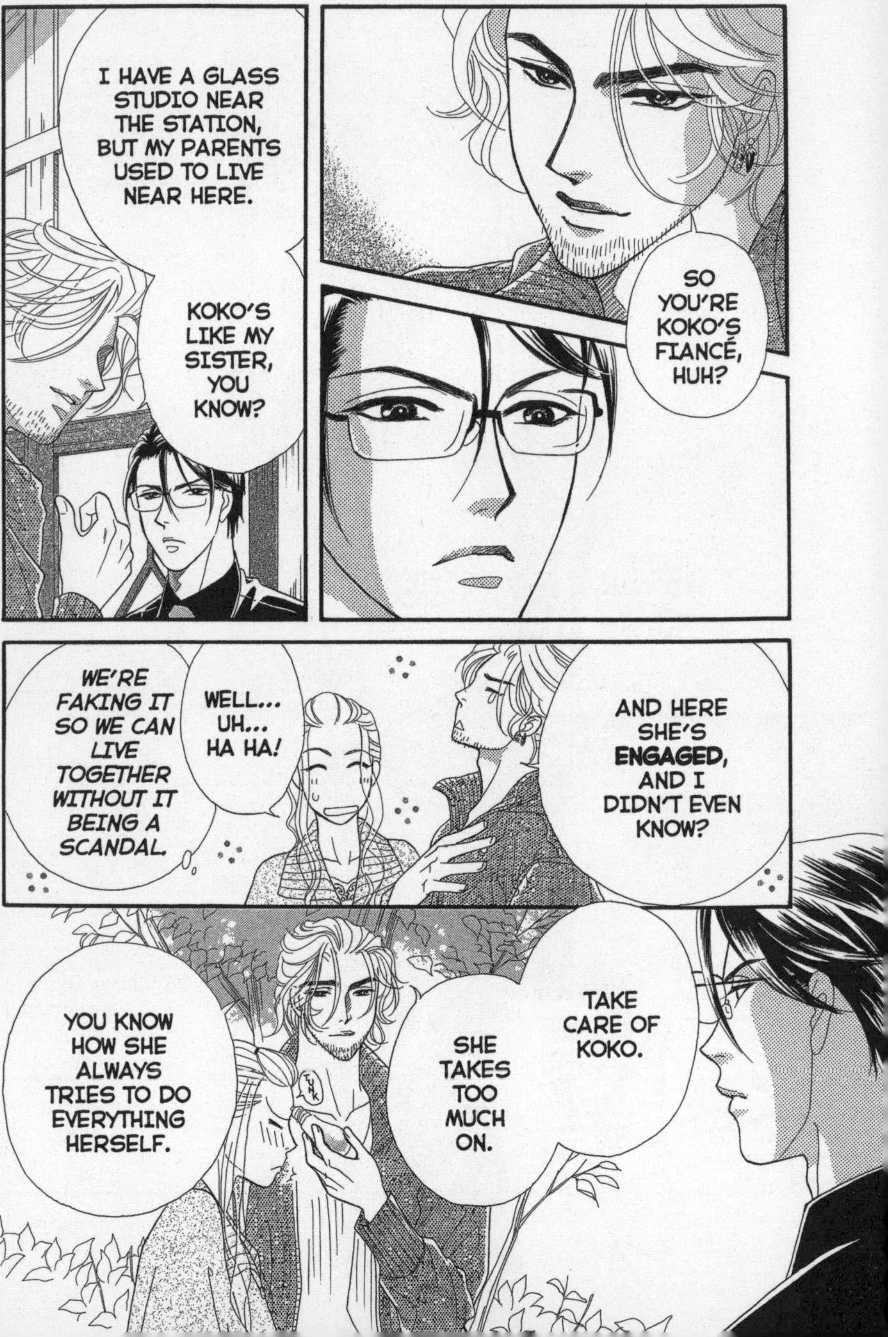
SO YOU'RE KOKO'S FIANCÉ, HUH?
I HAVE A GLASS STUDIO NEAR THE STATION, BUT MY PARENTS USED TO LIVE NEAR HERE.
KOKO'S LIKE MY SISTER, YOU KNOW?
AND HERE SHE'S **ENGAGED**, AND I DIDN'T EVEN KNOW?
WELL... UH... HA HA!
WE'RE FAKING IT SO WE CAN LIVE TOGETHER WITHOUT IT BEING A SCANDAL.
TAKE CARE OF KOKO.
SHE TAKES TOO MUCH ON.
YOU KNOW HOW SHE ALWAYS TRIES TO DO EVERYTHING HERSELF.
TUNK

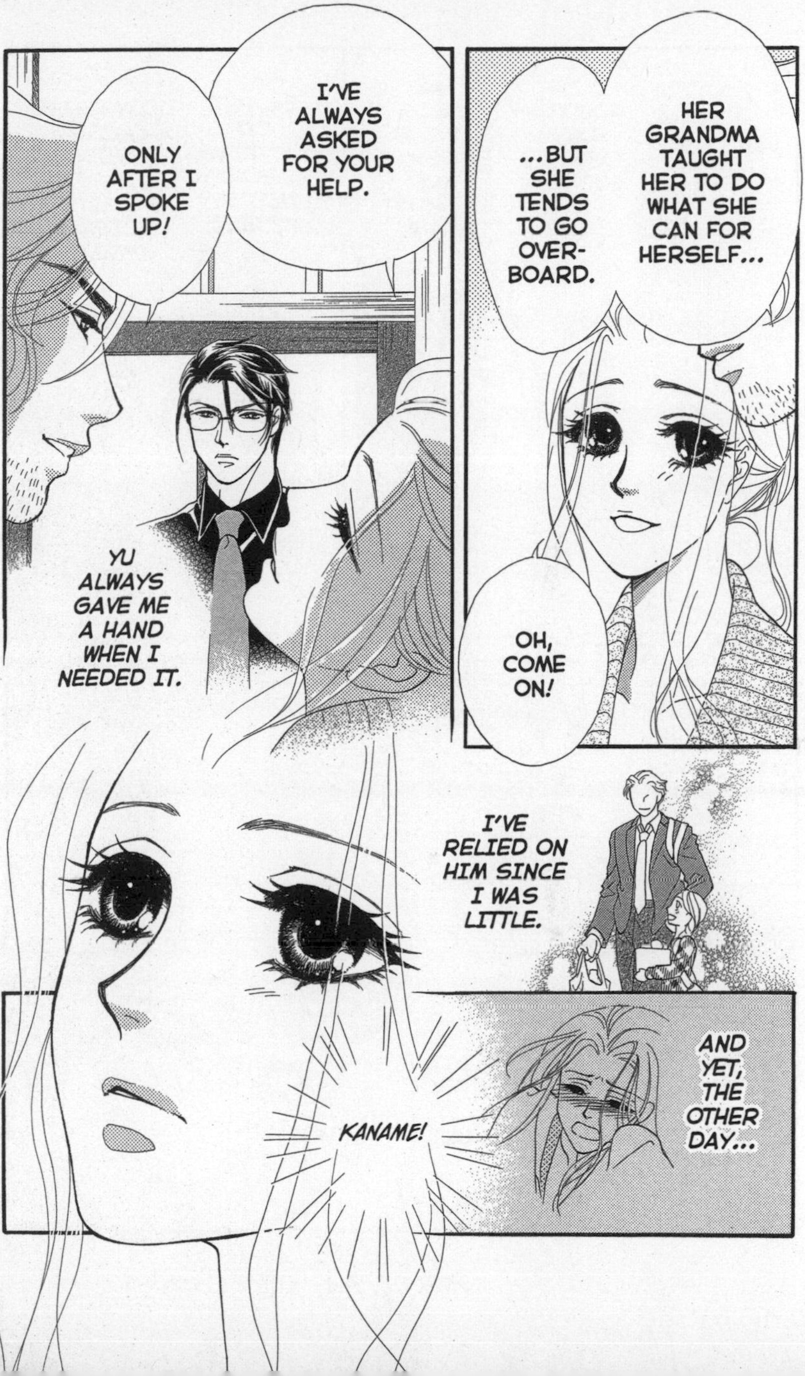
HER GRANDMA TAUGHT HER TO DO WHAT SHE CAN FOR HERSELF...
...BUT SHE TENDS TO GO OVER-BOARD.
OH, COME ON!
I'VE ALWAYS ASKED FOR YOUR HELP.
ONLY AFTER I SPOKE UP!
YU ALWAYS GAVE ME A HAND WHEN I NEEDED IT.
I'VE RELIED ON HIM SINCE I WAS LITTLE.
AND YET, THE OTHER DAY...
KANAME!

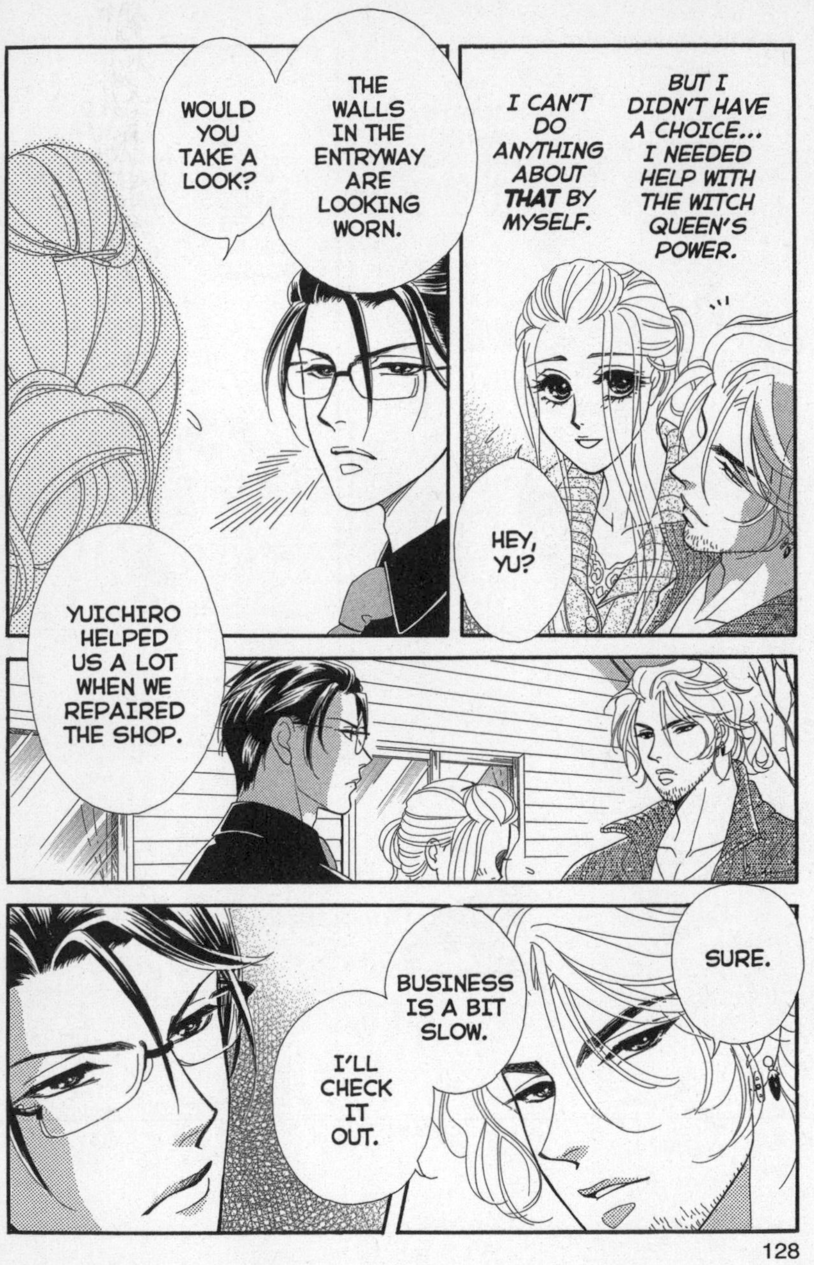
BUT I DIDN'T HAVE A CHOICE... I NEEDED HELP WITH THE WITCH QUEEN'S POWER.
I CAN'T DO ANYTHING ABOUT **THAT** BY MYSELF.
HEY, YU?
THE WALLS IN THE ENTRYWAY ARE LOOKING WORN.
WOULD YOU TAKE A LOOK?
YUICHIRO HELPED US A LOT WHEN WE REPAIRED THE SHOP.
SURE.
BUSINESS IS A BIT SLOW.
I'LL CHECK IT OUT.

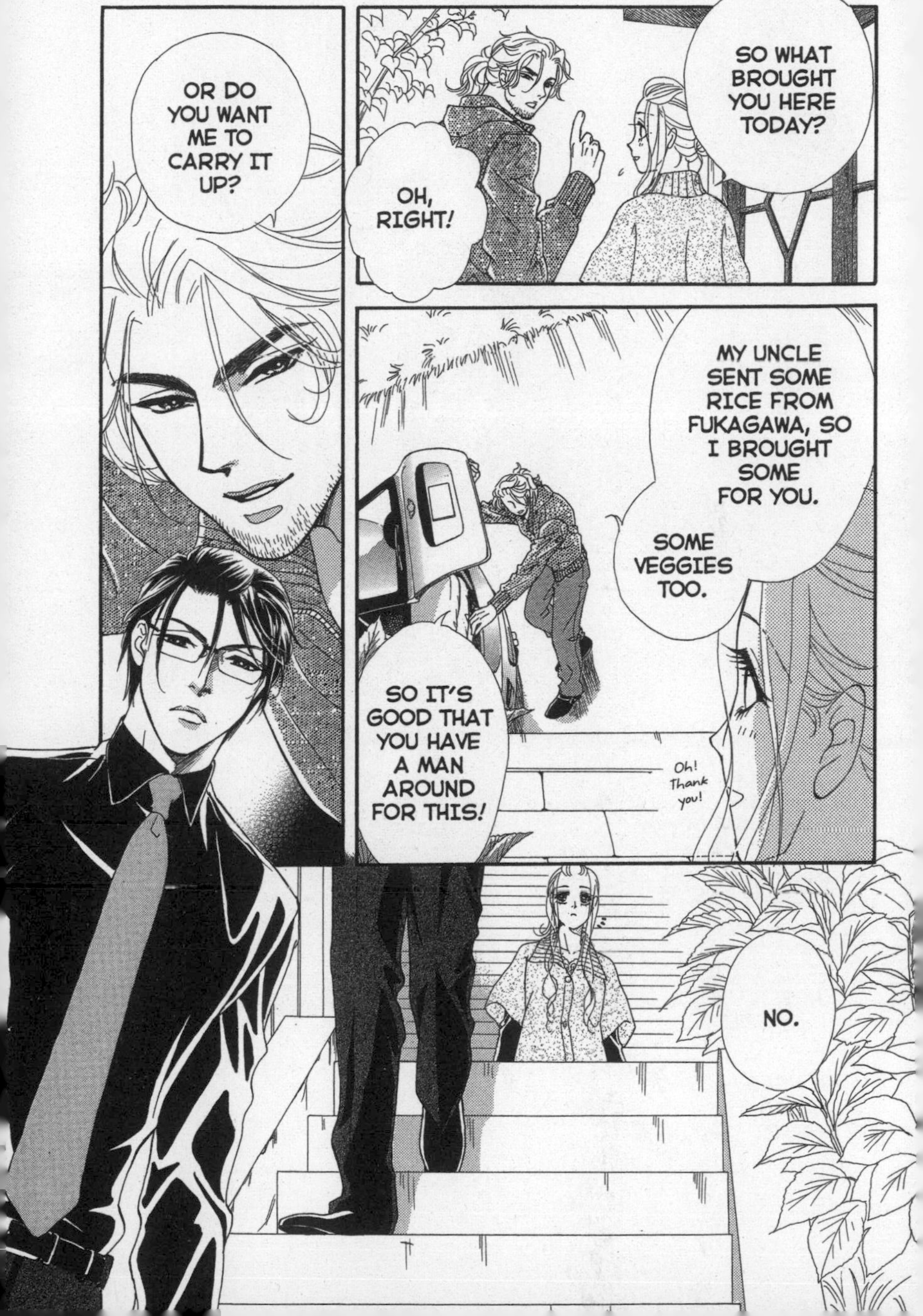
SO WHAT BROUGHT YOU HERE TODAY?
OH, RIGHT!
MY UNCLE SENT SOME RICE FROM FUKAGAWA, SO I BROUGHT SOME FOR YOU.
SOME VEGGIES TOO.
Oh! Thank you!
SO IT'S GOOD THAT YOU HAVE A MAN AROUND FOR THIS!
OR DO YOU WANT ME TO CARRY IT UP?
NO.

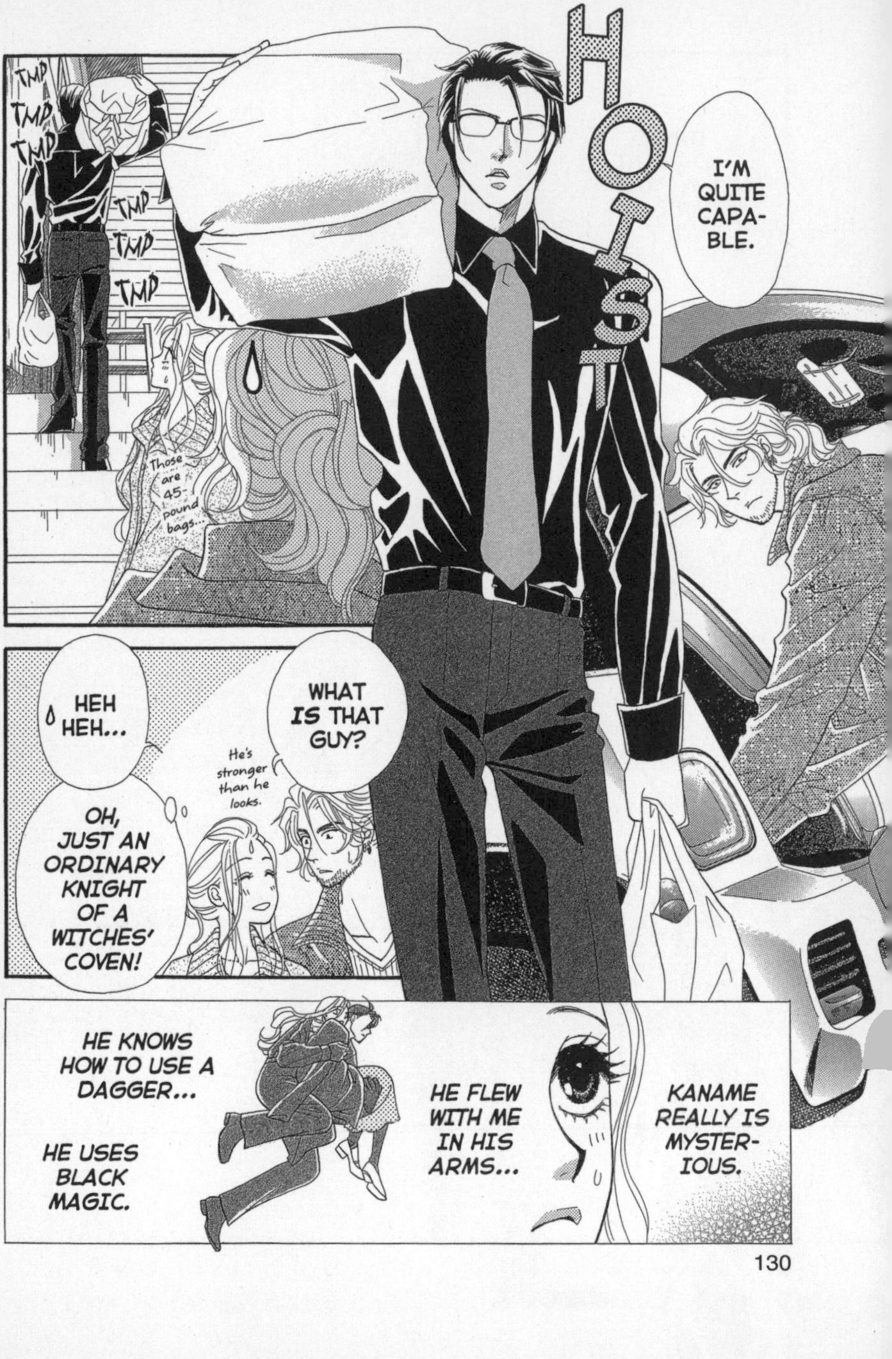
HOIST
I'M QUITE CAPABLE.
TMP TMP TMP TMP
TMP TMP TMP
Those are 45-pound bags...
WHAT *IS* THAT GUY?
He's stronger than he looks.
HEH HEH...
OH, JUST AN ORDINARY KNIGHT OF A WITCHES' COVEN!
KANAME REALLY IS MYSTERIOUS.
HE FLEW WITH ME IN HIS ARMS...
HE KNOWS HOW TO USE A DAGGER...
HE USES BLACK MAGIC.

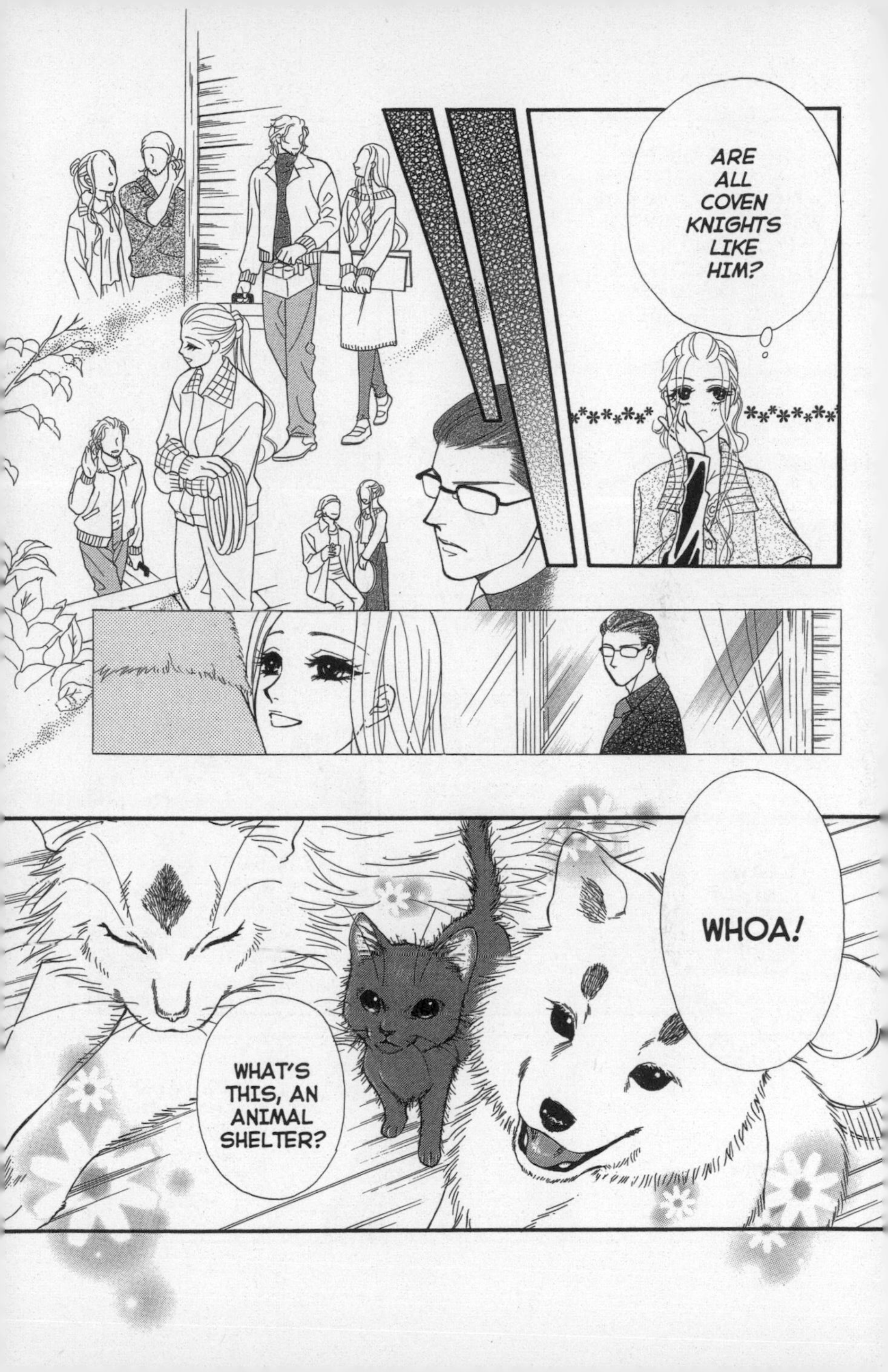
ARE ALL COVEN KNIGHTS LIKE HIM?
WHOA!
WHAT'S THIS, AN ANIMAL SHELTER?

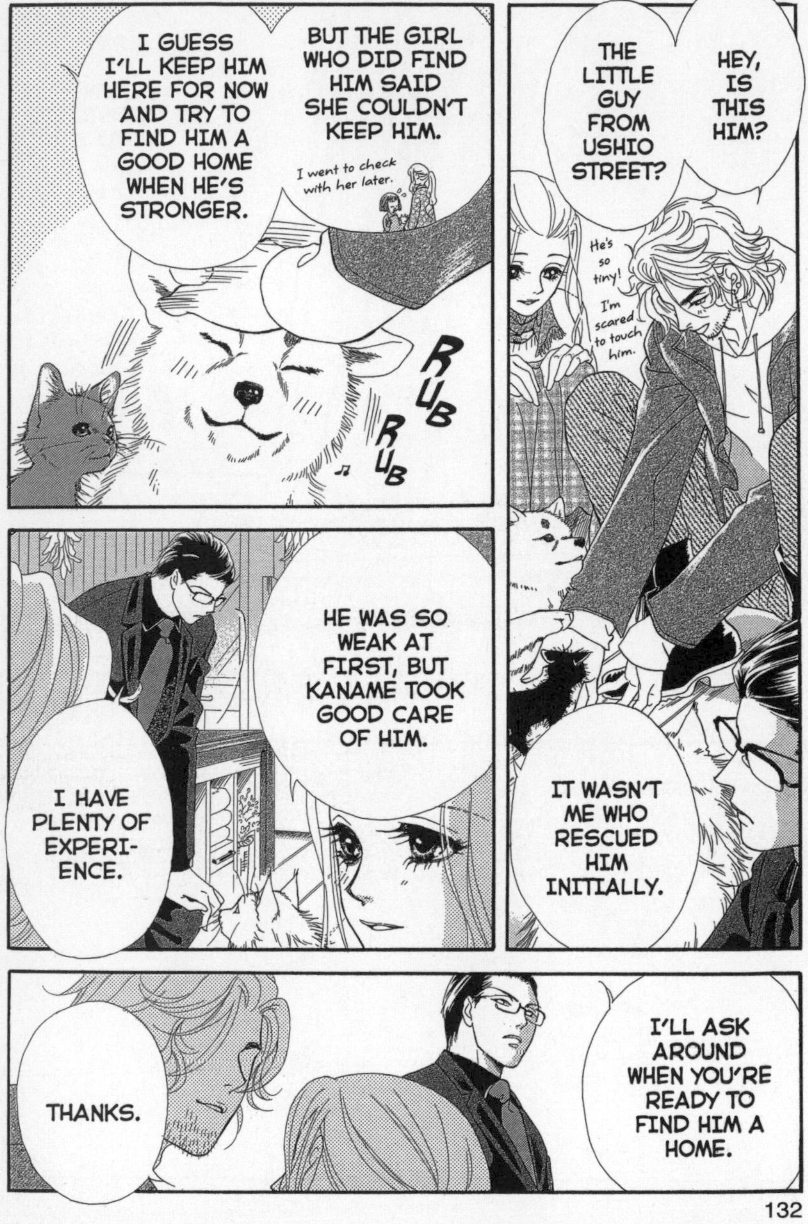
HEY, IS THIS HIM?
THE LITTLE GUY FROM USHIO STREET?
He's so tiny!
I'm scared to touch him.
IT WASN'T ME WHO RESCUED HIM INITIALLY.
BUT THE GIRL WHO DID FIND HIM SAID SHE COULDN'T KEEP HIM.
I went to check with her later.
I GUESS I'LL KEEP HIM HERE FOR NOW AND TRY TO FIND HIM A GOOD HOME WHEN HE'S STRONGER.
RUB
RUB
HE WAS SO WEAK AT FIRST, BUT KANAME TOOK GOOD CARE OF HIM.
I HAVE PLENTY OF EXPERI-ENCE.
I'LL ASK AROUND WHEN YOU'RE READY TO FIND HIM A HOME.
THANKS.

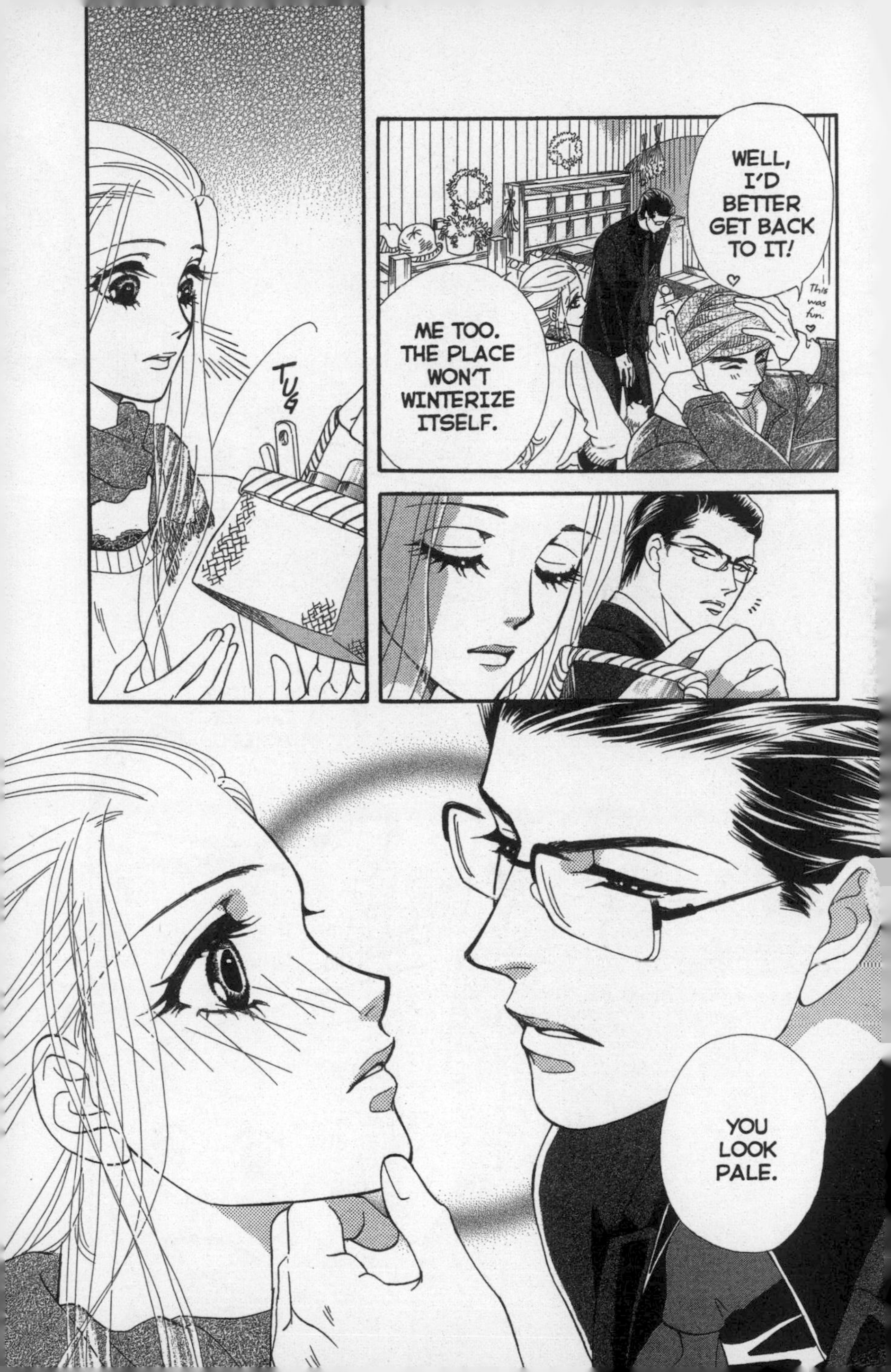
WELL, I'D BETTER GET BACK TO IT!
This was fun.
ME TOO. THE PLACE WON'T WINTERIZE ITSELF.
TUG
YOU LOOK PALE.

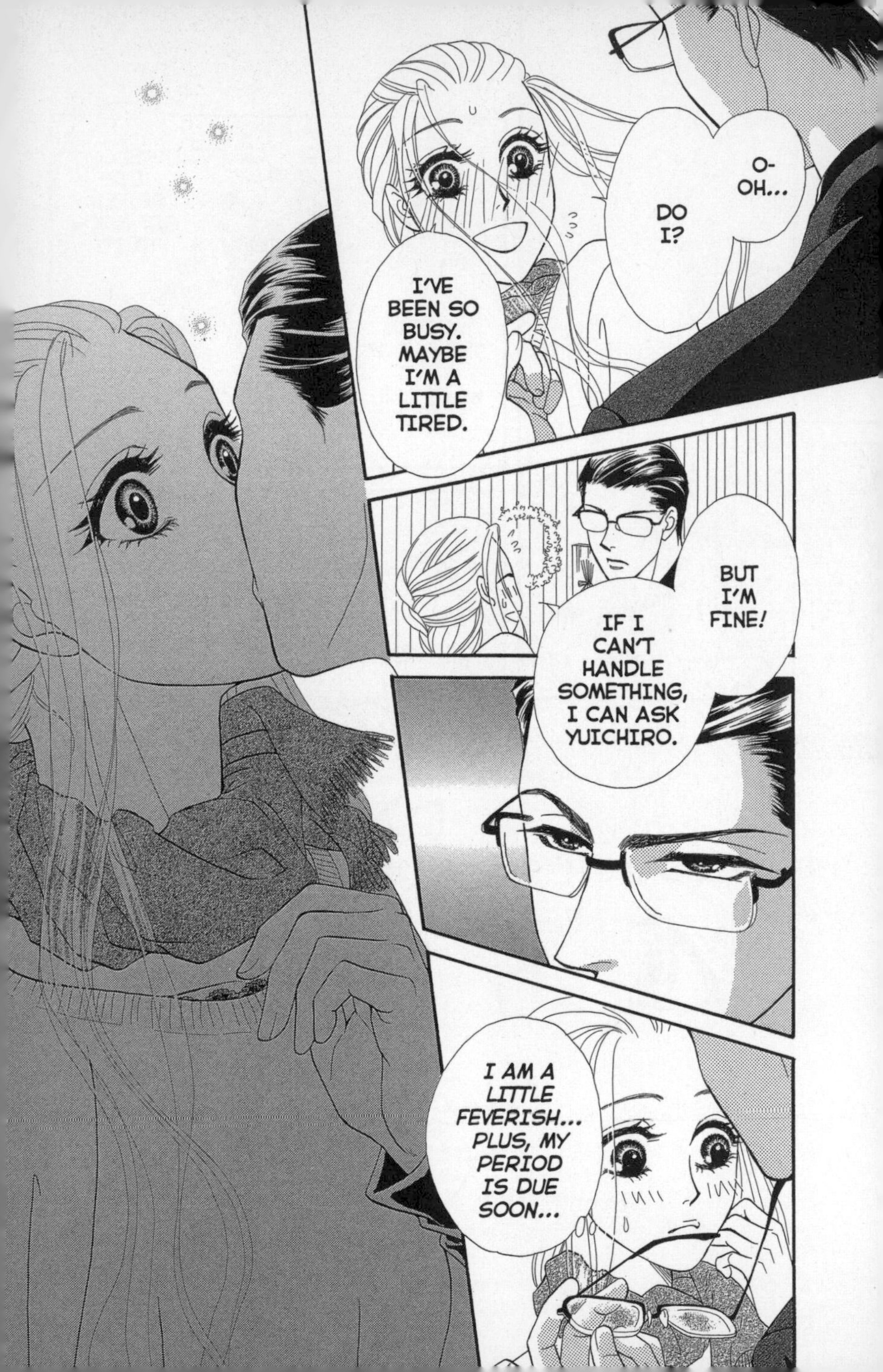
O-OH...
DO I?
I'VE BEEN SO BUSY. MAYBE I'M A LITTLE TIRED.
BUT I'M FINE!
IF I CAN'T HANDLE SOMETHING, I CAN ASK YUICHIRO.
I AM A LITTLE FEVERISH... PLUS, MY PERIOD IS DUE SOON...

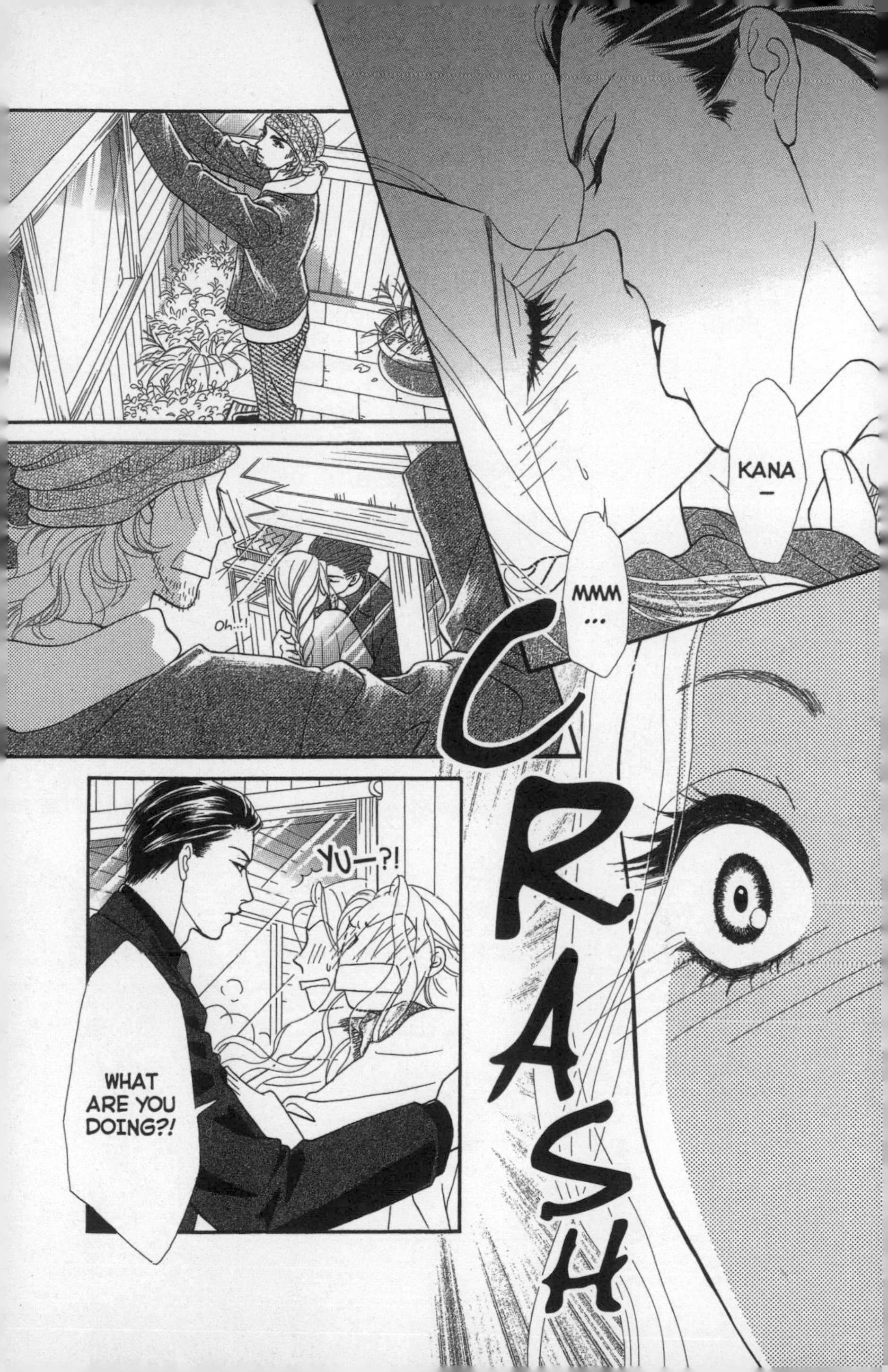
KANA —
MMM...
Oh...!
CRASH
YU—?!
WHAT ARE YOU DOING?!

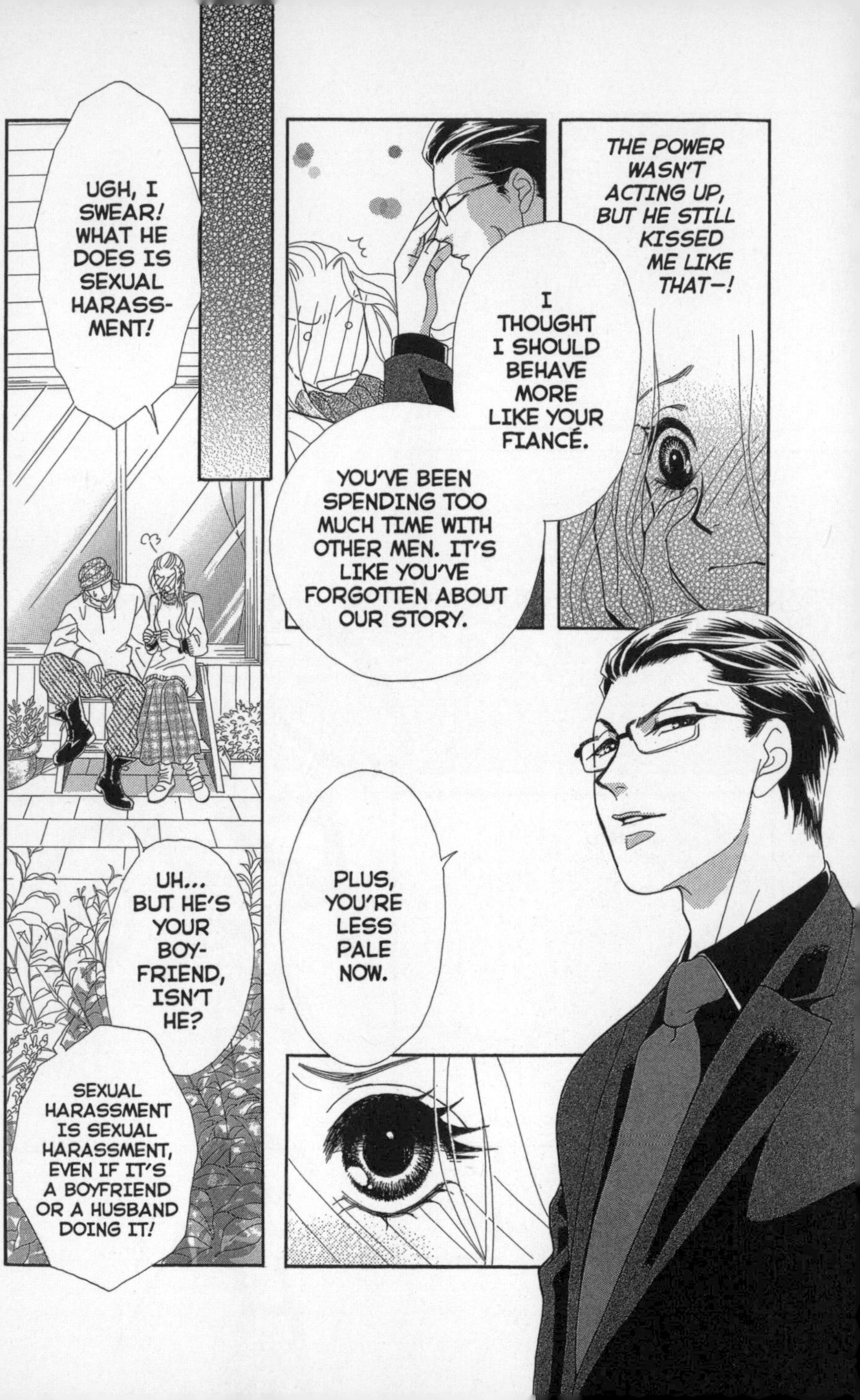
THE POWER WASN'T ACTING UP, BUT HE STILL KISSED ME LIKE THAT—!
I THOUGHT I SHOULD BEHAVE MORE LIKE YOUR FIANCÉ.
YOU'VE BEEN SPENDING TOO MUCH TIME WITH OTHER MEN. IT'S LIKE YOU'VE FORGOTTEN ABOUT OUR STORY.
PLUS, YOU'RE LESS PALE NOW.
UGH, I SWEAR! WHAT HE DOES IS SEXUAL HARASS-MENT!
UH... BUT HE'S YOUR BOY-FRIEND, ISN'T HE?
SEXUAL HARASSMENT IS SEXUAL HARASSMENT, EVEN IF IT'S A BOYFRIEND OR A HUSBAND DOING IT!

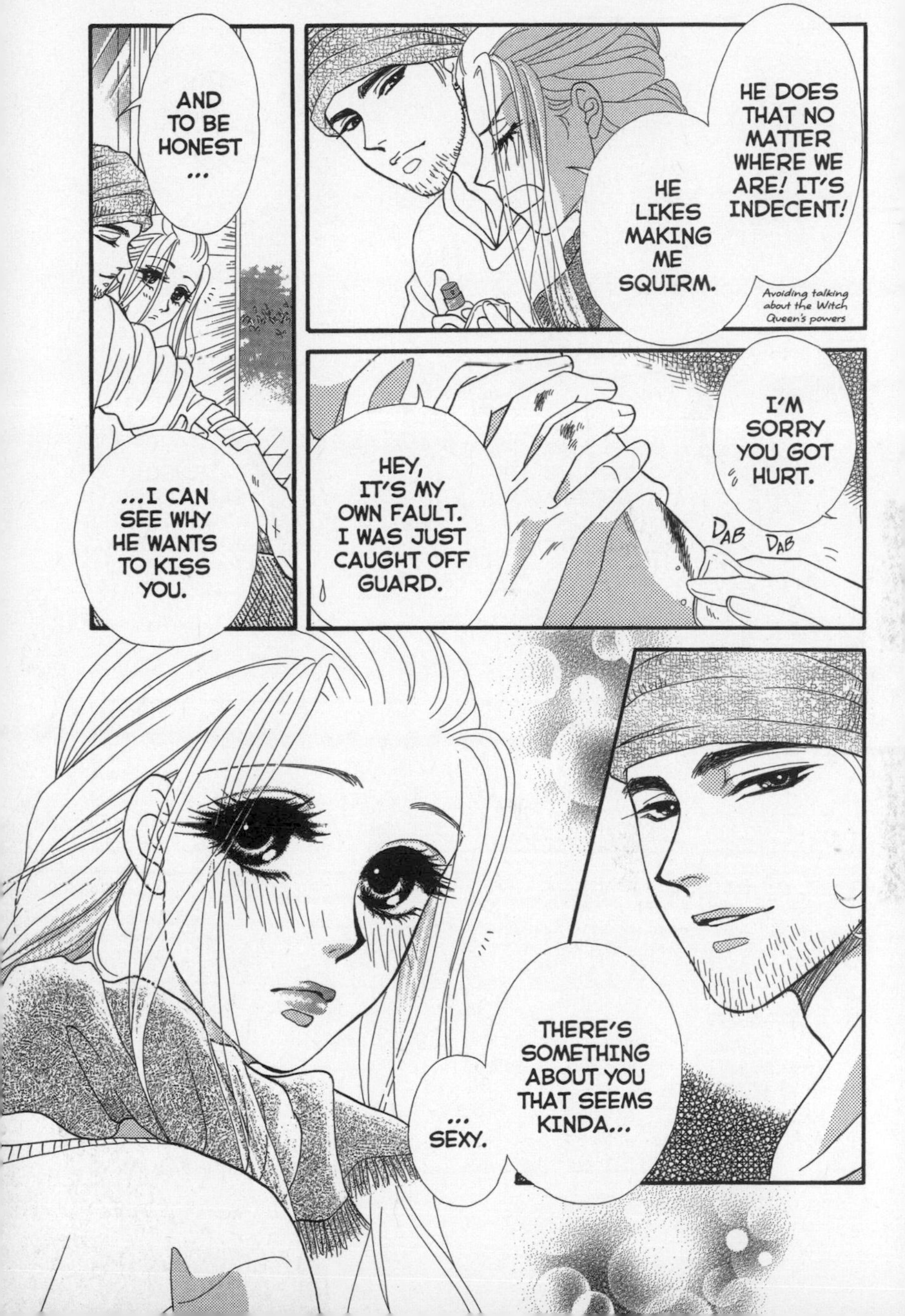
HE DOES THAT NO MATTER WHERE WE ARE! IT'S INDECENT!
HE LIKES MAKING ME SQUIRM.
Avoiding talking about the Witch Queen's powers
I'M SORRY YOU GOT HURT.
DAB DAB
HEY, IT'S MY OWN FAULT. I WAS JUST CAUGHT OFF GUARD.
AND TO BE HONEST ...
...I CAN SEE WHY HE WANTS TO KISS YOU.
THERE'S SOMETHING ABOUT YOU THAT SEEMS KINDA...
... SEXY.

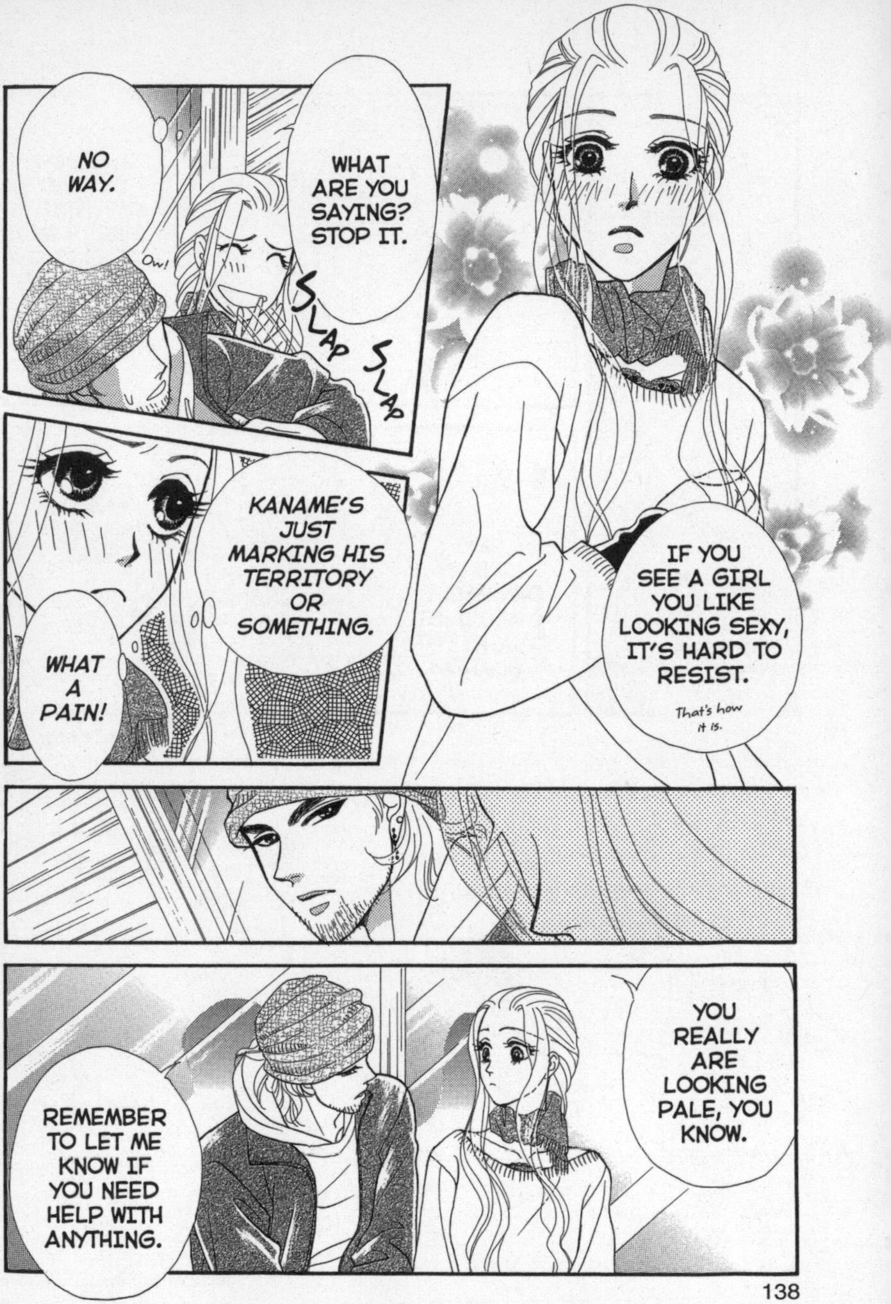
IF YOU SEE A GIRL YOU LIKE LOOKING SEXY, IT'S HARD TO RESIST.
That's how it is.
WHAT ARE YOU SAYING? STOP IT.
NO WAY.
Ow!
SLAP SLAP
KANAME'S JUST MARKING HIS TERRITORY OR SOMETHING.
WHAT A PAIN!
YOU REALLY ARE LOOKING PALE, YOU KNOW.
REMEMBER TO LET ME KNOW IF YOU NEED HELP WITH ANYTHING.

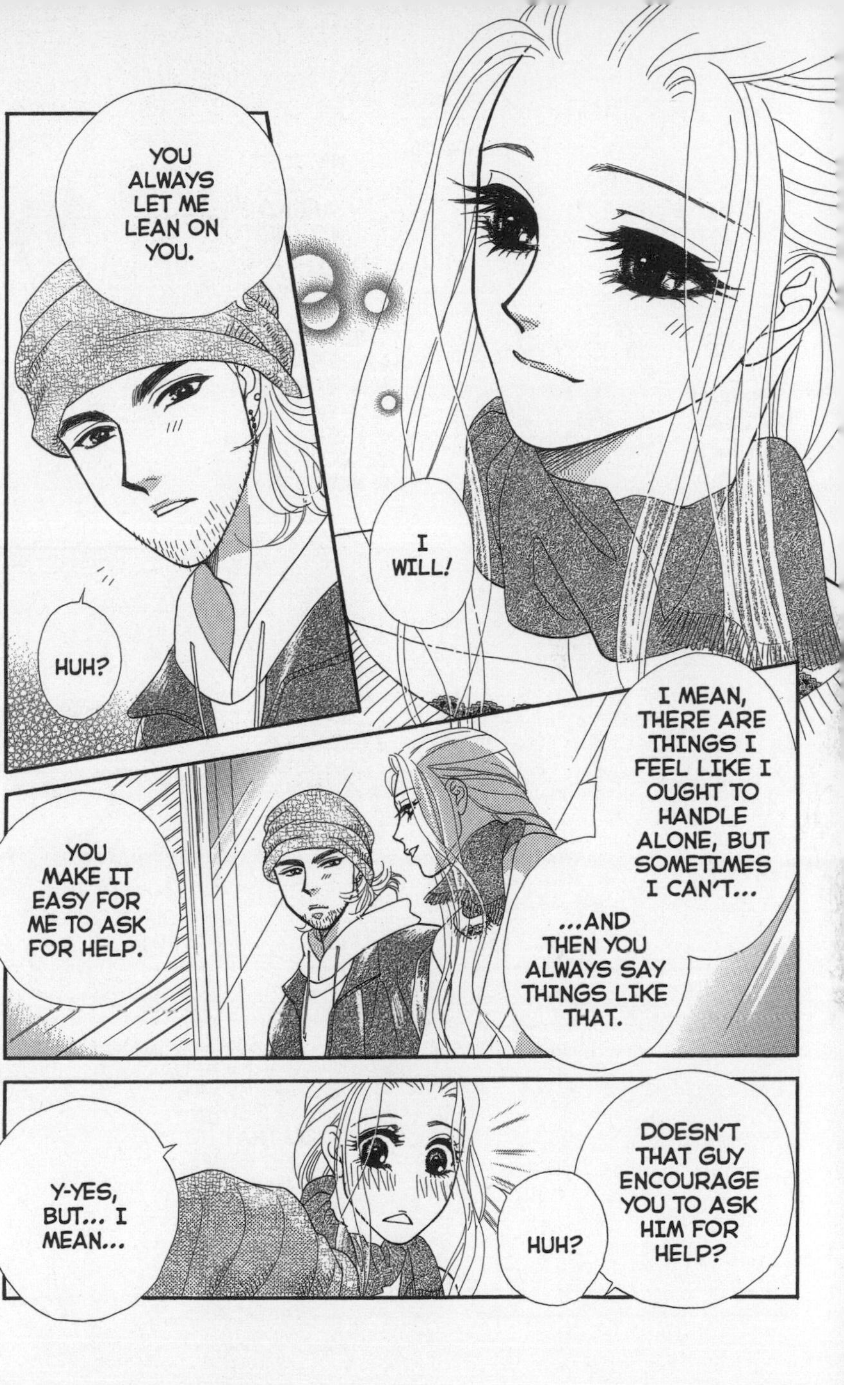
I WILL!
YOU ALWAYS LET ME LEAN ON YOU.
HUH?
I MEAN, THERE ARE THINGS I FEEL LIKE I OUGHT TO HANDLE ALONE, BUT SOMETIMES I CAN'T...
...AND THEN YOU ALWAYS SAY THINGS LIKE THAT.
YOU MAKE IT EASY FOR ME TO ASK FOR HELP.
DOESN'T THAT GUY ENCOURAGE YOU TO ASK HIM FOR HELP?
HUH?
Y-YES, BUT... I MEAN...

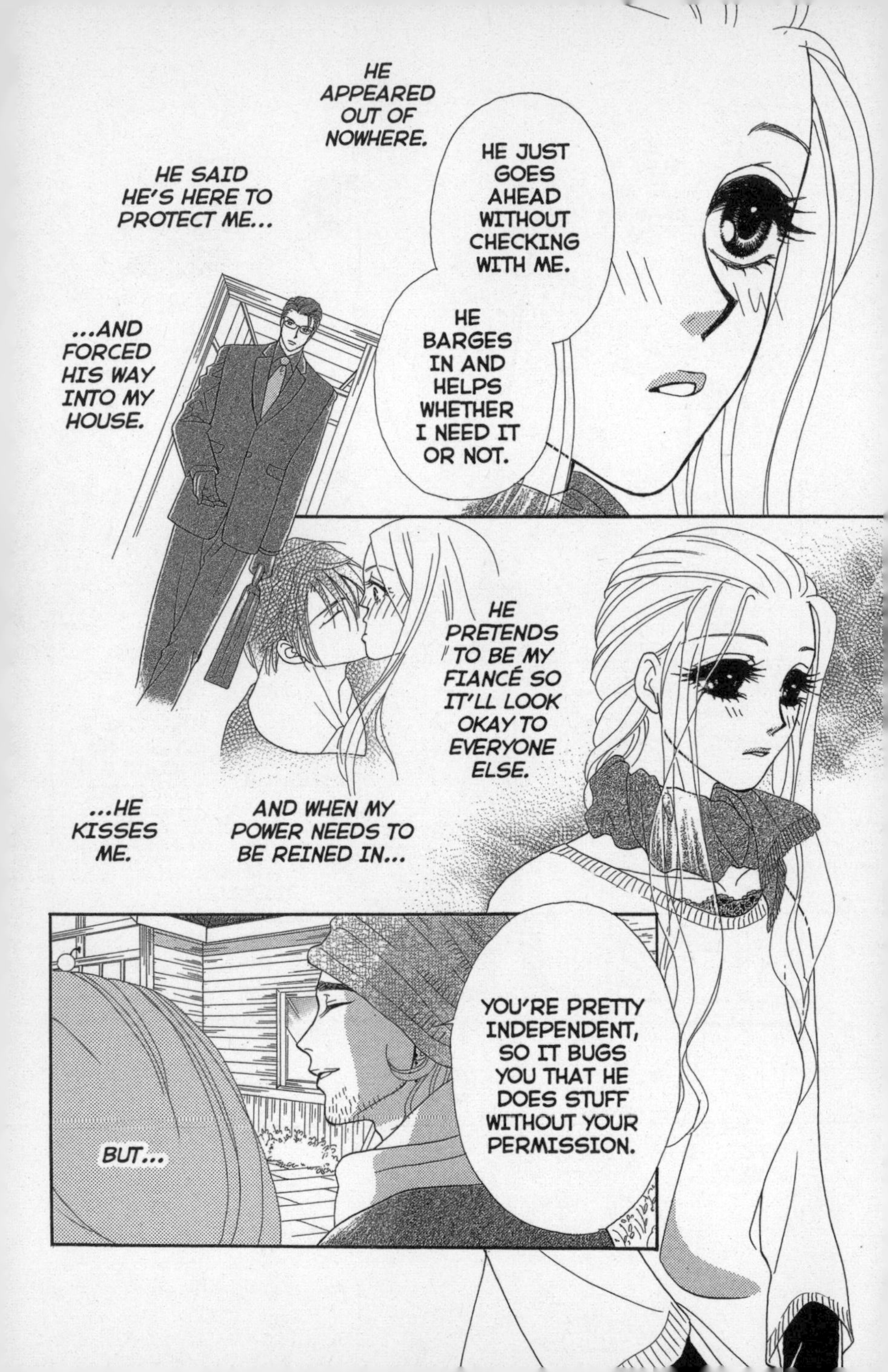
HE APPEARED OUT OF NOWHERE.
HE SAID HE'S HERE TO PROTECT ME...
...AND FORCED HIS WAY INTO MY HOUSE.
HE JUST GOES AHEAD WITHOUT CHECKING WITH ME.
HE BARGES IN AND HELPS WHETHER I NEED IT OR NOT.
HE PRETENDS TO BE MY FIANCÉ SO IT'LL LOOK OKAY TO EVERYONE ELSE.
AND WHEN MY POWER NEEDS TO BE REINED IN...
...HE KISSES ME.
YOU'RE PRETTY INDEPENDENT, SO IT BUGS YOU THAT HE DOES STUFF WITHOUT YOUR PERMISSION.
BUT...

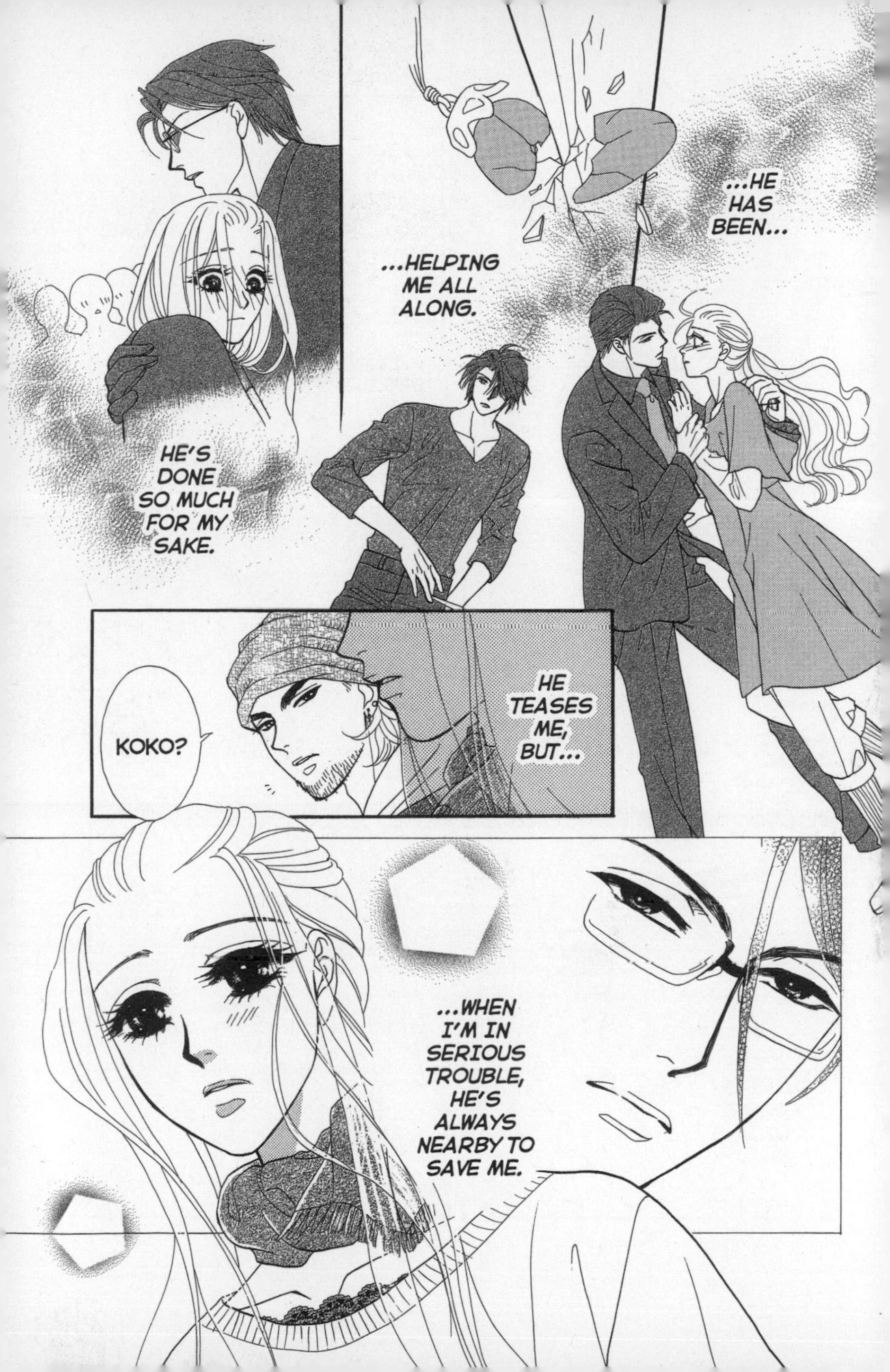
...HE HAS BEEN...
...HELPING ME ALL ALONG.
HE'S DONE SO MUCH FOR MY SAKE.
HE TEASES ME, BUT...
KOKO?
...WHEN I'M IN SERIOUS TROUBLE, HE'S ALWAYS NEARBY TO SAVE ME.

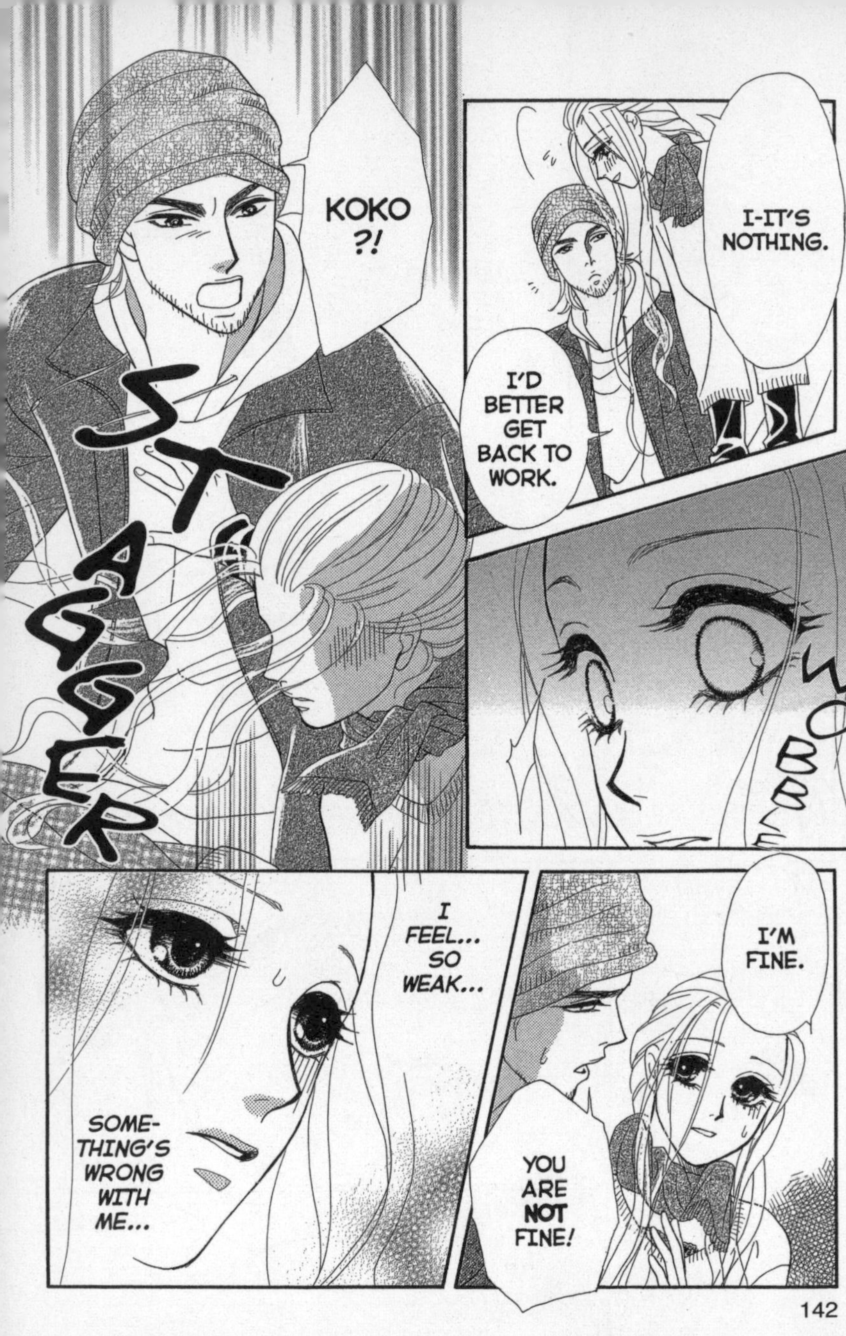
I-IT'S NOTHING.
I'D BETTER GET BACK TO WORK.
WOBBLE
KOKO ?!
STAGGER
I'M FINE.
YOU ARE **NOT** FINE!
I FEEL... SO WEAK...
SOME-THING'S WRONG WITH ME...

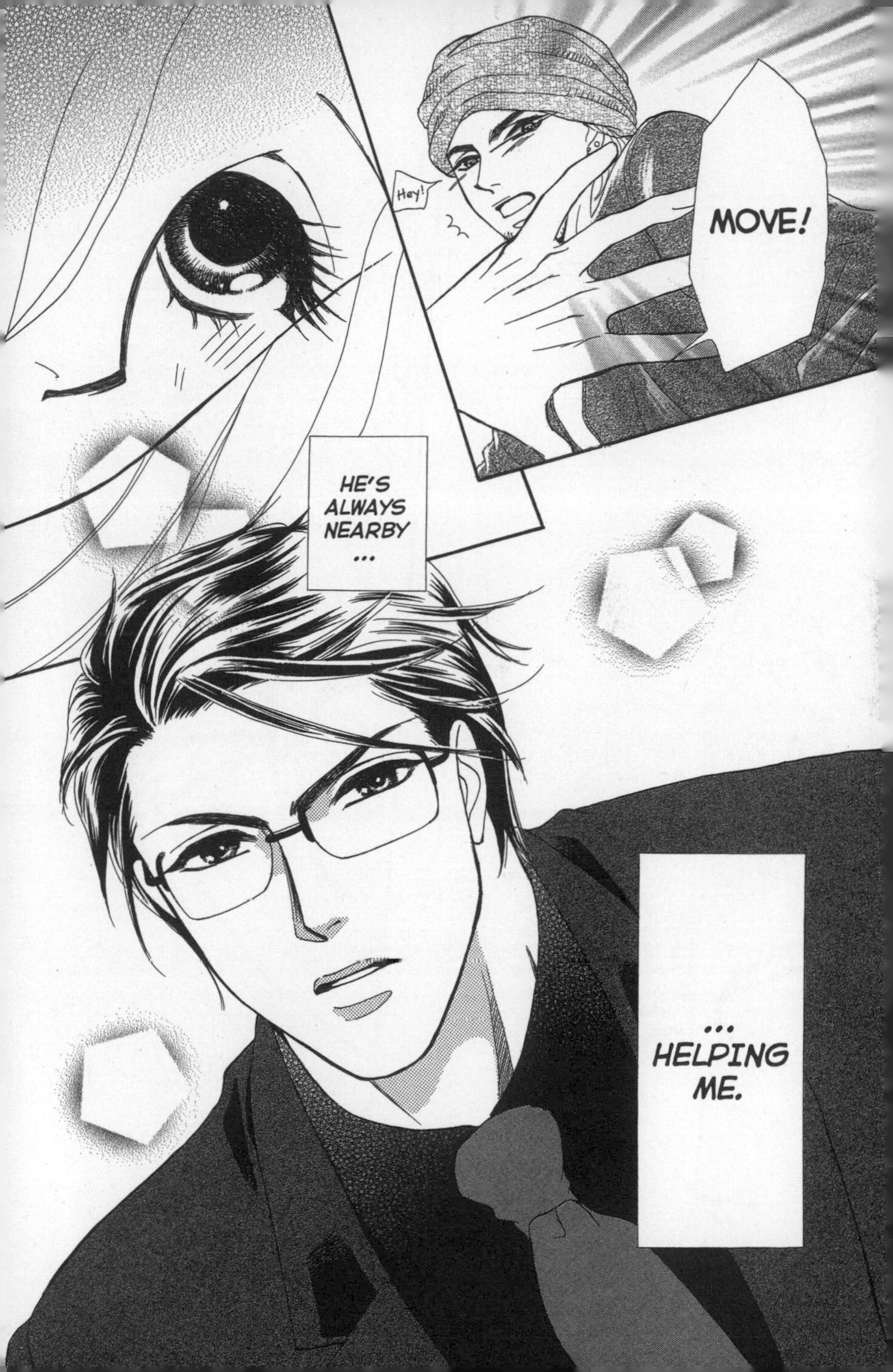
MOVE!
Hey!
HE'S ALWAYS NEARBY ...
... HELPING ME.

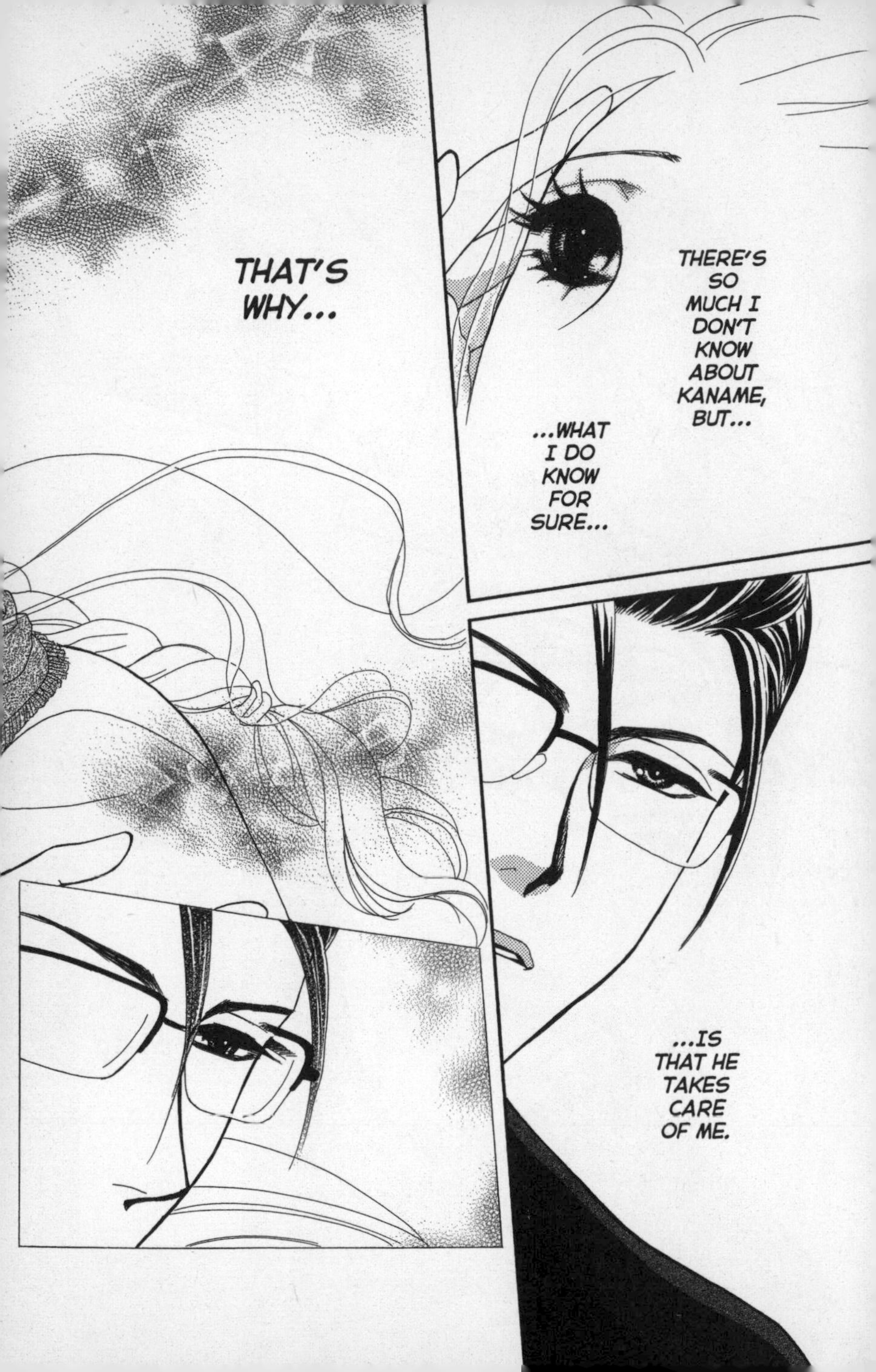
THERE'S SO MUCH I DON'T KNOW ABOUT KANAME, BUT...
...WHAT I DO KNOW FOR SURE...
...IS THAT HE TAKES CARE OF ME.
THAT'S WHY...

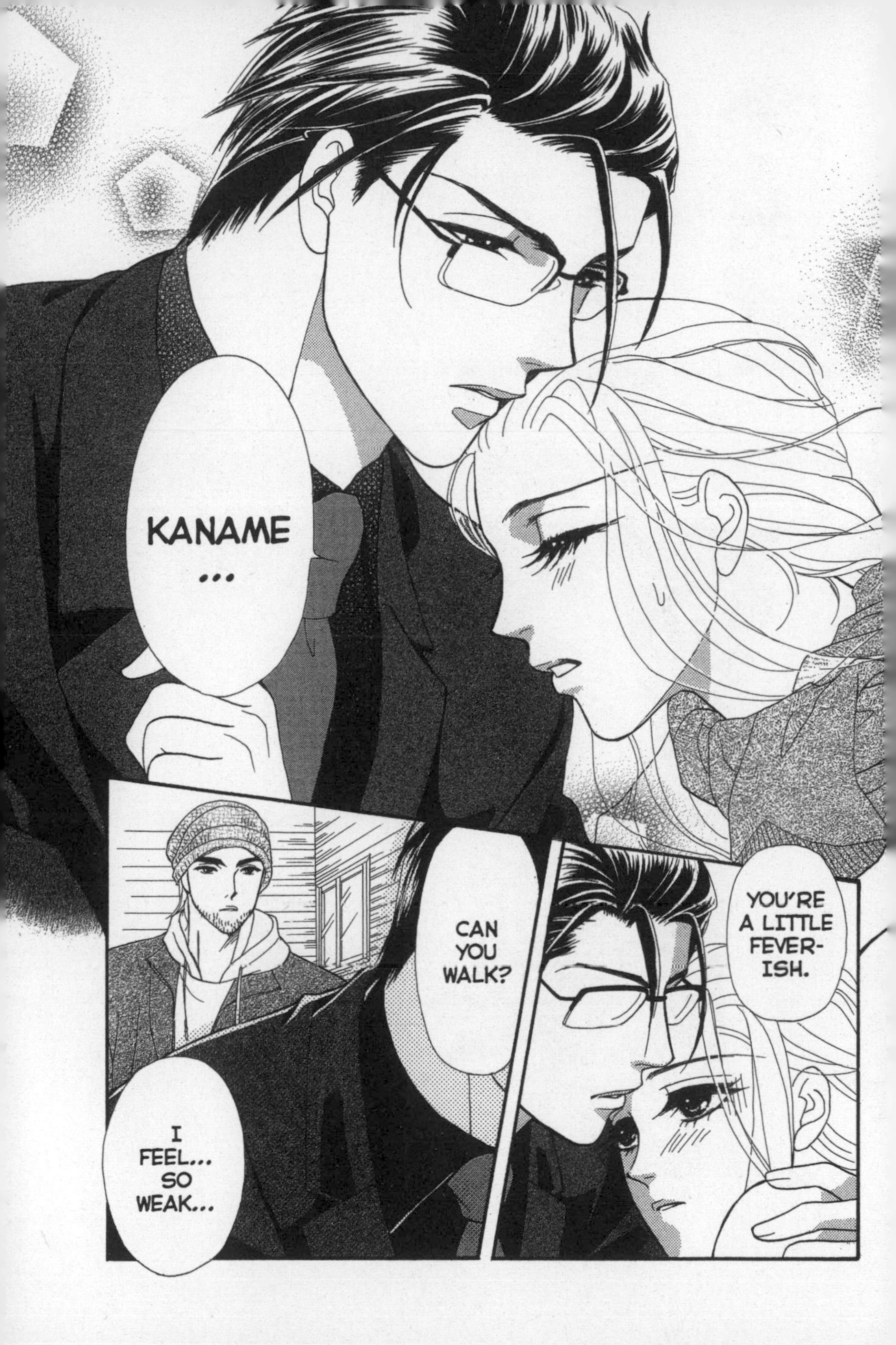
KANAME ...
YOU'RE A LITTLE FEVER-ISH.
CAN YOU WALK?
I FEEL... SO WEAK...

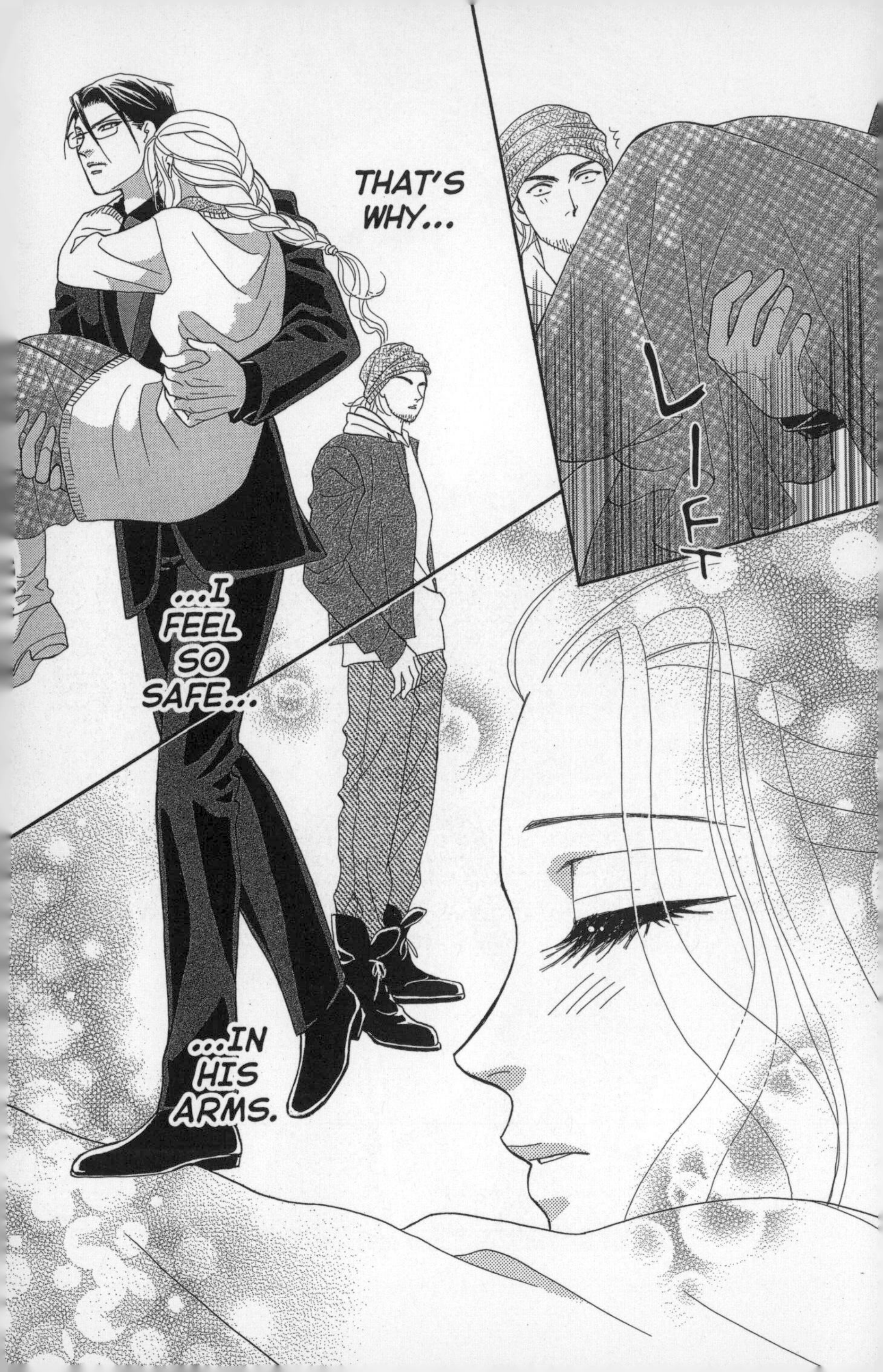
LIFT
THAT'S WHY...
...I FEEL SO SAFE...
...IN HIS ARMS.

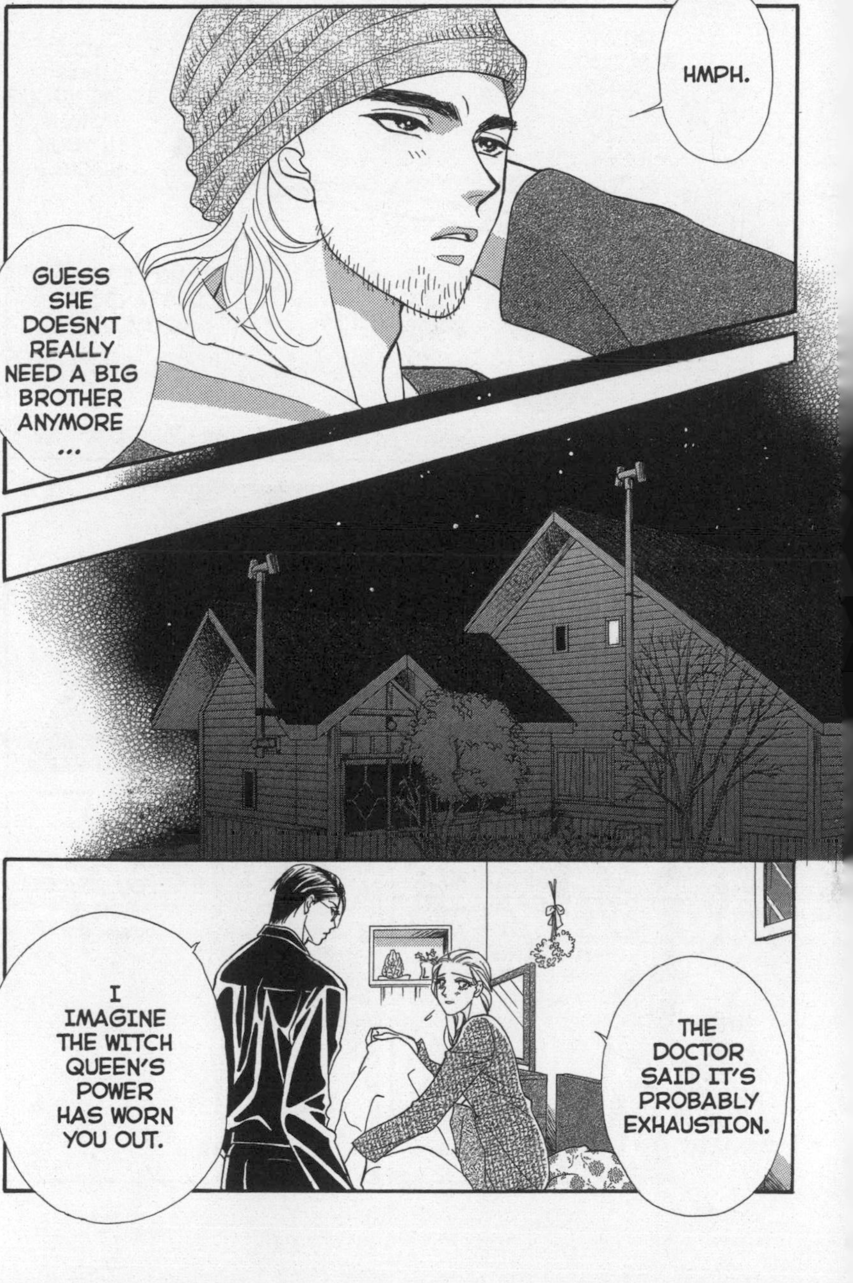
HMPH.
GUESS SHE DOESN'T REALLY NEED A BIG BROTHER ANYMORE...
THE DOCTOR SAID IT'S PROBABLY EXHAUSTION.
I IMAGINE THE WITCH QUEEN'S POWER HAS WORN YOU OUT.

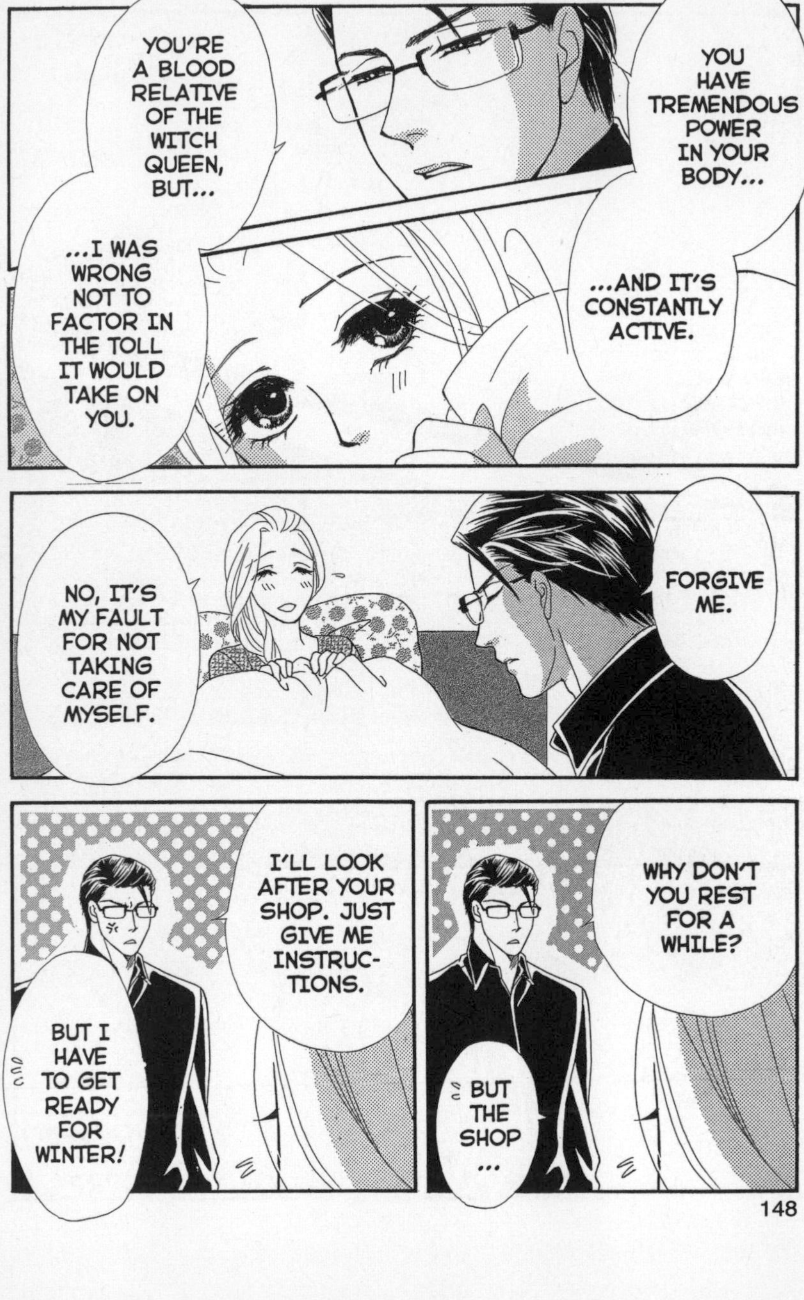
YOU HAVE TREMENDOUS POWER IN YOUR BODY...
...AND IT'S CONSTANTLY ACTIVE.
YOU'RE A BLOOD RELATIVE OF THE WITCH QUEEN, BUT...
...I WAS WRONG NOT TO FACTOR IN THE TOLL IT WOULD TAKE ON YOU.
FORGIVE ME.
NO, IT'S MY FAULT FOR NOT TAKING CARE OF MYSELF.
WHY DON'T YOU REST FOR A WHILE?
BUT THE SHOP ...
I'LL LOOK AFTER YOUR SHOP. JUST GIVE ME INSTRUC-TIONS.
BUT I HAVE TO GET READY FOR WINTER!

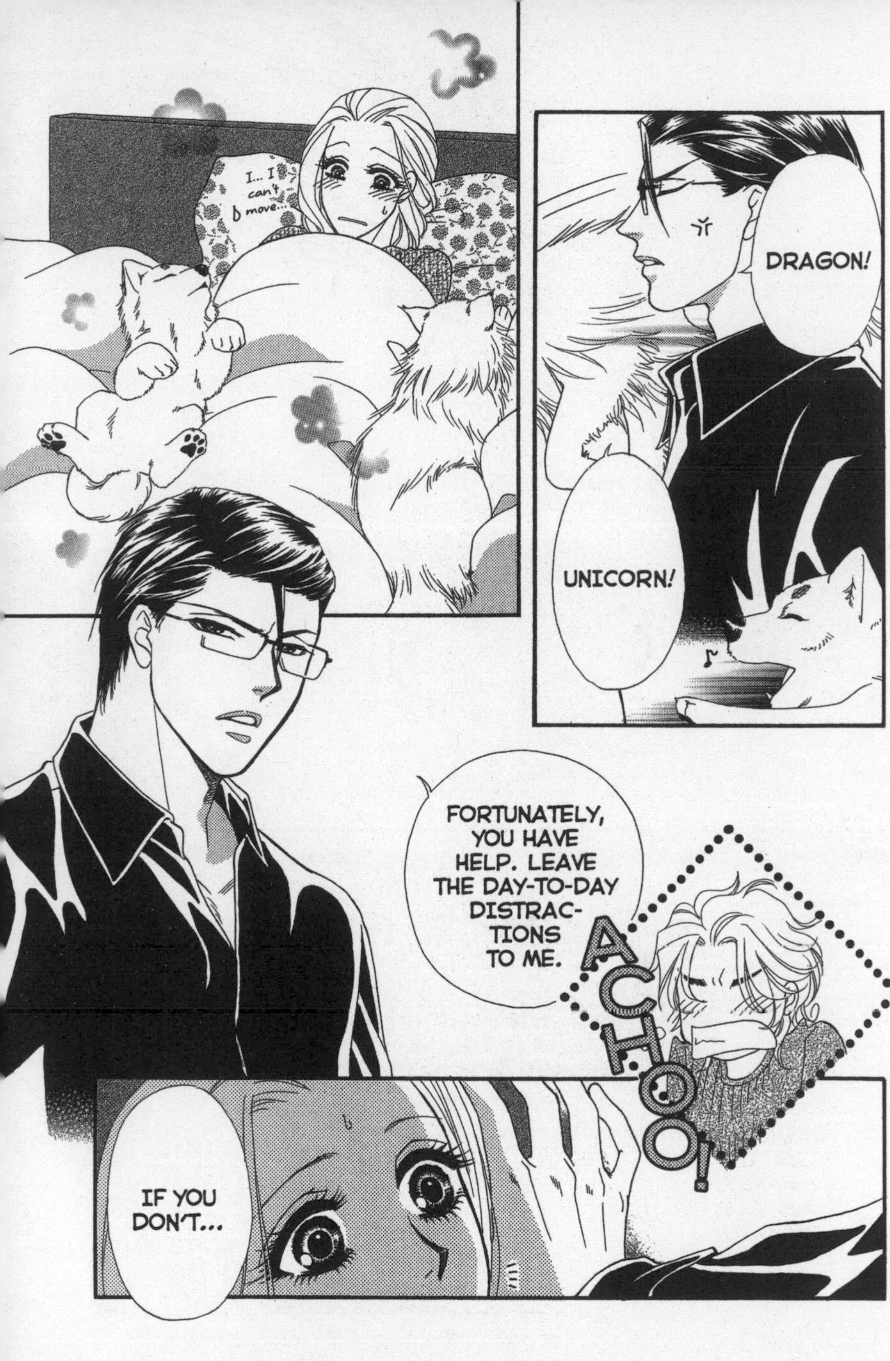
DRAGON!
UNICORN!
I... I can't move...
FORTUNATELY, YOU HAVE HELP. LEAVE THE DAY-TO-DAY DISTRACTIONS TO ME.
ACHOO!
IF YOU DON'T...

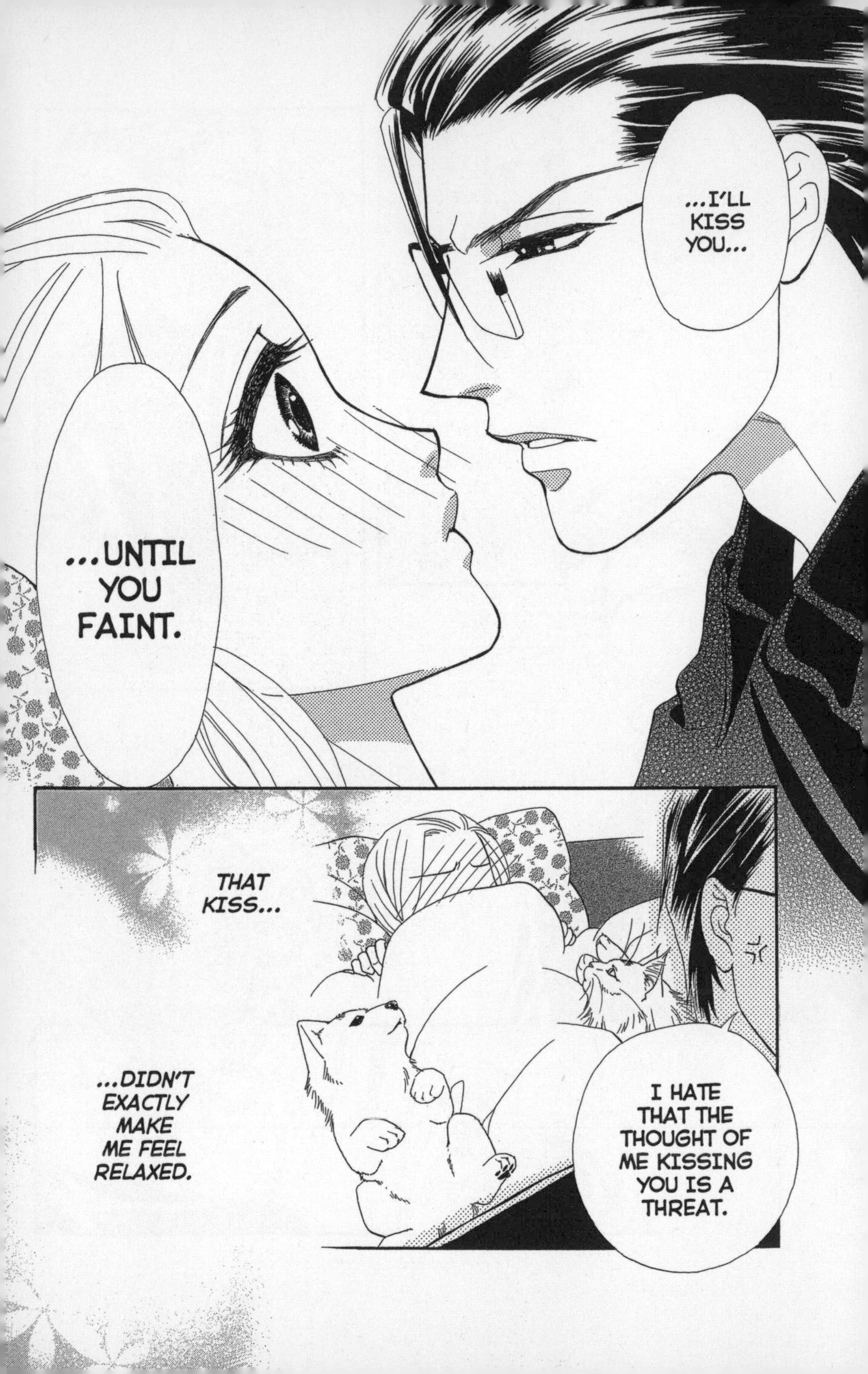
...I'LL KISS YOU...
...UNTIL YOU FAINT.
THAT KISS...
...DIDN'T EXACTLY MAKE ME FEEL RELAXED.
I HATE THAT THE THOUGHT OF ME KISSING YOU IS A THREAT.

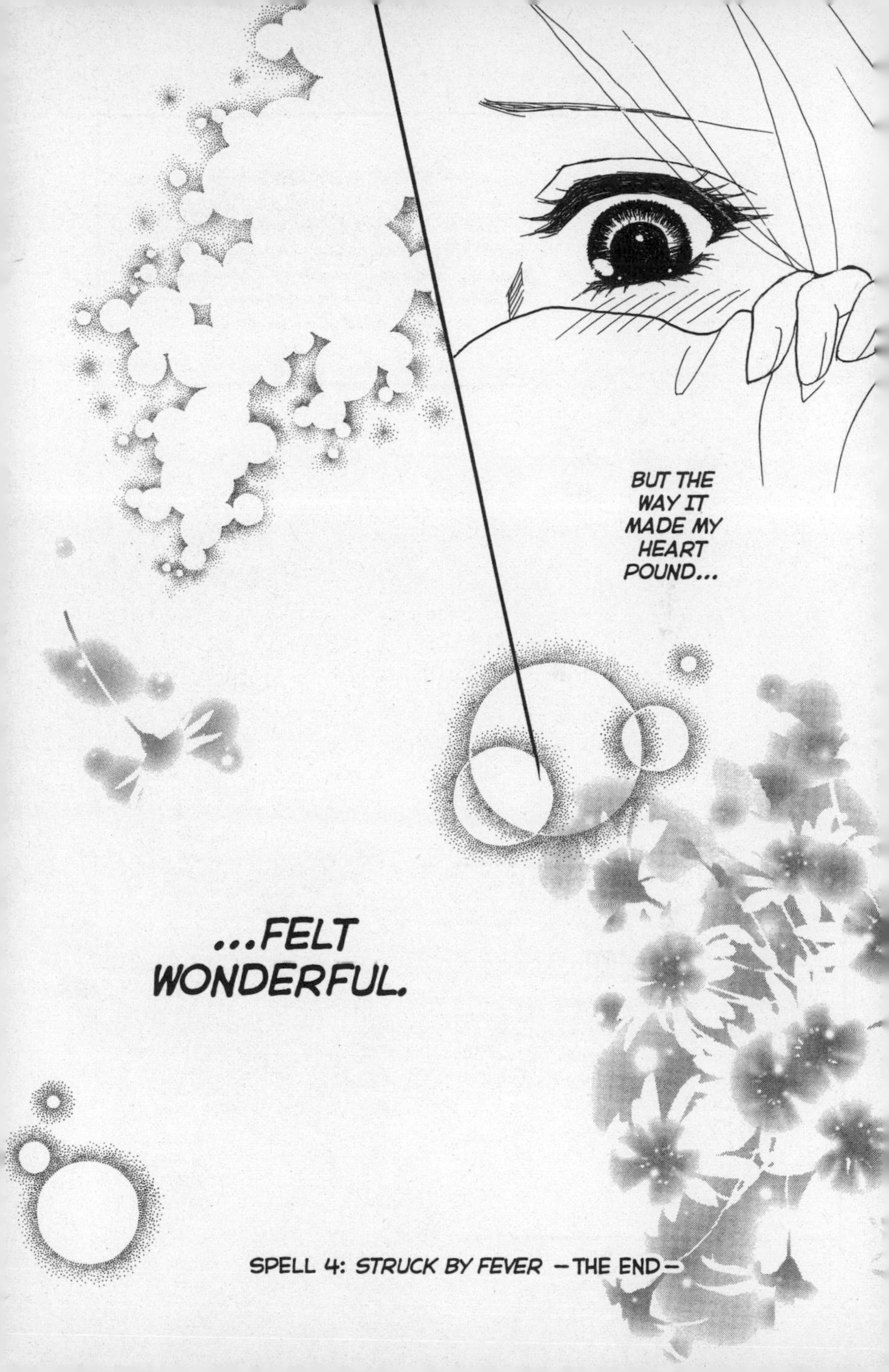
BUT THE WAY IT MADE MY HEART POUND...
...FELT WONDERFUL.
SPELL 4: STRUCK BY FEVER —THE END—

Hey, boy!

SHK SHK SHK SHK

YIp ♡

YIp! ♡

— STRUCK BY FEVER —

Yuichiro seems to get along better with Dragon than with Unicorn or Kitty, probably because Dragon can handle more roughhousing! (Ha ha) Actually, Dragon probably likes it more. (Heh)

— FAMILIARS —

It's so much fun drawing Kitty! But kittens are difficult. It seems easier to draw large animals. But that's okay! Kitty won't be little for long, so I'll have as much fun drawing him as I can!

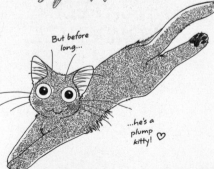

His face was triangular when he was found.

But before long...

...he's a plump kitty! ♡

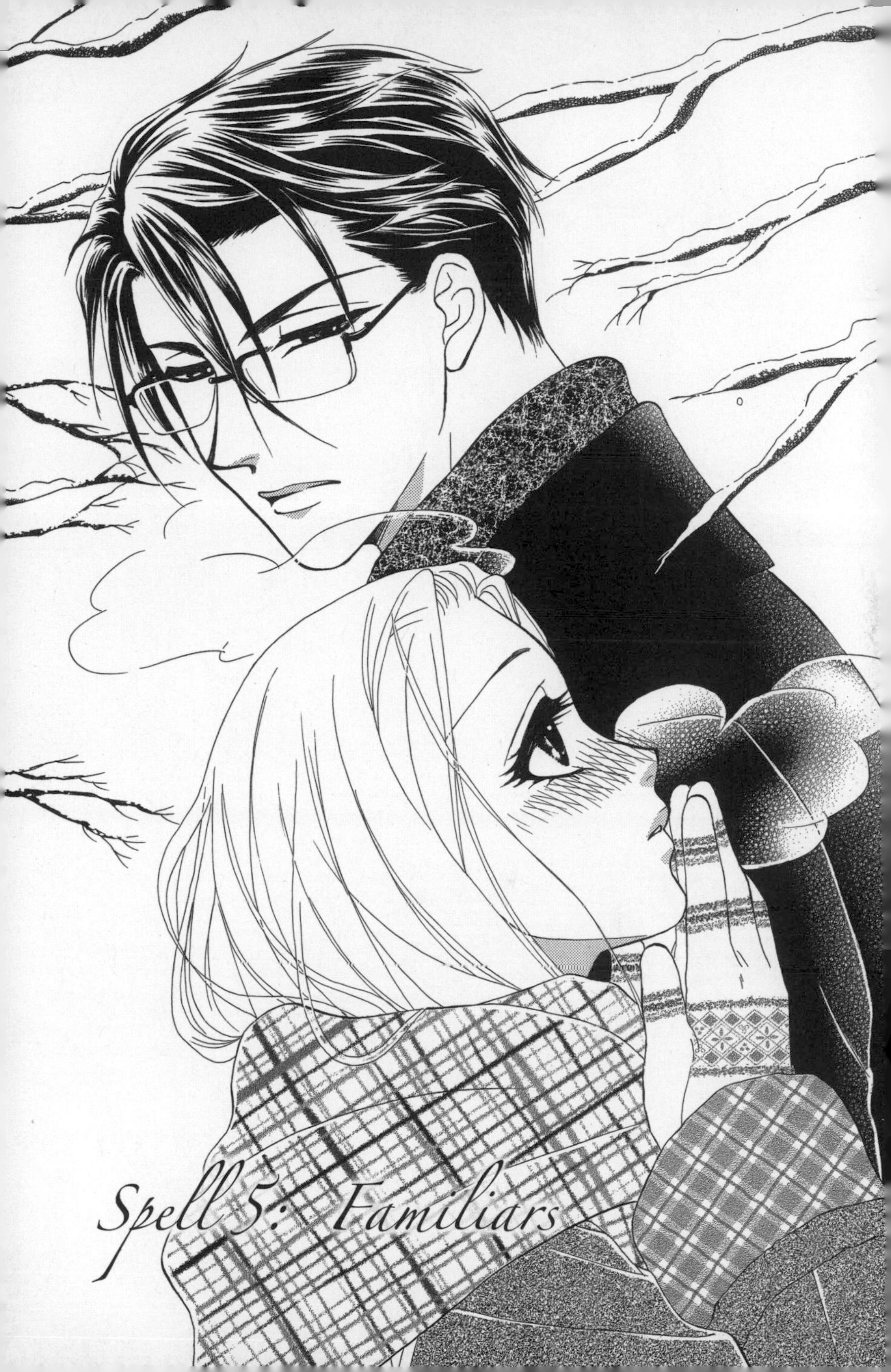
Spell 5: Familiars

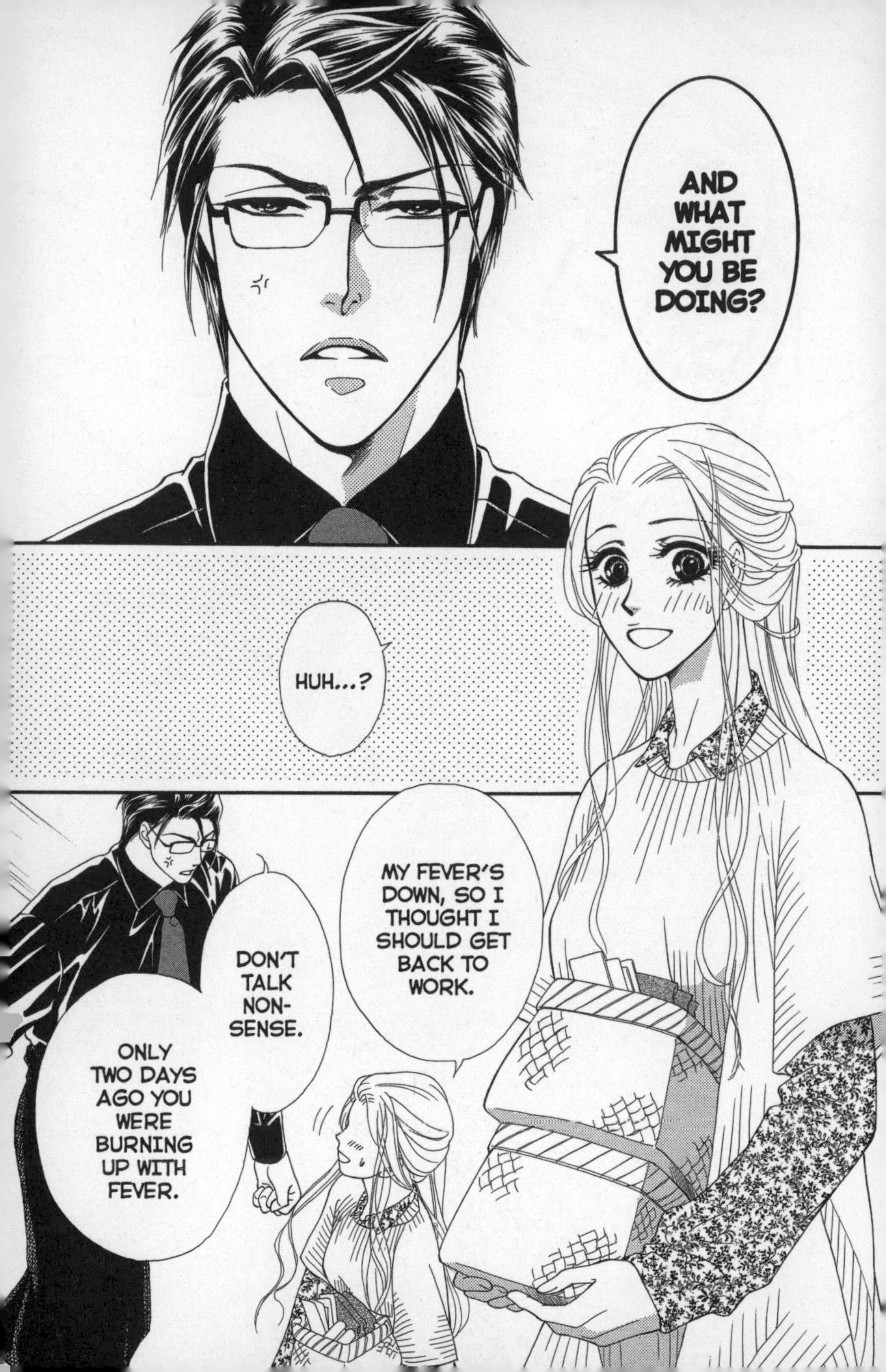
AND WHAT MIGHT YOU BE DOING?
HUH...?
MY FEVER'S DOWN, SO I THOUGHT I SHOULD GET BACK TO WORK.
DON'T TALK NON-SENSE.
ONLY TWO DAYS AGO YOU WERE BURNING UP WITH FEVER.

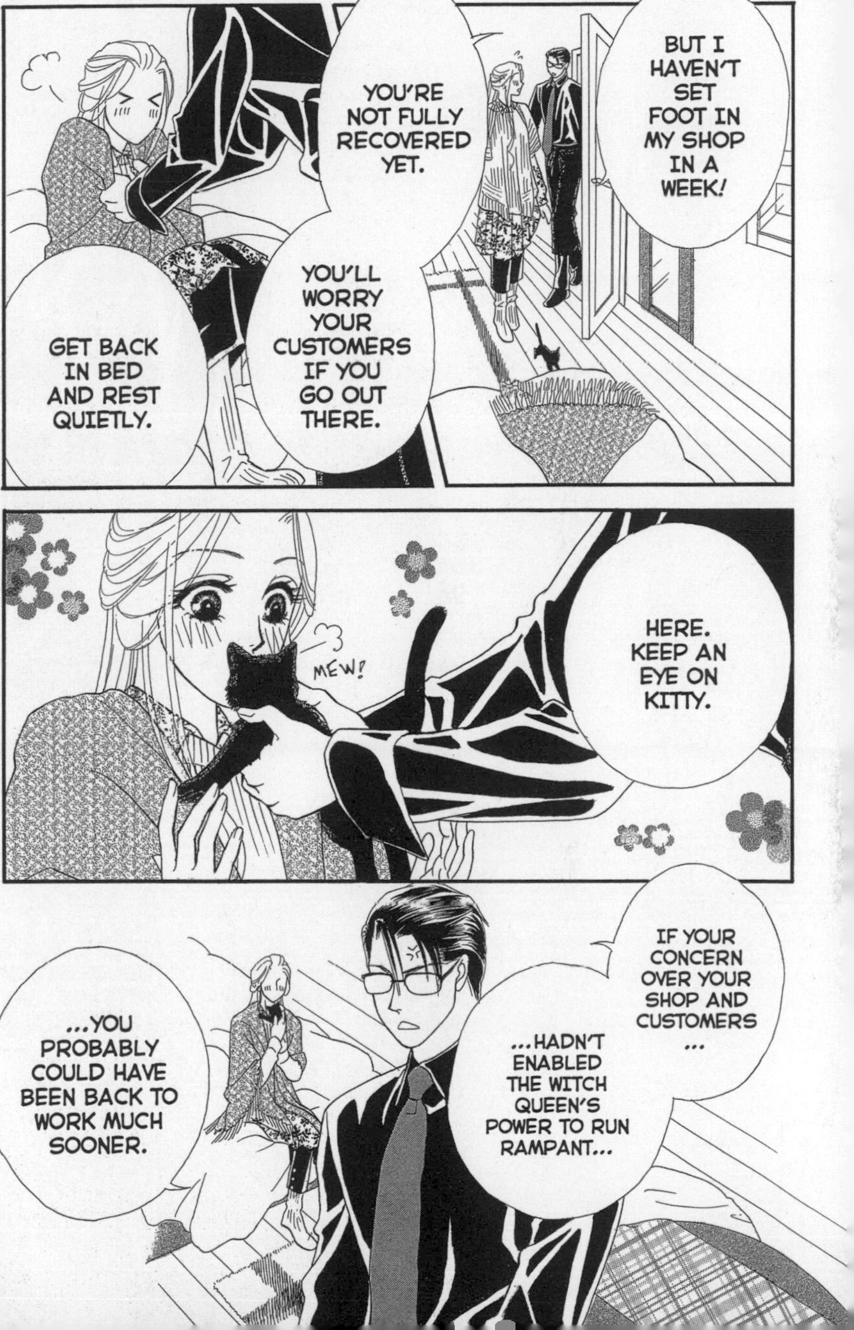
BUT I HAVEN'T SET FOOT IN MY SHOP IN A WEEK!
YOU'RE NOT FULLY RECOVERED YET.
YOU'LL WORRY YOUR CUSTOMERS IF YOU GO OUT THERE.
GET BACK IN BED AND REST QUIETLY.
HERE. KEEP AN EYE ON KITTY.
MEW!
IF YOUR CONCERN OVER YOUR SHOP AND CUSTOMERS ...
...HADN'T ENABLED THE WITCH QUEEN'S POWER TO RUN RAMPANT...
...YOU PROBABLY COULD HAVE BEEN BACK TO WORK MUCH SOONER.

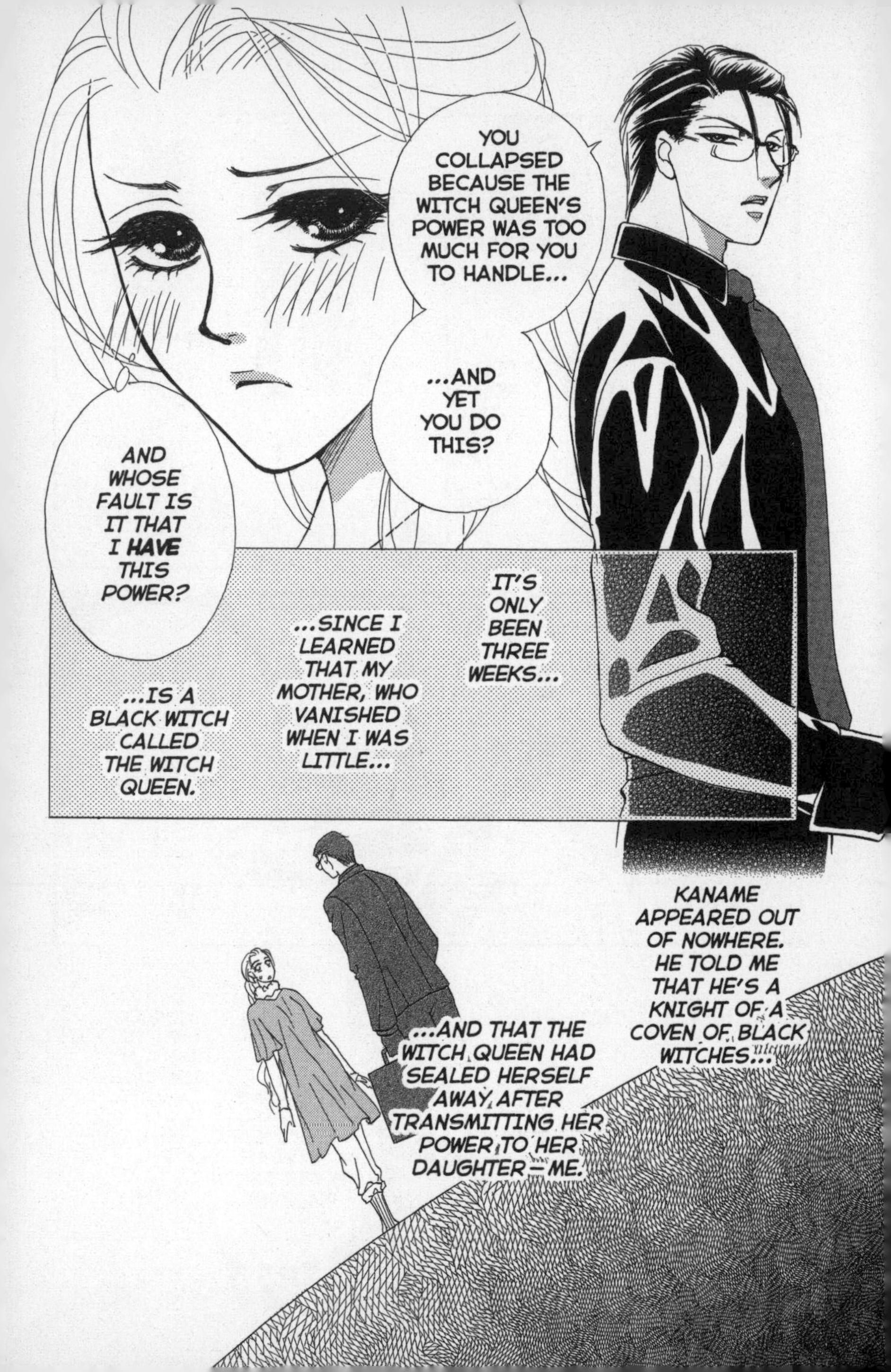
YOU COLLAPSED BECAUSE THE WITCH QUEEN'S POWER WAS TOO MUCH FOR YOU TO HANDLE...
...AND YET YOU DO THIS?
AND WHOSE FAULT IS IT THAT I **HAVE** THIS POWER?
IT'S ONLY BEEN THREE WEEKS...
...SINCE I LEARNED THAT MY MOTHER, WHO VANISHED WHEN I WAS LITTLE...
...IS A BLACK WITCH CALLED THE WITCH QUEEN.
KANAME APPEARED OUT OF NOWHERE. HE TOLD ME THAT HE'S A KNIGHT OF A COVEN OF BLACK WITCHES...
...AND THAT THE WITCH QUEEN HAD SEALED HERSELF AWAY AFTER TRANSMITTING HER POWER TO HER DAUGHTER—ME.

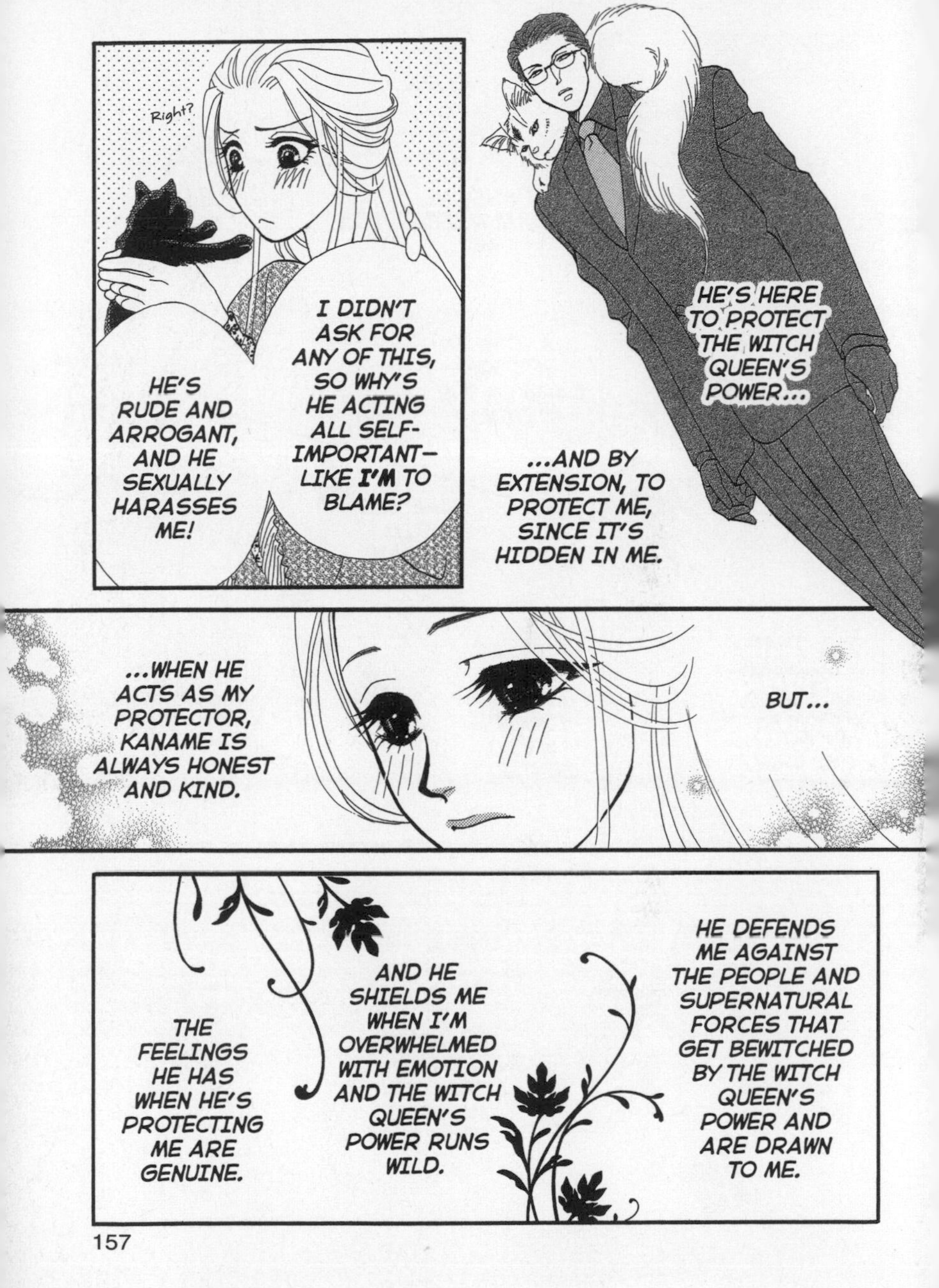
HE'S HERE TO PROTECT THE WITCH QUEEN'S POWER...
...AND BY EXTENSION, TO PROTECT ME, SINCE IT'S HIDDEN IN ME.
I DIDN'T ASK FOR ANY OF THIS, SO WHY'S HE ACTING ALL SELF-IMPORTANT—LIKE **I'M** TO BLAME?
HE'S RUDE AND ARROGANT, AND HE SEXUALLY HARASSES ME!
Right?
BUT...
...WHEN HE ACTS AS MY PROTECTOR, KANAME IS ALWAYS HONEST AND KIND.
HE DEFENDS ME AGAINST THE PEOPLE AND SUPERNATURAL FORCES THAT GET BEWITCHED BY THE WITCH QUEEN'S POWER AND ARE DRAWN TO ME.
AND HE SHIELDS ME WHEN I'M OVERWHELMED WITH EMOTION AND THE WITCH QUEEN'S POWER RUNS WILD.
THE FEELINGS HE HAS WHEN HE'S PROTECTING ME ARE GENUINE.

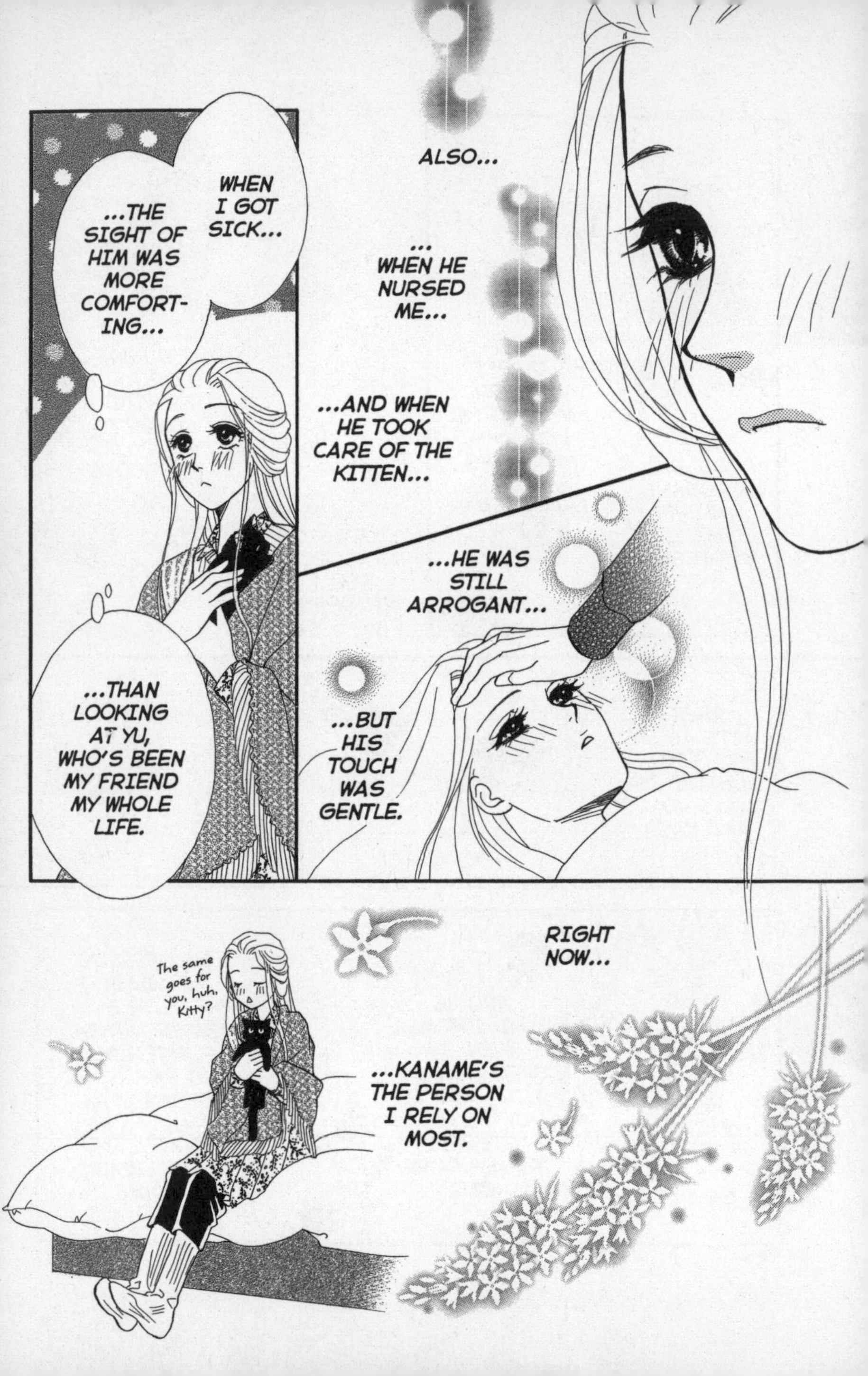
ALSO...
...WHEN HE NURSED ME...
...AND WHEN HE TOOK CARE OF THE KITTEN...
...HE WAS STILL ARROGANT...
...BUT HIS TOUCH WAS GENTLE.
WHEN I GOT SICK...
...THE SIGHT OF HIM WAS MORE COMFORTING...
...THAN LOOKING AT YU, WHO'S BEEN MY FRIEND MY WHOLE LIFE.
RIGHT NOW...
...KANAME'S THE PERSON I RELY ON MOST.
The same goes for you, huh, Kitty?

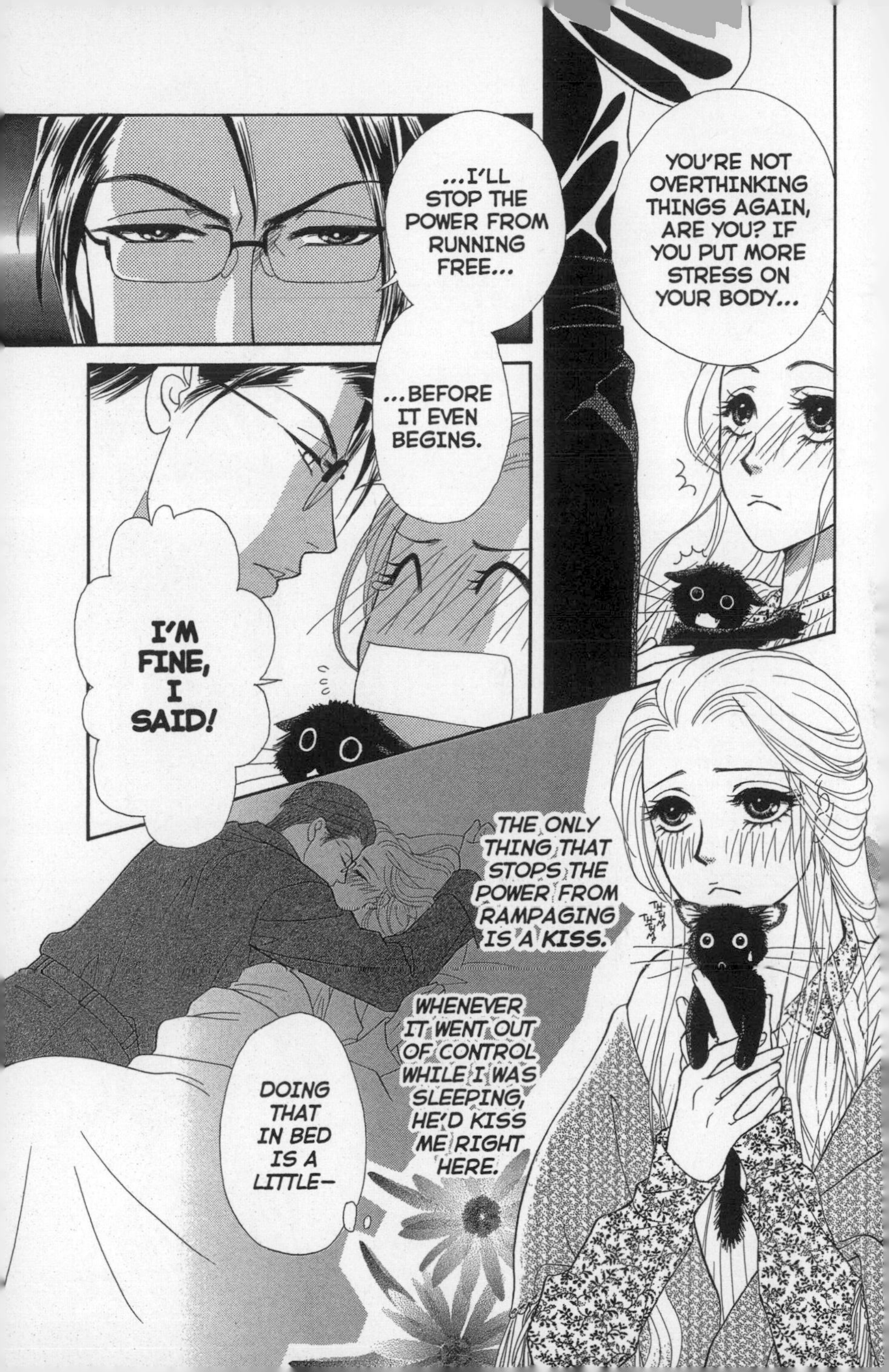
YOU'RE NOT OVERTHINKING THINGS AGAIN, ARE YOU? IF YOU PUT MORE STRESS ON YOUR BODY...
...I'LL STOP THE POWER FROM RUNNING FREE...
...BEFORE IT EVEN BEGINS.
I'M FINE, I SAID!
THE ONLY THING THAT STOPS THE POWER FROM RAMPAGING IS A KISS.
WHENEVER IT WENT OUT OF CONTROL WHILE I WAS SLEEPING, HE'D KISS ME RIGHT HERE.
DOING THAT IN BED IS A LITTLE—

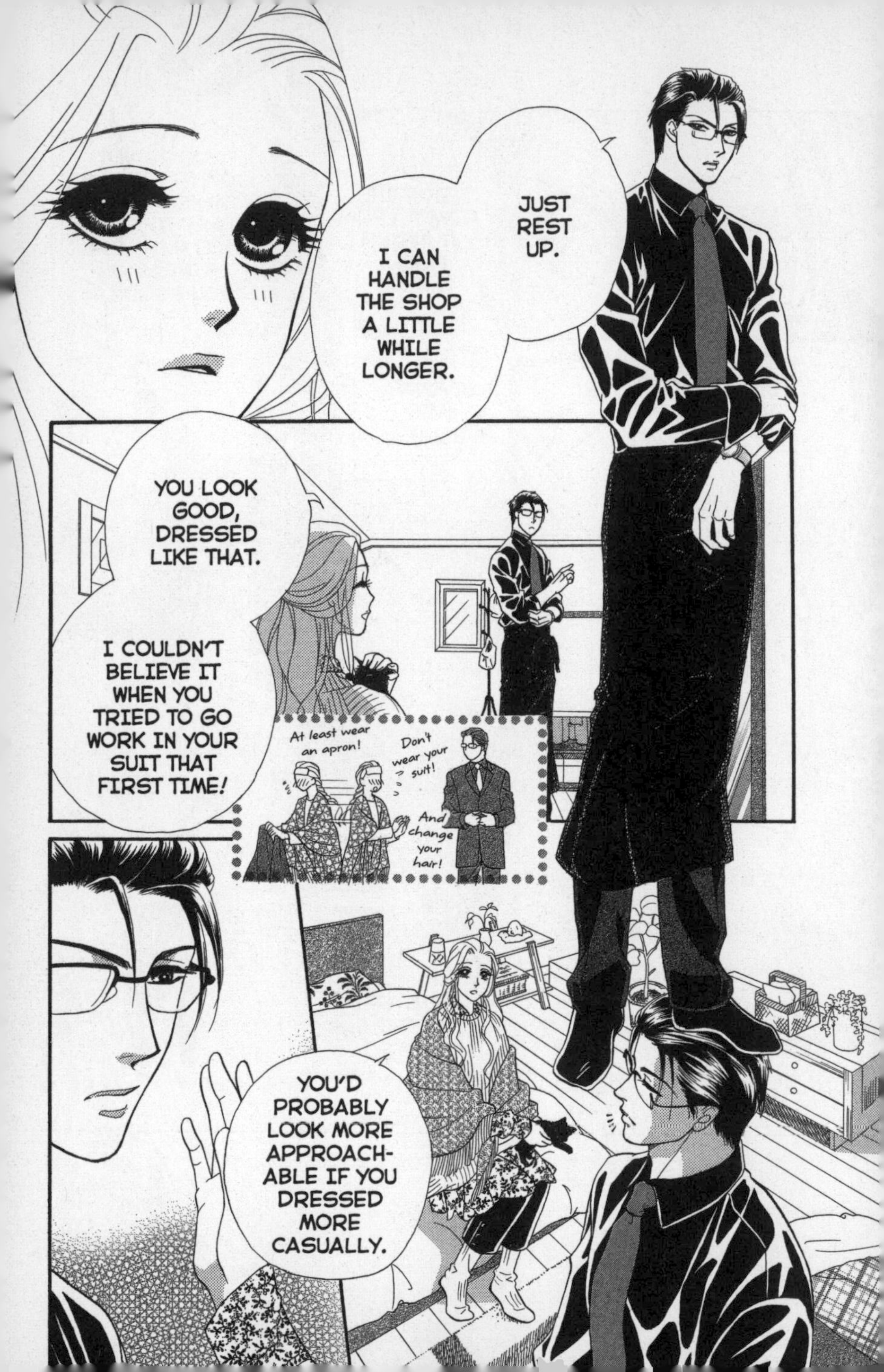
JUST REST UP.
I CAN HANDLE THE SHOP A LITTLE WHILE LONGER.
YOU LOOK GOOD, DRESSED LIKE THAT.
I COULDN'T BELIEVE IT WHEN YOU TRIED TO GO WORK IN YOUR SUIT THAT FIRST TIME!
Don't wear your suit!
And change your hair!
At least wear an apron!
YOU'D PROBABLY LOOK MORE APPROACH-ABLE IF YOU DRESSED MORE CASUALLY.

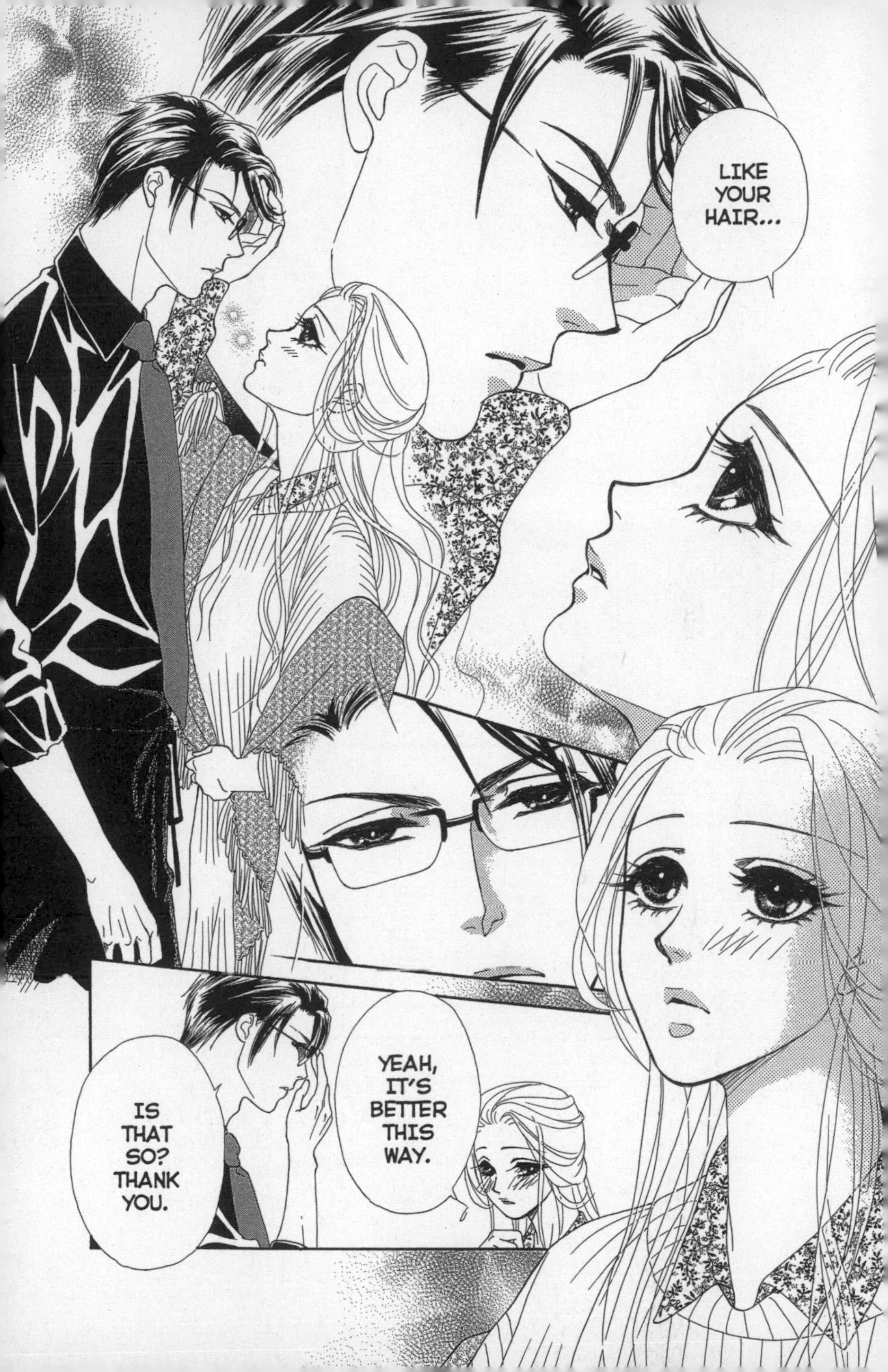
LIKE YOUR HAIR...
YEAH, IT'S BETTER THIS WAY.
IS THAT SO? THANK YOU.

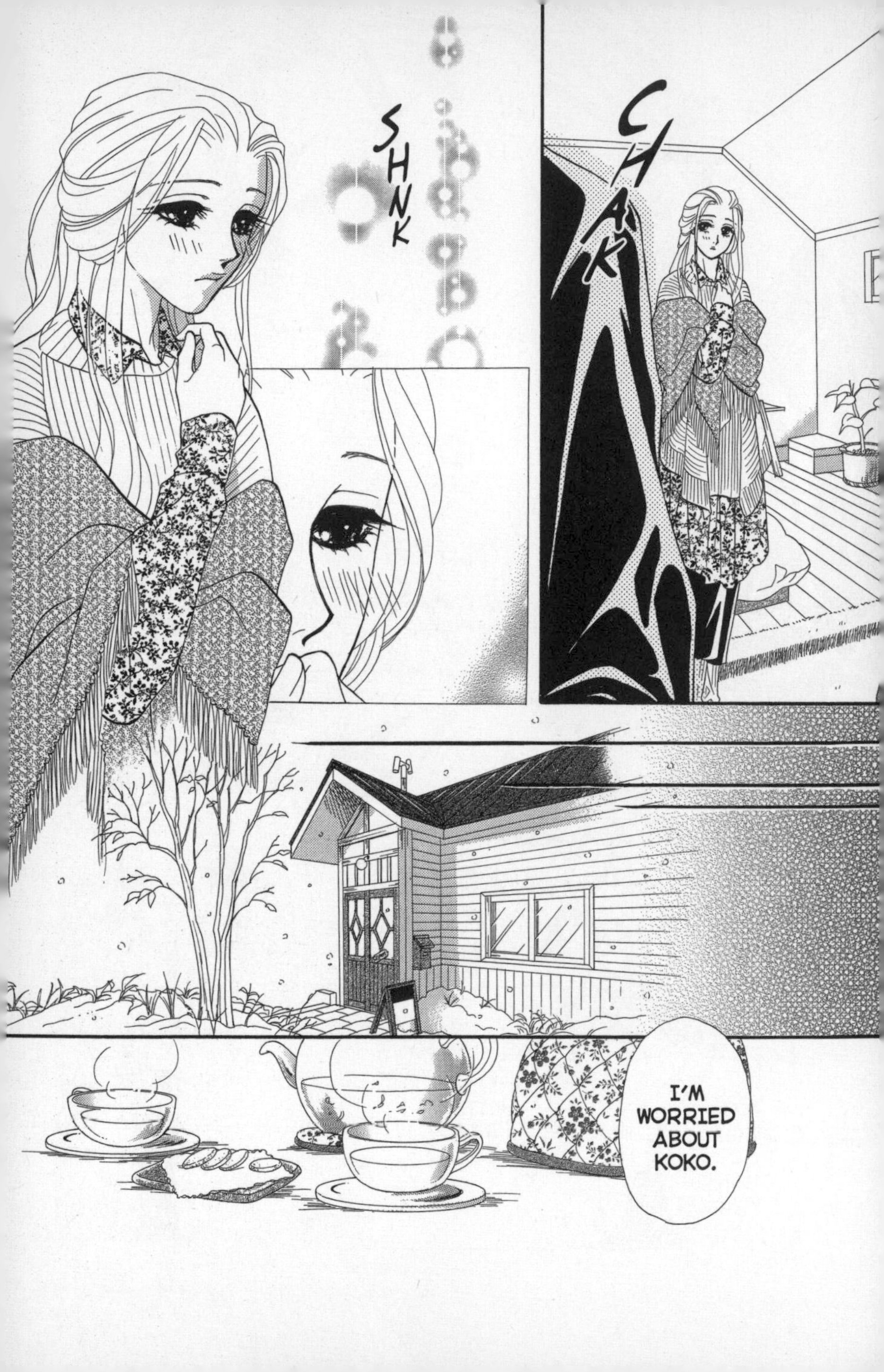
CHAK
SHNK
I'M WORRIED ABOUT KOKO.

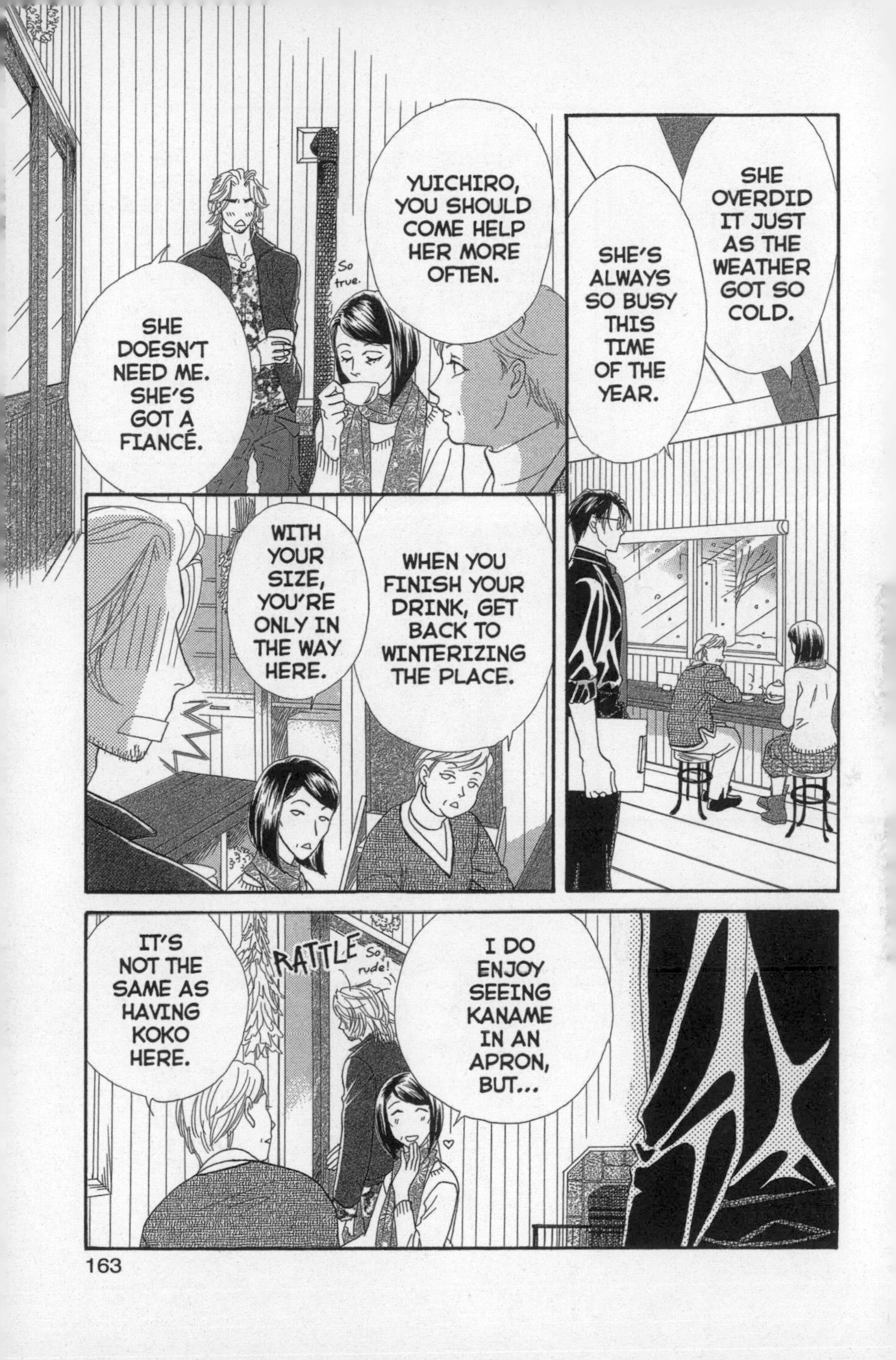
SHE OVERDID IT JUST AS THE WEATHER GOT SO COLD.
SHE'S ALWAYS SO BUSY THIS TIME OF THE YEAR.
YUICHIRO, YOU SHOULD COME HELP HER MORE OFTEN.
So true.
SHE DOESN'T NEED ME. SHE'S GOT A FIANCÉ.
WHEN YOU FINISH YOUR DRINK, GET BACK TO WINTERIZING THE PLACE.
WITH YOUR SIZE, YOU'RE ONLY IN THE WAY HERE.
I DO ENJOY SEEING KANAME IN AN APRON, BUT...
RATTLE
So rude!
IT'S NOT THE SAME AS HAVING KOKO HERE.

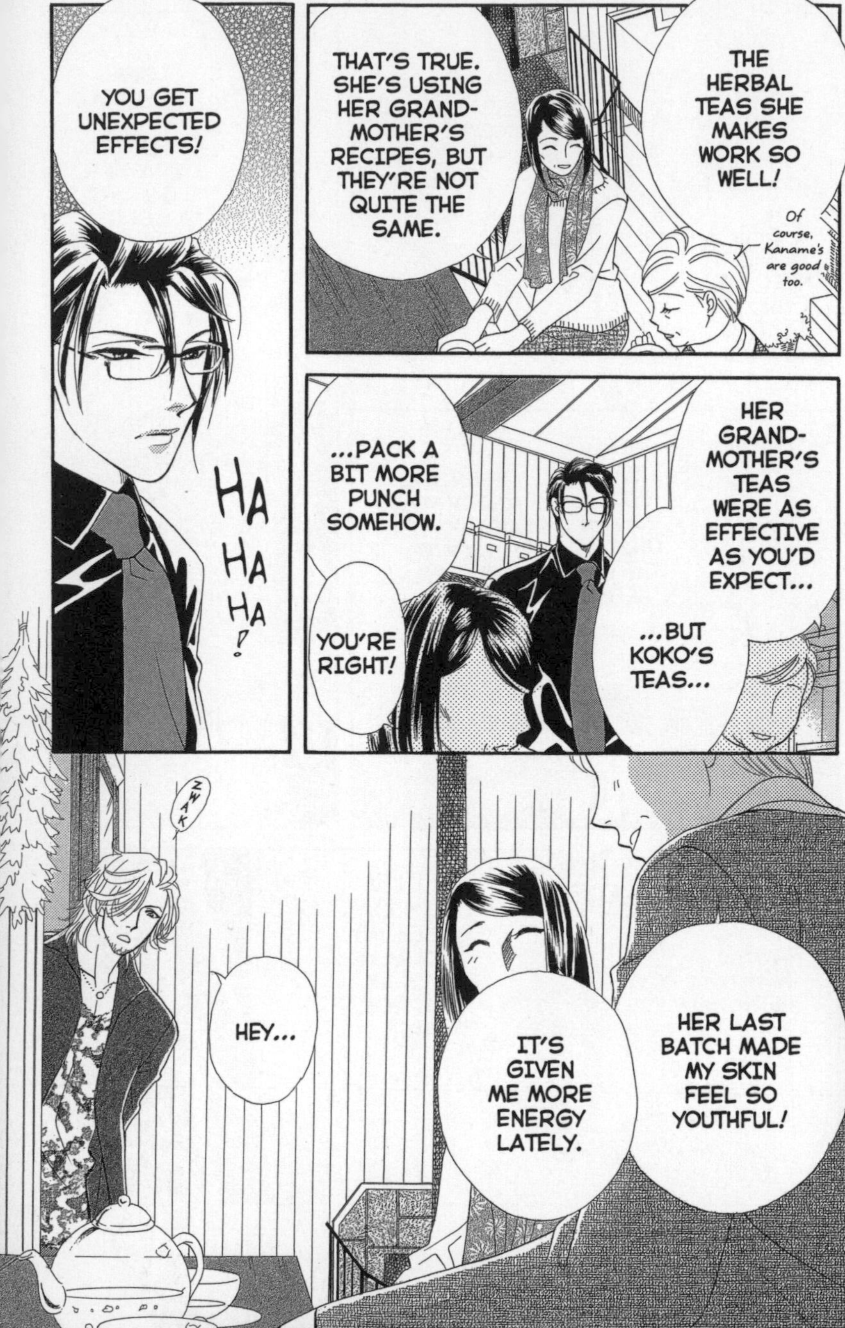
THE HERBAL TEAS SHE MAKES WORK SO WELL!
THAT'S TRUE. SHE'S USING HER GRAND-MOTHER'S RECIPES, BUT THEY'RE NOT QUITE THE SAME.
Of course, Kaname's are good too.
HER GRAND-MOTHER'S TEAS WERE AS EFFECTIVE AS YOU'D EXPECT...
...BUT KOKO'S TEAS...
...PACK A BIT MORE PUNCH SOMEHOW.
YOU'RE RIGHT!
YOU GET UNEXPECTED EFFECTS!
HA HA HA!
HER LAST BATCH MADE MY SKIN FEEL SO YOUTHFUL!
IT'S GIVEN ME MORE ENERGY LATELY.
ZWAK
HEY...

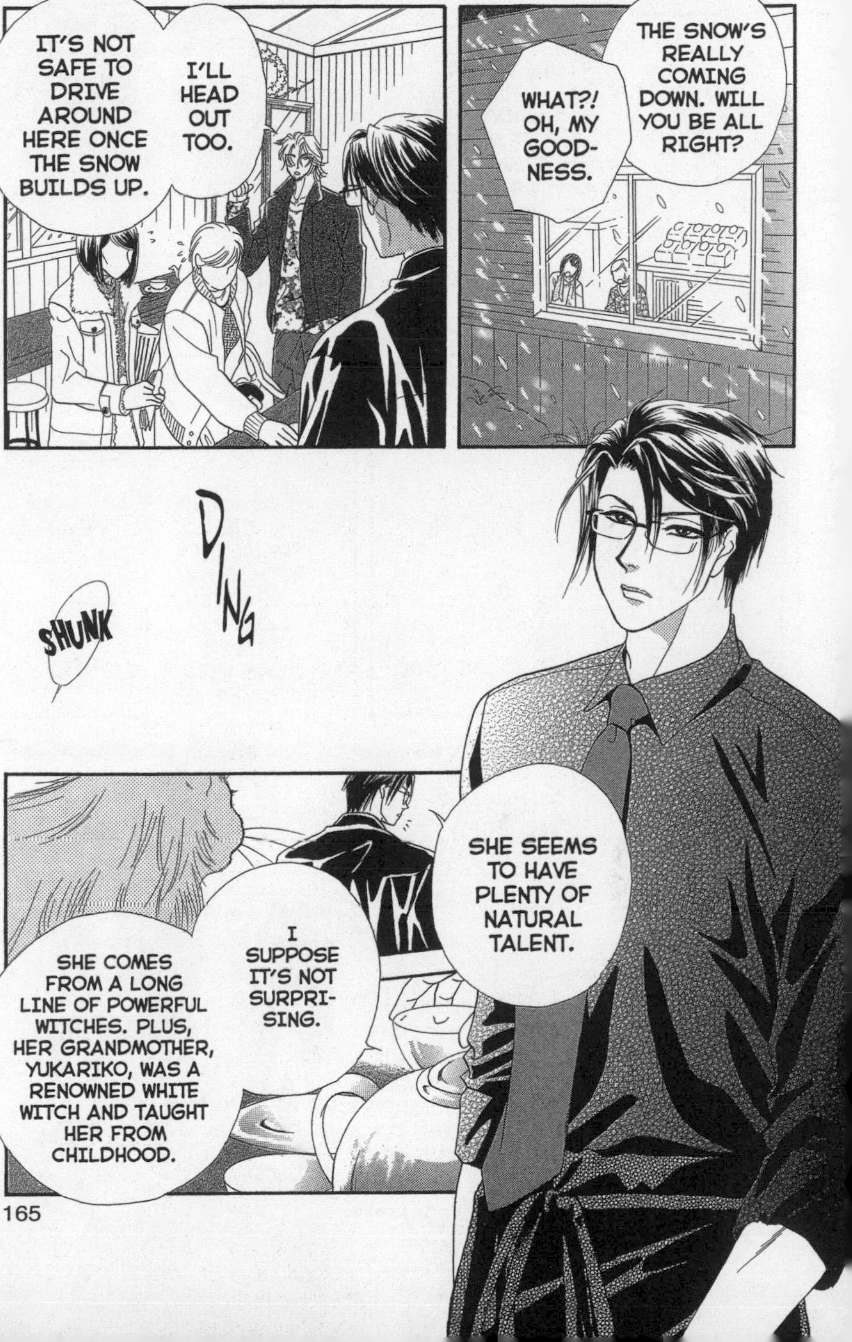
THE SNOW'S REALLY COMING DOWN. WILL YOU BE ALL RIGHT?
WHAT?! OH, MY GOODNESS.
I'LL HEAD OUT TOO.
IT'S NOT SAFE TO DRIVE AROUND HERE ONCE THE SNOW BUILDS UP.
DING
SHUNK
SHE SEEMS TO HAVE PLENTY OF NATURAL TALENT.
I SUPPOSE IT'S NOT SURPRISING.
SHE COMES FROM A LONG LINE OF POWERFUL WITCHES. PLUS, HER GRANDMOTHER, YUKARIKO, WAS A RENOWNED WHITE WITCH AND TAUGHT HER FROM CHILDHOOD.

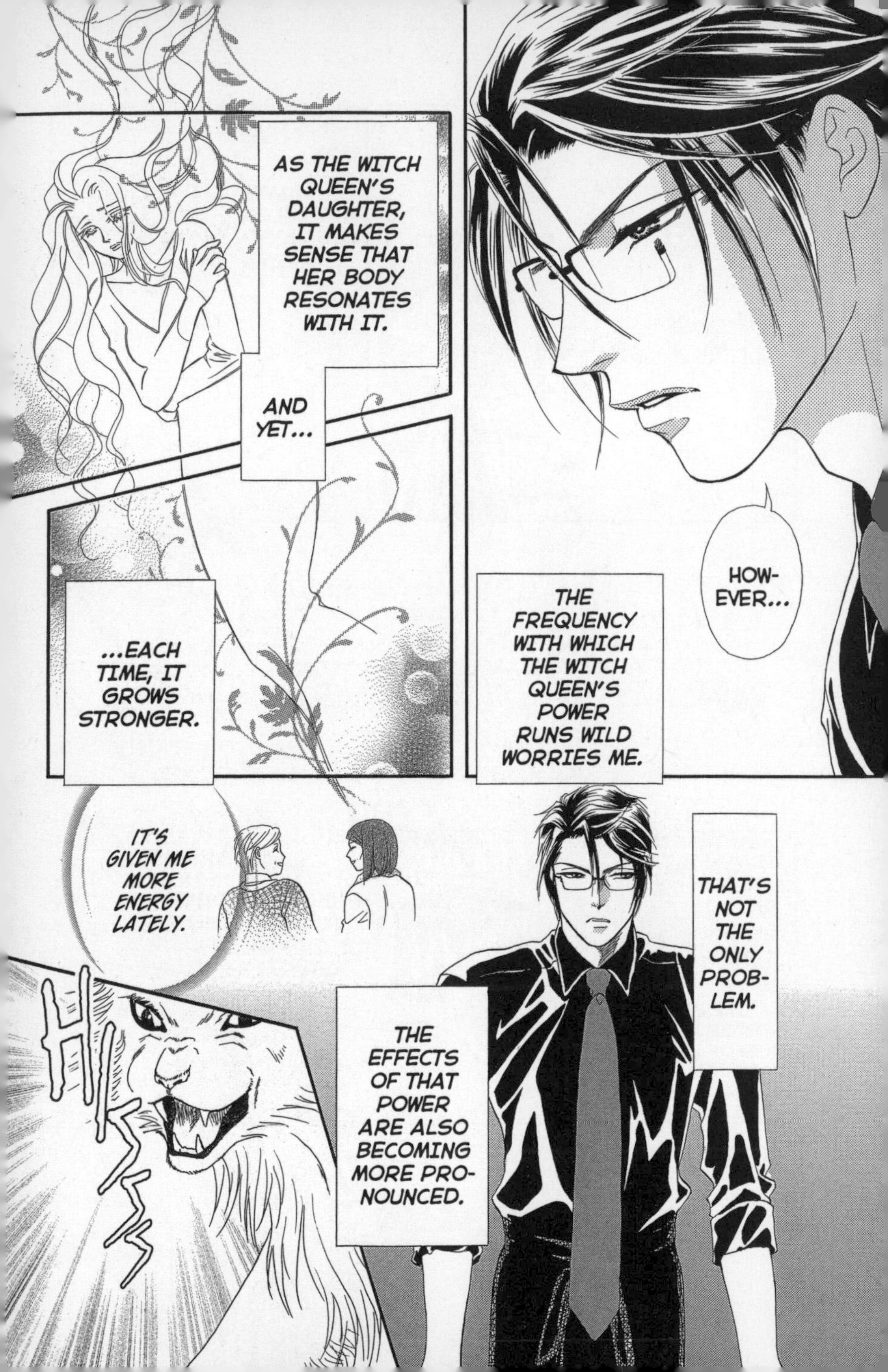
HOW-EVER...
THE FREQUENCY WITH WHICH THE WITCH QUEEN'S POWER RUNS WILD WORRIES ME.
AS THE WITCH QUEEN'S DAUGHTER, IT MAKES SENSE THAT HER BODY RESONATES WITH IT.
AND YET...
...EACH TIME, IT GROWS STRONGER.
THAT'S NOT THE ONLY PROB-LEM.
THE EFFECTS OF THAT POWER ARE ALSO BECOMING MORE PRO-NOUNCED.
IT'S GIVEN ME MORE ENERGY LATELY.

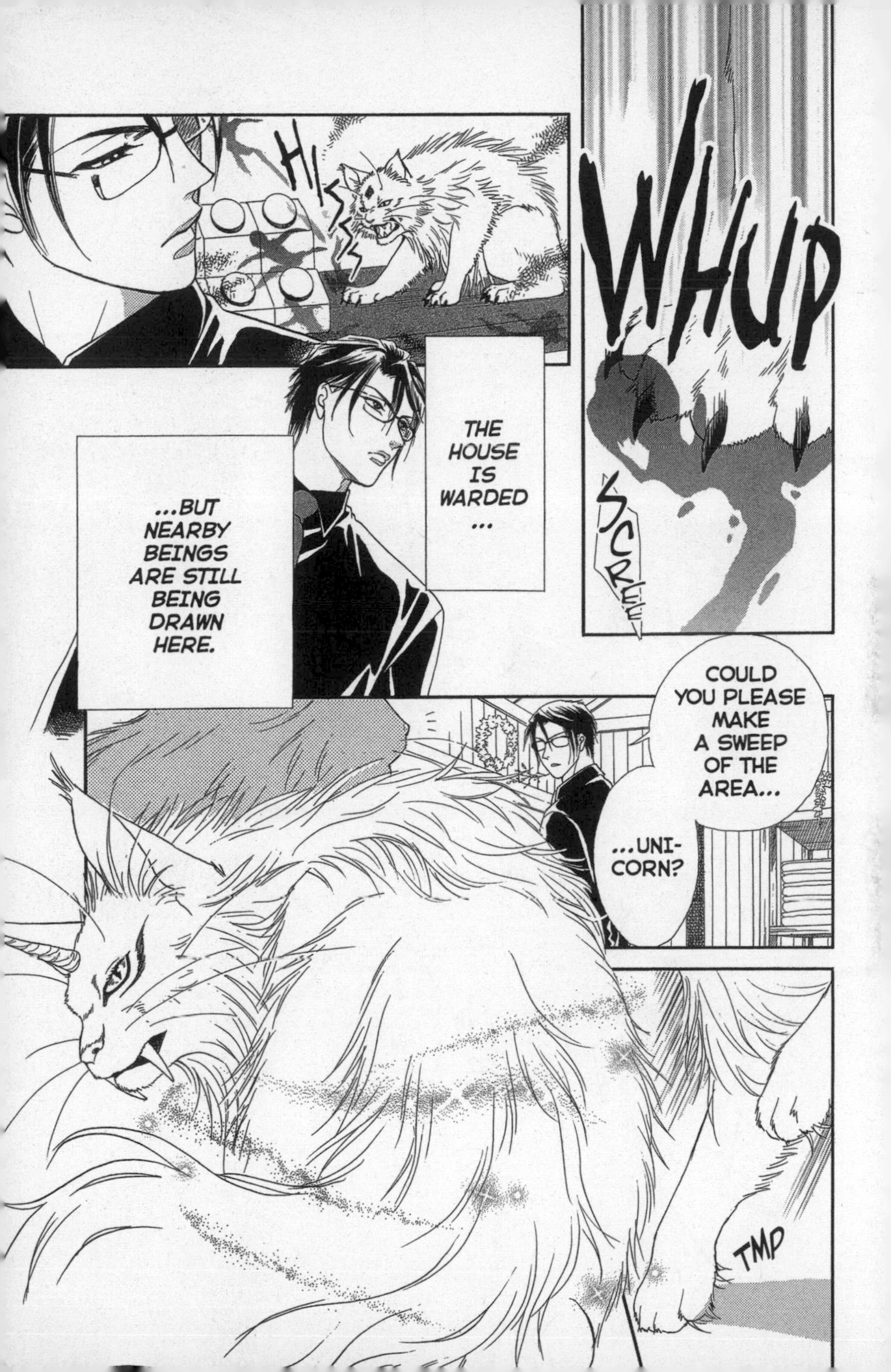

WHUP
SCREE
HISSS
THE HOUSE IS WARDED...
...BUT NEARBY BEINGS ARE STILL BEING DRAWN HERE.
COULD YOU PLEASE MAKE A SWEEP OF THE AREA...
...UNI-CORN?
TMP

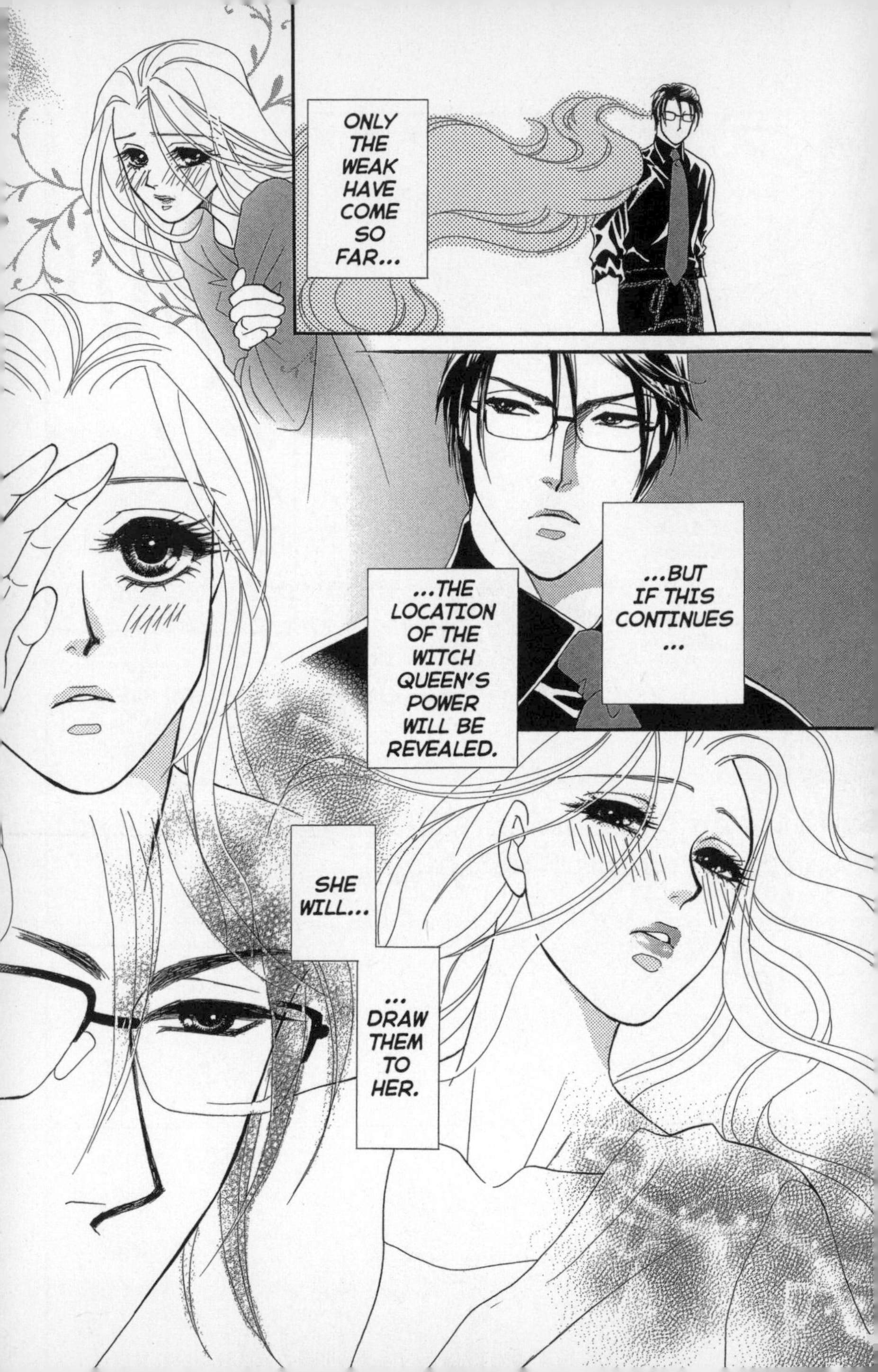
ONLY THE WEAK HAVE COME SO FAR...
...BUT IF THIS CONTINUES...
...THE LOCATION OF THE WITCH QUEEN'S POWER WILL BE REVEALED.
SHE WILL...
...DRAW THEM TO HER.

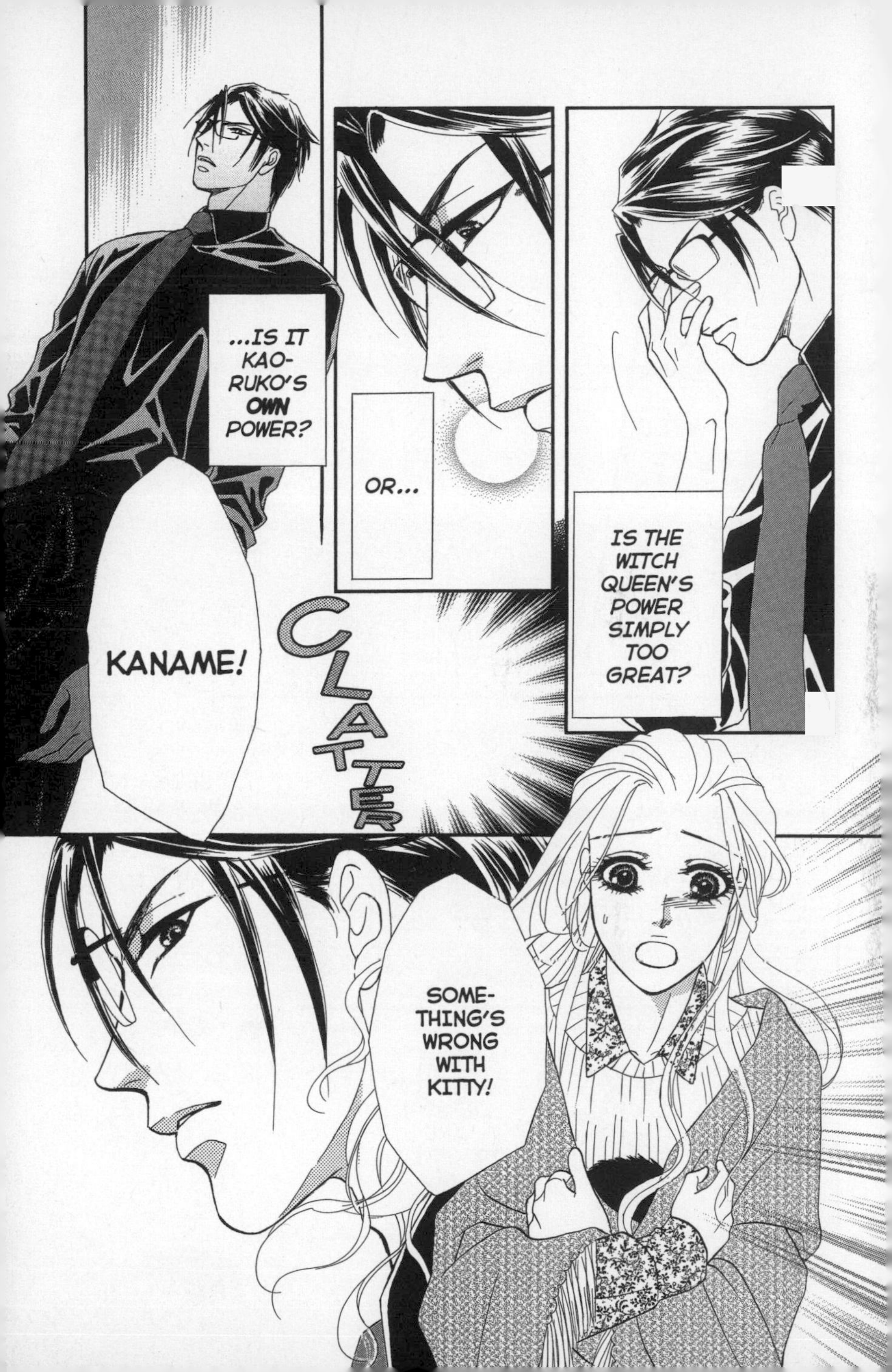
...IS IT KAO-RUKO'S OWN POWER?
OR...
IS THE WITCH QUEEN'S POWER SIMPLY TOO GREAT?
KANAME!
CLATTER
SOME-THING'S WRONG WITH KITTY!

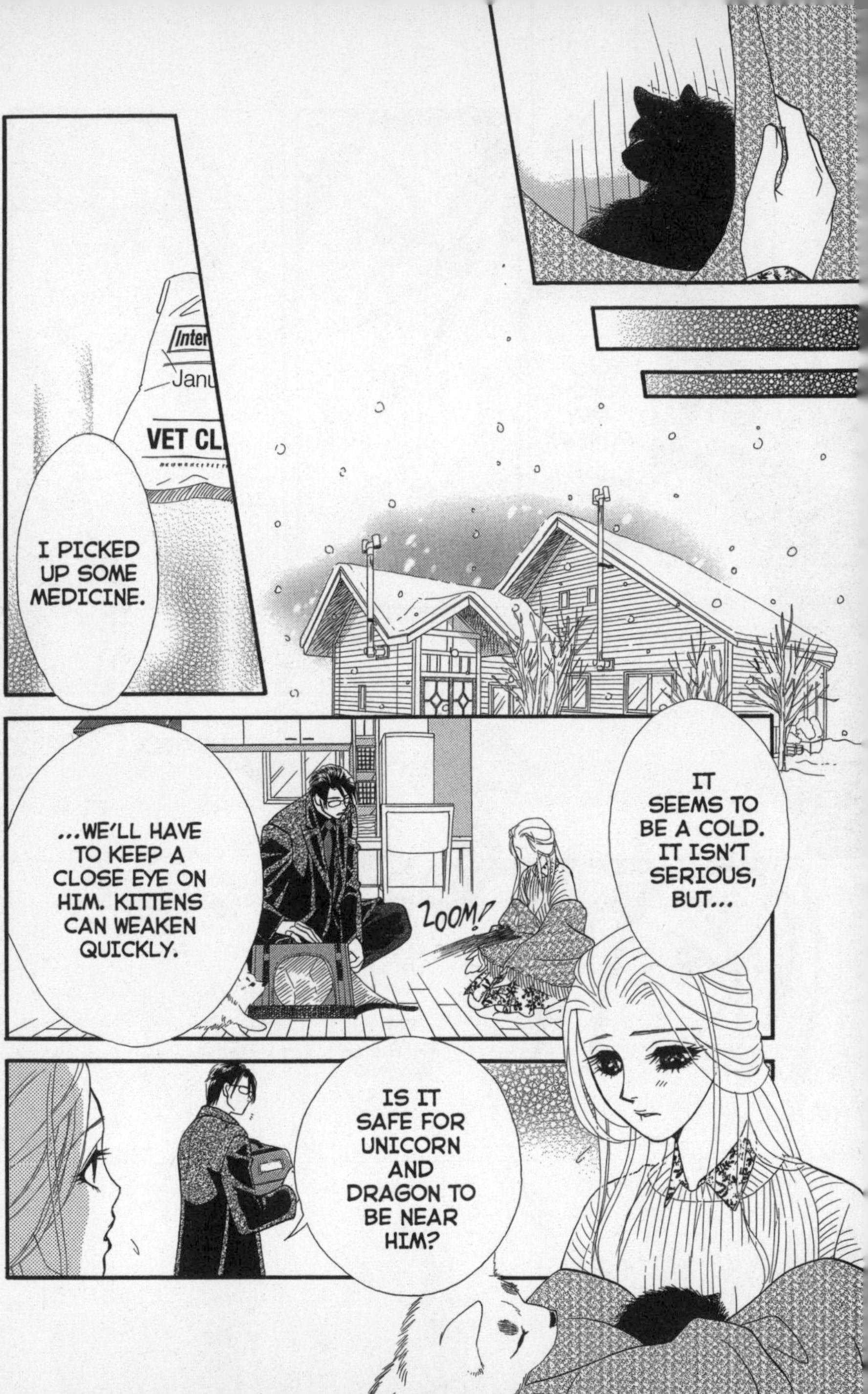
I PICKED UP SOME MEDICINE.
IT SEEMS TO BE A COLD. IT ISN'T SERIOUS, BUT...
ZOOM!
...WE'LL HAVE TO KEEP A CLOSE EYE ON HIM. KITTENS CAN WEAKEN QUICKLY.
IS IT SAFE FOR UNICORN AND DRAGON TO BE NEAR HIM?

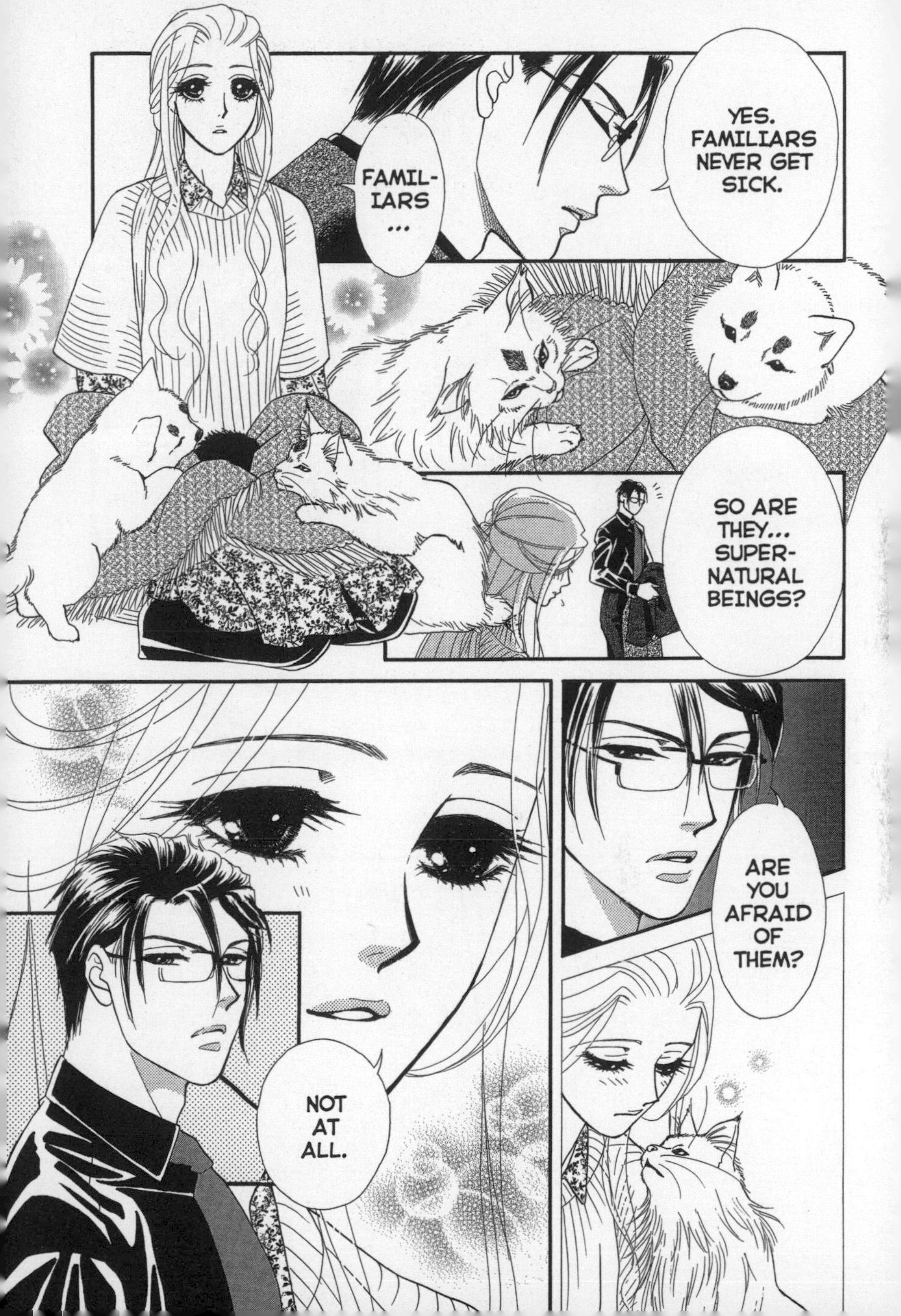
YES. FAMILIARS NEVER GET SICK.
FAMILIARS...
SO ARE THEY... SUPERNATURAL BEINGS?
ARE YOU AFRAID OF THEM?
NOT AT ALL.

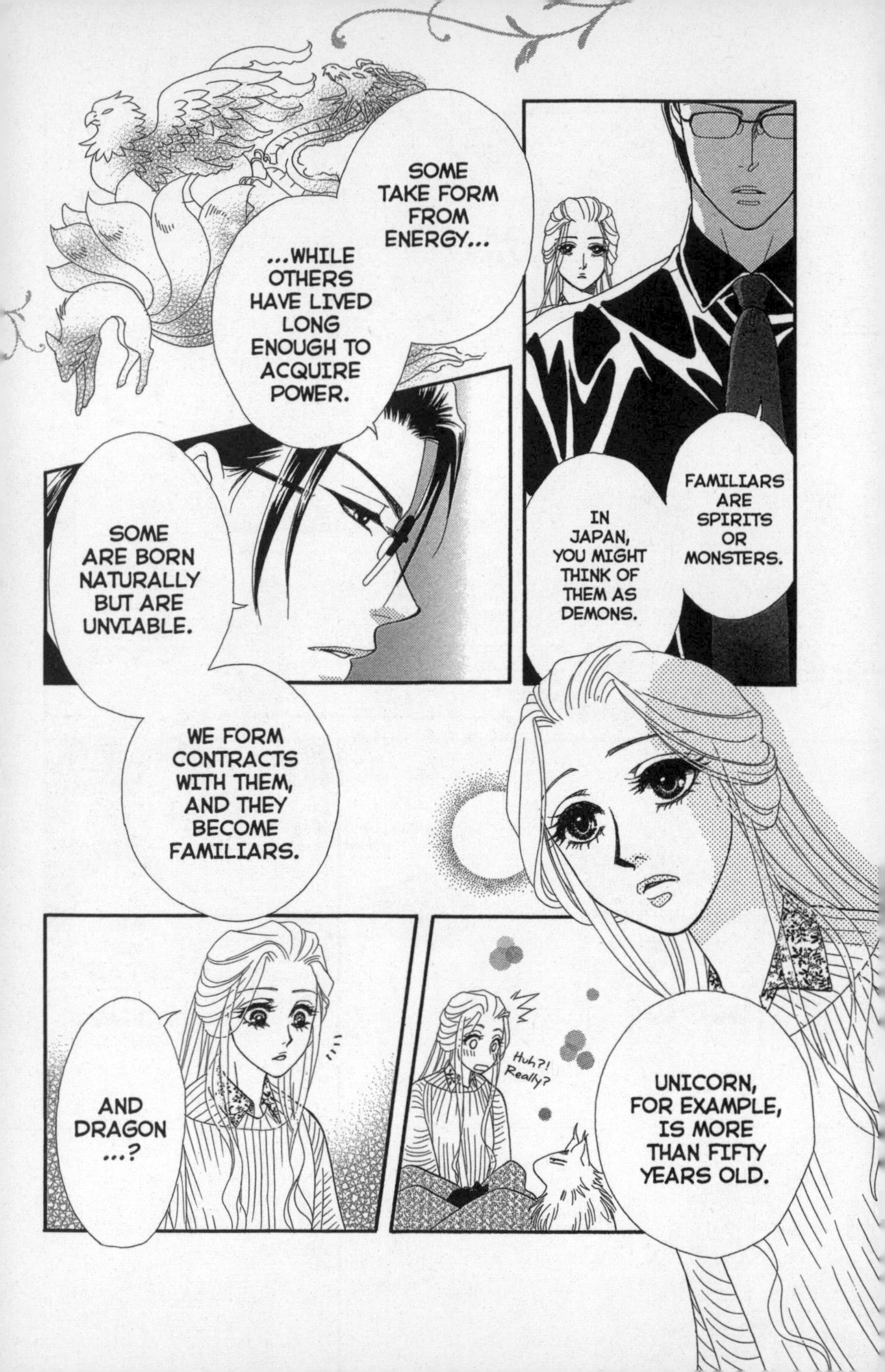
FAMILIARS ARE SPIRITS OR MONSTERS.
IN JAPAN, YOU MIGHT THINK OF THEM AS DEMONS.
SOME TAKE FORM FROM ENERGY...
...WHILE OTHERS HAVE LIVED LONG ENOUGH TO ACQUIRE POWER.
SOME ARE BORN NATURALLY BUT ARE UNVIABLE.
WE FORM CONTRACTS WITH THEM, AND THEY BECOME FAMILIARS.
UNICORN, FOR EXAMPLE, IS MORE THAN FIFTY YEARS OLD.
Huh?! Really?
AND DRAGON ...?

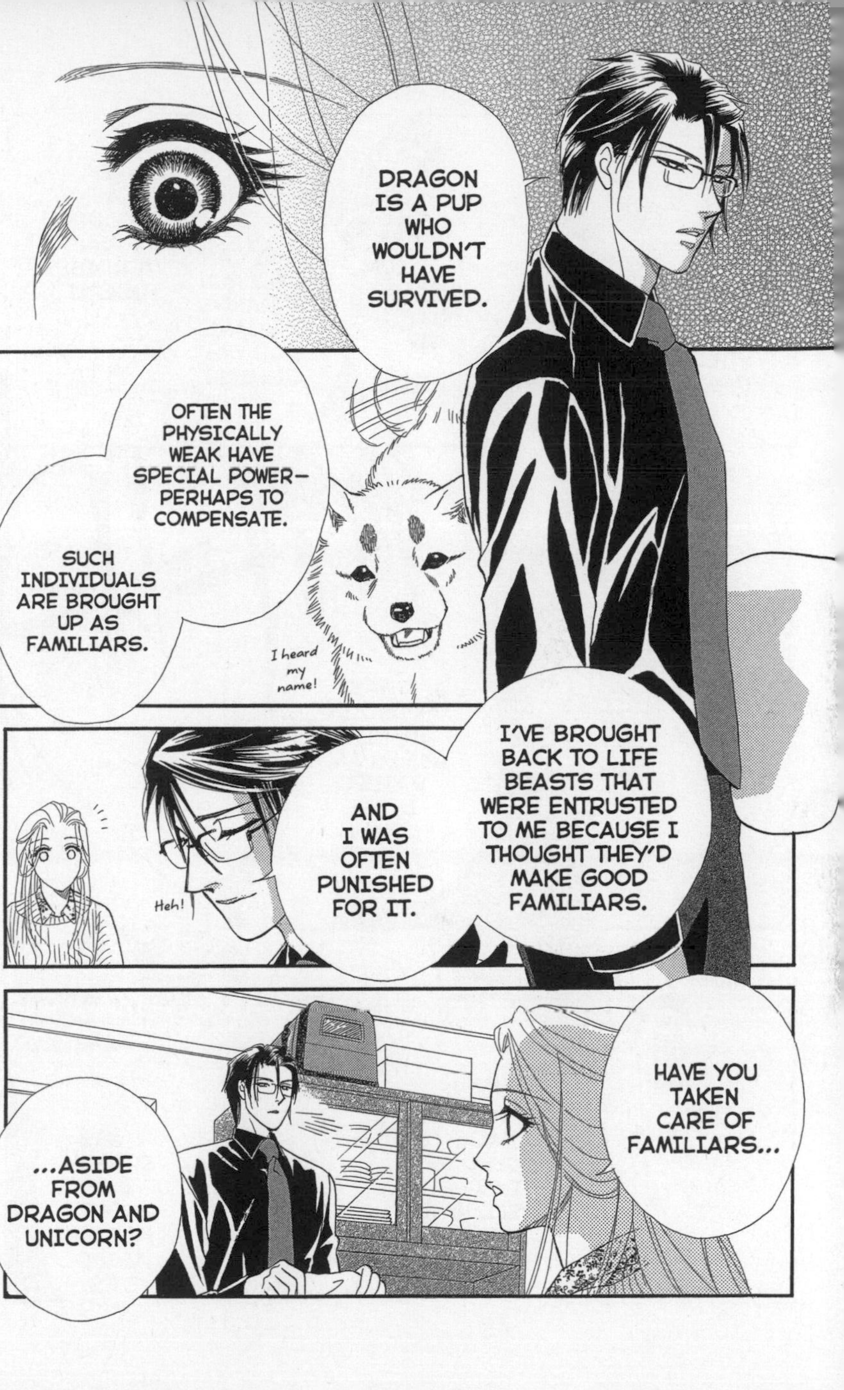
DRAGON IS A PUP WHO WOULDN'T HAVE SURVIVED.
OFTEN THE PHYSICALLY WEAK HAVE SPECIAL POWER— PERHAPS TO COMPENSATE.
SUCH INDIVIDUALS ARE BROUGHT UP AS FAMILIARS.
I heard my name!
I'VE BROUGHT BACK TO LIFE BEASTS THAT WERE ENTRUSTED TO ME BECAUSE I THOUGHT THEY'D MAKE GOOD FAMILIARS.
AND I WAS OFTEN PUNISHED FOR IT.
Heh!
HAVE YOU TAKEN CARE OF FAMILIARS...
...ASIDE FROM DRAGON AND UNICORN?

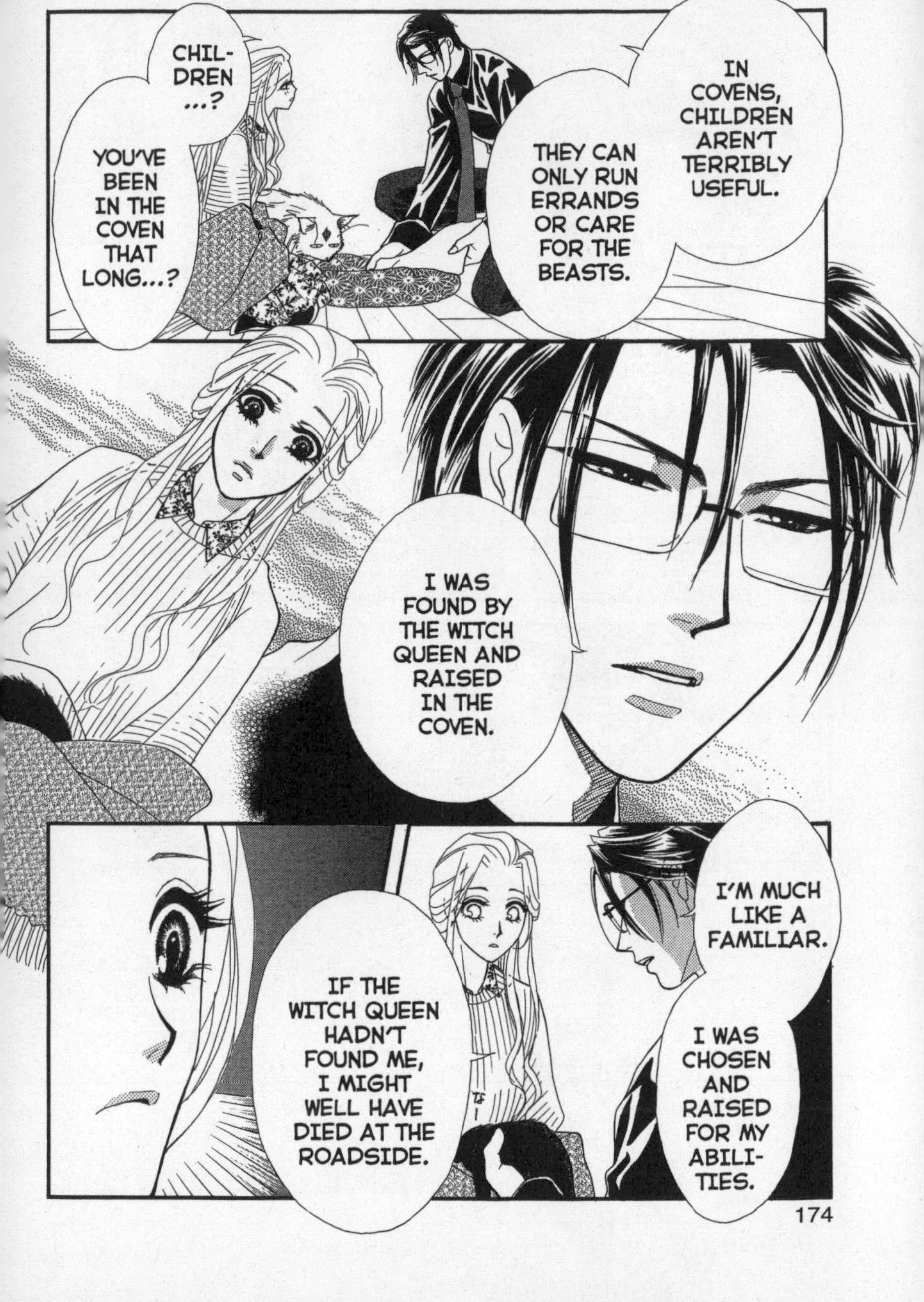
IN COVENS, CHILDREN AREN'T TERRIBLY USEFUL.
THEY CAN ONLY RUN ERRANDS OR CARE FOR THE BEASTS.
CHIL-DREN ...?
YOU'VE BEEN IN THE COVEN THAT LONG...?
I WAS FOUND BY THE WITCH QUEEN AND RAISED IN THE COVEN.
I'M MUCH LIKE A FAMILIAR.
I WAS CHOSEN AND RAISED FOR MY ABILI-TIES.
IF THE WITCH QUEEN HADN'T FOUND ME, I MIGHT WELL HAVE DIED AT THE ROADSIDE.

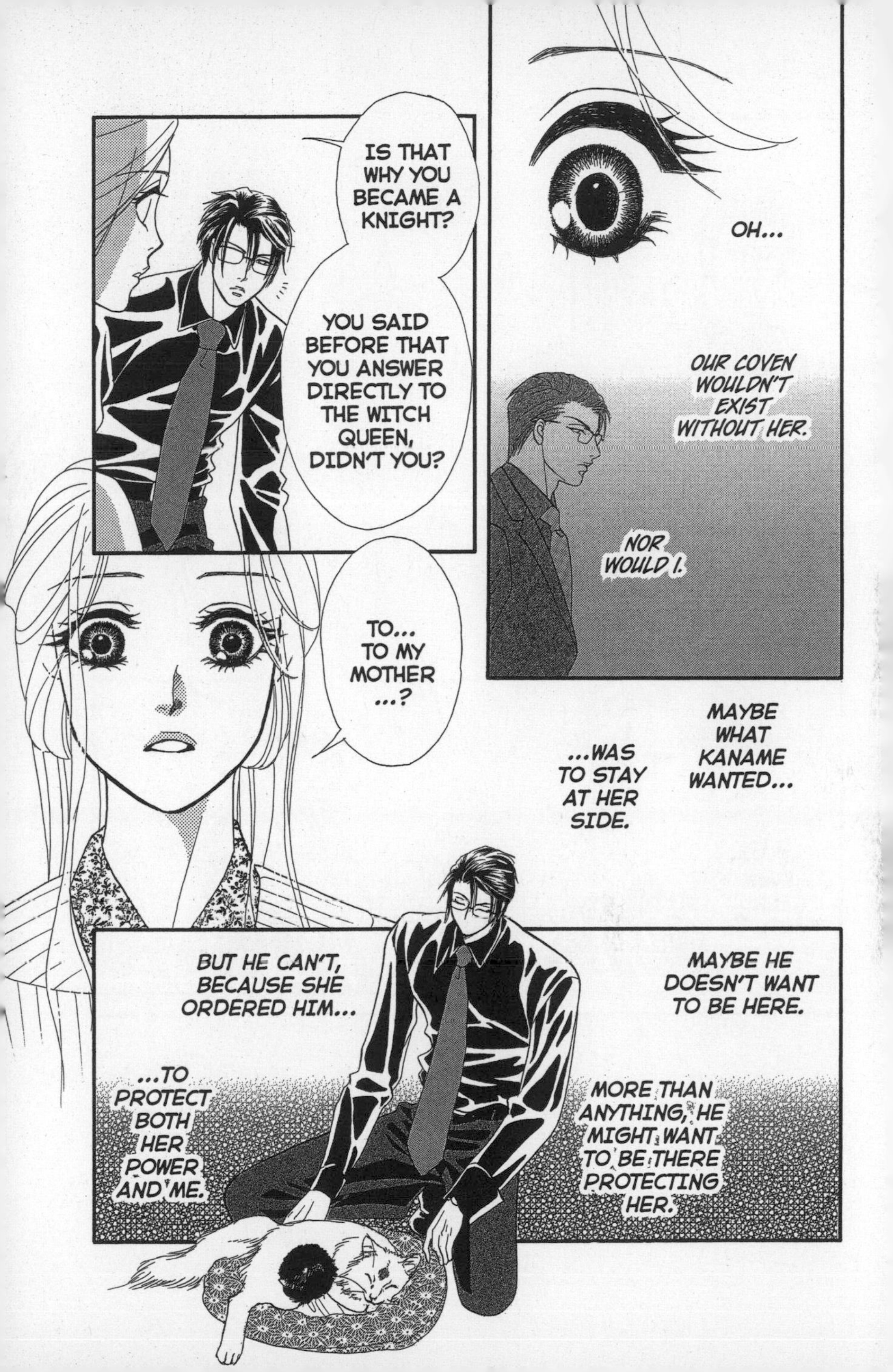
OH...
OUR COVEN WOULDN'T EXIST WITHOUT HER.
NOR WOULD I.
IS THAT WHY YOU BECAME A KNIGHT?
YOU SAID BEFORE THAT YOU ANSWER DIRECTLY TO THE WITCH QUEEN, DIDN'T YOU?
TO... TO MY MOTHER ...?
MAYBE WHAT KANAME WANTED...
...WAS TO STAY AT HER SIDE.
MAYBE HE DOESN'T WANT TO BE HERE.
MORE THAN ANYTHING, HE MIGHT WANT TO BE THERE PROTECTING HER.
BUT HE CAN'T, BECAUSE SHE ORDERED HIM...
...TO PROTECT BOTH HER POWER AND ME.

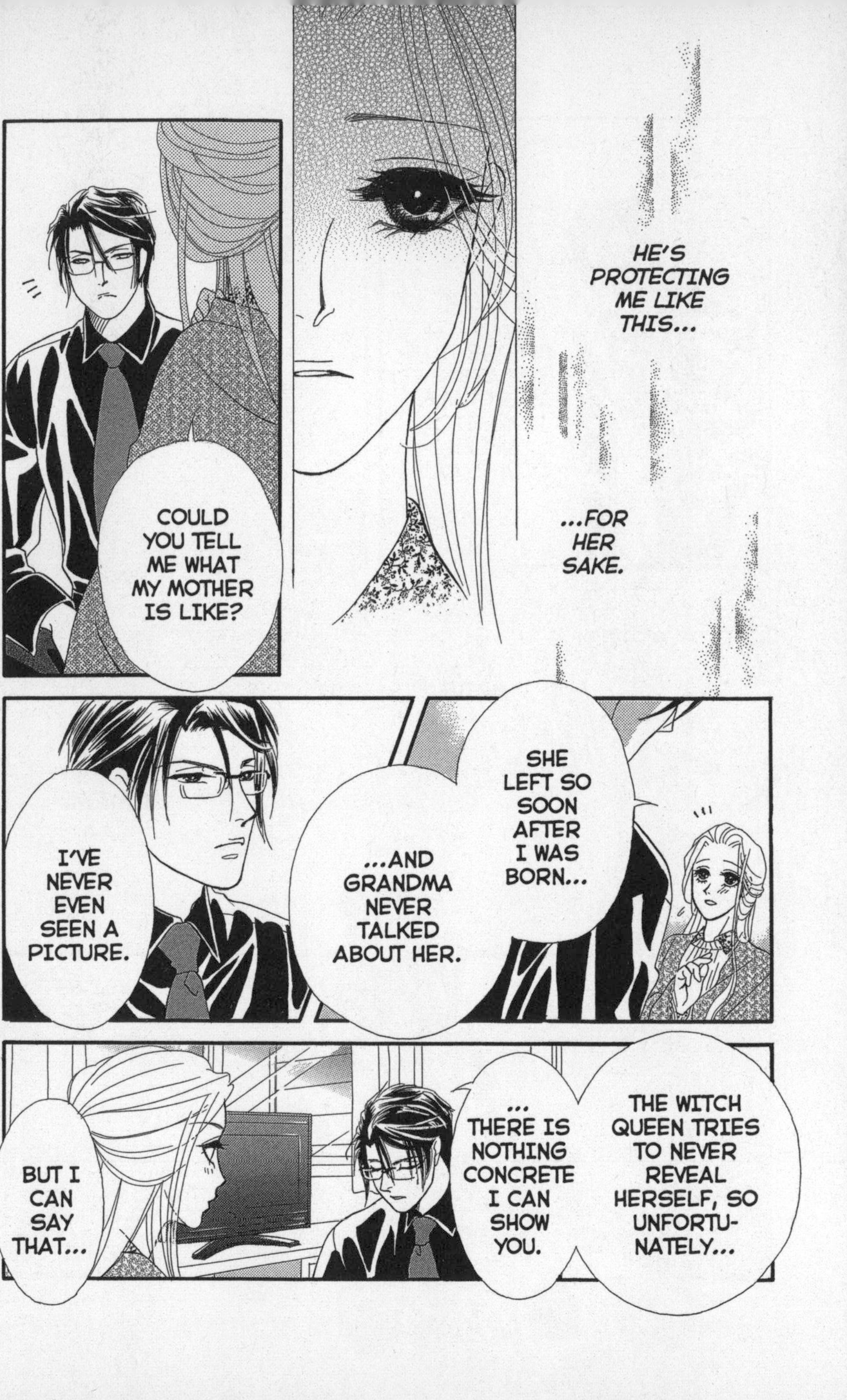
HE'S PROTECTING ME LIKE THIS...
...FOR HER SAKE.
COULD YOU TELL ME WHAT MY MOTHER IS LIKE?
SHE LEFT SO SOON AFTER I WAS BORN...
...AND GRANDMA NEVER TALKED ABOUT HER.
I'VE NEVER EVEN SEEN A PICTURE.
THE WITCH QUEEN TRIES TO NEVER REVEAL HERSELF, SO UNFORTU-NATELY...
...THERE IS NOTHING CONCRETE I CAN SHOW YOU.
BUT I CAN SAY THAT...

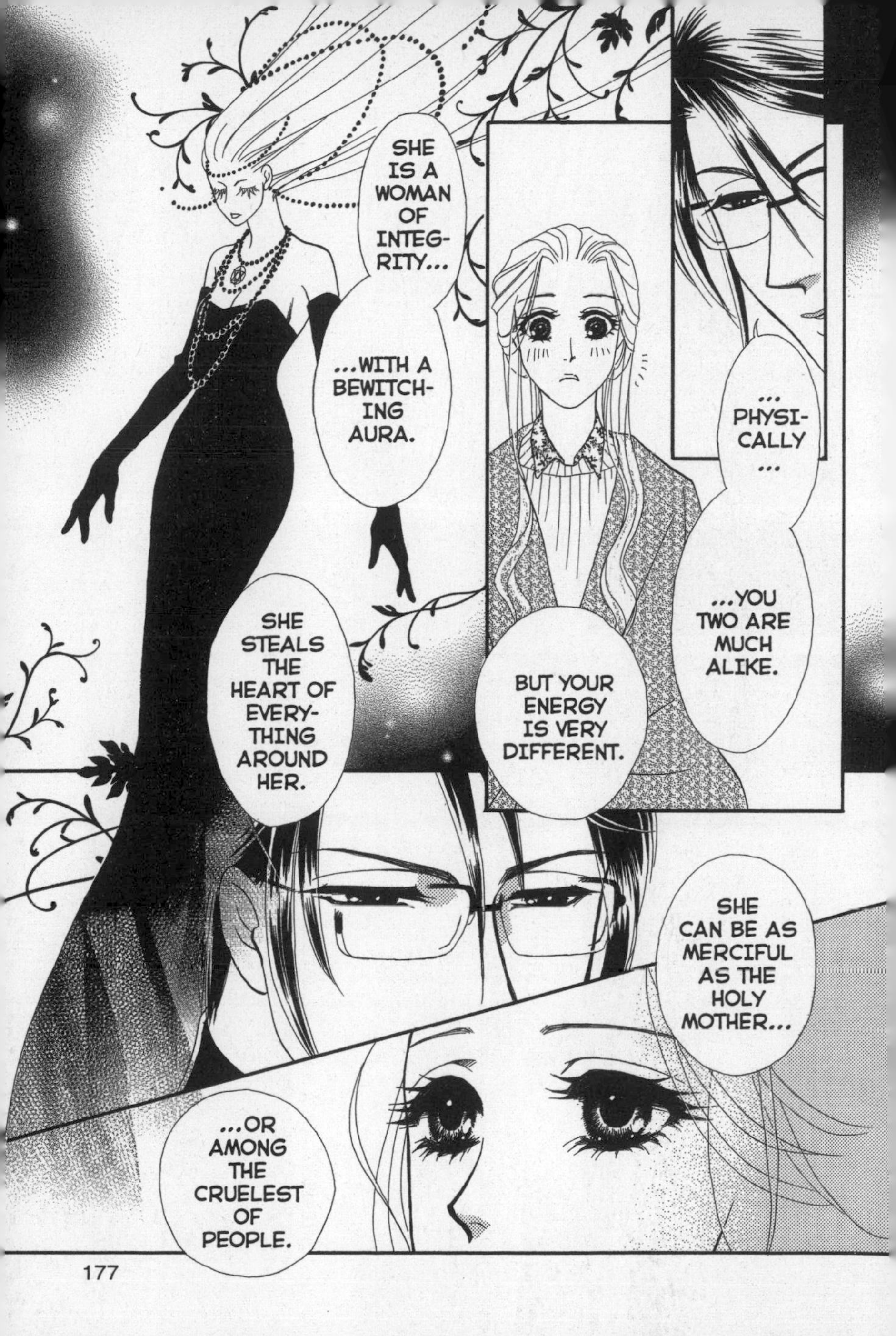
...PHYSICALLY...
...YOU TWO ARE MUCH ALIKE.
BUT YOUR ENERGY IS VERY DIFFERENT.
SHE IS A WOMAN OF INTEGRITY...
...WITH A BEWITCHING AURA.
SHE STEALS THE HEART OF EVERYTHING AROUND HER.
SHE CAN BE AS MERCIFUL AS THE HOLY MOTHER...
...OR AMONG THE CRUELEST OF PEOPLE.

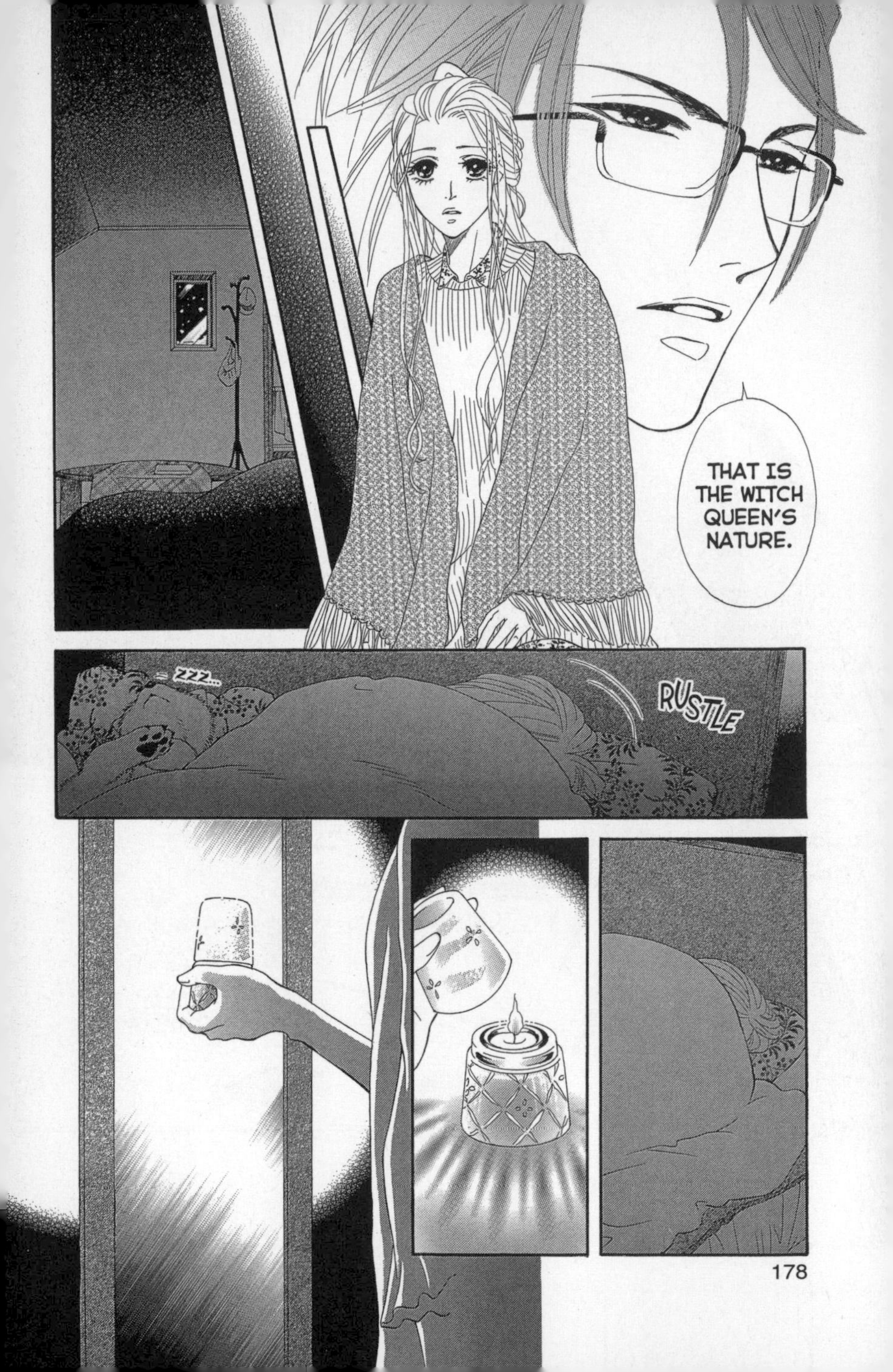
THAT IS THE WITCH QUEEN'S NATURE.
RUSTLE
ZZZ...

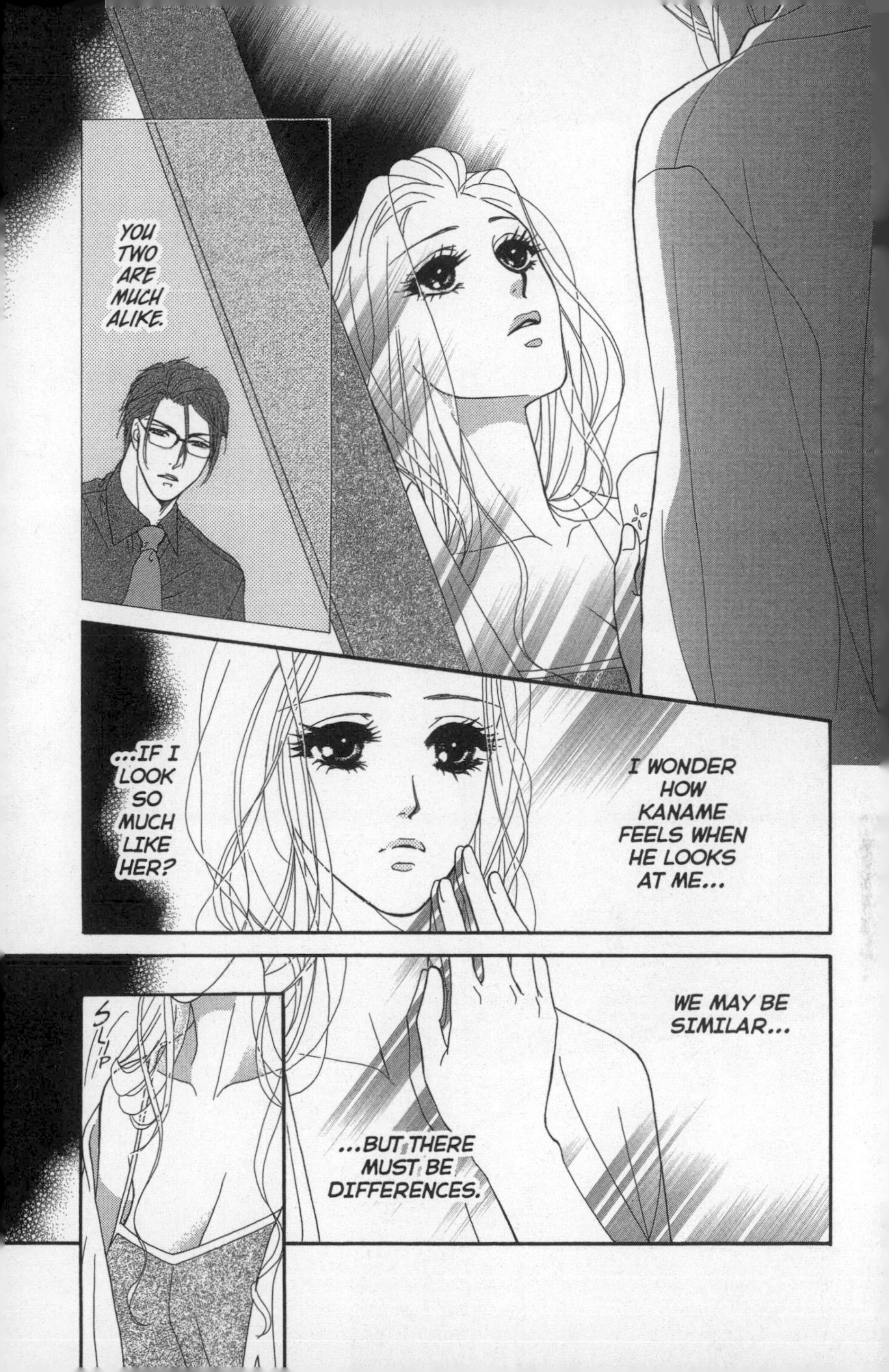
YOU TWO ARE MUCH ALIKE.
I WONDER HOW KANAME FEELS WHEN HE LOOKS AT ME...
...IF I LOOK SO MUCH LIKE HER?
WE MAY BE SIMILAR...
...BUT THERE MUST BE DIFFERENCES.
SLIP

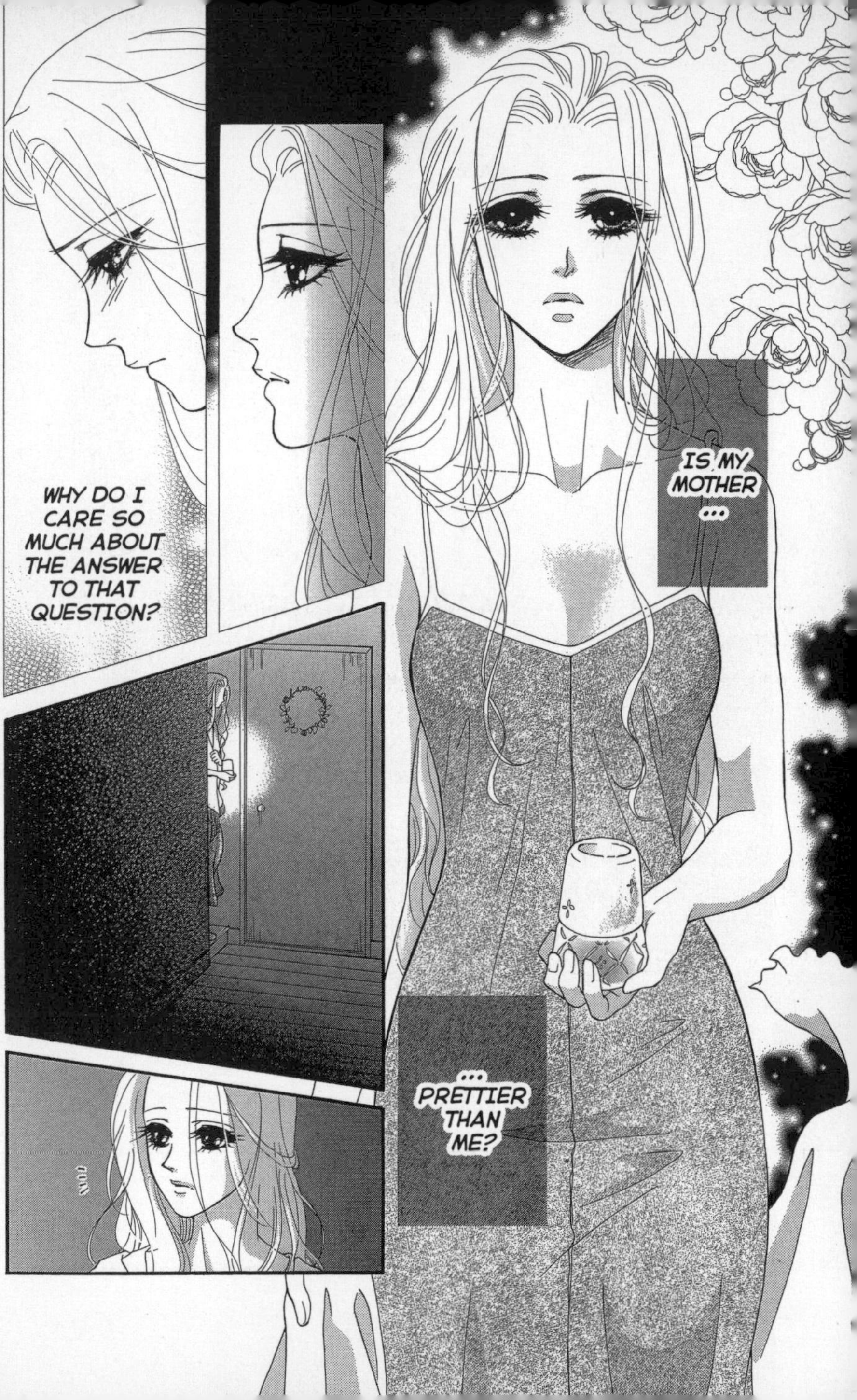
IS MY MOTHER ...
... PRETTIER THAN ME?
WHY DO I CARE SO MUCH ABOUT THE ANSWER TO THAT QUESTION?

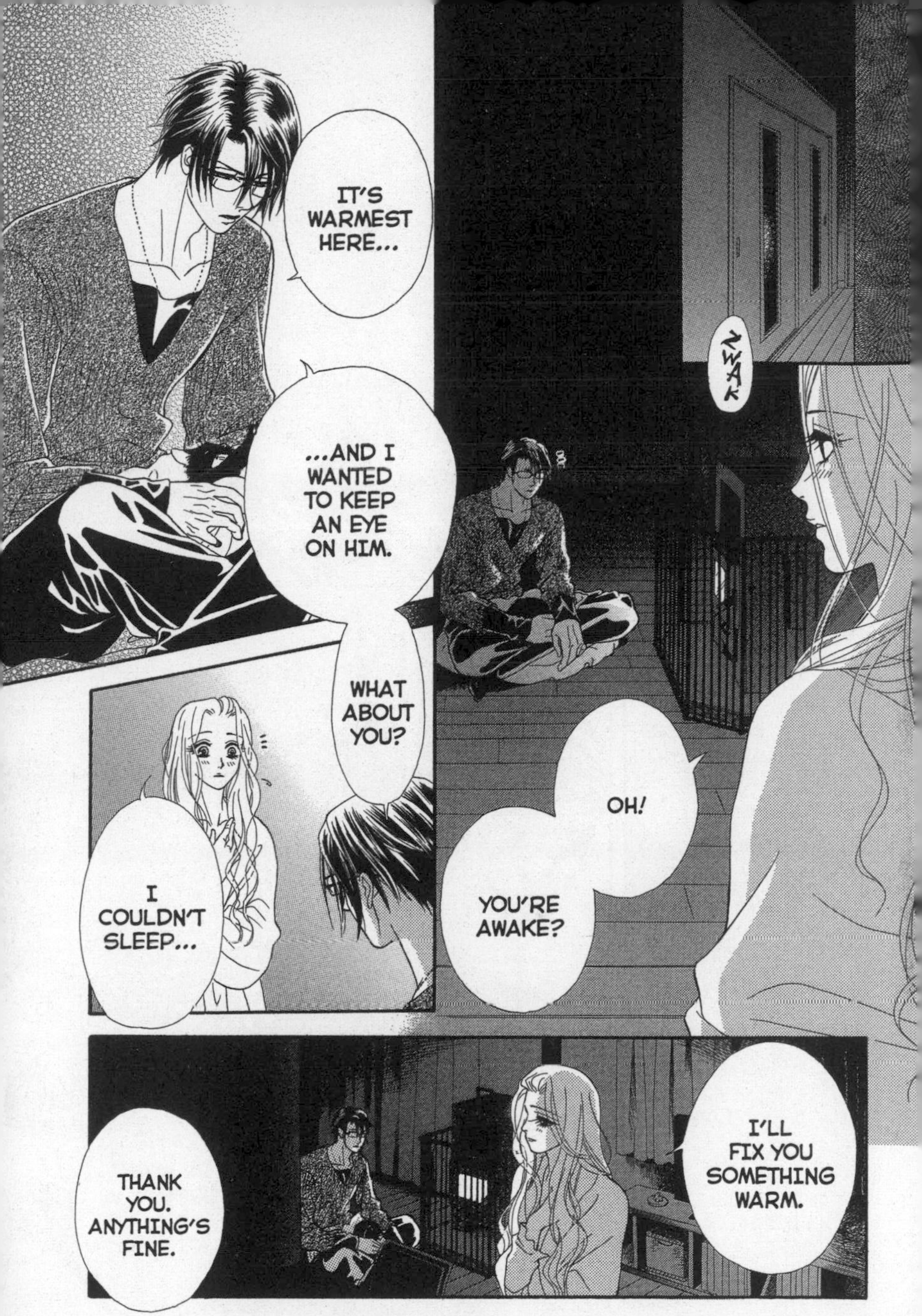
ZWAK
OH!
YOU'RE AWAKE?
IT'S WARMEST HERE...
...AND I WANTED TO KEEP AN EYE ON HIM.
WHAT ABOUT YOU?
I COULDN'T SLEEP...
I'LL FIX YOU SOMETHING WARM.
THANK YOU. ANYTHING'S FINE.

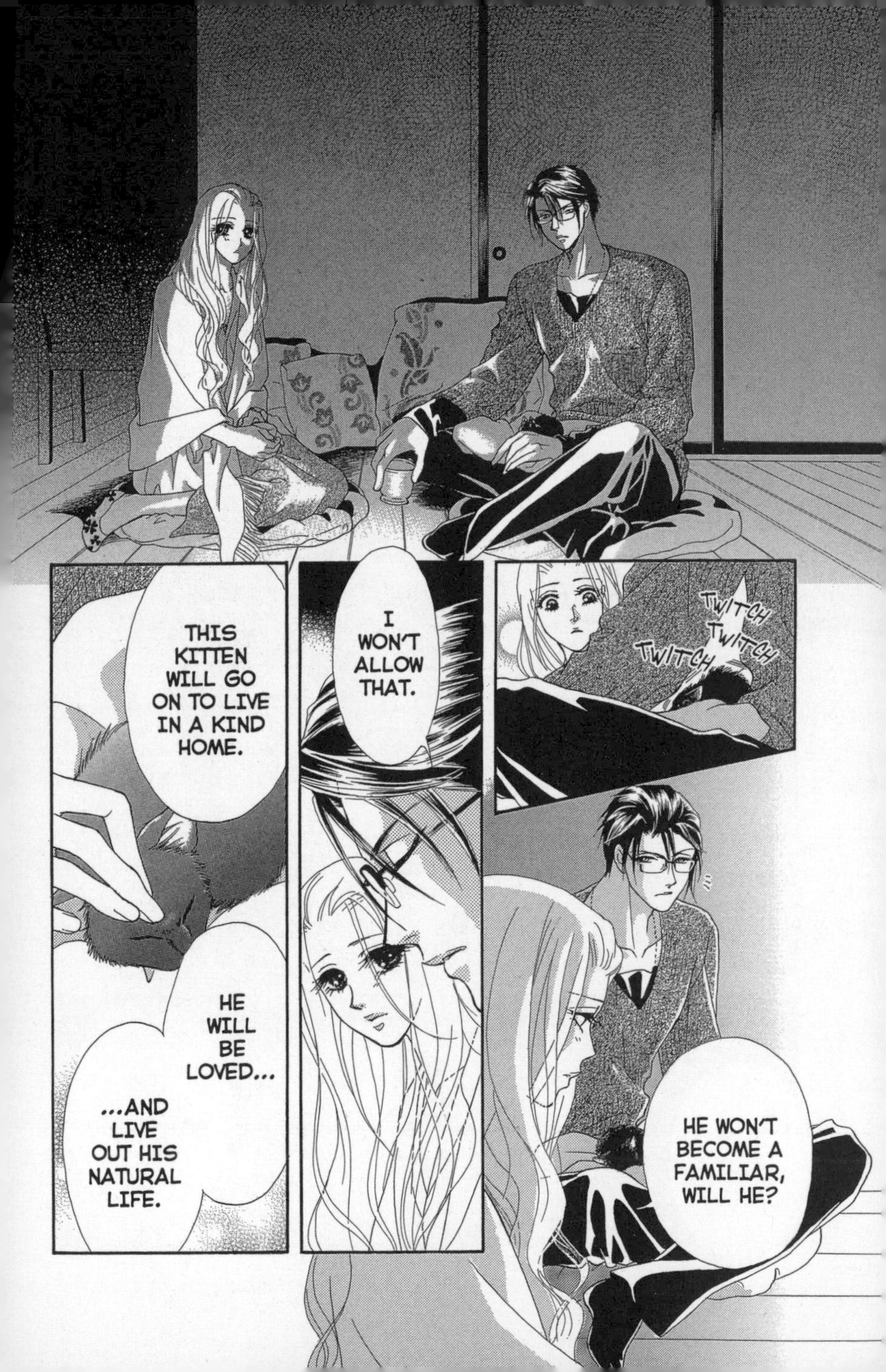
TWITCH TWITCH TWITCH
HE WON'T BECOME A FAMILIAR, WILL HE?
I WON'T ALLOW THAT.
THIS KITTEN WILL GO ON TO LIVE IN A KIND HOME.
HE WILL BE LOVED...
...AND LIVE OUT HIS NATURAL LIFE.

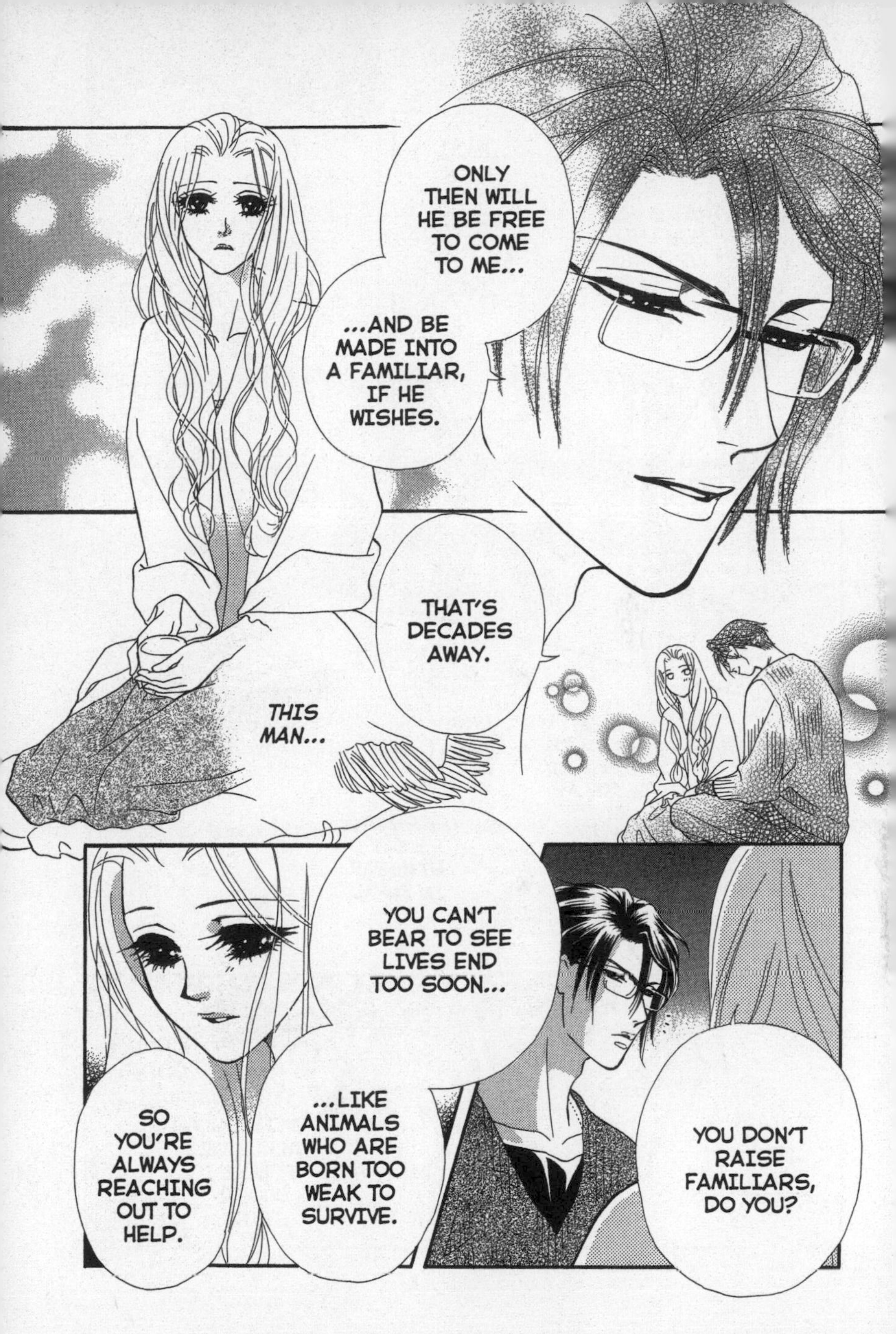
ONLY THEN WILL HE BE FREE TO COME TO ME...
...AND BE MADE INTO A FAMILIAR, IF HE WISHES.
THAT'S DECADES AWAY.
THIS MAN...
YOU DON'T RAISE FAMILIARS, DO YOU?
YOU CAN'T BEAR TO SEE LIVES END TOO SOON...
...LIKE ANIMALS WHO ARE BORN TOO WEAK TO SURVIVE.
SO YOU'RE ALWAYS REACHING OUT TO HELP.

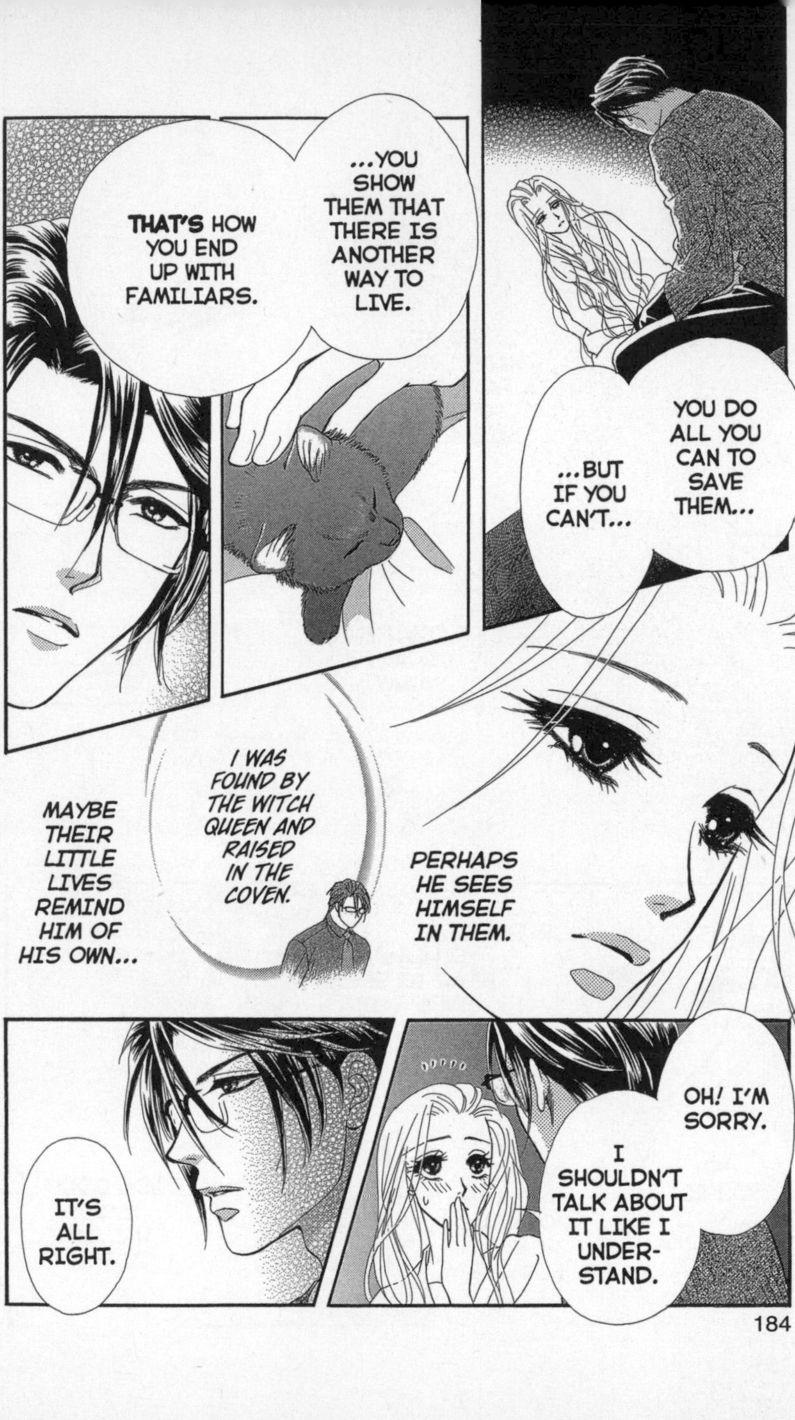
YOU DO ALL YOU CAN TO SAVE THEM...
...BUT IF YOU CAN'T...
...YOU SHOW THEM THAT THERE IS ANOTHER WAY TO LIVE.
THAT'S HOW YOU END UP WITH FAMILIARS.
PERHAPS HE SEES HIMSELF IN THEM.
I WAS FOUND BY THE WITCH QUEEN AND RAISED IN THE COVEN.
MAYBE THEIR LITTLE LIVES REMIND HIM OF HIS OWN...
OH! I'M SORRY.
I SHOULDN'T TALK ABOUT IT LIKE I UNDER-STAND.
IT'S ALL RIGHT.

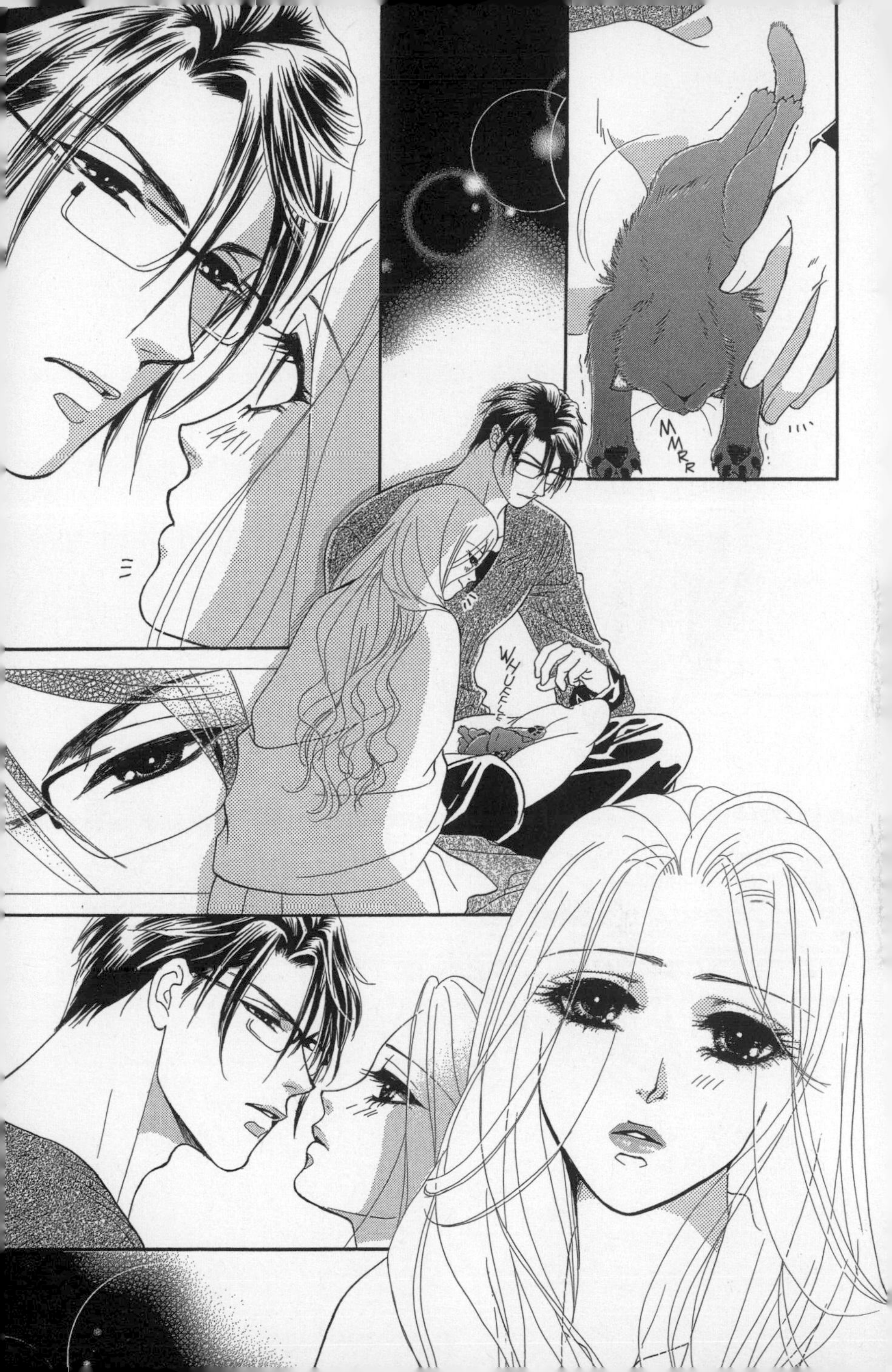
MMRR
WHUFFLE

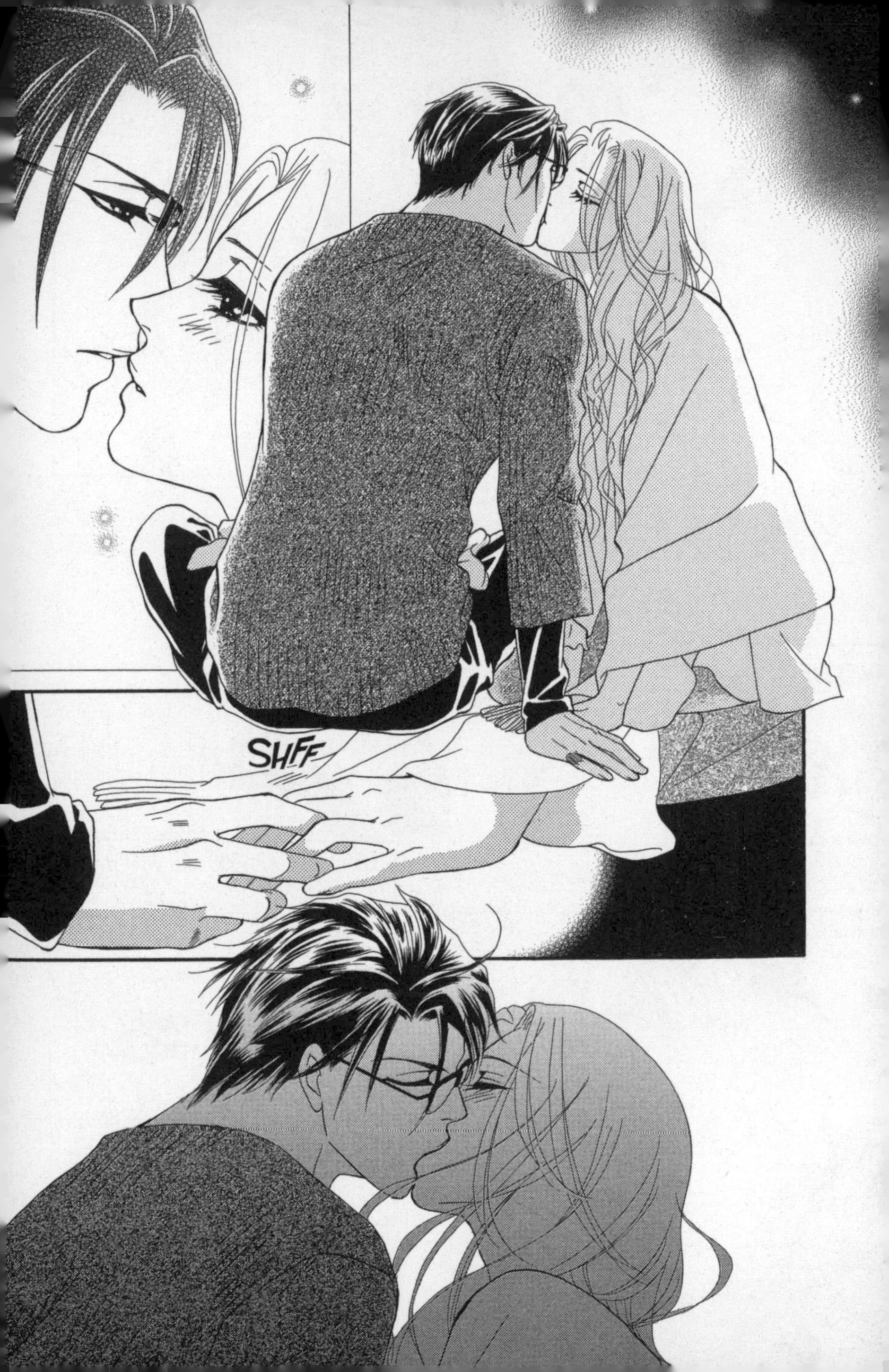
SHFF

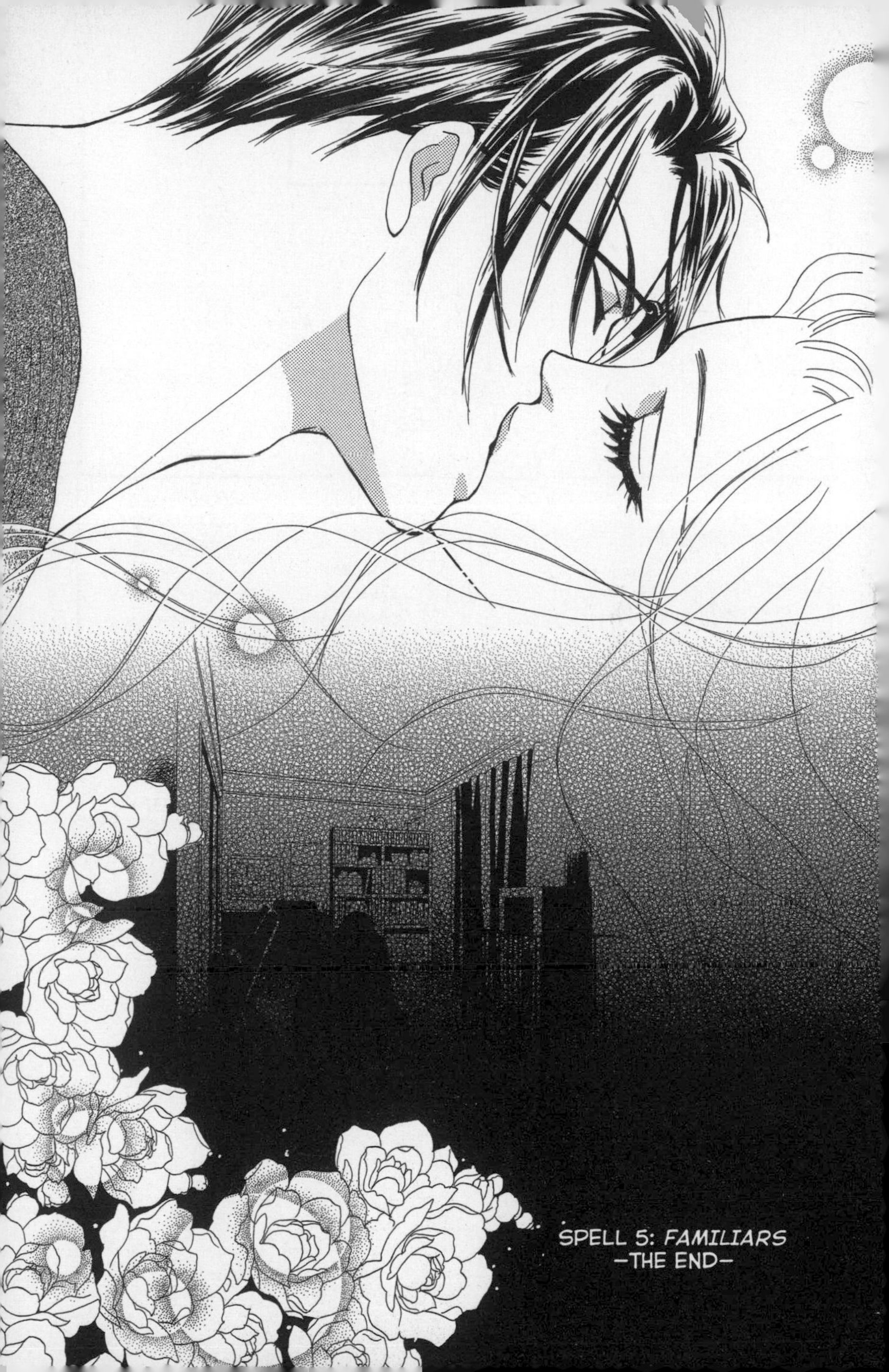
SPELL 5: *FAMILIARS*
—THE END—

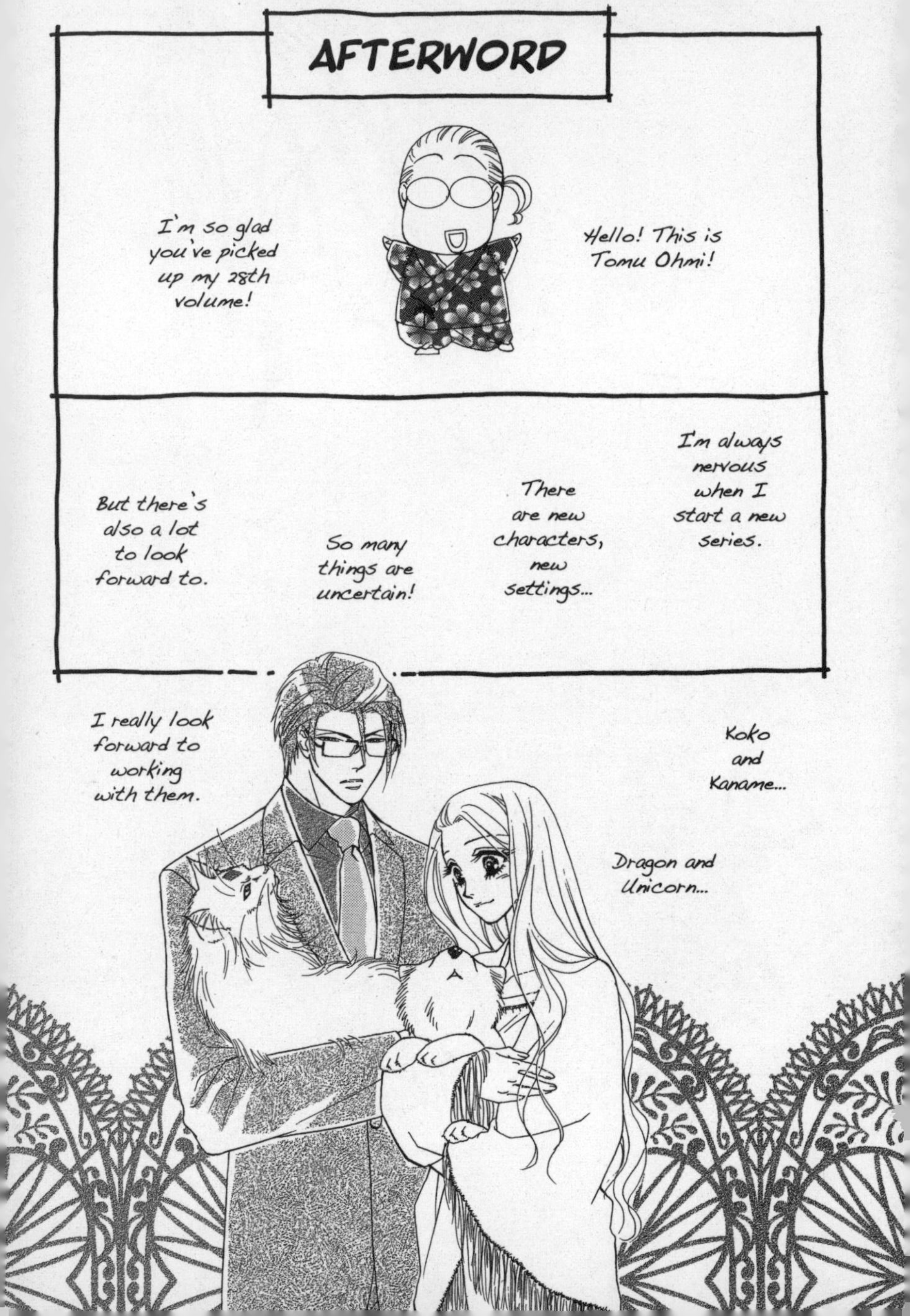
AFTERWORD
Hello! This is Tomu Ohmi!
I'm so glad you've picked up my 28th volume!
I'm always nervous when I start a new series.
There are new characters, new settings...
So many things are uncertain!
But there's also a lot to look forward to.
Koko and Kaname...
Dragon and Unicorn...
I really look forward to working with them.

When I begin a new series...
...the designs for the logo and the title page help create the right atmosphere.
← Like here!
And here!
I love it! ♡
*Note: These kanji characters are in the original Japanese logo.
The logo, the designs and the copy for each title page...
...are all so well done.
It would also be great if you looked at the original magazine publication!
They're lovely!
Please take a good look!

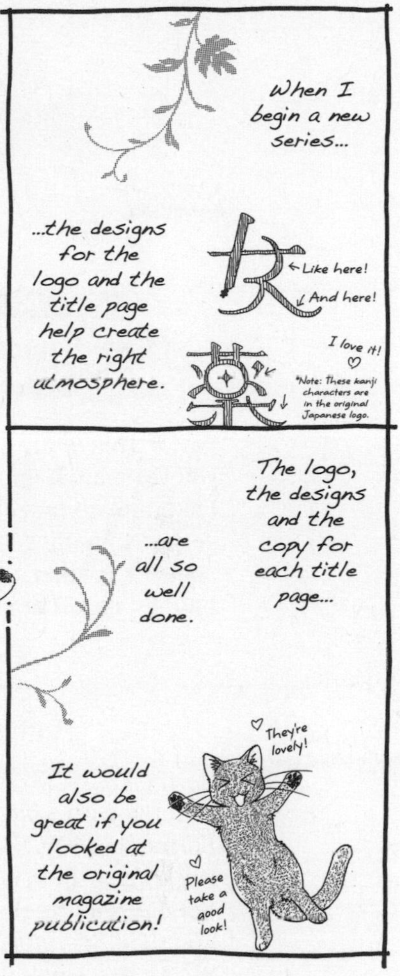

I'm looking forward to seeing you again, whether it's in **Petit Comic** magazine or in the graphic novel versions.

My thanks to everyone who helped me with this manga, and to all the readers.

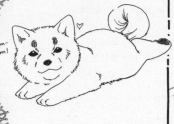

Mm-hm!

I may not be able to answer right away, but if possible, please let me know what you think!

Tomu Ohmi
c/o Spell of Desire Editor
Viz Media
P.O. Box 77010
San Francisco, CA 94107

You can also email your thoughts to the Petit Comics address. I shouldn't say this is in lieu of a reply, but I'd like to send you a New Year's greeting card, so please include your address.

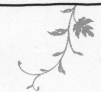

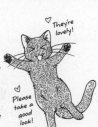

A WITCH'S FAMILIAR...

...IS A BLACK CAT, OF COURSE!

Yay! ♥ This is my 28th book!! Thank you very much for picking this up! I'm happy to meet you in this new series! I finally get to draw beasts again! ♥ It makes me very happy. ♥ I hope I can share this joy with you!

–Tomu Ohmi

∾ Author Bio ∾

Born on May 25, Tomu Ohmi debuted with *Kindan no Koi wo Shiyoh* in 2000. She is presently working on *Petit Comic* projects like *Spell of Desire*. Her previous series, *Midnight Secretary*, is available from VIZ Media. Ohmi lives in Hokkaido, and she likes beasts, black tea and pretty women.

Spell of Desire

VOLUME 1
Shojo Beat Edition

STORY AND ART BY
TOMU OHMI

MAJO NO BIYAKU Vol. 1
by Tomu OHMI
© 2012 Tomu OHMI
All rights reserved.
Original Japanese edition published by SHOGAKUKAN.
English translation rights in the United States of America, Canada, the
United Kingdom, and Ireland arranged with SHOGAKUKAN.

English Adaptation/Ysabet Reinhardt MacFarlane
Translation/JN Productions
Touch-up Art & Lettering/Monalisa de Asis
Design/Izumi Evers
Editor/Amy Yu

Printed in the U.S.A.

Published by VIZ Media, LLC
P.O. Box 77010
San Francisco, CA 94107

10 9 8 7 6 5 4 3 2 1
First printing, August 2014

www.viz.com

This is the last page.

In keeping with the original Japanese comic format, this book reads from right to left— so action, sound effects, and word balloons are completely reversed. This preserves the orientation of the original artwork—plus, it's fun! Check out the diagram shown here to get the hang of things, and then turn to the other side of the book to get started!